Nicola Meldrum

with **Fiona Aish, Gabrielle Lambrick, Jane Welberry Smith** and **Rawdon Wyatt**

Series Adviser **Catherine Walter**

Photocopiable Materials Adviser **Jill Hadfield**

Navigate

Teacher's Guide
with Teacher's Support and Resource Disc
and Photocopiable Materials

A2 **Elementary**

OXFORD
UNIVERSITY PRESS

OXFORD
UNIVERSITY PRESS

Great Clarendon Street, Oxford, OX2 6DP, United Kingdom

Oxford University Press is a department of the University of Oxford.
It furthers the University's objective of excellence in research, scholarship,
and education by publishing worldwide. Oxford is a registered trade
mark of Oxford University Press in the UK and in certain other countries

© Oxford University Press 2015

The moral rights of the author have been asserted

First published in 2015

2019 2018 2017 2016 2015

10 9 8 7 6 5 4 3 2 1

ISBN: 978 0 19 456526 4

Printed in China

This book is printed on paper from certified and well-managed sources

ACKNOWLEDGEMENTS

The publisher would like to thank the following for permission to reproduce photographs:
Alamy Images pp.228 (nurse/OJO Images Ltd), 233 (Mazzaro Bay/Rob Francis),
233 (hiker/Giulio Ercolani), 233 (tourists/Justin Kase zsixz), 245 (Singapore
Art Museum/MJ Photography), 245 (giraffe/Vipula Samarakoon); Corbis
pp.228 (businesswoman walking down street/Corbis), 228 (pilot/Corbis);
Getty Images pp.228 (chef holding plate/Jetta Productions/Dana Neely),
228 (musician/Hill Street Studios), 228 (cleaner/Eric Audras), 228 (student/John
Fedele), 228 (woman taking photo/Fotosearch), 228 (car mechanic/londoneye),
245 (pink river dolphins/Sara Pereira); Shutterstock pp.209 (businessman/
racorn), 209 (young woman/Goodluz), 228 (hairdresser/Tyler Olson), 228 (news
reporter/michaeljung), 245 (restaurant/Ariadna de Raadt).

Illustrations by: Paul Boston pp.38, 119; Vicki Gausden p.212; Dylan Gibson
p.216, 230, 231, 237, 250; Kerry Hyndman pp.229, 235, 247, 248; Joanna Kerr/
New Division pp.232; 234; 245; 246; 253

Vox pops worksheets written by: Sarah Walker.

Contents

Coursebook contents: Units 1–6

Contents

Oⁿ **Oxford 3000™** *Navigate* has been based on the *Oxford 3000* to ensure that learners are only covering the most relevant vocabulary.

2

4

3

Coursebook contents: Units 7–12

4

Introduction to *Navigate*

Navigate is an English language course for adults that incorporates current knowledge about language learning with concern for teachers' views about what makes a good course.

Many English language courses today are based on market research, and that is appropriate. Teachers know what works in their classrooms, out of the many kinds of materials and activities they have available. However, relying only on market research discourages innovation: it ignores the wealth of knowledge about language learning and teaching that has been generated. *Navigate* has been developed in a cycle which begins by calling on both market research and the results of solid experimental evidence; and then by turning back to classrooms once more for piloting and evaluation of the resulting materials.

A course for adults

This is a course for adults, whether they want to use English for study, professional or social purposes. Information-rich texts and recordings cover a range of topics that are of interest and value for adults in today's world. Learners are encouraged to use their own knowledge and experience in communicative tasks. They are seen as motivated people who may have very busy lives and who want to use their time efficiently. Importantly, the activities in the course are based on how adults best learn foreign languages.

Grammar: accuracy and fluency

Adults learn grammar best when they combine a solid conscious understanding of rules with communicative practice using those rules (Norris & Ortega, 2000; Spada & Lightbown, 2008; Spada & Tomita, 2010). *Navigate* engages learners in thinking about grammar rules, and offers them a range of communicative activities. It does not skimp on information about grammar, or depend only on communicative practice for grammar learning. Texts and recordings are chosen to exemplify grammar features.

Learners are invited, when appropriate, to consider samples from a text or recording in order to complete grammar rules themselves. Alternatively, they are sometimes asked to find examples in a text that demonstrate a rule, or to classify sentences that fall into different rule categories. These kinds of activities mean that learners engage cognitively with the rules. This means that they will be more likely to notice instances of the rules when they encounter them (Klapper & Rees, 2003), and to incorporate the rules into their own usage on a long-term basis (Spada & Tomita, 2010).

Navigate also offers learners opportunities to develop fluency in using the grammar features. Aspects of a grammar feature that may keep learners from using it easily are isolated and practised. Then tasks are provided that push learners to use the target grammar features in communicative situations where the focus is on meaning. For more on *Navigate*'s approach to grammar, see pages 24–25 of this book.

Vocabulary: more than just knowing words

Why learn vocabulary? The intuitive answer is that it allows you to say (and write) what you want. However, the picture is more complex than this. Knowing the most important and useful vocabulary is also a key element in reading and listening; topic knowledge cannot compensate for vocabulary knowledge (Jensen & Hansen, 1995; Hu & Nation, 2000), and guessing from context usually results in guessing wrongly (Bensoussan & Laufer, 1984). Focusing on learning vocabulary generates a virtuous circle in terms of fluency: knowing the most important words and phrases means that reading and listening are more rewarding, and more reading and listening improves the ability to recall vocabulary quickly and easily.

Navigate's vocabulary syllabus is based on the *Oxford 3000*. This is a list of frequent and useful vocabulary items, compiled both on the basis of information in the British National Corpus and the Oxford Corpus Collection, and on consultation with a panel of over seventy language learning experts. That is to say, an initial selection based on corpus information about frequency has been refined using considerations of usefulness and coverage. To build *Navigate*'s vocabulary syllabus, the *Oxford 3000* has then been referenced to the Common European Framework of Reference for Languages (CEFR; Council of Europe, 2001), so that each level of the course focuses on level-appropriate vocabulary. For more information on the *Oxford 3000*, see pages 26–27 of this book.

Adult learners typically take responsibility for their learning, and vocabulary learning is an area where out-of-class work is important if learners want to make substantial progress. *Navigate* focuses on giving learners tools to maximize the efficiency of their personal work on vocabulary. One way it does this is to teach not only individual vocabulary items, but also a range of vocabulary systems, for example how common prefixes and suffixes are used. Another is to suggest strategies for vocabulary learning. In this way, learners are helped to grow their vocabulary and use it with greater ease.

Speaking: putting it all together

Based on a synthesis of research about how adults learn, (Nation & Newton, 2009) demonstrate that different kinds of activities are important in teaching speaking. *Language-focused learning* focuses explicitly and in detail on aspects of speaking such as comprehensible pronunciation, appropriately polite language for a given situation or tactics for holding the floor in a conversation. *Fluency development* gives learners focused practice in speaking more quickly and easily. *Meaning-focused output* provides opportunities to speak in order to communicate meaning, without explicitly focusing on using correct language.

Navigate covers all three kinds of activities. The course systematically teaches aspects of pronunciation and intonation that contribute to effective communication; appropriate expressions for a range of formal and informal situations; and ways of holding one's own in a conversation.

It offers activities to help learners speak more fluently. Very importantly, it offers a wealth of meaning-focused activities. Very often, these activities are tasks: they require learners to do something together to achieve something meaningful. These tasks meet Ur's (1981) criteria for a task that works: straightforward input, a requirement for interaction, an outcome that is challenging and achievable, and a design that makes it clear when learners have completed the task. Learners are not just asked to discuss a topic: they are asked to do something with some information that involves expressing thoughts or opinions and coming up with a recognizable outcome.

Reading: not just a guessing game

Typical English language courses tend to test rather than teach reading; and they often concentrate on meaning-focused strategies that assume learners should be helped to puzzle out the meaning in the text on the basis of prior knowledge. There is a large body of evidence that shows why this is inefficient, discussed in the essay on reading on pages 20–21 of this book. Activities such as thinking about the topic of the text in advance or trying to guess unknown words have limited benefit in helping learners to understand the text at hand. These activities have even less benefit in helping learners understand the next text they will read, and as Paul Nation (2009) notes, that is surely the goal of the classroom reading activity. *Navigate* focuses on explicit teaching of things like sound-spelling relations, vocabulary that appears often in certain kinds of texts, the ways that words like pronouns and discourse markers hold texts together, and techniques for simplifying difficult sentences. These will give learners ways of understanding the text they are reading, but more importantly the next text they will read.

Listening: a very different skill

Too many books treat listening as if it were just another kind of reading, using the same sorts of activities for both. *Navigate* takes into account that listening is linear – you can't look back at the text of something you're hearing – and that listening depends crucially on understanding the sounds of English and how they combine (Field, 2008). Practice on basic elements of listening will lead to faster progress, as learners acquire the tools to hear English better. People who read can stop, read again, and go back in the text; but listeners can't do this with the stream of speech. For listening, language-focused learning means starting with building blocks like discriminating the sounds of the language, recognizing the stress patterns of words, distinguishing word boundaries, identifying stressed and unstressed forms of common words, and holding chunks of language in mind for short periods. Concentrating on knowledge and skills like these will pay off more quickly than only focusing on meaning, and will make listening for meaning much more efficient. Fluency development in listening is important too: this means activities that teach learners to understand language spoken at natural speed, and give them progressive practice in getting better at it. *Navigate* includes activities that focus systematically on each of these areas separately, as well as giving opportunities to deploy this knowledge and these skills in more global listening. John Field's essay, on pages 22–23 of this book, gives more detail on this.

Writing for different purposes

Adults learning English for professional, academic or leisure activities will need to write different kinds of texts at different levels of formality. The *Navigate* writing syllabus is based on a so-called *genre* approach, which looks at the characteristics of the different kinds of texts students may be called upon to write. It implements this syllabus by way of activities that allow students to express their own meanings in drafting, discussing and redrafting texts. This has been shown to be an effective means of developing writing skills for adults (Hyland, 2011).

Navigate offers an innovative approach to developing reading and listening skills. This, combined with a solid speaking and writing syllabus, gives learners a sound foundation in the four skills. Grammar and vocabulary have equal importance throughout the course and learning is facilitated through the information-rich and engaging texts and recordings. It is the complete course for the 21st-century adult learner.

Catherine Walter is the Series Adviser for the *Navigate* course. She is an award-winning teacher educator, materials developer and researcher. Catherine lectures in Applied Linguistics at the University of Oxford, where she convenes the distance MSc in Teaching English Language in University Settings, and she is a member of the Centre for Research and Development in English Medium Instruction.

References

Bensoussan, M. and Laufer, B. (1984). Lexical guessing in context in EFL reading comprehension. *Journal of Research in Reading*, 7(1), 15-32.

Field, J. (2008). *Listening in the Language Classroom*. Cambridge: Cambridge University Press.

Hyland, K. (2011). Learning to write. In Manchón, R. M. (Ed.), *Learning-to-Write and Writing-to-Learn in an Additional Language*, pp. 18-35. Amsterdam: John Benjamins.

Klapper, J. & J. Rees. 2003. 'Reviewing the case for explicit grammar instruction in the university foreign language learning context'. *Language Teaching Research* 7/3: 285-314.

Nation, I. S. P. (2009). *Teaching EFL/ESL Reading and Writing*. London: Routledge.

Nation, I. S. P. & Newton, J. (2009). *Teaching ESL/EFL Listening and Speaking*. London: Routledge.

Norris, J. M. and L. Ortega. 2000. Effectiveness of L2 instruction: a research synthesis and quantitative meta-analysis. *Language Learning* 50/3:417-528.

Schmitt, N. (2010). *Researching Vocabulary: A Vocabulary Research Manual*. Basingstoke: Palgrave Macmillan.

Spada, N. and Lightbown, P. M. 2008. Form-focused instruction: isolated or integrated? *TESOL Quarterly* 42/2, 181-207.

Spada, N. and Tomita, Y. 2010. Interactions between type of instruction and type of language feature: a meta-analysis. *Language Learning* 60/2:1-46.

Ur, P. (1981). *Discussions that Work: Task-centred Fluency Practice*. Cambridge: Cambridge University Press.

Navigate content overview

Coursebook lesson 1

Vocabulary & Speaking

Navigate has a strong emphasis on active vocabulary learning. The first lesson in each unit contains a *Vocabulary & Speaking*, a *Vocabulary & Listening* or a *Vocabulary & Reading* section in which essential vocabulary for the unit is introduced and practised. The vocabulary in lesson 1 and 2 is taught in topic sets, allowing students to build their vocabulary range in a logical and systematic way.

Unit topics

Navigate is created for adult students with content that appeals to learners at this level. The unit topics have been chosen with this in mind and vary from *My day* and *The past* to *The world around us*.

Goals

The goals show students what they will be working on and what they will have learnt by the end of the lesson.

Sample coursebook spread

2 My day

2.1 A day in the life of a scientist

GOALS ☐ Talk about everyday actions ☐ Use the present simple positive to talk about your day

Listening & Grammar present simple and adverbs of frequency

Location of Bird Island

1 Work with a partner. Look at the photos and information about Bird Island and answer the questions.
 1 Where is Bird Island?
 2 What animals live there?

2 2.1 Melanie Szabo is a scientist on Bird Island. Listen to her talking about her day in the summer and in the winter. Tick (✔) the activities she mentions.
 1 study penguins   7 have dinner
 2 get up early   8 work in the lab
 3 have breakfast   9 write emails
 4 go out in a boat   10 go to bed late
 5 visit different islands   11 relax
 6 take photos   12 read a book

3 2.1 Listen again and complete the sentences with the correct verbs. Is Melanie talking only about today, or things she does every day?
 1 In the summer, my days are long. I _____ early and _____ to the beach. I watch the penguins.
 2 We _____ different islands and we _____ photos.
 3 In the winter, we usually _____ more free time.

4a Work with a partner. Read the article about Melanie and her colleague, Sven. How are their jobs different?

SCIENTISTS ON BIRD ISLAND
Bird Island is an important scientific research centre. Every year lots of scientists visit the island, but Melanie Szabo, a professor of zoology, works there all year. Sven Olafsson, who is from Bergen in Norway, also works on the island. He studies seals and Melanie watches penguins. The penguins come to the beaches on the north of the island and Melanie often works there alone. Sven never works alone – he always works with the other scientists because the male seals are big and sometimes dangerous! Sven loves his job, but he works very hard and he hardly ever has free time. For Melanie, her favourite time is Saturday night. One of the scientists usually makes a big dinner for the group and they watch a movie together, relax or play games.

b Work with a partner. Would you like to work on Bird Island? Why/Why not?

5 Work with a partner. Read the sentences and complete the rules in the Grammar focus box.
 1 We visit different islands and we take photos.
 2 Sven loves his job, but he works very hard and he hardly ever has free time.
 3 Melanie watches penguins.

GRAMMAR FOCUS present simple positive
 • We use the present simple to talk about repeated actions and things that are always true.
 • To make the present simple positive, we use:
  I/You/_____/They + infinitive without to
  _____/She/It + infinitive without to + (e)s
 • When a verb ends in -ch, -sh, -ss, -s, -z, -x, we add _____ to the third person he/she/it form.
 • The third person he/she/it form of have is _____.
 → Grammar Reference page 138

16 Oxford 3000™

PRONUNCIATION third person -(e)s
 • The third person -s is pronounced /s/ or /z/ with most verbs, e.g. works, goes.
 • With verbs ending in -ch, -sh, -ss, -s, -z or -x, the third person he/she/it form is pronounced /ɪz/, e.g. watches, washes.

6a 2.2 Listen to three sentences and repeat.
 1 Melanie watches penguins. /ɪz/   3 Sven loves his job. /z/
 2 Sven also works on the island. /s/

b 2.3 Listen and circle the final sound you hear in verbs 1–6.
 1 goes /z/ /ɪz/   3 cooks /s/ /ɪz/   5 makes /s/ /ɪz/
 2 teaches /z/ /ɪz/   4 relaxes /s/ /ɪz/   6 plays /z/ /ɪz/

c 2.4 Listen, check and repeat.

7a Read the Grammar focus box about adverbs of frequency.

GRAMMAR FOCUS adverbs of frequency
 • Adverbs of frequency, e.g. always, never, sometimes, etc. tell us how often or how frequently something happens.
 • In the present simple, adverbs of frequency come after the verb to be, but before all other verbs.
  In the winter, the weather is always very cold.
  Melanie often works there alone all day.
 → Grammar Reference page 138

b Work with a partner. Underline the adverbs of frequency in exercise 4a. Write them in the correct place in the diagram.
 1 always   3 _____   5 hardly ever
 2 _____   4 _____   6 _____
 100%   50%   0%

8a Read the sentences about a scientist's week and complete the sentences with the correct form of the verbs in the box.

arrive be go (x2) got up have relax return work

 1 During the week, he _gets up_ early and he _____ at a volcano at seven o'clock. (always/usually)
 2 His work _____ dangerous and he _____ alone. (sometimes/never)
 3 He _____ to the research centre at about 1 o'clock and he _____ lunch in the lab. (usually/always)
 4 On Friday and Saturday nights he _____ at home. He _____ out with friends and he _____ to bed early. (usually/hardly ever/often)

b Read the sentences in exercise 8a again and put the adverbs in (brackets) in the correct places.

c 2.5 Listen and check your answers.

2.1 2.2 2.3 2.4 2.5

Vocabulary & Speaking daily activities

9a Work with a partner. Match illustrations 1–12 to the phrases in the box.

get up go home go to bed go to work/college
have a shower have lunch/dinner listen to music
make breakfast play video games read a book
see friends watch TV/a film

b 2.6 Listen, check and repeat.

10a TASK Tell your partner five things about your day, using the phrases in exercise 9a and adverbs of frequency. Give more information when you can.
  I get up at about eight o'clock.
  I (sometimes/always/never) have a shower …, etc.

b Work with a different partner. Tell them about your first partner's day.
  Alexa gets up at eight o'clock. She always has a shower.

▶ VOX POPS VIDEO 2

17

Penguins on the beach on Bird Island

Seals on Bird Island

Listening & Grammar

Grammar forms the 'backbone' of *Navigate*. Lesson 1 introduces the first grammar point of the unit. It is always combined with a skill, either reading or listening. See page 24 of this book for more information.

Grammar focus box

At this level of *Navigate*, grammar is introduced deductively when a new topic is introduced or inductively when the students are extending their knowledge on a particular area (see the Grammar focus box in lesson 2.2). Students are asked to complete the information in the Grammar focus box based on what has been introduced in previous exercises in the *Grammar & Listening* or *Grammar & Reading* exercises. The Grammar focus box is followed by a number of spoken and written exercises in which the grammar is practised further.

Vox pops video

Most units contain a prompt to the Vox pops videos. The videos themselves can be found on the Coursebook DVD or Coursebook e-book, and the Worksheets that accompany them are on the Teacher's Support and Resource Disc. The videos themselves feature a series of authentic interviews with people answering questions on a topic that has been covered in the lesson. They offer an opportunity for students to hear real people discussing the topics in the Coursebook.

Coursebook lesson 2

Listening & Vocabulary

Navigate has a strong emphasis on everyday vocabulary that allows students to speak in some detail and depth on general topics. Here students work on telling the time. All target vocabulary in the unit can also be found in the wordlists on the Teacher's Support and Resource Disc, the e-book and the DVD packed with the Coursebook.

Reading & Grammar

Lesson 2 provides the second grammar point of the unit. It is always presented through a reading text or audio extract, and is practised through both controlled and freer exercises.

Task

Each lesson ends with a task which allows students to practise with others what they have learnt in the lesson. They often work in pairs or groups to complete the task.

2.2　Spending time

GOALS ■ Tell the time ■ Use the present simple negative

Listening & Vocabulary　telling the time

1a　Work with a partner. Do you think sentences 1–3 are true (T) or false (F)?
1　It takes about a year to learn to be an astronaut. T / F
2　Some astronauts stay in space for over a year at a time. T / F
3　Astronauts don't need perfect eyesight. T / F

b　Turn to page 127 and check your answers.

2　2.7 🔊 Sanaa Diya is a trainee astronaut at the European Astronaut Centre (EAC) in Cologne, Germany. Listen and answer the questions.
1　What does she think about the training?
2　What subjects does she learn?

3　2.7 🔊 Listen again and match activities 1–6 in Sanaa's day to times a–f.
1　She gets up
2　She has breakfast in the canteen
3　She goes to morning classes
4　She stops for a break in the morning
5　Classes finish in the evening
6　She goes to sleep

a　at quarter to eight.
b　at ten to seven.
c　at quarter to six.
d　at five past ten.
e　at quarter past eleven.
f　at half past eight.

4a　Work with a partner. Write the times under the clocks.

1　*It's three o'clock.*　2　　3
4　　5　　6
7　　8　　9
10　　11　　12

b　2.8 🔊 Listen, check and repeat.

PRONUNCIATION saying the time
• When we say the time, we don't stress *past* or *to*, e.g. *twenty-five past three, ten to seven.*
• We don't pronounce the letter *l* in *half*, so we say /hɑːf/.
• *Quarter* begins with a /k/ sound, so we say /ˈkwɔːtə/.

5a　2.9 🔊 Listen to the times. Circle the words you hear.
1　*quarter* / *half* past eight　4　*five* / *quarter* to six
2　*quarter* to / *past* three　5　*twenty* to / *past* three
3　*ten* to / *past* ten　6　*twenty* / *twenty-five* to four

b　2.9 🔊 Listen again and repeat.

6　Work with a partner. Talk about what time you do these things or what time they happen where you live.
• the sun rises in summer　• you have lunch
• you get up　• the shops close
• the shops open　• public transport stops
• your favourite TV programme starts
The sun rises at about half past six.
Shops like the baker's open early, at eight o'clock.

18　Ⓞ Oxford 3000™

Reading & Grammar　present simple negative

7　Work with a partner. What's different about life on earth and life in space? Use the ideas in the box.

daytime and night-time　washing　sleeping

8a　Read the article about Canadian astronaut Chris Hadfield and life in space. Check your ideas in exercise 7.

A perfect day

When Chris Hadfield goes into space, he <u>doesn't have</u> a lot of free time. He works twelve hours a day and also does two hours' exercise. Life in space is very different to life on earth. Astronauts don't have showers like people on earth do – they wash with a cloth. They don't sleep in a bed – they sleep in special sleeping bags on the walls. It is difficult to know the time because in space the sun doesn't rise once a day – it rises once every 45 minutes. It's hard work, but most astronauts love being in space. Chris says it is amazing and he doesn't want to sleep. For him, every day in space is a perfect day!

b　<u>Underline</u> the negative verb forms in exercise 8a, e.g. *doesn't have*, and complete the rules in the Grammar focus box.

GRAMMAR FOCUS present simple negative
To make the present simple negative, we use:
I/You/We/They + *do not* (＿＿＿＿＿＿) + infinitive without to
He/She/It + *does not* (＿＿＿＿＿＿) + infinitive without to

→ Grammar Reference page 139

9a　Change these sentences from positive to negative. Use contractions.
1　They have a lot of free time.
　They don't have a lot of free time.
2　I go to classes in the evening.
3　Chris has a shower in the morning.
4　Sanaa sleeps in a sleeping bag.
5　They speak to their families every day.
6　He works eight hours a day.

b　2.10 🔊 Listen, check and repeat.

10a　Work with a partner. Do you think these things usually happen or not in space?
A　*I don't think astronauts get sick on their first trip into space.*
B　*Really? I disagree. I think they usually get sick.*
1　get sick on their first trip into space
2　wear special clothes in the space station
3　change their clothes every day
4　exercise a lot
5　go on a spacewalk every day
6　sleep a lot

b　2.11 🔊 Listen and check your ideas.

11a　**TASK** Chris says every day in space is a perfect day for him. Describe a perfect day for you. Write down three things you do and three things you don't do.
On a perfect day, I don't go to work. I have breakfast in bed at about half past nine – fresh fruit, coffee and a croissant – and I get up at ten o'clock.

b　Compare your sentences with a partner. Is their perfect day similar or different to yours?

c　Work with a different partner. Tell them about your first partner's perfect day.

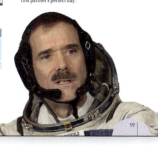

19

Pronunciation

Most units contain pronunciation work in either lesson 1 or lesson 2. Pronunciation in *Navigate* is always relevant to the grammar or vocabulary input of the lesson. The pronunciation exercises in the first two lessons focus mostly on speech production to improve intelligibility (for instance, minimal pairs and word stress). Pronunciation also appears in some Speaking and writing lessons and there it focuses mostly on teaching aspects of pronunciation that cause problems and confusion for listening comprehension (pronunciation for receptive purposes).

Grammar Reference

At the end of the Coursebook, the Grammar Reference section offers more detailed explanations of grammar and a series of practice exercises. This can be set as homework and then reviewed in class.

Navigate content overview

Coursebook lesson 3

Reading & Speaking
Navigate contains reading texts covering a wide variety of topics, text types and sources. As well as comprehension of interesting reading and listening texts, in this section students work on decoding skills to develop their reading or listening. These decoding skills, for example, predicting, connected speech, linking words, referencing words, etc., drill down to the micro level of reading and listening, and enable students to develop strategies to help them master these skills. See pages 20 and 21 of this book for more information.

Vocabulary and skills development
This lesson works on vocabulary and skills development. Students will, for instance, practise collocations, word building and word stress. The lesson also contains reading, writing, listening and/or speaking exercises.

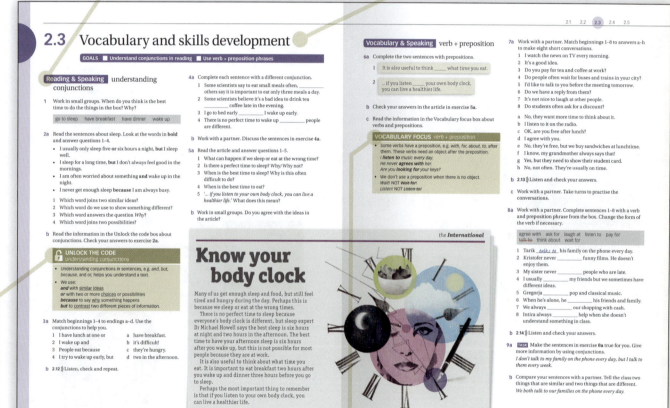

Unlock the code
This section describes the decoding skill that is being taught in the reading or listening skills lesson. They are general tips which can be used as tactics for understanding when reading or listening to texts. This Unlock the code box is about understanding conjunctions.

Vocabulary focus
Vocabulary focus boxes appear in this lesson to draw attention to a particular vocabulary area, in this case verbs and their prepositions. The students go on to do some exercises where they use the information in this study tip. In other units, Vocabulary boxes deal with pre- and suffixes, adjectives, etc.

Coursebook lesson 4

Speaking and writing

Navigate understands that classes can be made up of adults learning English for many different reasons. In lesson 4 of every unit, *Speaking and writing*, *Navigate* provides appropriate communication practice for work, study or social life with an emphasis on language production. At the end of the speaking and writing sections, students complete a speaking or writing task. The lesson also contains two language focus boxes: *Language for speaking* and *Language for writing*.

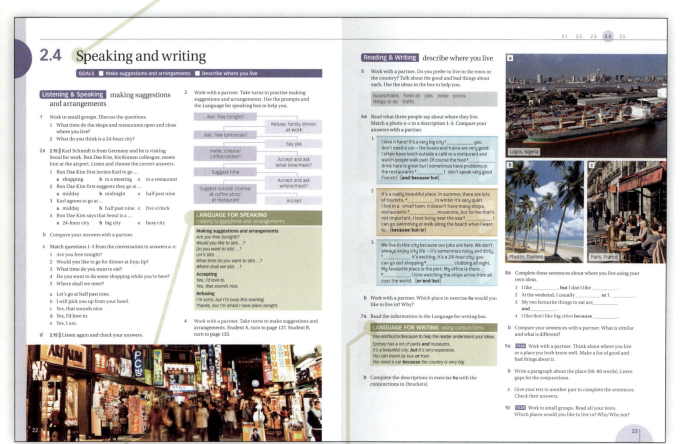

Language for speaking

The *Language for speaking* box contains phrases that students can use to complete a task about a particular topic. Here they have to make suggestions and arrangements and they can use the phrases in the box. Other language for speaking boxes cover *Making requests*, *Asking for and giving directions* and *Showing interest*.

Language for writing

The *Language for writing* box contains suggestions which students can use to complete their task in the writing section. There are various topics in this box throughout the Coursebook; here the focus is on conjunctions. In other units, the boxes focus on topics such as *Opening and closing an email*, *Imperatives* and *Using a comma in lists*.

Navigate content overview

Coursebook lesson 5

Video

The Video page contains activities that accompany the unit video. This video is a documentary video or authentic interview. The video page starts with one or two warmer activities which set the scene before the students watch the video, followed by two activities which check understanding of the video. The final activity is a task based on what the students have just watched.

In A2 the video topics are:

Unit 1: Brighton language exchange
Unit 2: The Menna family
Unit 3: An Iranian doctor in the USA
Unit 4: Almas Tower
Unit 5: Camden Market
Unit 6: Istanbul
Unit 7: Health and fitness in New York

Unit 8: Adventure holidays
Unit 9: Making a pizza
Unit 10: The Grand Canyon
Unit 11: Silicon Fen
Unit 12: Park Theatre

---

21   22   23   24   2.5

2.5 Video

The Menna family

1 Work with a partner. Look at the people in the photos and think about …
 • what nationality they are
 • where they live
 • what they like eating
 • how old they are
 • what jobs they do
 • what they do at weekends

2 ▶ Watch the video about the Menna family. Check your ideas in exercise 1. What other information do you find out about the family?

3 ▶ Watch the video again. Choose the correct option. Sometimes more than one answer is possible.
 a Roberto works *for a television network / for Channel 9 / at home.*
 b Gabriela goes to work at *5.30 / 6.30 / 7.30 a.m.*
 c Milagros and Julieta go to *school by bus / go to the same school / go to different schools.*
 d The girls get up at *8 a.m. / 9 a.m. / 10 a.m. on Saturdays.*
 e Gabriela drinks *chocolate milk / mate / coffee.*
 f After breakfast the girls play *football / tennis / video games.*
 g They go to the park *in the evening / in the afternoon / before lunch.*
 h The family usually visits the girls' *aunt and uncle/ cousins / grandparents* on Sundays.
 i They eat *salad / pasta / rice* with their barbecue.
 j On Sundays they go to bed *early / late / at 11 p.m.*

4a TASK Work with a partner. You are going to do a class survey to find out whose weekend is the most different to yours. Write 6-8 questions to find out about other students' weekend routines.
 Do you work at the weekend?
 What time do you get up on Saturdays?

 b Ask other students in the class about their weekend routines. Whose weekend is the most different to yours?

24

Review

1a Complete the sentences with the present simple positive form of the verbs in the box.

go   have   like   live   study   work

 1 I _____ classical music.
 2 After class, I _____ home by bus.
 3 My friend _____ in a bank.
 4 We _____ English on Mondays and Wednesdays.
 5 In my country, people _____ their main holiday in August.
 6 My classmate _____ in a flat in the city centre.

 b Work with a partner. Make the sentences in exercise 1a true for you. Give more information.
 I don't like classical music. I like rock.

2a Look at the information and write sentences about people in the UK. Use words from the box.

always   never   sometimes   hardly ever   usually   often

 They never have fish for breakfast.

 0%   10%   50%   75%   85%   100%

 [have fish for breakfast]   [go to a different city to study]   [eat lunch at work]

 [be late for meetings]   [have more than one TV at home] [talk about the weather]

 b 2.16 🎧 Listen and check your answers.

 c Change the adverbs of frequency to make the sentences true for where you live. Compare your sentences with a partner. How many sentences are the same?

3a Put the daily activities in the order people usually do them.

 go to bed   go to work   get up   have a shower
 have dinner   go home   have lunch   watch TV

 b Work with a partner. Think of three more daily activities. Decide where they go in your order from exercise 3a.

4 Work with a partner. Say what time you usually do the activities in exercise 3a. Do you do things at the same time as your partner?
 I usually get up at six o'clock, but at weekends …

5a Match beginnings 1-6 to endings a-f to make questions.
 1 What radio station do you
 2 Do you usually agree
 3 Do you normally
 4 Do you like waiting
 5 Who's the first person
 6 Do you pay

 a for public transport?
 b for things in shops by cash or by credit card?
 c with everything your family/colleagues say?
 d you talk to in the morning?
 e listen to?
 f ask for directions when you are lost?

 b Work with a partner. Ask and answer the questions in exercise 5a.

6a Complete the conversation with the words in the box.

busy   free   like   love   let's   plans   shall   want

 A Are you 1 _____ after class today?
 B I'm sorry, but I'm 2 _____ this evening. But I don't have any 3 _____ tomorrow.
 A Would you 4 _____ to go out for a pizza?
 B Yes, I'd 5 _____ to. What time 6 _____ we meet?
 A Eight o'clock at Gino's? Or do you 7 _____ to meet at the station?
 B Yes, 8 _____ meet there at 7.45.
 A OK, see you then!

 b 2.17 🎧 Listen and check your answers.

 c Work with a partner. Use your own ideas and have a similar conversation.

25

Task

The Task on the Video page is an outcome task which focuses on fluency. It can be a writing or speaking task. Here the students compare weekend routines with their class mates. Other tasks on Video pages are, for instance, discussing jobs, thinking about and discussing a famous building, a presentation about shopping, writing an email about a trip to Istanbul.

Review

The Review page contains revision of grammar, vocabulary and the skills practised in the unit. The Review activities can be set for homework, but are also specifically designed to be done in class incorporating pairwork and group work tasks to give learners additional opportunities to practise key language from the unit.

Workbook

Unit structure
The Workbook follows the Coursebook lessons. The first two spreads each have two pages of exercises which correspond with the Coursebook contents of the same lessons. Spreads 3 and 4 of the Workbook each have a page of extra practice which corresponds to the material in lessons 3 and 4 of the Coursebook. The Workbook also contains lessons for extensive reading and listening, review exercises, audioscripts of the listening material in the Workbook and answer keys (with key version only).

Vocabulary
In the Workbook, students find further practice of the vocabulary which they learnt in the corresponding lesson of the Coursebook. They can do this individually and at their own pace. On this page students practise vocabulary to do with daily activities.

I can …
At the end of each Workbook spread, the *I can* statements remind students which goals they should have reached. If they feel they need more practice, they can use the Online Practice materials (see page 19 of this book).

Grammar
In the Workbook, students find further practice of the grammar which they learnt in the corresponding lesson of the Coursebook. This page contains more exercises on the present simple and adverbs of frequency as introduced in the Coursebook.

Also in the Workbook

Reading for pleasure
The *Reading for pleasure* and *Listening for pleasure* pages appear once every two units in the Workbook. They offer students an opportunity for extensive reading or listening supported by a few exercises to ensure understanding. Here the students read an extract from a book about New York.

Review
As well as a Review page in every unit of the Coursebook, *Navigate* Workbook offers another chance for students to check what they have learnt with a Review page once every two units.

Navigate content overview

Teacher's Guide and Teacher's Support and Resource Disc

The Teacher's Guide and Teacher's Support and Resource Disc Pack is a complete support package for teachers. It is designed for both experienced and new teachers and offers a wealth of resources to supplement lessons with *Navigate*.

What's in the Teacher's Guide?

The Teacher's Guide contains thorough teaching notes for teachers to follow as they go through the Coursebook in their lessons. Answer keys are provided to all activities where appropriate and the audioscripts are embedded within the teaching notes for ease of reference.

As well as this, though, the Teacher's Guide offers numerous ideas and extra support in the shape of the following features, to be found throughout the teaching notes:

- **Lead-in:** an extra activity at the start of every unit to encourage engagement with the topic of the unit.
- **Extra activity:** an activity that offers an alternative approach to the one in the Coursebook for variety or to tailor the material to a specific teaching situation.
- **Extension:** an idea on how to extend the activity in the Coursebook, useful especially if learners have shown a strong interest in that topic.
- **Extra support/Extra challenge:** These are alternative ways of doing an activity where more staging may be required for learners who are struggling, or to keep stronger learners occupied in mixed-ability classes.
- **Pronunciation:** tips and notes for teaching pronunciation.
- **Watch out!:** potentially problematic language points or language that learners might ask about.
- **Feedback focus:** guidelines on what to monitor in an activity and how to give feedback.
- **Dictionary skills:** moments when it may be useful to develop learners' dictionary skills and ideas on how to do it.
- **Smart communication:** tips on small talk, appropriacy, and communication strategies.
- **Critical thinking:** strategies to analyse and evaluate what learners read and hear, their work and that of their peers.
- **Study tips:** tips to help learners assimilate what they have learnt.

The Teacher's Guide also includes the following features:

- Essays by influential authors and experts in the fields of reading, listening, grammar, the CEFR, testing and photocopiable materials. These essays have been written by people who have contributed to the development of material used in *Navigate*.
- Photocopiable materials: Extra grammar, vocabulary and communication activities as photocopiable worksheets.
- Photocopiable worksheets to accompany the Vox pops videos found on the Coursebook DVD.

What's on the Teacher's Support and Resource Disc?

- **Lesson overview videos:** Catherine Walter, *Navigate* Series Adviser, offers one-minute overviews of each of the main lessons of the Coursebook, including the methodology behind it and the benefit to the learner.

- **Tests:** a full range of Unit, Progress and Exit tests to enable you and your students to monitor progress throughout their course. Available in PDF and Word format, and in A/B versions. See page 32 of this book for more details.
- MP3 audio for all of the tests.
- All of the photocopiable material that is found at the back of the Teacher's Guide as downloadable PDFs.
- Wordlists (A-Z and unit-by-unit)
- Audioscripts in Word of all Coursebook, Workbook and Test audio.
- Student study record: a self-assessment form to be filled in by the student after each unit is completed.

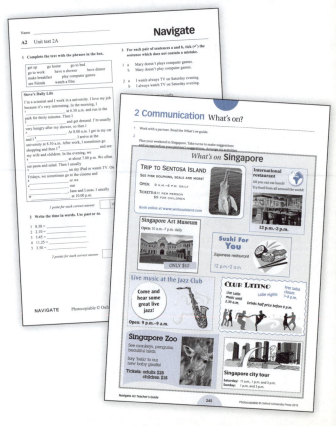

e-books

The *Navigate* e-books are digital versions of the Coursebooks and Workbooks. Learners study online on a computer or on a tablet, and their work is safely saved in the Cloud. The *Navigate* e-book Teacher's edition is the Coursebook with integrated teacher's notes as well as selected pop-up images. You can use it as a classroom presentation tool.

To access an e-book:

1 Go to **www.oxfordlearnersbookshelf.com**.

2 To use your e-books on a tablet, download the app, and register or log in.

   To use your e-books on a computer, register or log in to the website.

3 **Note:** After you register, you can use your e-books on both a computer and a tablet.

4 Choose **Add a book**.

5 Enter your access code.

Watch this video for help on registering and using e-books: **www.brainshark.com/oup/OLBgetstarted**

In the *Navigate* e-book Teacher's edition, the teacher's notes from the Teacher's Guide can be called up on the page where the information is needed.

Draw on the page or highlight text.

Find units quickly, jump to a page, or bookmark a page.

The listening materials that go with the course play straight from the page and are placed with the exercise where they are needed. The user can slow the material down to hear each word clearly and then speed up again. In addition, learners can improve pronunciation by listening to the audio, record their own and then compare to the original. The e-books also contain video material which can be played straight from the Video lesson page. The video material can be played full screen, or split screen to move around the pages and complete activities as you watch.

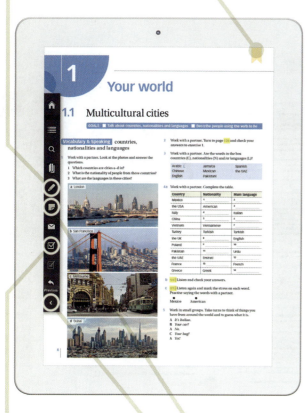

Automatic marking helps learners check progress and learn from their mistakes. They can also email a page to you to mark or to add to their learning portfolio.

The sticky note can be used to place comments with an exercise. These comments can either be written or recorded and can be placed anywhere on the page.

This tool allows the user to move back to the original page. For instance, if the user has moved from a lesson page to a Grammar reference page, clicking on this arrow will move the reader automatically back to the page they came from.

Many images in the *Navigate* e-book Teacher's edition can be enlarged by clicking on the image. This functionality can be used in class to discuss particular images in detail or to aid completion of exercises that go with the photos.

Navigate content overview

iTools

Navigate iTools is a digital tool, specifically designed for use on whiteboards, that can also be used with data projectors, and PCs or laptop computers. Pages from the Coursebook and Workbook are seen on screen with various tools to help the teacher present the material in class.

This tool appears with each exercise and allows the teacher to discuss an exercise in class whilst calling up the answers. Clicking on the key will pop up a box containing the exercise rubric and spaces which can hold the answers when you click on the relevant buttons in the bottom of the box. There are three options: 'see next answer', 'see all answers', and 'hide all answers'.

The Grammar reference page can be reached by clicking on the book icon placed near the Grammar focus box. The user jumps to the relevant Grammar reference page and can return to the original page again by using the arrow button at the bottom of the page.

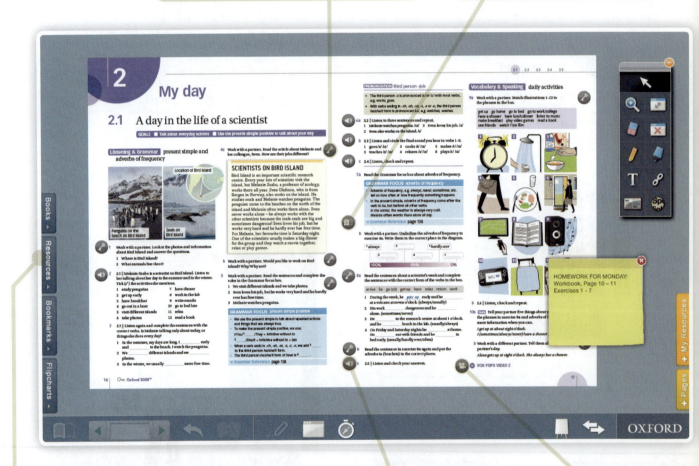

Resources

Navigate iTools includes a number of resources for use in the classroom:

- The Vox pops worksheets.
- Photocopiable materials from the Teacher's Guide are available to download here, as are wordlists.
- New Grammar Powerpoint presentations for display on your whiteboard help you teach the grammar from the Coursebook in a more interactive way.

This tool allows the teacher to play the audio material that is relevant to the exercise. The teacher can also reveal the audio script so that students can read along whilst they listen.

Video can be played on your whiteboard by clicking the icon.

Online practice

Our online practice courses give your learners targeted extra practice at the level that's right for them. Supported by the online Learning Management System, teachers and administrators can assign media-rich activities for the classroom or at home, and measure learners' progress.

Each learning module uses a step-by-step process, engaging learners' interest, then encouraging them to explore, practise and reflect on their learning.

Learners can study independently with a wide range of support materials: Cultural glossaries, Language models, Wordlists, Grammar and Vocabulary Reference, hints and tips, automatic marking and instant feedback.

You can monitor your learners' progress with a variety of management tools, including a Gradebook and User Progress statistics.

Create your own new content to meet the needs of your learners, including speaking and writing tasks, tests, discussions and live chat. You can also upload videos, audio and Powerpoint® presentations.

Oxford Online Skills

(General English, Bundle 2)
Helps learners focus on developing their Listening, Speaking, Reading and Writing skills, in the classroom or at home

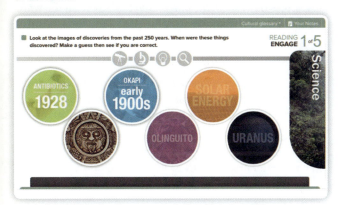

- Engage learners with 30 hours of media-rich activities per level, including videos, interactive infographics and striking photography, on culturally diverse topics.
- Topics complement those found in *Navigate*. For example: My family, the past, giving opinions, writing emails or blog posts.
- Learners' access codes come on a special card included with their Coursebook.
- Variety of top-up materials if you'd like more skills practice for your learners. Choose more modules for general English with General English Bundle 1, or focus on Academic English, all four skills or paired skills (Reading & Writing, Listening & Speaking). The choice is yours. Find out more at **www.oup.com/elt**.

Oxford Online Language Practice

Puts the spotlight on building up learners' vocabulary and grammar

- With a topic-based approach, grammar and vocabulary is integrated in a meaningful and contextualized learning journey.
- Topic areas reflect those commonly found in Adult general English courses, and include Education, Personality, Work, Holidays, Storytelling, Crime and Entertainment.
- Comprehensive support for learners in every Module, with printable grammar and vocabulary references and wordlists, and notes on key differences in American and British English.
- Each CEFR level includes 12 Modules and 25 hours of learning and practice material.

Learners' access codes come on a special card included with *Navigate* Pack 3. If you do not have Pack 3, you can buy this course online from **www.oup.com/elt**.

Oxford English for Work

Telephoning, Socializing and Writing Skills

- Each level includes three skills: Telephoning, Socializing and Writing.
- Activities are highly practical and immediately transferable to the workplace.

Learners' access codes come on a special card included with *Navigate* Pack 3. If you do not have Pack 3, you can buy this course online from **www.oup.com/elt**.

The *Navigate* approach – Reading

Reading tomorrow's text better – Catherine Walter

Learning to play beautiful music does not start with playing beautiful music. No one would expect to start learning the cello by trying to play a concerto; rather, they would learn how to use the bow and to finger the notes, to transition quickly and accurately from one note to another, to relate the musical notation on the page with the physical movements needed to play, and to work on making all that happen smoothly.

In the same way, becoming skilled at reading comprehension in a second language is not best achieved solely by practising comprehension. Of course, the goal of reading activities in an English language course is to help learners achieve better comprehension of the English language texts that they read. However, this does not mean that all of the activities in the classroom should be comprehension activities.

To read well in a second language, readers need to decode written text accurately and fluently (Grabe, 2009). Accurate decoding means being able to make a connection between the words on the page, how they sound and what they mean. Making a connection between the written words and how they sound is important because readers of alphabetic languages immediately convert what they read to silent speech in their minds, using that silent speech to build a mental representation of the text (Gathercole & Baddeley, 1993).

- *Second language readers need practice in matching common spellings and the way they sound, and they need to recognize common words that are spelt irregularly.*

Just as fluent playing of a piece of music is not only achieved by playing it again and again, but by playing scales and doing other exercises, fluency in reading comprehension is not best achieved only by extensive reading – although this has a part to play. Fluency development activities can help (Nation, 2009).

- *Second language readers need to focus on reading fast and without hesitation.*

Knowing how the words sound is useless if the reader does not know what the words mean. Contrary to popular myth, skilled readers who are reading a text for information or pleasure do not spend a lot of time guessing unknown words, because they already know all the words. Skilled readers do not sample bits of the text and deduce what the rest of the text means; they process the entire text, rapidly and automatically (Grabe, 2009). Skilled readers do not use context to infer meaning as often as less-skilled readers do: they do not need to, because they know the words (Juel, 1999). Second language readers who guess unknown words usually guess them wrongly (Bensoussan & Laufer, 1984). To read a text comfortably without using a dictionary, second language readers need to know the meanings of 98% of the words in a text (Hu & Nation, 2000). Note that topic familiarity cannot compensate for second language proficiency (Jensen & Hansen, 1995).

- *Second language readers need to learn the most common and useful words at their level, and they need to be able to recognize them quickly and automatically.*
- *They need to be aware of vocabulary systems, such as how prefixes and suffixes work, so that they can recognize word families, and can learn more vocabulary independently.*
- *More time should be spent on learning vocabulary than on learning to guess unknown words; teaching about guessing unknown words should be strategic.*
- *Activating learners' prior knowledge about a text they are about to read has a very limited effect on how well they will understand it.*

To read well, second language readers need to be able, accurately and fluently, to break down the grammar of the sentences they are reading. They also need to know how these sentences are put together to make a text. Recognizing how sentences are assembled in a text means, for example, recognizing the uses of determiners like *this* and *that*, of words like *which* that link one part of a sentence to another, of expressions like *on the other hand* that say what the writer thinks about what follows.

- *Texts for language learners should contain high-frequency grammatical features in natural contexts.*
- *Second language readers should learn how ideas are linked within texts, e.g. with pronouns, lexical links and discourse markers.*

Paul Nation (2009) points out that what happens in many second language reading activities is that the learners are helped to understand the text in front of them. Nation says that the question for the teacher of reading should rather be:

How does today's teaching make tomorrow's text easier to read?

This is the aim of many of the teaching activities in *Navigate*. Some of the activities that contribute to better reading are not specifically labelled as reading activities. For example, there is work on matching spelling and sounds. There is a carefully staged vocabulary syllabus based on the Oxford 3000™ list of frequent and useful words (Oxford University Press, 2014). There is regular work on vocabulary systems.

In addition, each reading text

- has intrinsic interest, so that learners will want to read it
- contains high-frequency, useful vocabulary
- contains useful grammatical features in natural contexts
- exemplifies features of natural connected texts.

Generally, the reading texts in *Navigate* are the starting point for intensive language-focused learning of reading skills. That is to say, the activities surrounding them are part of a structured programme which aims to prepare learners to read the next text they will encounter more skilfully.

The activities do this by

- helping learners to read more accurately and/or more fluently
- focusing on aspects of the current text that commonly occur in other texts
- prompting learners to understand and reflect upon the ways in which important grammar and discourse features are exemplified in the text
- concentrating on working with features that occur more often in written than spoken language
- providing activities that help learners to understand the text as a whole
- providing teacher and learner with information about the learner's performance, as a basis for future work.

All these teaching activities contribute to a structured programme which will move learners more efficiently towards becoming better readers of English.

References

Bensoussan, M. and Laufer, B. (1984). Lexical guessing in context in EFL reading comprehension. *Journal of Research in Reading*, 7(1), 15-32.

Gathercole, S. E. & Baddeley, A. D. (1993). *Working Memory and Language*. Hove, England: Lawrence Erlbaum Associates Ltd.

Grabe, W. (2009). *Reading in a Second Language: Moving from Theory to Practice*. Cambridge: Cambridge University Press.

Hu, M. H. & Nation, P. (2000). Unknown vocabulary density and reading comprehension. *Reading in a Foreign Language* 13/1:403-430.

Jensen, C. & Hansen, C. (1995). The effect of prior knowledge on EAP listening-test performance. *Language Testing* 12:99-119.

Juel, C. (1999). The messenger may be wrong, but the message may be right. In J. Oakhill & S. Beard (Eds.), *Reading Development and the Teaching of Reading*, 201-12. Malden, MA: Blackwell.

Nation, I. S. P. (2009). *Teaching ESL/EFL Reading and Writing*. London: Routledge.

Reading in *Navigate*

Navigate includes micro-skills work on reading, helping learners to identify common aspects of reading texts, which in turn enables them to develop their reading skills in general. These Unlock the code boxes identify some specific areas of reading skills that are exploited in lesson 3 in six of the units.

🔓 UNLOCK THE CODE
understanding conjunctions

- Understanding conjunctions in sentences, e.g. *and*, *but*, *because*, and *or*, helps you understand a text.
- We use:
  and with <u>similar ideas</u>
  or with two or more <u>choices</u> or possibilities
  because to say <u>why</u> something happens
  but to <u>contrast</u> two different pieces of information.

🔓 UNLOCK THE CODE
pronoun referencing

The first time we talk about a thing or person we usually use the noun. After that we often refer to it using a pronoun because we don't want to repeat the same noun.

Where's my **pen**? I can't find *it*.
it = pen

My grandparents are French. *They* live in Paris.
They = my grandparents

🔓 UNLOCK THE CODE
time sequencers

Writers often use time sequencers to show the order in which something happens, e.g. *first*, *next*, *then*. If you understand these phrases, it is easier to understand what comes next in the text.

TWIN VILLAGE

Kodinhi is a small village in Kerala in south India. It's a typical village, but *its* people are not typical. Two thousand families live here and 290 families have twins. In India seven babies in 1,000 are twins, but in Kodinhi, forty-five babies in 1,000 are twins.

Mohammed Rāshin's family is from Kodinhi. He and *his* wife have seven boys. Four of *their* sons are twins. Mohammed says, '*My* wife and I are very happy with *our* family. Everyone in the village is happy.'

But why are there so many twins in Kodinhi? How is it possible? No one really has an answer, but the village doctor says it isn't genetic; he thinks it's something in the water or the food.

- **typical** a good example of something that's usual, normal, average
- **genetic** things that come from your parents, like blue eyes or brown hair

This approach is used in combination with a more top-down approach to reading where students read content-rich texts as vehicles for grammar or vocabulary learning, and to stimulate discussion on a topic of general interest to adults. All reading texts have been carefully graded. Vocabulary level in the texts is checked against CEFR levels to ensure that only a minimum number of words are above the level expected to be understood by learners at the level of the Coursebook.

The *Navigate* approach – Listening

Training better listeners – John Field

In the early days of ELT, listening was mainly employed as a means of presenting new language in a dialogue context. In time, teachers and teacher trainers came to recognize the importance of teaching the four skills for their own sake, but there remained the problem of precisely how to do it. For listening, they fell back on a method widely used in L1 and L2 reading, as well as in early listening tests – namely the comprehension question. More enlightened teachers played short sections of a recording and asked oral comprehension questions; but coursebook materials often relied on a conventional lesson format where the teacher sets comprehension questions in advance of listening, plays a three- or four-minute recording and then checks answers.

This approach became very entrenched in ELT methodology, but it was not without its critics. The most commonly expressed reservation was that it *tested* listening rather than *teaching* it. Other drawbacks were less often mentioned. The method is very teacher centred. The comprehension questions are often in written form so that the task taps into reading as well as listening. The focus on 'comprehension' diverts attention from the fact that there is much more to listening than just the end-product. Above all, if a learner gives the right answer to a question, it tells us nothing about the way in which they arrived at that answer, so we cannot help them to listen better.

Today, listening instruction has moved on. Current approaches treat listening as a form of expertise, like driving a car or learning chess. A novice trying to acquire expertise in any skill starts out by needing to focus a lot of attention on the basic processes that make up the skill (in the case of listening, an L2 learner might need to concentrate on just recognizing words). With time and practice, however, these basic processes become more and more automatic and demand less attention. This enables the novice to perform more efficiently – in the case of the L2 listener, to switch attention from word recognition to building up a wider picture of the speaker's purpose and the conversation as a whole.

This perspective suggests the need to practise the fundamentals of the listening skill as intensively as possible in the early stages of a teaching programme. It also suggests the wisdom of reserving some of the more complex processes associated with context, interpretation or line of argument for higher-level learners.

L2 listeners' needs can be tackled in three ways

Exposure to the input

Learners need to hear short clips which illustrate some of the phonetic features of English that prevent listeners from recognizing words. Words in connected speech do not have standard forms like they do in writing. Because speakers take short cuts in producing them, they are often subject to elision (*didn't* → *'dint'*), assimilation (*ten pounds* → *'tem pounds'*), liaison (*tie up* → *'tieyup', go out* → *'gowout'*) or resyllabification (*find out* → *'fine doubt'*). Words that are of lesser importance in an utterance are often reduced. Function words in English have weak forms (*have, of, a* and *are* can all be represented by the single weak sound schwa /ə/), and words in commonly occurring chunks of language often get downgraded in prominence (*Do you know what I mean?* can be reduced to as little as '*Narp mean?'*).

The best way of dealing with these perceptual problems is by using small-scale exercises that focus on examples of just one of the features mentioned. The teacher reads aloud these examples or plays a recording of them and learners transcribe them. But this is no conventional dictation exercise: it employs speech that is as natural as possible, not read-aloud; and learners are not penalized for spelling errors. For examples, see Field, 2008: Chap. 9.

Training in expertise

Psycholinguistic models of listening have demonstrated that the skill demands five distinct operations:

- Decoding: matching the signals that reach our ears to the sound system of the language
- Lexical search: matching groups of sounds to words in our oral vocabulary
- Parsing: combining groups of words into grammatical units to obtain a simple point of information
- Meaning construction: interpreting the information in terms of context and the goals of the speaker
- Discourse construction: adding the information to what has gone before.

All five can be practised by means of small-scale exercises. In terms of lexical search, a major challenge when listening to any language is that there are no consistent gaps between words in connected speech like those in writing. It is the listener who has to decide where one word ends and the next begins (Field, 2003). A useful exercise is therefore for the learner to listen to a short passage of natural speech and write down any words that he/she has recognized, then to replay the passage several times, each time adding more words. This kind of task is best done at the learner's own pace – for homework or in a listening centre. Parsing can be practised by playing half of a sentence and asking learners to use what they have heard so far to predict the rest. Discourse construction can be practised by asking learners to fill in a blank Table of Contents form. For multiple examples of these exercise types, see Field 2008: Chaps. 10–13.

Compensating for gaps

It has been suggested that lower-level L2 learners need a great deal of practice in cracking the code of speech before they can move on to building more complex meanings. This takes time, and learners feel frustrated when, despite their listening instruction, they find they understand little of what they hear on the internet or on TV, DVD and film. There is thus a further need to train learners (especially adults) in strategies which enable them to make the most of the little they are able to extract from a piece of real-world speech, at least until their listening improves. In one type of strategy practice, they listen to a short recording, try to work out the gist of what they have heard, share ideas in pairs, and then listen again (perhaps more than once) in order to check if they were right and to add new information. This type of task helps learners who dislike the uncertainty of not recognizing every single word, by encouraging them to make guesses. It also helps those who are more willing to take risks, by making them check their (sometimes rash) guesses against what comes next. The fact is that listening to speech (even in one's first language) is always a highly approximate process. Because words in speech vary so much, all listeners keep having to form hypotheses about what they have heard and revising those hypotheses as they hear more.

The tasks that have been suggested in this three-pronged approach focus on particular components of listening and are mainly small scale (some constituting just 5 minutes of intensive practice). So where does that leave the conventional comprehension task? Well, we do still need it. We need it in order to integrate many of the processes that have been mentioned. They do not operate in isolation and a listener has to learn to use them in conjunction with each other. The traditional comprehension recording also provides exposure to a wide range of voices, either in conversation or monologue. Adjusting to unfamiliar voices is a part of listening that we take for granted in our first language; but it can be demanding when the speaker is talking in a second language.

But we should perhaps rethink some aspects of the traditional comprehension task. Teachers and materials providers need to draw more heavily on authentic material – or at least use studio material that resembles natural speech in its pausing patterns, hesitations, overlaps, false starts, etc. Careful thought also needs to be given to the role of the comprehension question. It is quite possible to design questions that tap specifically into one of the five levels of processing identified above. This should be done in a way that reflects the capabilities of learners, with an emphasis at lower levels on questions that target word-level cues and factual information.

References

Field, J. 2003. Promoting perceptions: lexical segmentation in L2 listening. *ELT Journal* 57/4: 325–34

Field, J. 2008. *Listening in the Language Classroom*. Cambridge: Cambridge University Press

John Field is Senior Lecturer in the CRELLA research unit at the University of Bedfordshire, UK. He is especially known for his work on second language listening; and his *Listening in the Language Classroom* (CUP, 2008) has become a standard work in the field. His background in psycholinguistics (on which he has also written widely) informs much of his thinking. He is currently applying it to the notion of cognitive validity in L2 testing; and is developing new types of listening test which more accurately reflect the components of the skill. In another life, John was a materials writer and teacher trainer: writing coursebook series for Saudi Arabia and Hong Kong, radio programmes for the BBC World Service, and TV programmes for the Open University of China. He continues to advise publishers on materials design.

Listening in *Navigate*

The approach to listening in *Navigate* draws significantly on John Field's research, through a carefully graded listening skills syllabus focusing on features of the spoken language. These decoding skills for listening can be found in the skills development lessons and include the following areas:

🔓 UNLOCK THE CODE
positive and negative contractions

- When we speak, we often use contractions, e.g. *I'm, she isn't*, etc. It is important to understand the difference between the positive and negative forms of the verb.
- The verb *to be* is not stressed in positive sentences.

  He's Australian.   I'm Chinese.

- In negative sentences *not*, *isn't* and *aren't* are stressed.

  She's not Polish. It isn't my family name. They aren't friends.

🔓 UNLOCK THE CODE (1)
the schwa /ə/ sound in words

Many words have an unstressed syllable that is usually pronounced with a **schwa** /ə/ sound. The sound is often (but not always) on the last syllable.

farmer, woman, hairdresser, salary, agree

🔓 UNLOCK THE CODE
understanding similar vowel sounds

- Vowel sounds can sound very similar to each other when you listen.

/æ/	/eɪ/	/e/
man	main	men
/ɒ/	/ʌ/	/əʊ/
not	nut	note
/e/	/ɪ/	/iː/
set	sit	seat

- Listening for the general meaning of the sentence can help you understand the correct word.

  The not/nut/note says 'Wait here'.

The *Navigate* approach – Grammar

Grammar: What is the best way to learn it? – Catherine Walter

Attitudes towards planned grammar teaching vary across the world. Some attitudes derive from theoretical stances that have not stood the test of time; yet they persist, here and there, in teacher education programmes, in national advice to teachers and in some language teaching materials.

One of the problems here may well be memories of classrooms where students learnt grammar rules, but didn't use them in communicative activities. It became clear that this was not a good way for learners to become good communicators in their second language. This led to proposals in which learning of grammar rules was seen as counterproductive.

One idea that emerged was that grammar should be taught only when the need for a particular grammar feature emerged spontaneously. The idea was that in the course of a communicative activity, the learner would want to say something, but lacked the necessary grammar. This was seen as the perfect time for the teacher to offer that grammar. However, there are three problems here. Firstly, in a classroom, different learners may be ready for a grammar point at different times. Secondly, it is not possible to construct a series of tasks from which every important grammar feature will emerge. Thirdly, classrooms are unpredictable. If the teacher is depending on what emerges in class for the whole grammar syllabus, they need to be able to give a clear, accurate, level-appropriate explanation of any feature that happens to emerge. This is not an easy task, and the chances of a teacher's improvising consistently good rules are small.

Some writers have proposed eliminating the teaching of grammar altogether. Krashen (1982) held that learners only need *comprehensible input*, a bit more advanced than the language they can already produce. He claimed that this would lead learners progressively towards proficiency. This approach has been clearly shown not to work, in careful studies by researchers such as Swain (1985) and Genesee (1987).

Another proposal is the Natural Order Hypothesis (Meisel, Clahsen & Pienemann, 1981): the idea that there is a natural developmental sequence for acquiring second language grammar features, no matter the order of teaching. This hypothesis has some evidence behind it, although only for a very few structures of the language. Even for those few structures, Goldschneider and DeKeyser (2005) demonstrated in a rigorous meta-analysis that the developmental order is strongly predicted by salience – how much the feature stands out in the language. Given this finding, it is clear that making a grammar feature more salient to the learner, for example by explicit teaching, should be a way of fostering learning.

It has also been claimed that peer-peer support, where students in a class help one another to learn, is an effective way of teaching grammar. This is based on a sound framework (Vygotsky, 1978), but the framework supposes an expert-novice pair, not two novices. Research has described some interesting interactions; but the peers almost always come up with a non-standard grammar form.

One respected framework for language acquisition that supports explicit grammar teaching is the input-interaction-output framework, in which the learner is gradually pushed to restructure their internal second language grammar so it approaches standard grammar more closely. Here, explicit grammar teaching is seen as valuable because it

- helps learners to notice grammar features in the input

- encourages learners to notice the differences between how they say something and how proficient speakers say it

- provides information about what *doesn't* happen in the language.

Another strong current approach, *task-supported instruction*, holds that it is important for learners to use their language in tasks, where the main focus is on meaning, but where the learners need to interact in their second language to reach an outcome. Early on, it was hoped that tasks would be enough to make grammar emerge. However, all serious scholars working in this paradigm (e.g. Skehan, 2003; Willis & Willis, 2007) now agree that pre-task and post-task explicit focus on grammar is necessary.

In a skills-based approach, where language learning is seen like learning to drive or to play a musical instrument, teaching grammar rules is highly valued. Learning the rules is seen as a precursor to being able to use those rules. As DeKeyser (1998) says, while you are learning to walk the walk, the rule is a crutch to lean on.

However, these are theories. What about the evidence? There have been rigorous meta-analyses finding that:

- explicit teaching of grammar rules yields better results than implicit teaching (Norris & Ortega, 2000)

- explicit teaching yields better results for both simple and complex forms (Spada and Tomita, 2010)

- explicit teaching of rules, combined with communicative practice, leads to unconscious knowledge of the grammar forms that lasts over time (Spada and Lightbown, 2008)

- there is no difference in results between integrating the teaching of rules with a communicative activity and teaching them separately (Spada and Tomita, 2010). In other words, presentation-practice-production works just as well as more integrated methods.

To summarise: there is theoretical support and hard evidence that teaching grammar rules, combined with communicative practice, is the best way for adults in classrooms to learn to use the grammar of their new language.

Navigate often teaches rules 'inductively': learners are given a bank of examples of the rule. Then they see part of the rule and are guided to think about how to complete it. There is evidence that for appropriate rules this works as well, and perhaps better, than giving the rule first (e.g. VanPatten & Oikkonen, 1996; Ming & Maarof, 2010).

Navigate also provides a wealth of communicative activities where the focus is on meaning, but which are structured so as to encourage the use of the rules that have been taught. This provides the second ingredient of the recipe that has been shown to be the best way for adults to learn to become more proficient users of second language grammar.

References

DeKeyser, R. 1998. 'Beyond focus on form: cognitive perspectives on learning and practicing second language grammar' in C. Doughty & J. Williams (eds.). *Focus on Form in Classroom Second Language Acquisition*. Cambridge: Cambridge University Press.

Genesee, F. 1987. *Learning through Two Languages*. New York: Newbury House.

Goldschneider, J. M. & DeKeyser, R. M. (2005). Explaining the "Natural Order of L2 Morpheme Acquisition" in English: A Meta-analysis of Multiple Determinants. *Language Learning* 55(S1):27-76

Krashen, S. 1982. *Principles and practice in second language acquisition*. Oxford: Pergamon Press.

Meisel, H., J. Clahsen & M. Pienemann. 1981. 'On determining developmental stages in natural second language acquisition'. *Studies in Second Language Acquisition* 3:109-135.

Norris, J. M. & L. Ortega. 2000. 'Effectiveness of L2 instruction: a research synthesis and quantitative meta-analysis'. *Language Learning* 50/3: 417-528.

Skehan, P. 2003. 'Task-based instruction'. *Language Teaching* 36/ 1:1-14.

Spada, N. & Lightbown, P. (1999). Instruction, first language influence, and developmental readiness in second language acquisition. *The Modern Language Journal* 83(i):1-22.

Spada, N. & P. M. Lightbown. 2008. 'Form-focused instruction: isolated or integrated?' *TESOL Quarterly* 42: 181-207.

Spada, N. & Y. Tomita. 2010. 'Interactions between type of instruction and type of language feature: a meta-analysis'. *Language Learning* 60/2: 1-46.

Swain, M. 1985. 'Communicative competence: some roles of comprehensible input and comprehensible output in its development', in S. Gass & C. Madden (eds.). *Input in Second Language Acquisition*. Rowley MA: Newbury House, 235-253.

VanPatten, B. & S. Oikkonen. 1996. 'Explanation versus structured input in processing instruction'. *Studies in Second Language Acquisition* 18/4: 495-510.

Vygotsky, L. S. 1978. *Mind in Society: the Development of Higher Psychological Processes*. Cambridge, MA: Harvard University Press.

Willis, D. & Willis, J. 2007. *Doing Task-Based Teaching*. Oxford: Oxford University Press.

Grammar teaching in *Navigate*

Grammar is taught in context through texts and audio recordings, and then followed up with Grammar focus boxes which offer the rules of the grammar point in a succinct and level-appropriate way.

Exercises to practise the grammar point offer controlled practice, and a speaking task gives learners the opportunity to reproduce the grammar point in a semi-controlled way.

The Grammar reference section at the back of the Coursebook offers more detailed grammar explanations and further controlled practice, to give learners as much opportunity as possible to assimilate the grammar point.

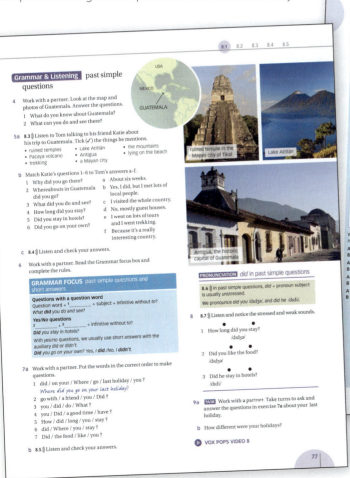

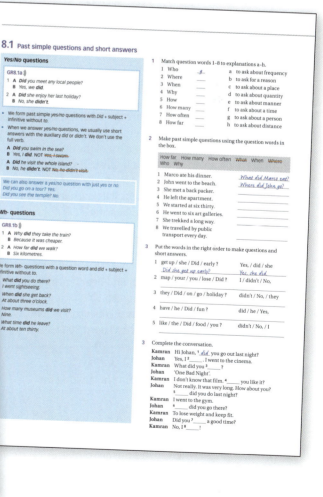

The *Navigate* approach – Vocabulary

Vocabulary and the Oxford 3000

Vocabulary is a crucial area of adult language learning and *Navigate* puts a strong emphasis on it. As well as useful and transferable vocabulary sets that allow students to speak in some detail and depth on general topics, there is a dedicated page in every unit on vocabulary development which covers areas like word families, prefixes or suffixes, collocations and fixed expressions.

In developing the vocabulary syllabus across the six levels of *Navigate*, special attention was paid to the Oxford 3000 – a tool to help teachers and learners focus on the key vocabulary needed to become proficient in English. The Oxford 3000 is integrated into the vocabulary syllabus and items from the coursebook that appear in the Oxford 3000 are indicated by a key symbol in the wordlists found on the Student's DVD, the Coursebook e-book, and on the Teacher's Support and Resource Disc. As you would expect, at the lower levels of *Navigate* a high proportion of words on these wordlists are in the Oxford 3000, and as students progress through the course to higher levels they will learn more vocabulary that sits outside this core 3000.

But what exactly is the Oxford 3000? Read on to find out.

The Oxford 3000 – The words students need to know to succeed in English

Which words should students learn to succeed in English?

The English language contains literally thousands of words and, as language teachers or language learners, it is often difficult to know which words are the most important to learn. To help with this, Oxford University Press's ELT dictionary team created the Oxford 3000 - a list of the 3000 words that students really need to know in English. It was drawn up in collaboration with teachers and language experts. The Oxford 3000 words are included in most OUP learner's dictionaries, including the Oxford Advanced Learner's Dictionary.

The Oxford 3000 words are marked with a key in OUP's learner's dictionaries, and are available on the **www.oxfordlearnersdictionaries.com** website. You can look up the entry for each word, and hear it pronounced in either British or American English. At elementary level OUP learner's dictionaries focus on the Oxford 2000, which includes 2000 of the words on the Oxford 3000 list.

How was the Oxford 3000 created?

There were three key requirements in creating the Oxford 3000:

1 sources – to provide evidence of how the English language is actually used

2 criteria – to use when analysing the sources

3 expertise – to provide insights into the vocabulary needs of learners of English.

1 Sources

The Oxford 3000 is a corpus-based list. A corpus is an electronic database of language from different subject areas and contexts which can be searched using special software. When lexicographers analyse a particular word in the corpus, the corpus shows all of the occurrences of that word, the contexts in which it is used, and the grammatical patterns of the surrounding words.

The Oxford 3000 is informed by the:

- British National Corpus (100 million words)
- Oxford Corpus Collection (developed by Oxford University Press and including different types of English – British English, American English, business English, etc.)

By using this combination of corpora, we can understand how English is currently used, and which words are used most frequently.

2 Criteria

When deciding which words should be in the Oxford 3000, corpus frequency alone was not used as a guide to inclusion. Three core criteria were identified:

- frequency – the words which appear most often in English
- range – the words which appear frequently AND across a broad range of different contexts
- familiarity – words that are not necessarily used the most frequently, but are important in general English.

The combination of frequency, range and familiarity means that the Oxford 3000 is more pedagogically informed than a list of words based on frequency alone. For example, when the corpus was analysed, it was found that we talk about 'Friday' and 'Saturday' more frequently than 'Tuesday' or 'Wednesday'. However, when learning the days of the week, it is useful to learn all of them at the same time – not just the most frequent ones. For this reason, all the days of the week appear in the Oxford 3000.

3 Expertise

A group of lexicographers and around 70 English language teachers from English language schools all over the world worked together on the Oxford 3000, bringing classroom experience and linguistic expertise together to create a list that truly supports the needs of language learners.

Why use the Oxford 3000?

When the research team looked at the corpora using the criteria mentioned above, they found that around 3000 words covered 80–85% of vocabulary in a general English text.

Here are the results of the research into frequency and coverage – that is, how much text is covered by the thousand most frequent words, the next thousand most frequent words, the third thousand most frequent words, and so on.

most frequent word families	coverage	total
1st 1000	74.1%	
2nd 1000	7.2%	2000 = 81.3% coverage (74.1% + 7.2%)
3rd 1000	3.9%	3000 = 85.2% coverage (81.3% + 3.9%)
4th 1000	2.4%	4000 = 87.6% coverage (85.2% + 2.4%)
5th 1000	1.8%	5000 = 89.4% coverage (87.6% + 1.8%)

12,500 word families cover 95% of text.

By learning the first 3000 words, students build a very strong vocabulary base which covers a significant majority of the words they will see in texts. The *Oxford 3000* therefore provides a useful springboard for expanding vocabulary and is a valuable guide in vocabulary learning. If a learner comes across a new word and it is in the *Oxford 3000*, they can be sure that it is important to learn it.

Beyond the *Oxford 3000*

As students advance in their learning, the vocabulary they need will depend on the areas of English that they are interested in. The *Oxford 3000* will give them a good base for expanding their lexical knowledge.

Dictionaries and the *Oxford 3000*

The *Oxford 3000* app

Oxford 3000 is a list of the most important and useful words to know in English informed by corpus-based research. In a recent survey, over 60% of teachers told us they believe that learning the *Oxford 3000* expands their students' vocabulary. The new Learn the *Oxford 3000* app for iPad/iPhone™ helps students learn the *Oxford 3000* with practice exercises and tests to check progress.

Oxford Wordpower Dictionary 4th edition

Updated with over 500 new words, phrases and meanings, *Oxford Wordpower Dictionary* is a corpus-based dictionary that provides the tools intermediate learners need to build vocabulary and prepare for exams. *Oxford 3000* keyword entries show the most important words to know in English. This edition includes Topic Notes, Exam Tips and Writing Tips, and a 16-page Oxford Writing Tutor. Students can search the A-Z dictionary by word or topic on the CD-ROM, and use the exercises to practise for international exams.

Oxford Advanced Learner's Dictionary 9

The *Oxford Advanced Learner's Dictionary* is the world's best-selling advanced learner's dictionary. The new ninth edition, featuring 185,000 words, phrases and meanings, develops the skills students need for passing exams and communicating in English. It is the ultimate speaking and writing tool, with brand new resources including the Oxford iSpeaker and Oxford Speaking Tutor.

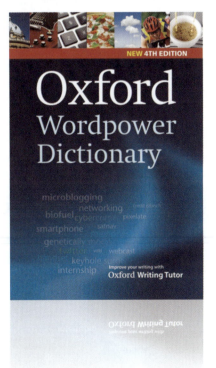

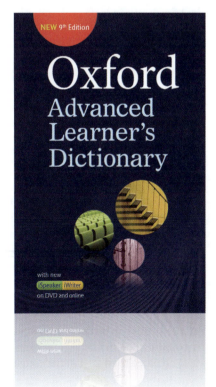

The *Navigate* approach – Photocopiables

Photocopiable Teacher's Resource Materials – Jill Hadfield

What are photocopiable resource materials?

The resource materials in *Navigate* Teacher's Guide are one-page photocopiable activities that can be used to provide further practice of the target language in this book. There are 36 activities, divided into three sections: Grammar, Vocabulary and Communication, and they practise the target grammar, lexis and functions in the book.

What types of activity will I find?

There are two main types of activity in the photocopiable materials: linguistic activities and communicative activities.

Linguistic activities focus on accuracy and finding the right answer, inserting the correct word in a gap-fill, for example. These are familiar exercise types and require correct answers which are given in the Answer Key in the Teachers' Notes.

Communicative activities have non-linguistic goals: solving a puzzle or finding differences in two pictures, for example. The emphasis is more on fluency and on using the target language as a means to an end. The communicative activities in this book fall into two types: open-ended activities such as discussions or role plays with no fixed end-point or goal, and closed-task, game-like activities, such as board games or guessing games with a fixed goal.

Why use them?

The activities can be used to provide extra practice or revision in speaking, reading and writing the target language in each unit. The different types of activity provide different types of practice, which will appeal to different learner preferences. The linguistic activities provide practice in recalling the target language and using it accurately, and the communicative activities provide practice in recalling the target language and using it, integrated with other language, to complete a task. Some of these activities are designed with a game-like element: that is, they have a goal such as guessing or solving a problem, which students have to work together to achieve. This provides variety and a change of focus for the students and makes the practice fun and enjoyable. The element of play is also relaxing and lowers the affective filter (Krashen 1987) which makes learners less inhibited and more willing to use the language, and the fact that the activities have a goal is motivating for the learners and gives them a sense of satisfaction when they have achieved the goal. Other activities have a personalization element which is also motivating for the learners and leads to positive affect. Both personalized and playful activities involve the learners in investing more of themselves in the language, leading to deeper processing which helps retention of language items (Schmitt 2000).

When should I use them?

The activities can be used immediately at the end of each relevant section in the book for extra practice. Alternatively, they could be used later in the course for revision or review.

How should I use them?

The activities are for pair, group or whole class mingling work. This means you will have to think carefully about:

- how to arrange the groupings
- how to set up the activities and give instructions
- what your role will be during the activities
- what the different requirements of the 3 different activity types will be regarding monitoring, finishing off the activity and giving feedback.

Classroom layout

If you have desks arranged in groups of tables, you probably will have 4–6 students at each group of tables. This makes pairwork and groupwork easy. Mingling activities can be done in the spaces between the tables, or in a space at the front of the class if tables are pushed back a bit.

If you have desks in a U-shape, adjacent pairs can easily work together. Groups of three and four are best arranged by asking one or two students to move and sit opposite another pair of students. This makes it much easier for students to listen and talk to each other than if they are sitting in a line. Whole class mingling activities are easily arranged by asking students to move to the space in the centre of the U.

Even if you have fixed and immovable desks arranged in rows, you can adapt the arrangement to pair and group work by asking adjacent students to work with each other, or those in the row in front to turn around and work with the students behind them. Whole class mingling activities may cause more of a problem if space is limited, but you can adapt the activities so that only half the class is standing up and moving while the other half remain seated.

Setting up the activities

The activities often have several stages. This means you will have to be very clear in your own mind about how the stages follow each other. Here are some tips for giving instructions:

- Use simple language: simple vocabulary and simple sentence structure.

- One step, one sentence, then pause and make sure they have understood. Very often you may have to give an instruction, then wait for each group or pair to carry it out, before going on with the next, e.g. *Take a counter each … OK … have you all got a counter? … Place your counter on the START square …*

- Use checking questions, for example, *Are you working in pairs or on your own?*

- Use demonstration: show how to carry out an activity by doing it yourself for the class to watch, or by playing the first round of the game with one group while the class watches.

Teacher's role

Your role during the activity will vary. At the start you will be an Instruction Giver. During the activity you will have to be a Monitor, circulating and listening to the students in order to monitor progress, give help where needed, and note errors for feedback at the end of the activity. Depending on your class you may also have to be an Explainer if students have misunderstood what to do (if a number of them have misunderstood, you will need to stop the activity and give the instructions again), or a Controller, if students are off-task or not speaking English. Finally, you will need to stop the activity and give feedback. Your exact role during and at the end of the activities will vary according to the type of activity.

Linguistic activities

Some of these activities are to be done in pairs and some individually. If students are working individually (e.g. for a gap-fill), get them to check their answers in pairs before you give feedback. If they are working in pairs, get them to check with another pair. These activities are accuracy based and have one right answer. This means that you will need to go through the correct answers with the class at the end and explain any problems. It is a good idea to have visual support in the form of answers on the board or on a handout for students who may misunderstand the oral answers.

Communicative activities – open-ended

These activities do not have an outcome or come to a pre-arranged end. You will therefore have to keep a close eye on students to see when they are running out of ideas. If they come to a stop early while you feel the activity has more mileage, you may have to encourage them, or suggest new ideas. You will have to decide when to stop the activity – make sure students have come up with enough ideas, but don't let it go on so long that they get bored. There are no 'right answers' to these activities, so feedback is a matter of 'rounding off' the activity by asking students to share ideas.

Communicative activities – closed task

These game-like activities will come to an end automatically when the goal has been achieved. Some groups may achieve their goal earlier than others. You can keep them occupied by putting groups together and asking them to compare solutions. These activities often have an answer or 'solution', so feedback will involve going through solutions and checking answers in much the same way as for the linguistic activities.

References

Hadfield, J *Elementary Communication Games* Pearson 1987.

Krashen, S. *Principles and Practice in Second Language Acquisition* Prentice-Hall International, 1987.

Schmitt, N. *Vocabulary in Language Teaching* Cambridge: Cambridge University Press, 2000

Jill Hadfield has worked as a teacher trainer in Britain, France and New Zealand and worked on development projects with Ministries of Education and aid agencies in China, Tibet and Madagascar. She has also conducted short courses, seminars and workshops for teachers in many other countries. She is currently Associate Professor on the Language Teacher Education team in the Department of Language Studies at Unitec, New Zealand and has been appointed International Ambassador for IATEFL. She has written over thirty books, including the *Communication Games* series (Pearson), *Excellent!*, a 3 level primary course (Pearson), the *Oxford Basics* series, *Classroom Dynamics* and *An Introduction to Teaching English* (OUP). Her latest book, *Motivating Learning*, co-authored with Zoltan Dornyei, was published in 2013 by Routledge in the *Research and Resources in Language Teaching* series, of which she is also series editor.

Photocopiable Teacher's Resource Materials in *Navigate*

The photocopiable Teacher's Resource Materials for *Navigate* can be found at the back of this Teacher's Guide, as well as on the *Teacher's Support and Resource Disc*, packaged with the *Teacher's Guide*, as downloadable PDFs. They are also available to download from the *Navigate iTools* classroom presentation software product.

The *Navigate* approach – The CEFR

The CEFR – Anthony Green

The *Common European Framework of Reference for Languages* (or CEFR), published by the Council of Europe in 2001, is intended to help teachers and others to develop and connect language syllabuses, curriculum guidelines, examinations and textbooks. It takes what it describes as an 'action-oriented approach' to language education: the purpose of learning a language is to enable the learner to communicate increasingly effectively in a growing range of social situations that are relevant to his or her individual needs.

For many educational systems, the CEFR's concern with effective communication represents a shift in emphasis. Instead of focusing on what learners know about a language – how many words they know or how accurately they can apply grammar rules – the key question for the CEFR is what learners might actually want to do with the language or languages they are learning – the activities they might need to carry out and the ideas they might want to express. Achievement in language learning is measured by the learner's degree of success in using languages to negotiate their way through the world around them.

Although practical communication is seen to be a fundamental goal, the CEFR does not try to suggest how this goal should be reached. It is not a recipe book that tells course designers what to include or that tells teachers how to teach. Instead, it offers a common set of terms that can apply to learners of different languages in different countries within a variety of educational systems. These common terms make it easier to draw comparisons and connect what happens in language education in one setting to what happens elsewhere.

It is part of the Council of Europe's educational philosophy of lifelong learning that learners should be able to move easily between informal learning, schools, universities and workplace training courses in different places to pick up and keep track of the practical skills that they need. This is much easier if everyone shares the same basic terms for talking about teaching and learning. If a 'Beginner' level class in one school is like an 'Elementary' level class in another school, or a 'Preliminary' class in a third and the 'Getting Started' book in textbook series X is like the 'Grade 2' book in series Y, life in the English classroom can soon get very confusing.

Having a shared descriptive language is very useful for course designers because it helps us to see how a particular course can fit into a learner's individual language learning career. In the CEFR, levels of language ability are set out – running from *Basic* (A1 and A2), through *Independent* (B1 and B2) up to *Proficient* (C1 and C2). These levels are based on teachers' judgements of the relative difficulty of 'Can Do' statements describing how learners are able to use language. For example, at the A1 level a learner, 'can use simple phrases and sentences to describe where he/she lives and people he/she knows', but at B2 'can present clear, detailed descriptions on a wide range of subjects related to his/her field of interest'. The system helps learners to monitor their progress, find suitable learning materials and identify which qualifications might be within their reach.

Of course, not every learner will need or want to 'present clear, detailed descriptions on a wide range of subjects'. The framework is not a specification of what learners ought to know, it simply provides examples of what is typically taught and learned at each level. Users are free (in fact they are encouraged) to add to the comprehensive, but far from exhaustive range of Can Do activities presented. People do not all choose to learn languages for the same reasons: they prioritise different skills and aspire to reach different objectives. Nor does everyone progress in their language learning in quite the same way. Someone who has learned a language informally while living in a country where that language is spoken may chat confidently with friends and colleagues, but find it more difficult to read a novel. On the other hand, someone who has learnt from books may read and translate with assurance, but struggle to keep up with the dialogue in films.

The framework captures such differences by providing a terminology for the range of social situations where learners may need to use languages and the kinds of knowledge, skills and abilities – competences – they might bring into play to achieve effective communication. Developing language abilities can involve 'horizontal' growth – coping with new contexts for language use – as well as 'vertical' progression through the CEFR levels. Horizontal progress could include shifts in the focus for learning between the written and spoken language, between more receptive language use (reading and listening) to more interactive (exchanging text messages and emails or participating in conversation) as well as shifts between different social domains (such as shifting from more academic to more occupational, workplace related language use).

Increasingly, English language textbooks include Can Do objectives derived from the CEFR in each unit. However, unlike *Navigate*, most have only incorporated the CEFR retrospectively, often after publication. This can certainly help to situate them in relation to other courses and systems of qualifications, but using the framework in the development process can bring much greater benefits. This is because in addition to providing a shared terminology, the framework poses challenging questions that help designers and other users to think about, describe and explain why they choose to learn, teach or assess language abilities in the way that they do. These questions keep the language learner at the heart of every decision. Examples of the wide range of issues that developers are invited to consider include, 'the communicative tasks in the personal, public, occupational and/or educational domains that the learner will need to tackle', 'how communicative and learning activities relate to the learner's drives, motivations and interests' and the 'provision ... made for learners to become increasingly independent in their learning and use of language'.

Although the CEFR can provide us with shared terms, it is clear that people working in different places may sometimes understand the framework in quite different ways. The Can Do statements are inevitably open to a range of interpretations. For example, phrases and sentences that are considered 'simple' by one teacher may seem rather 'complex' to another. There have been complaints that the A2 level represented in one text book is as difficult as the B1 level in another. This has serious implications: if there is not at least a similar understanding of the levels among users of the framework, many of the potential benefits of the CEFR will be lost.

Recognizing the need to build shared interpretations and to provide more concrete guidance, the Council of Europe has called for the production of 'Reference Level Descriptions' which can show in much greater detail how the CEFR applies to specific languages. For English, a good deal of work has already been done. *Threshold* (first published in 1975, but updated in 1990) is effectively a specification of B1 level objectives. Other books cover CEFR A1 (*Breakthrough*), A2 (*Waystage*) and B2 and above (*Vantage*). All of these are available in print or as free e-books via the English Profile website at **www.englishprofile.org**. At the same site, you can find information about the ongoing work of English Profile

which aims to further build our shared understanding of the CEFR as it applies to English.

To make the most of the CEFR and its place in the *Navigate* series, I would encourage teachers to learn more about the framework and the ways in which it can help to guide the teaching and learning process (as well as some of the many criticisms that have been made of its use). It is worth taking the time to find out about the overall descriptive scheme as well as the more familiar levels. The best place to start is the Council of Europe Language Policy Division website (**www.coe.int/t/dg4/linguistic**) where the rather more reader-friendly *Guide for Users*, the CEFR itself and many related resources can be downloaded free of charge.

Anthony Green is Professor of Language Assessment at the University of Bedfordshire, UK. He has published widely on language assessment issues and his recent book *Language Functions Revisited* (2012) sets out to fill the gap between the broad descriptions of levels provided in the CEFR and the level of detail required for applications such as syllabus or test design. His main research interests concern the design and use of language assessments and relationships between assessment, teaching and learning.

Reference to the CEFR in *Navigate*

The contents pages of *Navigate* Coursebook show not only what language points are taught in each unit, but also what the communicative goals are. Teachers and learners can relate their learning to real-world situations and see at a glance what Can-do activities they will become competent in.

Each lesson shows clear communicative goals.

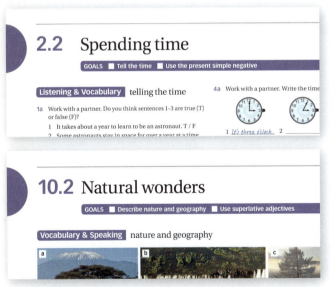

The *Navigate* Workbook allows students to self-assess on Can-do statements at the end of every section, giving them the opportunity to check their progress and manage their learning.

Teachers can also download a CEFR mapping document from the *Navigate* Teacher's website (**www.oup.com/teacher/navigate**) to see full details of how the competencies from the CEFR are covered in each level of *Navigate*.

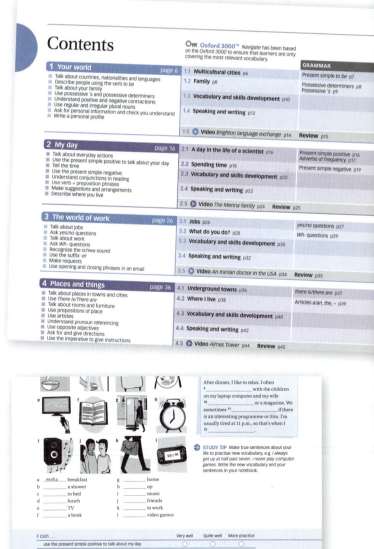

The *Navigate* approach – Testing

The *Navigate* Testing Package – Imelda Maguire-Karayel

As all teachers know, assessment is central to effective syllabus design and is an essential part of effective teaching and learning. It not only allows learners to recognize their achievements and make progress, but it enables instructors to shape and adapt their teaching to specific needs. This is especially true in the case of busy adult learners who often have limited time for attending language courses. Two of the main constructs in modern language testing are validity and practicality. Validity is key, a test has to measure what it claims to, and practicality is essential as tests should be easy both for teachers to administer and learners to take.

The *Navigate* course comes complete with its own testing package. This is included in the Teacher's Guide and is published in both Word and PDF formats. At each of the six levels, the teacher is provided with a complete set of tests designed to test learners' understanding and proficiency: twelve Unit tests, four Progress tests and one End-of-course test. Reflecting the course ideology, the tasks in the tests present learners with content that is both information rich, and international in flavour, while allowing them to practise newly acquired language in a range of contexts.

Unit tests

The Unit tests measure learners' understanding of the key grammar, vocabulary and decoding skills presented in the unit, the latter being tested in a similar context to the one in the unit. Unit tests are intended to last up to sixty minutes and comprise ten tasks. Greater weight is given to vocabulary and grammar which is tested across five different task types. Vocabulary is typically tested through tasks such as multiple-choice questions, matching sentence endings, gap fill, word formation or first letter tasks. Grammar is tested through tasks such as multiple-choice cloze, open cloze, or right/wrong questions, sentence transformation. The reading and listening decoding skills covered in the third lesson of each unit are tested across two tasks so that teachers and learners can see how effectively they have attained a command of potential blockages to comprehension. The functional language taught in the fourth lesson is also tested in an authentic context.

Each Unit test also includes two exam-style tasks, modelled on those in Cambridge Main Suite exams or IELTS. Tasks include those found in Cambridge English: Key, Preliminary and First, and have been especially written to reflect the theme of the unit. As they give exposure to task format and simulate exam conditions to some extent, the inclusion of the exam-style tasks is likely to be very beneficial for learners who go on to take certified exams. The exam-type tasks learners will do in the Unit tests include multiple matching, matching headings, note-taking, true/false/not given, sentence transformation, multiple-choice reading comprehension, gapped text, short answer questions and open cloze. The accompanying Answer Key to each test allows busy teachers to mark unit tests quickly and accurately, thereby reducing demands on teachers' time.

Learners take Unit tests once they have completed the corresponding unit, and teachers and learners alike can evaluate if the learning objectives for that particular unit have been achieved. Teachers can then, if necessary, spend more time covering language points which need more attention. If they think it is more appropriate for their learners, teachers may also administer certain sections of the test only to match the sections of the unit that have been covered in class. Times can be adjusted accordingly.

Progress tests

There are four Progress tests in the *Navigate* testing package, each one intended to last approximately 60 minutes and to be administered after every three units. Progress tests are designed to test learners' proficiency. The content of each Progress test relates to the material covered in the units, but the Progress tests differ from the Unit tests in that they more closely resemble established international English Language exams. The vocabulary and grammar of the three units is tested by task types such as open or multiple-choice cloze. All four language skills are tested in the Progress tests. The Listening tasks comprise two question types, such as true/false, gap fill and multiple choice questions, and it can also cover some of the functional language from the three units. The Reading tasks also comprise two different task types, such as multiple matching, true/false/not given or multiple choice. Writing is tested through two tasks; the first is a short task testing discrete language items and the second is a longer task which requires the learner to produce a piece of extended written discourse. Writing tasks are authentic in that they reflect the real-world communication likely to be undertaken by learners. Genres include emails, text messages, form completion and social media posts. The Speaking task also assess learners' grasp of the units' functional language by asking them to carry out a transactional role-play based on a set of prompts. It appears at the end of the Progress test on a separate page and can be done at a later time than the rest of the test, either in pairs or with the teacher acting as one of the speakers in the task.

General mark schemes are provided to assist teachers in marking both the Speaking and Writing tasks. Care has been taken to ensure that the topic in each of the tested skills relates to as many units, thereby keeping the face validity of the Progress test high. For example, the content of the Listening section will usually relate to a different unit to the content of the Reading task. The same usually applies in the case of the Speaking and Writing skills.

End-of-course test

The End-of-course test also focuses on the four skills and tests target language from the entire course. As vocabulary and grammar are at the heart of the *Navigate* syllabus, these language systems are rigorously tested in the End-of-course test through task types such as gap-fill, open cloze and multiple-choice questions, with the course's functional language incorporated across tasks. The main part of the test covers tasks on Vocabulary, Grammar, Reading and Listening. There are 100 points available for the main test. Teachers are also provided with optional Speaking and Writing tests worth 20 points each, so if students take all parts of the test, they can achieve a maximum score of 140. The Writing task can easily be set along with the main test, but this will increase the time needed to complete the test, so teachers may prefer to set that part on a separate occasion. The Speaking tasks can be done at a time that is convenient for the teacher and students. This could be during normal class hours, by giving the class an extended task to do, and then taking pairs of students to a quiet space to do the Speaking test. Or the teacher may wish to set aside a different time for the Speaking test. It is advisable to do the Speaking test as soon as possible after the main test. As in the Progress tests, all tasks are exam-like in nature and general mark schemes are provided.

The *Navigate* tests are written by experts in the field of language assessment, many of whom also have years of EFL-teaching experience. As the test writers have extensive experience of writing for leading exam boards or assessment bodies, they bring knowledge of good practice in language assessment. The use of assessment experts also means that a consistent approach has been applied throughout the production of the tests. The test writers also contribute a deep understanding of aligning language to the CEFR. The result is a reliable, robust end-to-end testing package, which we are confident teachers and students using *Navigate* will find useful and rewarding as they work their way through the various levels of the course.

Imelda Maguire-Karayel has over twenty years' experience in ELT. She is an EFL/EAP teacher and teacher-trainer, a materials writer, and an educational consultant for adapting a BBC language education series for television.

She has taught in private language schools, ECIS-accredited schools and universities in Hong Kong, Greece, Turkey and the UK.

She has worked for Cambridge English and now works as an English language assessment consultant in the production of exam materials, exam practice materials, course-based assessment materials, and course books.

She has written course-based assessment and exam practice materials for *New Headway* (OUP), *English File* (OUP), *Touchstone* (CUP), and *Foundation IELTS Masterclass* (OUP)

The *Navigate* tests

All the tests for *Navigate* can be found on the Teacher's Support and Resource Disc that is packaged with the Teacher's Guide.

Tests are supplied as PDFs and as Word documents for those occasions where teachers may wish to edit some sections of the tests. There are A and B versions of each test – the B version containing the same content as the A version but in a different order, to mitigate potential cheating if learners are sitting close to each other whilst doing the test.

Audio MP3 files for the tests are also available on the Teacher's Support and Resource Disc. All tests that contain a listening task begin with this task so that there are no timing issues with the listening during a test.

1 Your world

Unit overview

Language input

Present simple *to be* (CB p7)	• *He's from Nigeria.* • *I'm not from Brazil.* • *Are they Italian? No, they aren't.*
Possessive determiners (CB p8)	• *my, your, his, her, its, our, their*
Possessive *'s* (CB p9)	• *His son's name is Rudolfo.*
Grammar reference (CB pp136–137)	

Vocabulary development

Countries, nationalities and languages (CB p6)	• *Mexico, Mexican, Spanish*
Family (CB p9)	• *father, mother, sister-in-law …*
Regular and irregular plural nouns (CB p11)	• *cousin – cousins* • *knife – knives*

Skills development

Listening: understanding positive and negative contractions (CB p10)

Speaking: asking for personal information and checking you understand (CB p12)

Writing: a personal profile (CB p13)

Video

Documentary: Brighton language exchange (CB p14)

Vox pops (Coursebook DVD & TG p256)

More materials

Workbook	• Language practice for vocabulary, pronunciation, grammar, speaking and writing
Photocopiable activities	• Grammar: All over the world (TG p203 & TSRD) • Vocabulary: Who's Marcos? (TG p221 & TSRD) • Communication: Something in common (TG p238 & TSRD)
Tests	• Unit 1 test (TSRD)
Unit 1 wordlist (TSRD)	

1.1 Multicultural cities

Goals

- Talk about countries, nationalities and languages
- Describe people using the verb *to be*

Lead-in

Closed book. To check students' existing knowledge of the language they will cover in this lesson.

- Ask students these questions:
  What country are we in? What nationalities live here? What is/are the language(s) of this country?
- Write answers on the board and correct any errors.

Vocabulary & Speaking countries, nationalities and languages

Exercise 1

- You could demonstrate this with the class using the first photo – show the photos on an IWB or projector if you have one.
- Put students in pairs. Ask students to discuss questions 1–3. To prepare for feedback, ask students to write their ideas on the board for each photo, e.g. Photo 1: England; Nationalities: British (also many Asian, European, African, West Indian nationalities); English is the main language. Other languages include Polish and Urdu.

Exercise 2

- Ask students to work with a partner. Refer them to p126. Ask students to check their answers. You could ask students to correct any errors they made on the board in exercise 1.

ANSWERS

1 a the UK   b the USA   c Australia
  d the United Arab Emirates (UAE)
2 a British   b American   c Australian   d Emirati
3 a English   b English   c English   d Arabic

CRITICAL THINKING All these cities have many different nationalities living in them. You can see this in the communication activity for this lesson. Open a class discussion. Students can share knowledge and discuss the positive aspects of living in a place with many nationalities and cultures.

Exercise 3

- Use the answers from exercise 2 to lead in to this. Ask for an example of a country, nationality and language from one of the photos. Direct students to the first example, which is completed.
- Prepare the board for answers while students work in their pairs. Ask fast finishers to add their answers to the board.
- Check answers.

ANSWERS

Arabic L Chinese N, L English N, L Jamaica C
Mexican N Pakistani N Spanish N, L the UAE C

Exercise 4a

- Put students into pairs, grouping faster and slower learners where possible to encourage peer teaching.

- Do the first example together (Mexico, Mexican, Spanish).
- Ask students to work together and complete the table.

Exercise 4b 1.1 🔊

- Play track 1.1 and ask students to check their answers.
- Pause on any difficult examples to focus on spelling. Add the correct spelling to the board.

WATCH OUT! Some students will have trouble with punctuation. In some languages such as Spanish, the names of countries do not have capital letters.

Exercise 4c 1.1 🔊

- Add *Italian* to the board and ask students how many syllables it has. Check they understand *syllable* (= a part of a word that has one vowel sound).
- Ask which syllable is stressed (spoken louder and a bit longer). Mark this clearly on the board. For example, oOo helps students to see how many syllables there are and which is stressed.
- Play track 1.1 and ask students to mark the stressed syllable; direct them to the examples in the Coursebook to help.
- Check answers and drill the correct pronunciation.

ANSWERS/AUDIOSCRIPT 1.1

● Mexico	● Mexican	● Spanish
● the USA	● American	● English
● Italy	Ital●ian	Ital●ian
● China	Chi●nese	Chi●nese
● Vietnam	Vietnam●ese	Vietnam●ese
● Turkey	● Turkish	● Turkish
● the UK	● British	● English
● Poland	● Polish	● Polish
● Pakistan	Pakist●ani	● Urdu
● the UAE	Em●irati	● Arabic
France	French	French
Greece	Greek	Greek

DICTIONARY SKILLS Show students how word stress is marked in dictionaries. It usually appears like this: 'Arabic with a small apostrophe-like mark before the stressed syllable.

Exercise 5

- Demonstrate with a student. Tell them you are thinking of an object you have at home/in your bag/in this class, etc. Tell them where it's from (It's Chinese). Ask them to guess what it is.
- Put the students into groups of three or four. Tell them to think of three or four objects from different countries and to repeat the activity.

Go over mistakes with pronunciation of countries and nationalities. You can use your fingers to help students identify the stressed syllable. Clearly indicate the number of syllables to the class by holding up your fingers and holding the stressed finger.

Grammar & Listening present simple to be

> **Background notes:** London is a very multicultural city. There are many second/third generation families from different countries living there. Many families are a mix of nationalities as children born in Britain have British nationality but their parents have their original nationality. This means there is a rich mix of cultures. English is used to describe somebody from England, but British is the official nationality of anyone born in Britain (England, Scotland and Wales).

Exercise 6a 1.2 🎵

- Tell students to look at the photo and factfile of Godwin.
- Ask questions to introduce the listening: *Where is Godwin from?* (Nigeria) *So, what is his nationality?* (Nigerian) *Where does he live?* (North London)
- Play track 1.2 and ask students to write the countries, nationalities and languages they hear.

Exercise 6b

- Ask students to compare their lists in pairs.

ANSWERS

the UK   Nigeria   French   half-French   Brazil   England   British   English   Iraq   Polish   Lebanese   American   Turkish   Japanese

Exercise 6c

- Check students understand *boss* (= a person who tells people what to do at work), *wife* (= the woman a man is married to), *saxophone* (= a musical instrument made of metal).
- Tell students to read the factfile and think about what information goes in the gaps. They should work in pairs to complete this task.

Exercise 6d 1.2 🎵

- Play track 1.2. Ask students to listen again and check their answers.
- Ask where Godwin's saxophone is from for an extra challenge. (It's Japanese.)

EXTRA ACTIVITY Ask students to compare where Godwin lives with their own city. Do they live in a multicultural place? What type of restaurants and shops are there?

ANSWERS

1 French   2 Brazil   3 British   4 English   5 Polish
6 restaurant   7 American   8 Turkish

AUDIOSCRIPT 1.2

Interviewer: So, … Tell us about your life here in Britain. Are you from London?
G: Well, my name is Godwin. I'm from Nigeria originally. My wife, Sylvie, is French. Actually, she's half-French: her mother's French and her father's from Brazil. Our two children were born in England, so they're British … We speak English at home. Our home's in north London. Many different nationalities live here. The neighbours are a family from Iraq. Next to our house is a Polish supermarket and the restaurant across the road is Lebanese. I work for an American organization – but my boss isn't American; she's Turkish … What else? … I play football and I play the saxophone and, oh yeah, my saxophone's Japanese.

Exercise 7a

- Do the first example with the whole class. Check contractions – do students know the full form of the contractions?
- Ask students to work in pairs to choose the correct form of the verb *to be*.

ANSWERS

1 Are   2 is   3 'm   4 're   5 are   6 is   7 isn't

Exercise 7b 1.3 🎵

- Play track 1.3. Ask students to listen to the sentences and check their answers to exercise 7a, correcting any mistakes. Check answers with the class.
- Play the track again and ask students to say the sentences with the recording. If they find this difficult, stop the recording and tell the students to repeat with you. Do group, pair and group repetition. Make sure students use the contracted forms and sound as natural as possible.

AUDIOSCRIPT 1.3

1 Are you from London?
2 My name is Godwin.
3 I'm from Nigeria.
4 Our two children were born in England, so they're British.
5 The neighbours are a family from Iraq.
6 The restaurant across the road is Lebanese.
7 My boss isn't American.

PRONUNCIATION Focus on long and short vowel sounds in *are* (ɑː(r)) and *am* (æm). You could also help students sound natural by asking them which syllables are stressed in the sentence. Help them to notice that the nouns and main verbs tend to be stressed. The grammar words are usually not stressed, e.g.

*Are you from **Lon**don?*
*The **neigh**bours are a **fam**ily from I**raq**.*

Exercise 8

- Ask students to work in pairs and use the examples from exercise 7a to complete the rules.

ANSWERS

1 'm   2 're   3 isn't   4 are not   5 Are   6 'm not   7 is
8 aren't

EXTENSION To assess progress and understanding, ask students to make sentences about themselves and friends or other people in the class, e.g.
We're from Colombia. We're not Spanish. She's French. Our teacher's Scottish. Anna's Polish.

- Refer students to *Grammar reference* on p136. There are four more exercises here that students can do for homework.

Exercise 9 1.4 🔘

- Ask students what instrument Godwin plays (the saxophone).
- Write *Andy* and *Murielle* on the board. Tell students they are going to listen for information about these people. Play track 1.4. Ask students to compare ideas in pairs before you check answers together.

ANSWERS

Andy is Godwin's saxophone teacher. Murielle is a student in Godwin's class. She is from Senegal. French is her first language.

AUDIOSCRIPT 1.4
T (Teacher) **G** (Godwin) **M** (Murielle)
T Come in. Oh, hello. What's your name?
G Hi, I'm Godwin.
T I'm Andy, the saxophone teacher. Are you a student?
G No, I'm not. I have a job.
T No … I mean, are you a student for the saxophone class?
G Oh, sorry, yes. Yeah, I am.
T Where are you from, Godwin?
G I'm from Nigeria, but London's my home now.
T Is it your first class?
G Yes, it is.
T OK. Well, let me introduce you to the other students.
G OK.
T This is Murielle. She's a student here, too.
G Hi Murielle. Nice to meet you. I'm Godwin.
M Nice to meet you, too.
G Murielle's a French name. Are you French?
M No, I'm from Senegal. But my first language is French.

Exercise 10a

- Do the first example together.
- Ask students to work in pairs to complete the conversation.

ANSWERS

1 What's 2 Are 3 from 4 Is 5 introduce 6 This
7 too 8 meet 9 I'm 10 too

Exercise 10b 1.4 🔘

- Play track 1.4 again and ask students to check their answers, correcting any mistakes.
- Check students understand *Let me introduce you*, and the use of *This is* to introduce people.

Exercise 11

Put students into groups of three. Demonstrate the exercise with two students so they see how to change the language to make it true for them. Ask students to practise the conversation using their own names and countries.

EXTRA CHALLENGE Tell students to close their books. Project or write the conversation from exercise 10a on the board. Slowly make sections of it disappear. Students have to start to memorize the conversation. Encourage them to change roles as they repeat the conversation.

EXTENSION Refer students to the factfile. Tell them to think of questions to find out the information that they haven't talked about so far in their groups, e.g. *Where do you live? Have you got children? What languages do you speak?* You don't have to insist on 100% accuracy on question formation here but this will allow stronger, more confident students to experiment with language.

Students could create a factfile for someone else in the class after they have asked questions or before they do this extension activity to help them revise and extend the questions they ask. You could simplify or adapt the factfile to the level of your group.

GRAMMAR REFERENCE ANSWERS

Exercise 1
1 am – I'm
2 is – She's
3 are – They're
4 is – She's not/She isn't
5 am – I'm
6 are – You're
7 is – It's

Exercise 2
1 Q: Are you Russian?   A: No, I'm not.
2 Q: Is your name Ben?   A: Yes, it is.
3 Q: Am I late for class today?   A: Yes, you are.
4 Q: Are they British?   A: No, they're American.
5 Q: Are you from Austria?   A: No, we aren't.
6 Q: Is she a teacher?   A: No, she isn't.

Exercise 3
1 Is / Yes, he is.
2 Are / No, I'm not.
3 Am / No, you're not.
4 Is / Yes, it is.
5 Are / Yes, we are.

Exercise 4
1 A: Hi, my name's Luigi.
3 A: No , I'm Italian.
2 B: Hi, I'm Asli. Are you from Spain?
5 A: No, not Rome. I'm from Naples in the South. Where are you from?
4 B: Oh , are you from Rome?
9 A: Oh good!
8 B: Yes, they are, and the teacher is nice.
6 B: I'm from Istanbul in Turkey. Are you a student in this class?
7 A: Yes, I am. It's my first day. Are the students friendly?
10 B: OK! Let me introduce you to my friends.

1.2 Family

Goals

- Talk about your family
- Use possessive 's and possessive determiners

Lead-in

1 Closed book. Review countries and nationalities.

- Ask students to think back to countries and nationalities from lesson 1.1. Ask a student to write them on the board with help from the class.
- Check spelling and correct any mistakes.
- Check pronunciation.

2 Open book. Test before you teach.

- Refer students to the title of the lesson: Family. Ask students to work in pairs. Set a time limit and ask them to write down as many things as they can that the word *family* makes them think of. Two minutes is long enough.
- Ask them to compare their words with another pair.
- Ask two or three students to share any interesting words they heard with the class and go over unknown words.

Reading & Grammar possessive determiners

> **Text summary:** This text is an extract from an article about the high number of twins in a village in India. It asks some questions about why this has happened but does not give any firm answers.

Exercise 1

- If you can, project the photo in the classroom and ask students what is special about it. You can do this exercise in pairs or as a quick whole-class activity.
- As you get ideas from students, add vocabulary to the board and check understanding with the class. Teach the meaning of *twins* (= two people who have the same mother and were born at the same time).

ANSWERS
The children in the photo are special because they are all pairs of twins.

Exercise 2

- Tell students to read the text quickly and focus on the main ideas. Give them a one-minute time limit.
- Ask students if their ideas were correct. Encourage them to refer to ideas from the text to support their answers.

Exercise 3

- Tell students to work in pairs and discuss the questions. Question 3 asks students to interpret the text. According to the text, no one knows why there are lots of twins. The village doctor says there is something in the food or water, but this is possibly not a serious answer. Explain that in English when you can't explain something, people sometimes say that it's because 'there must be something in the water'.

- Check answers.

ANSWERS
1 Kodinhi is not a typical village because there are more twins than the average in India.
2 Yes, they are.
3 The village doctor thinks there are so many twins because there is something in the water or the food.

Exercise 4

- Put students in groups of three or four. Tell them to discuss questions 1 and 2. Encourage students to give reasons and explanations for their ideas as they speak.

FEEDBACK FOCUS Listen to the conversations for examples of good language and mistakes with possessive determiners. Make a note of any examples you hear. Use your notes to adapt how you teach the grammar. If students are using this language very well, you can move quickly over to the next activity. For example:
*My sister has twin girls. **Her** husband has twins in **his** family.* = good use of possessive determiners.
My sister has twin girls. ~~She's husband family has twins.~~ = incorrect use.

Exercise 5

- Write *He and _____ wife* on the board and ask students to fill the gap. Ask them what kind of word it is. (It's a possessive determiner.)

WATCH OUT! Some students find these determiners confusing. In some languages a more usual construction would be *She is the mother of my wife* instead of *She is my wife's mother*. It may be useful to compare possessive determiners with the students' first language.

- Ask students to work individually and complete the Grammar focus table using the examples in the article to help them. Tell them to compare answers in pairs, and then check with the class that they know the correct form and use of the grammar.

ANSWERS
1 my   2 his   3 its   4 our   5 their

- Refer students to *Grammar reference* on p137, exercise 1. Students can do this for homework. (The others are to be done after exercise 12.)

Exercise 6a

- Ask students to work individually and complete the exercise. Tell them to identify which words are possessive determiners and which are personal pronouns.

ANSWERS
1 Her   2 your   3 I   4 they   5 His   6 our

Exercise 6b

- Ask students to compare answers with the person sitting next to them. Afterwards, check answers with the class.

EXTENSION To check how well students remember this language, you could tell them to close their books and do a quick oral test. Shout out personal pronouns and ask students to tell you the possessive determiner, or vice versa. Students could also test each other quickly in pairs for one minute.

Exercise 7

- Tell students to read the example and then complete the exercise individually. Tell them to identify what the determiner is replacing: a man, woman, group of people, or thing.
- Ask them to check their answers with a partner before you check answers with the whole class.

1b their 2b our 3b his 4b Your 5b Her 6b its
7b My

Vocabulary & Speaking family

Exercise 8

- Put students into pairs. Tell them they have two minutes to think of as many family member words as they can. Ask for ONE example to get them started. You could do this activity in two teams with one writer each. Give the teams a big piece of paper and a board pen. They have to work together to add as many words as they can to their paper. Display the pieces of paper after two minutes and see who has the most words. Each word earns a point for the team. You could deduct points for incorrect spelling. This will help you assess their current knowledge and use of this vocabulary area.

Exercise 9a

- Add an example of a male word from the previous activity to the board. Ask students to tell you the female word, e.g. brother ➜ sister
- Ask students to work in pairs to complete the matching activity. Give them a time limit to keep the pace of the lesson up.

ANSWERS
1 c 2 f 3 j 4 g 5 i 6 b 7 h 8 e 9 a 10 d

Exercise 9b 1.5 💿

- Play track 1.5 and check answers. Ask students to listen once to correct their answers, then listen again and repeat. Also ask individuals to repeat, to check pronunciation of more difficult words.

EXTRA ACTIVITY To check students' understanding and use of the vocabulary, ask students to work in pairs and tell each other sentences using the words, e.g. *I don't have a brother but I have a sister. My aunt is called Maria and my uncle is called Pepe.*

PRONUNCIATION There are some difficult vowel and consonant sounds here. The spelling makes the pronunciation more difficult. Check these sounds. You could ask students to look up the words in the dictionary and use the phonemic script to help them remember the spelling–sound combinations.
The *th* in *brother, father, grandfather, mother* and *grandmother* is pronounced /ð/
the second syllable in *husband* is pronounced with a schwa ('hʌzbənd)
the *u* sound in *husband* is pronounced as in *up, run* /ʌ/
the *ph* spelling in *nephew* is pronounced /f/ /nefjuː/
the *gh* in *daughter* is not pronounced /dɔːtə(r)/ – students often think this is a pronounced sound when in fact it's silent.

AUDIOSCRIPT 1.5

1	brother	c	sister
2	son	f	daughter
3	husband	j	wife
4	father	g	mother
5	uncle	i	aunt
6	grandfather	b	grandmother
7	grandson	h	granddaughter
8	nephew	e	niece
9	stepfather	a	stepmother
10	brother-in-law	d	sister-in-law

Exercise 9c

This activity focuses on commonly confused words and introduces more vocabulary of extended family members.

- Do the first question with the whole class.
- Ask students to work in pairs to choose the correct words. Tell them to read the whole sentence to understand the meaning.
- Check answers, and then further extend their vocabulary by testing students with some questions.
  What's the opposite of stepfather? (stepmother)
  What's the opposite of sister-in-law? (brother-in-law)
  Who is your husband's mother? (your mother-in-law)
  What's the male word for mother-in-law? (father-in-law)

ANSWERS
1 children
2 cousin
3 brother-in-law
4 parents
5 stepfather

EXTENSION You could extend this by asking students to make a quiz in pairs for another team to test this vocabulary.

Exercise 10

- Model this task by describing a person in your family. You could ask students to guess who you are describing. Here is an example:
  She's young. She's not married. She's single. We have the same grandmother. She's not my sister. My mother is her father's sister. Answer: my cousin.
- Ask students to work in pairs and to tell each other about three people in their family.

Grammar & Speaking possessive 's

Exercise 11 1.6 💿

- Draw your own family tree on the board. Describe your family and encourage students to ask you questions about it.
- Tell students to look at the family tree on p9. Tell them to predict what might go in the gaps in the description of the tree.
- Play track 1.6. Ask students to listen and complete the tree. You may need to replay the recording to help students catch the possessives. If they can't answer 4 and 5, add a gapped word to the board and ask them to fill in the letters: R a _ _ _ _ _ (Rafina's), S _ _ _ (She's).

ANSWERS
1 son 2 his 3 married 4 Rafina's 5 She's

AUDIOSCRIPT 1.6

Zafar and his wife have two children: a son, Hasan, and his twin brother, Tariq. Tariq is married to Rafina. Sahala is Tariq and Rafina's daughter. She's three years old.

Exercise 12

- To lead in to exercise 12, add the example of the possessive from exercise 11 to the board (*Rafina's*). Ask students to discuss with a partner what the *'s* means. Elicit *possessive*, or something similar.
- Ask students to read the Grammar focus box individually and complete the exercise.
- Check answers together.

ANSWERS

1 Zafar is **Rashida's** husband.
2 Hasan is **Tariq's** brother.
3 Rafina is Tariq's **wife**.
4 Their **daughter's** name is Sahala.
5 Sahala is Zafar's **granddaughter**.
6 Rashida is **Sahala's** grandmother.

EXTENSION To further check the grammar, you could try this fun game. Tell the students to close their eyes. Go around the class and take some items from their tables – pens, pencil cases, bags, etc. and hide them. Tell students to open their eyes, and say that you have taken things from the class when they weren't looking. Ask students to work together to write a list of all the things that are missing. Give them a time limit – two minutes is usually enough. Answers should look like this:
Anna's bag
Hasan's mobile phone
Cinta's pencil case

- Refer students to *Grammar reference* on p137 (exercises 2, 3 and 4). Students can do these for homework.

Pronunciation similar sounding words

Exercise 13a 1.7 🎧

- This exercise focuses on words which sound the same or similar in connected speech. It's an opportunity to show students how words with different spellings can sound the same.
- Tell students to listen and complete the exercise.

ANSWERS

1 same   2 same   3 different   4 same   5 different

Exercise 13b 1.7 🎧

- Play the track again and ask students to repeat each sentence.

Exercise 14a

- To create interest in this exercise, you could refer students to your own family tree on the board again, but this time rub out some names to leave some gaps. Students ask you questions in order to complete it. Example questions:
  What's your grandfather's name? Is Amy your daughter's name? Is your sister married? What's your sister's husband's name?
- Ask students to then draw their own tree with or without gaps. Adapt this to suit your group.

Exercise 14b

- Ask students to work with a partner to describe their trees and find out more information about their partner's family.
- Listen and make a note of good language and mistakes with the target language from this lesson. Go over your notes with the whole class and ask them to correct the mistakes, without isolating individual students' mistakes.

EXTENSION Tell students to find a new partner and repeat the activity without making the same mistakes.

EXTRA ACTIVITY To give further practice of family vocabulary, possessive determiners and possessive *'s*, put students into new pairs or groups of three. Tell them to explain and describe their previous partner's family, e.g. *Aisha's family is quite big. She has three sisters and two brothers. Her sisters live near her. One of her brothers lives in London and another brother lives in Singapore. Her oldest sister's a nurse. She's married. Mmm, I can't remember more.*

GRAMMAR REFERENCE ANSWERS

Exercise 1
1 Her   2 Their   3 its   4 his   5 your   6 our
7 my   8 your

Exercise 2
1 's   2 '   3 's   4 's   5 '   6 's   7 '

Exercise 3
1 mechanic's car   2 aunt and uncle's   3 He's   4 her
5 Magda's nephew   6 Jane's children   7 My glasses
8 its

Exercise 4
1 I'm   2 is   3 its   4 child's   5 are   6 their   7 Our
8 names   9 mother's   10 father's   11 husband's

1.3 Vocabulary and skills development

Goals

- Understand positive and negative contractions
- Use regular and irregular plural nouns

Lead-in

1 Closed book. Vocabulary check.

- Write the names of four or five people in your family on the board.
- Tell students to ask you yes/no questions to guess their relation to you. For example:
  Is Malik your brother? Is Shaheen your cousin?
- Ask students to repeat the activity in pairs or groups of three.
- Go over any mistakes with vocabulary and pronunciation.

2 Closed book. Speaking activity to practise family vocabulary, possessive determiners and possessive *'s*.

- Ask students what they remember about each other's families from the last lesson. Choose one student and tell them what you remember: *Your mother's name is Sheila. Mmm, I think your sister's name is Claudia and you don't have any brothers. Your sister has a daughter and her name is Susana. Am I correct?*

- Ask students to stand up and (if there is space) walk around the room talking to each other and saying what they remember. Alternatively, they can do this in pairs or small groups.
- Listen and make notes of good language and errors and go through this after the speaking activity has finished.

Listening & Speaking positive and negative contractions

Exercise 1a
- Ask students to write down the names of three of their friends, teachers, family members or other people they know.

Exercise 1b
- Put students into pairs. Demonstrate the activity by writing the name of someone you know on the board and telling the class about them. Encourage students to ask you questions.

EXTRA SUPPORT/CHALLENGE This will help students ask questions in exercise 1b to make it more of a conversation. Write the questions you are asked on the board. Work with the class to correct and improve the questions, keeping things simple. You could do some drilling to help consolidate the question forms. Leave the questions on the board for the next activity.

- Give students three to five minutes to think about what they will say about the three people they chose. Tell them not to write full sentences but to make notes to help them speak.

STUDY TIP Students may have to learn new words for jobs. Encourage students to use dictionaries. Remind them to focus on the pronunciation displayed in the dictionaries and to make a note of the pronunciation of a new word when they add it to their notes, including word stress. If they do not know phonemic script, then encourage them to note the pronunciation in a way that will help them remember it. You could discuss this with the whole class before they start preparing to talk about their friends and family.

- Ask students to tell their partner about the three people they know.

FEEDBACK FOCUS Listen as students tell each other about the people they chose and make a note of good examples and errors of contractions (positive and negative). You can use this to help you adapt the focus you give to the grammar section.

Exercise 2 1.8 🔘
- In this Unlock the code activity the focus is on sentence stress. By helping students understand where we place emphases in a sentence with a contraction in it, we can help improve their listening skills.
- Write *She's Polish. She isn't Hungarian.* on the board and read the sentences to the class. Ask if they can hear a difference in the stress patterns.
- Play track 1.8 and tell students to read and listen to the Unlock the code box.

EXTENSION This short activity will give further practice of the pronunciation of contractions. Ask students to work in the same pairs as in exercise 1b. Students should first work individually and write sentences to describe the people they heard about in that exercise. Demonstrate this with the class using information about one person a student spoke about in exercise 1b. Write four sentences, two positive and two negative, on the board, making sure you use contractions, e.g. *Your friend's American. She isn't British. She's a nurse. She isn't a dentist.*

Ask students to read their sentences to their partners and check if the information they remembered is correct or not. The partner should correct the sentences if they are wrong. This will give further practice of the sentence stress.

PRONUNCIATION To help students with sentence stress, you could try back-chaining. Start with the last syllable in the sentence. Ask students to listen and repeat. Then say the last two syllables, the last three, etc., building up until students are saying the whole phrase. Students could choose one or two sentences from the previous activity and drill them in pairs to practise this.

Exercise 3 1.9 🔘
- Tell students to listen and underline the correct contraction.
- Play track 1.9.
- Go through the answers together.

ANSWERS
1 I'm 2 It isn't 3 That's not 4 They aren't 5 It's
6 She isn't 7 It's 8 He isn't

AUDIOSCRIPT 1.9
1 I'm Russian.
2 It isn't an Arabic name.
3 That's not a girl's name.
4 They aren't brothers.
5 It's the same.
6 She isn't French.
7 It's a long name.
8 He isn't married.

Exercise 4 1.10 🔘
- Ask students to read through the sentences and think of possible answers. This will help them think of the correct person – *am/is/are* – before they listen. For example, in number 1, the options are *is* or *isn't*.
- Show them how to write the contracted form answers, e.g. That's …
- Play track 1.10. Ask students to listen and write the correct answers. Check answers.
- Ask students to work in pairs and practise saying the sentences with the correct emphasis.

ANSWERS
1 's not 2 's 3 's 4 's 5 isn't 6 isn't 7 's not 8 's

AUDIOSCRIPT 1.10

1 It's not a female name.
2 Their name's Spanish.
3 She's called Sarah.
4 His family name's Ramirez.
5 That isn't a boy's name.
6 My name isn't very long.
7 Their family's not large.
8 He's my friend.

EXTENSION Ask students to work in pairs and write four to eight sentences about people in the class without mentioning their names. For example, *His family name's …. She doesn't speak Turkish*. Put the students together in groups of four. Tell them to read their sentences. The other pair has to guess who they are describing. Students who guess correctly get a point.

Exercise 5a

• Students work individually to match the nationalities and the names.

Exercise 5b 1.11 ⊚

• Play track 1.11. Ask students to listen and check their matches.

ANSWERS
1 b   2 c   3 a   4 d

Exercise 5c 1.11 ⊚

• Tell students to look at the pairs of countries. Working with a partner, students quickly discuss which pairs might have something in common. This allows them to check their understanding of the first recording.

• Play track 1.11 again and ask students to listen and tick or cross the pairs. Check answers.

ANSWERS
1 ✗   2 ✓   3 ✗   4 ✗

AUDIOSCRIPT 1.11

B I'm Bülent and I'm Turkish. In my country we say or write our personal name and then our family name, so I'm Bülent Sadik. It's the same in some other countries, for example, the UK, the USA and Thailand.
N Oh, it isn't the same in China. We use the family name first. My first name's Na and my family name's Li. So I'm called Li Na.
T Well, I'm not from China but we're the same as you, Na, with names. I'm Hungarian, and my family name's Antalek. So please call me Antalek Tamás.
B So Tamás is your personal name?
T That's right.
M Well … Spanish names are different. I'm Manuela García Gómez. We say our first name, then our father's family name and then our mother's family name!
T Wow!
M Yes – it isn't short!

Exercise 6a

• Ask students to remember the names of people you talked about in the lesson lead-in. Ask them what they remember.

• Tell students to read the exercise.

• Demonstrate the activity by telling the class about your name and the names of people you know. Encourage students to ask you questions.

EXTRA SUPPORT When a student asks a good question, you could add it to the board or ask them to write it on the board. This will provide extra support for students when they speak, and help to make it more of a conversation than a monologue.

• Ask students to prepare some ideas using the prompts. They should write notes rather than full sentences. Encourage students to refer to the vocabulary and grammar in the previous two lessons to help them.

• If you feel students need extra support, ask a confident student to tell you their information and model the activity by asking questions, referring to the ones on the board, to find out more information.

• Put students into pairs and ask them to complete the activity.

Exercise 6b

• Put students into different pairs and ask them to tell their new partners three things their first partners told them.

FEEDBACK FOCUS Listen for examples of good language and errors in the use of contractions, family vocabulary, possessive determiners and possessive *'s*. Write the examples on cut-up strips of paper. When the students have finished, distribute the strips among the groups. Tell students to divide the papers into two categories: correct language and errors/mistakes. Check their papers are in the correct category and move any incorrect examples. Tell students to correct the papers with errors on them.

Vocabulary & Speaking regular and irregular plural nouns

Exercise 7a

> **Cultural note:** *What's in a name* is a line from the Shakespeare play *Romeo and Juliet*. In the play their names meant they couldn't be together because their families were at war. As a lead-in here, you could ask what importance names have in students' own culture.

> **Text summary:** This is a magazine article about names. It describes some interesting things about the way names and titles are formed in different countries.

• Refer students to the title of the article. Check that they know the difference between a *title* and a *name*. (A title is what comes before the name: Mr, Mrs, Miss, Ms, Sir, Lady, Lord, etc.) Note that some titles (Sir, Lord, Baron, etc.) are usually a feature in cultures that have a king or queen. You could discuss this with the class if they are interested.

• Tell students to read the article and discuss the question with a partner to compare their understanding of the text.

ANSWERS
Titles: In English, men are Mr and women are Mrs (married), Miss (single), or Ms (married or single).
Surnames: In Greece, women can have their husband's surname. In Iceland, most surnames have -*sson* or -*dottir* at the end.

Exercise 7b

- Ask students to work with their partner to discuss the question.

Exercise 7c

- Write *name, country, man, person* on the board and ask how many of each thing you are talking about. Answer: one. Elicit the plural nouns (names, countries, men, people).
- Ask students to work alone at first to complete the table and then check their answers with their partner.

Exercise 7d 1.12 ⊙

- Play track 1.12. Ask students to check their answers and repeat.

1 a name   2 countries   3 men   4 a woman   5 people

AUDIOSCRIPT 1.12

a name	names
a country	countries
a man	men
a woman	women
a person	people

PRONUNCIATION   Note that it can be difficult to hear the difference between *woman* and *women*. Write the words in phonemic script (ˈwʊmən and ˈwɪmɪn) on the board and ask students to listen and recognize the vowel sounds. Ask them to look at you and see how the mouth changes shape.

Test receptive pronunciation by saying the words. Students listen and put up their left hand if you say *woman* and their right if you say *women*. Repeat these words, getting quicker as you say them. Students can also do the activity in pairs. You could also try the same activity with silent drilling. This helps students to focus on the mouth position. They could then try this in pairs.

Exercise 8

- Tell students to read the Vocabulary focus box. Tell them you are going to test them on the information.

Exercise 9

- Ask students five to ten questions to test their memory of the rules. For example, *What's the plural of* child? *How do you spell it? What's the singular of* women? *How do you spell it?*
- Put students into pairs. Refer them to the information on p126 and p131 and ask them to complete the activity.

Student A
Table A
1 a story   2 glasses   3 a life   4 dresses   5 a child
Table B
6 knives   7 a person   8 cities   9 a match   10 women

Student B
Table B
1 a knife   2 people   3 a city   4 matches   5 a woman
Table A
6 stories   7 a glass   8 lives   9 a dress   10 children

EXTRA ACTIVITY   Ask students to work in pairs and write five to eight sentences with an error in each. For example, *Henry the 8th had eight wifes.* Students should then swap papers and find the errors. You could make it a race.

Exercise 10a

EXTRA ACTIVITY   As an alternative or addition to the illustrations, you could use objects in the classroom and use a cloth, or a coat/jacket, to cover the items. Show the items on a tray to the class for thirty seconds. Cover them and give students two minutes to write the items correctly. Teams get one point for each correct item.

- Tell students to look at the photos for one minute. They are not allowed to write anything.

Exercise 10b

- Ask students to close their books and give them a time limit to write all the items they can remember. Remind them to use the articles *a/an* for single items.
- Ask students to compare their lists with a partner.

Exercise 10c

- Ask students to open their books, check their lists and see how many items they got right. You could ask them to write the lists on the board and go over any errors with articles. Remember to praise correct answers too.

seven knives   a brush   an umbrella   two men
three watches   three children   two dictionaries
six glasses   five pencils   a box

1.4 Speaking and writing

Goals

- Ask for personal information and check you understand
- Write a personal profile

Lead-in

1 Closed book. Class discussion to lead in to the topic of profile writing.

- Ask students what a *personal profile* is (= a short description of yourself) and where you find one. Give examples to start ideas: on social media sites such as Facebook and LinkedIn.

> **Background note:** Facebook is a website where you can connect with other people to share news and photos, comment on each other's activities and discuss things. It's usually for friends and family and it's informal. LinkedIn is a website where you can post professional information about yourself, connect with other professionals and join different groups. People use it to find jobs, and companies use it to find employees.

- Put students into pairs. Ask them to think of what information is included in profiles. Give a time limit for this.
- Write their ideas on the board. Check understanding of new vocabulary.

2 Closed book. Test before you teach.

- Ask students to imagine it is the first time they have met each other. What questions would they ask each other? Tell them to think of some questions and write them down.

- Put students into groups of four and tell them to ask each other the questions. Listen and make a note of their questions to go over after the Language for speaking exercise. You could add in some of their questions to help build their confidence.

Listening & Speaking asking for personal information and checking you understand

Exercise 1

- Ask students to work in pairs and answer the questions.

- You could ask students if they would be interested in a course like this or if they have done a similar course and what it was like.

Exercise 2   1.13

STUDY TIP Ask students what information they would have to give if they went to the college to join this course. Ask students how they would prepare to do this in English. Discuss the idea that students can prepare for situations by predicting the conversation and learning useful phrases and vocabulary.

- Tell students to read the form and think about what information they will need to write in the gaps. Ask for examples. You could teach them the language for @ *at* and **.** *dot* to help them with the email question.

- Play track 1.13. Ask students to listen and write answers.

- Check answers.

AUDIOSCRIPT 1.13

R Hi. Can I help you?
A Yes, I'm here for the 'Create a Website' course.
R Oh yes, at six o'clock. What's your name?
A Antonio Russo.
R Ah yes. Your name's here on the list. I just need some other details. What's your nationality?
A I'm Italian but my home is here in Toronto.
R OK, and what's your job?
A I'm a restaurant owner.
R Mmm … So, is the website for business or for fun?
A It's for business.
R For your restaurant?
A Yes, that's right.
R And, finally, what's your email address?
A It's antonio@russorest.com
R Sorry, can you repeat that please?
A Yes, Antonio – A-N-T-O-N-I-O – at russorest dot com.
R How do you spell russorest?
A R-U-double S-O-R-E-S-T.
R OK. Great. Thanks. Now the cost of the course is …

Exercise 3a   1.14

- Tell students to read through the questions and predict what word goes in each gap.

- Play track 1.14 and tell students to listen and fill in the gaps.

Exercise 3b

- Refer students to the Language for speaking (1) box to check their answers.

Exercise 3c   1.15

- Play track 1.15 and ask students to listen and repeat.

PRONUNCIATION To help students use the correct emphasis (sentence stress) you could write the sentences on the board and ask them to mark the stressed syllables. This will review the Unlock the code activity in lesson 3. Tell students to remember that usually it's the nouns and verbs that are stressed and not the grammar words.

What's your name?

Work on intonation here, too. Students tend to go up at the end of questions. Explain that in *Wh-* questions our voice usually goes down. Drill the questions to focus on sentence stress and intonation.

Exercise 4a   1.16

- Ask students to read the sentences and predict what goes in the gaps.

STUDY TIP To help students use their grammar knowledge to improve their listening skills, you could ask them what part of speech they are listening for. Students should be able to identify if a noun, verb or adjective is needed in each sentence, for example.

- Play track 1.16 and ask students to listen and write the words that go in the gaps.

AUDIOSCRIPT 1.16

A It's antonio@russorest.com.
R Sorry, can you repeat that, please?
A Yes, Antonio – A-N-T-O-N-I-O – at russorest dot com.
R How do you spell russorest?
A R-U-double S-O-R-E-S-T.
R OK. Great. Thanks. Now, the cost of the course is …

Exercise 4b

- Refer students to the Language for speaking (2) box to check their answers.

Exercise 4c   1.17

- Play track 1.17 and tell students to listen to double-check their answers. Then they should listen one more time and repeat the questions.

AUDIOSCRIPT 1.17

Sorry, can you repeat that, please?

How do you spell that?

How do you spell 'russorest'?

EXTRA ACTIVITY To practise pronunciation of letters for spelling their names.

Write these phonemes in a line across the top of the board and drill the phoneme sounds:

eɪ biː siː diː iː ef dʒiː eɪtʃ aɪ jeɪ keɪ el em en əʊ piː kjuː ɑː es tiː juː viː dʌbljuː eks waɪ ʒed

Tell students to copy them into their notebooks and then add the letters of the alphabet below each sound. Do the first few letters as an example:

eɪ	biː	siː
A	B	C

Tell students to practise spelling their names to each other in pairs.

Exercise 5a

- Tell students to match the questions to the answers to consolidate the language they have seen so far in the lesson.
- Check answers together.

ANSWERS

1 e   2 g   3 f   4 d   5 c   6 a   7 b

Exercise 5b

- Ask students to work in pairs and to take turns asking and answering the questions. Listen and correct pronunciation of email vocabulary and letters of the alphabet.

Exercise 6

- Put students into new pairs. Refer them to the information on p126 and p132.
- Ask students to complete the tables with their personal information. Model the exercise by drawing a similar table on the board and asking one student questions to find the information, e.g. *What's your name? What's your job?*

EXTRA SUPPORT Write the questions they need to ask on the board if you think they will find it difficult to use the correct questions.

Reading & Writing a personal profile

Exercise 7

- Refer students to the advert in exercise 1 again. Ask students to read and answer the question.

ANSWER

They want personal information and your reason for attending the course.

- Elicit ideas and add *profile* and *reason(s)* to the board. Ask students to work in pairs and brainstorm what information might go under each heading. Get one example from the class to start. e.g. Profile – name, age, location, nationality. Reason: For my photography club, etc. Go over any vocabulary which comes up. You could use this moment to teach *skills* (= things that you can do well) as students need to understand this for the reading exercise.

Exercise 8a

- Ask students to work individually to read the profile and fill in the gaps.

STUDY TIP To help develop scanning skills, ask students to read the categories with the gaps first and think about what kind of information they are reading to find. Do the first example with the class. Tell them to think about what part of speech the gap is, to further support this skill development.

- Ask students to compare and check answers in pairs and then with the class.

ANSWERS

1 Cristina   2 Australian   3 artist   4 designer   5 art
6 design   7 Portuguese   8 art and design work

Exercise 8b

- This exercise requires students to read in more detail. Tell them to read the questions carefully before they read Cristina's profile to find the answers. Encourage them to think about what kind of information they are looking for.
- Check answers with the class.

ANSWERS

1 She is an artist and designer. At the moment she is unemployed.
2 Portuguese a French c

EXTRA SUPPORT If students need support, teach them the key words from the text: *unemployed* (= to not have a job), *skills* (= things that you do well), *beginner* (= a person who is learning or doing something new), *fluent* (= can speak a language well).

Exercise 9

- Write *cristina oliveira* on the board, all lower case. Ask students what is wrong with the punctuation. Elicit *no capital letters*.
- Ask students to use Cristina's profile to complete the exercise. Check answers.

ANSWERS

1 Cristina Oliveira
2 My …, I'm …, My …, The …
3 Toronto, Canada
4 Australian, Portuguese
5 Portuguese, French
6 November

Exercise 10

- Refer students to the text in the box. Tell them to find nine mistakes with capitals. Refer them to the Language for writing box to use as a guide.

ANSWERS

I am a student at Columbia University. My Saturday job is at a Chinese supermarket called Jing Jing Foods.

EXTENSION To give further practice and to consolidate the rules in the Language for writing box, ask students to create their own texts with mistakes to test their classmates. Students could work in pairs or individually. Tell them to write a similar length text with at least five mistakes with capitals in it. Students swap texts and correct them. To make this more interesting you could set a time limit for making the corrections.

Exercise 11a

- Tell students to read through the form and check the meaning of *owner*.
- Ask students to work in pairs for this activity. Tell them to write a profile similar to Cristina's. Word length: forty to fifty words. Set a time limit suitable to your group. Tell students to imagine they are Antonio and write in the 1st person, using *I*.

Exercise 11b

- Tell students to work in new pairs and swap texts. Ask students what kinds of things they could look for to give feedback on the texts: things that are the same or different, missing information, mistakes with capitals and spelling mistakes are some suggested areas to focus on.
- Tell students they have two to three minutes to read the texts and find examples of good language and any mistakes. Tell them to give their classmates feedback and to help correct any mistakes.

WATCH OUT! Some students are not used to peer reviewing and might react negatively to getting or giving feedback on their classmates' work. Discuss this with your group and focus on the positive learning opportunities. Noticing mistakes and good language in someone else's work can help us learn.

Exercise 12a

- Students should work alone for this activity.
- Tell them to think of the information they need to write a profile about themselves. Encourage them to note this information down so that they don't forget to include anything.
- Refer students to the Language for writing box. Encourage them to check this as they write and to do one final check when they have finished.
- Word limit: 40–60 words. Time limit: 15 minutes.

Exercise 12b

- Put students into pairs. Think about pairs where students can help each other – a good mix of levels and personalities. Students should feel comfortable giving and receiving feedback.
- Ask students to swap texts. Tell them to read the texts and check the capital letters, underlining any places where they think there might be a mistake.
- Students swap texts again and correct their mistakes based on the comments made by their partner.

EXTRA ACTIVITY To encourage students to read each other's work and to consolidate the use of capital letters through reading, you could have a reading gallery activity. Place students' work around the room, on the walls if possible. Tell students to walk around and read all the texts and try to find someone they have something in common with. When they find something, they can find that person and talk to them about it to find out more information.

1.5 Video

Brighton language exchange

VIDEOSCRIPT

Welcome to Brighton. My name's Rebecca and I'm a student here. I'm English but I'm not from Brighton. I come from London. But I live here now and I love it!

Brighton is an exciting and multicultural town. It has a population of 270,000, and many of these people are from different countries.

A lot of people are here for Brighton's great beach and fantastic atmosphere. But many are here for the language. Learning English is now a huge global business. There are over one and a half billion English learners around the world and Brighton is a very popular English-speaking destination.

There are now English language schools all over the town with lots and lots of students.

But of course learning isn't just for the classroom. It's important to chat in English outside of class too.

This is the Jubilee Library. English language learners come here to practise speaking. Every day there is a 'conversation exchange' here. You can teach other people your language and learn English from them.

There's a table for every language. Each person speaks their own language for the first 45 minutes and English for the last 45 minutes. Today it's an open exchange, so there are people from all over the world here. But sometimes the exchange is for specific languages. On Monday, for example, there's an Italian exchange, and on Tuesday there's a Spanish exchange.

Language exchanges are great places to meet people and make friends.

These conversations aren't long but they're only the beginning. After the language exchange, learners socialise together. They go to the beach and walk along Brighton Pier. They also see some of the town's famous sights, like the Brighton Clock Tower and the Royal Pavilion. Social events like these are a fantastic way to practise English in a friendly environment.

It isn't surprising that Brighton is such a popular destination for English language learners. There are great facilities like the conversation exchange, and lots of people to talk to. Learning a language isn't easy but with friendly people in a relaxed atmosphere, it's lots of fun!

VIDEO ANSWERS

Exercise 1

beach, conversation, flag, library, pavilion, pier

Exercise 3

1 T
2 F The population of Brighton is 270,000.
3 T
4 F There are conversation exchanges every day at the Jubilee Library.
5 T
6 F The language exchange is free.
7 T
8 F Brighton is famous for Brighton Clock Tower and the Royal Pavilion.

Review

Exercise 1a
1 Are   2 're not   3 'm   4 's   5 Is   6 're not   7 Are
8 'm not

Exercise 1b   1.18

AUDIOSCRIPT 1.18
A Are you and your wife from England?
B No, we're not. I'm from Edinburgh in Scotland and my wife's Canadian.
A Canadian? Is she from Montreal? My sister's at university in Montreal.
B No, she's from Vancouver. What about you? You're not English. Are you Australian?
A No, I'm not. I'm from Wellington in New Zealand.

Exercise 2a
1 your   2 you   3 his   4 she   5 her   6 their   7 our

Exercise 3a
My **name's** Memed. I'm from Izmir. **It's** a city in Turkey. I have two **sisters**. Their **names** are Sevil and Fatima. Sevil is 10 and **Fatima's** 14. My **brother's** name is Cem. **He's** a doctor. His **wife's** name is Eda.

Exercises 4a & b   1.19

	Country	Nationality	Main language
1	the UK	British	English
2	the UAE	Emirati	Arabic
3	Pakistan	Pakistani	Urdu
4	the USA	American	English

AUDIOSCRIPT 1.19
1 British
2 the United Arab Emirates
3 Urdu
4 American

Exercise 4c
1 the UAE   2 Emirati   3 the USA   4 Pakistan
5 Arabic   6 English

Exercise 4d   1.20

AUDIOSCRIPT 1.20
Dubai is a very multicultural city in the United Arab Emirates. People come here to work from many different countries. Only 10% of people in Dubai are Emirati: 90% of the city's population are from other countries. Some people come from the UK and the USA, but many people are from Asia. India is home for most of Dubai's workers, but people come from Pakistan and the Philippines, too. The language of the United Arab Emirates is Arabic, but because of its international population, lots of people use English.

Exercise 5   1.21
1 aunt   2 grandfather   3 niece   4 granddaughter
5 uncle   6 cousin

AUDIOSCRIPT 1.21
1 Your mother's sister.
2 Your father's father.
3 Your sister's daughter.
4 Your son's daughter.
5 Your mother's brother.
6 Your aunt's son.

Exercise 6
1 nationalities
2 language
3 children
4 wives
5 woman
6 addresses

Exercise 7a
1 What's your name?
2 How do you spell that?
3 What's your nationality?
4 What's your job?
5 What's your email address?
6 Sorry, can you repeat that?

My day

Unit overview

Language input

Present simple positive (CB p16)	• *I get up early in the summer.* • *Sven loves his job.*
Adverbs of frequency (CB p17)	• *always, usually, often, sometimes, hardly ever, never*
Present simple negative (CB p19)	• *They don't have a lot of free time.* • *She doesn't go out on Fridays.*
Grammar reference (CB pp138–139)	

Vocabulary development

Daily activities (CB p17)	• *get up, go to work, have a shower …*
Telling the time (CB p18)	• *It's three o'clock.* • *It's twenty-five past three.*
Verb + preposition (CB p21)	• *listen to, agree with, looking for …*

Skills development

Reading: understanding conjunctions (CB p20)

Speaking: making suggestions and arrangements (CB p22)

Writing: describe where you live (CB p23)

Video

Documentary: The Menna family (CB p24)

Vox pops (Coursebook DVD & TG p256)

More materials

Workbook	• Language practice for grammar, vocabulary, pronunciation, speaking and writing • Listening for pleasure • Review: Units 1 & 2
Photocopiable activities	• Grammar: My day (TG p203 & TSRD) • Vocabulary: Telling the time (TG p221 & TSRD) • Communication: What's on? (TG p238 & TSRD)
Tests	• Unit 2 test (TSRD)
Unit 2 wordlist (TSRD)	

2.1 A day in the life of a scientist

Goals

- Talk about everyday actions
- Use the present simple positive to talk about your day

Lead-in

1 Closed book. To check students' existing use of verbs in the present simple and to recycle vocabulary from Unit 1.

- Ask students to work in groups of three or four and remember the jobs they spoke about in the last unit, when they talked about their families. Write the jobs on the board. Check understanding.
- Ask students to discuss this question in their groups: *What activities does a person do in that job every day?*
- Listen to their discussions and note examples of the present simple and any useful vocabulary. Add language to the board, check meaning and encourage peer teaching. Focus on the meaning of the verbs, not the form of the present simple at this stage.

STUDY TIP To remember vocabulary, students need to *see* it at least seven times according to some experts. Ask students to write sentences using some of the vocabulary you think is relevant and useful for extra practice. Check sentences for correct grammar and meaning.

2 Open book. To create interest in the topic of the lesson.

- Tell students to read the title of the lesson and talk to a partner about what they think they are going to learn.
- Discuss some ideas with the whole class. Write the most common predictions on the board. (At the end of the lesson, go over their ideas and see who was correct.)

Listening & Grammar present simple and adverbs of frequency

Exercise 1

WATCH OUT! Students often have problems with the pronunciation of 'island' ('aɪlənd) and this might affect their listening. Check the pronunciation before they listen.

- If you have an IWB or projector, show the images to the class.
- Put students into pairs and tell them to discuss the questions with a partner.
- Listen and add any relevant, useful vocabulary to the board. This will help pre-teach vocabulary for the listening and reading in this lesson, e.g. *penguin, seal, island, beach, research* (= the study of materials and information to find an answer to something). Go over this with the class to check understanding after they finish speaking.

STUDY TIP As you write vocabulary on the board, add any *collocations* (= words that often go together) – verbs + nouns, adjectives + nouns, etc., e.g. *do research, free time*. Ask students to note the collocations and then create example sentences with the vocabulary in their notebooks. Check the pronunciation and encourage students to note this as well. You could discuss the benefits of recording vocabulary in similar contexts.

ANSWERS
1 Bird Island is in the southern Atlantic Ocean, near South Georgia, north of the Antarctic.
2 Seals and penguins live there.

Exercise 2 2.1 🔘

Audio summary: A scientist who does research on Bird Island describes her daily life there. Bird Island is a small island in South Georgia, in the southern Atlantic Ocean. It is a station for research on the birds and seals living there.

- Ask students to read the instructions and then read through activities 1–12. Tell them to work in pairs and predict which activities they think Melanie does or doesn't do.
- Play track 2.1. Tell students to listen and tick the actions she does. Students could compare answers in pairs.
- Check answers with the class.

ANSWERS
1 ✓ 2 ✓ 3 ☐ 4 ✓ 5 ✓ 6 ✓ 7 ✓ 8 ✓
9 ☐ 10 ✓ 11 ✓ 12 ☐

AUDIOSCRIPT 2.1
I'm a scientist. I study penguins on Bird Island and I'm very happy here. In the summer my days are long. I get up early and go to the beach. I watch the penguins with their babies. I sometimes go out in a boat with the other scientists on the island. We visit different islands and take photos of the birds and animals there.
I often work all day and I only stop in the evening to have dinner. I sometimes go back to the beach after dinner to spend more time with the penguins. Then I work in the lab. I always go to bed late! In the winter, the weather is always very cold, but we usually have more free time and I can relax.

Exercise 3 2.1 🔘

- Tell students to work individually. Ask them to read the sentences and think about what words go in the gaps – some might remember the verbs from the first listening. Don't confirm answers.
- Play track 2.1 again. Ask students to listen and write verbs in the gaps.
- Check answers and write the verbs on the board. Ask students to discuss if these sentences describe today or things she does every day. Elicit that the verbs are describing actions that are repeated or done every day. In fact, she is talking about her job in different seasons and how these habits change.

ANSWERS
1 get up; go 2 visit; take 3 have
EXTENSION Ask students to read through the audioscript on p161 and find more examples of everyday actions. To check and reinforce understanding, ask students what parts of Melanie's job they think are interesting/fun/difficult. Would they like to have her job?

Exercise 4a

> **Text summary:** This article is about two scientists who live on Bird Island. It describes their daily life and what they like and don't like about life on the island.

- Tell students to read the instructions. Check they understand *colleague* (= someone you work with).
- Ask students to read and discuss the question.

SUGGESTED ANSWERS

Melanie works there all year; studies penguins; works alone on the beaches. Sven studies seals and never works alone on the beaches.

EXTRA CHALLENGE Set a short time limit (e.g. two minutes) as this is a scanning exercise.

EXTRA SUPPORT This will pre-teach some vocabulary from the text. Read out the following definitions of words and ask students to read the text and find the word you are defining.
1 to study something carefully to learn more about it (research)
2 with no people around you (alone)
3 the man animal, the opposite of female (male)
4 the opposite of *often* (hardly ever)

EXTENSION Tell students to read the text again and think about the advantages and disadvantages of the jobs described. Encourage them to remember information in the recording too.

Exercise 4b

- Put students into pairs. Ask them to discuss the questions. Focus on meaning and fluency here.

CRITICAL THINKING Students relate information from the reading to themselves. Encourage them to give reasons and explanations for their opinions. You could model this, e.g. *I'd love to have Sven or Melanie's job. It seems exciting and interesting. I enjoy taking photos. I would like to see the images and remember the experience. I don't like the winter. I don't like cold weather. I'd like to work with the animals. It's an experience you can't forget.*

Exercise 5

- Tell students to read the sentences and underline the verbs. Write them on the board and ask these questions: *What's different about the form of* visit/take *and* loves/works/watches? (The second group has *s* or *es* on the end.) *When do we add* s *or* es *to verbs?* (When we are referring to third person singular – *he/she/it.*)
- Tell students to work with a partner and complete the Grammar focus box. Check answers together.

ANSWERS

1 We 2 He 3 -es 4 has

- Refer students to *Grammar reference* p138. There are more exercises here students can do for homework.

Pronunciation third person *-(e)s*

- Ask students to read the information in the Pronunciation box.
- This drill, practising the *-s/-es* endings, will help you assess the students' pronunciation and lead in to the pronunciation focus in the next exercise. In this type of

drill the teacher drills a starter sentence and then a cue word or phrase. The students add the cue into the starter sentence.

Example:	*I like seals.*
Cue: *She*	*She likes seals.*
Cue: *Love*	*She loves seals. And so on:*
They	*They love seals.*
Visit	*They visit seals.*
He	*He visits seals.*
Watch	*He watches seals.*
We	*We watch seals.*
You	*You watch seals.*

Exercise 6a 2.2

- Play track 2.2. Ask students to listen to the recording. Focus on recognition of the sounds first, before you ask them to produce the sentences. Ask students to listen again and repeat. To ensure all students are getting it right, ask students to repeat without the recording in pairs and as individual drills.
- Isolate the phonemes and check pronunciation by asking students to say just the sounds /s/ /z/ /ɪz/

Exercise 6b 2.3

- Play track 2.3. Ask students to listen and complete the exercise.

Exercise 6c 2.4

- Play track 2.4 and ask students to check their answers. Then they should repeat the words. Make sure students notice the spelling to reinforce the rules in the pronunciation box.

ANSWERS

1 /z/ 2 /ɪz/ 3 /s/ 4 /ɪz/ 5 /s/ 6 /z/

AUDIOSCRIPT 2.4
/s/ cooks, makes
/z/ goes, plays
/ɪz/ teaches, relaxes

Exercise 7a

- As a lead-in, write *Ivan* (or another name) _____ *gets up late* on the board and ask students to think of words that can go in the gap (books closed or covered). Write different suggestions on the board.
- Tell students to read the Grammar focus box. Point out that these adverbs can go in the gap.
- Refer students to *Grammar reference* on p138. There are more exercises here that students can do for homework.

Exercise 7b

- Put students into pairs. Ask students to read and underline the adverbs in the text in exercise 4a and complete the diagram.
- Ask students to make the sentence on the board that is true for them: *I _____ get up late*, and compare their answer with a partner.

ANSWERS

1 always 2 usually 3 often 4 sometimes
5 hardly ever 6 never

Exercise 8a

- Ask students to read the instructions and the example. Check understanding with some concept-checking questions, e.g. *What does the scientist do? What does he research? Do you think his job is dangerous? How is his job different to Melanie's?*
- Ask students to complete the sentences.

ANSWERS

1 gets up, arrives	3 returns, has
2 is, works	4 stays, goes, goes

Exercise 8b

- Ask students to complete the sentences in exercise 8a and check answers with the person next to them.

EXTRA SUPPORT Use sentence 2 from exercise 8a. Ask students if the sentence makes sense. They should say no, because if his work is dangerous he shouldn't work alone. Ask students to come to the board and write the sentence with the adverbs in the correct place. Check with the class.

ANSWERS

1 always gets up; usually arrives
2 is sometimes dangerous; never works
3 usually returns; always has
4 usually relaxes; hardly ever goes; often goes

Exercise 8c 2.5 🎧

- Play track 2.5 and tell students to listen to check answers.

WATCH OUT! Note that it can sometimes be difficult to pronounce *usually*. The *s* is pronounced /ʒ/. Use the listening to draw attention to the pronunciation of this and any other sounds your students have problems with. For example, some students may have problems with the /v/ in *never* and *ever*.

AUDIOSCRIPT 2.5

1 During the week, he always gets up early and he usually arrives at a volcano at seven o'clock.
2 His work is sometimes dangerous and he never works alone.
3 He usually returns to the research centre at about one o'clock and he always has lunch in the lab.
4 On Friday and Saturday nights he usually relaxes at home. He hardly ever goes out with friends and he often goes to bed early.

Vocabulary & Speaking daily activities

Exercise 9a

- Ask students to match the illustrations to the phrases.

Exercise 9b 2.6 🎧

- Ask students to listen to track 2.6 and check their answers. Ask them to listen again and repeat the expressions. For extra support, check pronunciation of the third person form by saying the verb in the infinitive and asking students to repeat in the third person. Students could quickly drill each other this way in pairs.

ANSWERS/AUDIOSCRIPT 2.6

1 get up   2 have a shower   3 make breakfast
4 go to work/college   5 have lunch/dinner
6 go home   7 watch TV/a film   8 read a book
9 listen to music   10 play video games   11 go to bed
12 see friends

EXTRA ACTIVITY Tell students to draw a nine-box grid to fill a side of A4. In each box they should draw one of their daily activities with stick figures. They can use the ideas in exercise 9a and add their own activities.

Put students into pairs. Tell them to swap drawings and write in the activities they think the drawings are showing. They should then tell their partner about the day: *You get up, and then you have a shower, …* Ask students to correct each other.

Students can then work with a different partner and report the day of the previous partner: *She gets up, and then she has a shower*. They can take the drawings to help them.

Exercise 10a

- This is primarily a speaking activity so encourage students not to write. While students may feel confident, it may help to give them some preparation time. Give them two minutes to think about what they will say.
- Put students into pairs, and ask them to tell each other about their day. You could demonstrate the exercise by telling them about your day.

Exercise 10b

- Put students into new pairs and ask them to tell their new partner what they heard from the first partner. Listen and note examples of good and incorrect pronunciation.

EXTRA ACTIVITY Get students to work in groups of four. Ask them to tell each other about their days and about the other students they talked to. Their goal is to find things everyone agrees on and to make five sentences. Encourage them to think of specific examples, e.g. *specific TV shows, local newspapers*. Ask the groups lots of questions as they work to prompt this, e.g. *What do you watch? How do you read, online, on a smartphone?* etc.

Example sentences:
We sometimes read the same newspaper. We usually get up early. We never watch (name of a TV show). *We always watch the news. We sometimes read the news on our smartphones.*

STUDY TIP Encourage students to reflect on their learning. Ask them to work in pairs and discuss what they learnt in this lesson. They could even quiz each other on vocabulary and/or content they have learnt.

GRAMMAR REFERENCE ANSWERS

Exercise 1

1 work	5 relaxes
2 love	6 read
3 takes	7 watches
4 have	8 wash

Exercise 2

1 We often go to the beach.
2 He always makes a big dinner.
3 They sometimes visit other islands. (OR They visit other islands, sometimes.)
4 You usually work in the lab. (OR You work in the lab, usually.)
5 We never have enough sleep.
6 I never listen to music at work.
7 It hardly ever rains on the island.
8 It is never cold in my city.
9 I am hardly ever worried.
10 The houses are sometimes cold in winter. (OR The houses are cold in winter, sometimes.)

Exercise 3

1 studies 2 goes 3 usually 4 works 5 enjoy
6 finishes 7 has 8 listen 9 never 10 hardly

2.2 Spending time

Goals

- Tell the time
- Use the present simple negative

Lead-in

1 Closed book. To test/review present simple positive.

- Ask students to work with a partner.
- Tell them to think back to lesson 2.1. What can they remember about the scientists on Bird Island?
- Tell them to write at least three things the scientists do every day. Remind them of the names: Melanie and Sven. Ask fast finishers to write their sentences on the board. Ask others to add other, different examples when they have finished.
- Ask the class to correct any errors in the use of the present simple.

2 Closed book. To create interest in the topic and elicit useful vocabulary.

- Display or draw an image of an astronaut on the board and teach students the word.
- Ask students to work in small groups and write down words they think of when they see an astronaut, e.g. *space, rocket, job, dangerous*. You could give a time limit. Write vocabulary on the board and check the meaning of any unknown words.

Listening & Vocabulary telling the time

Exercise 1a

- Ask students to work in pairs and discuss the questions. Elicit answers from the class. Encourage students to give reasons for their ideas, e.g. *I think number one is false. One year is a short time. I think it takes about five years to study.*

Exercise 1b

- Ask students to check answers on p127.

ANSWERS

1 False. The basic training takes about two years. Then, before each trip into space, they need to do another two–three years of training.
2 True. Valeri Polyakov stayed in space for 437.7 days in 1994–5. Sergei Avdeyev stayed in space for 379.6 days in 1998–9.
3 True. Astronauts can wear glasses.

EXTENSION Start a class discussion on the answers: Are they surprised? Would they like to do this job? Encourage students to share any knowledge they have on the topic.

Exercise 2 2.7 💿

- Check understanding of *trainee n.* (= a person who is training for a job). Ask students to read the instructions and questions and to discuss with a partner what they think she will say. Ask for some examples before they listen and write useful vocabulary on the board.

EXTRA SUPPORT Pre-teach *hard* (= not easy, difficult), *canteen* (= a place where people eat when they are at work or school), *engineering* (= planning and making machines, bridges, roads or railways, etc.), *physics* (= the science of things like heat, sound and light), *equipment* (= the things you need for doing something), *machine* (= a thing with moving parts that does a job, e.g. a washing machine washes clothes) before students listen.

- Tell students to listen and answer the questions. Play track 2.7. Ask students to check their ideas in pairs and then with the class.

ANSWERS

1 It's hard, but interesting. She loves it.
2 Engineering and physics, Russian

AUDIOSCRIPT 2.7
All astronauts in Europe learn their job at the European Astronaut Centre in Cologne in Germany. The training is hard, but it's interesting and I love it. My day starts at ten to seven when I get up. I have a shower and then have breakfast in the canteen at quarter to eight. Classes begin at half past eight. In the mornings, we study things like engineering and physics. At quarter past eleven, we stop and have a break. I usually have a coffee and I also try and learn some Russian vocabulary. We all learn Russian here. Classes start again at half past eleven.
Lunch is at one o'clock, and in the afternoons we have more classes from quarter past two. We learn to use the space equipment and machines and we also have language classes. Classes finish at quarter to six. I always feel really tired, but I often go to the gym in the evening. I'm in bed by ten o'clock and by five past ten I'm usually asleep.

Exercise 3 2.7 💿

- Ask students to read through the sentences and guess the matches. Check the meaning of *stop for a break* (= stop working for a short time).
- Play track 2.7 again and tell students to listen and complete the exercise. Check answers.

ANSWERS
1 b 2 a 3 f 4 e 5 c 6 d
EXTENSION To test students' understanding of time vocabulary, draw a clock face on the board and ask students to come to the board and draw the six times from sentences 1–6 on it.

Exercise 4a

- Tell students to work in pairs to complete the exercise.

Exercise 4b 2.8 💿

- Play track 2.8 and ask students to check their answers.
- Then play track 2.8 again and ask them to repeat the phrases.

EXTRA SUPPORT Teach the alternative system of telling the time, which some students may find easier. For example, *14.30 is two thirty, 08.15 is eight fifteen, 10.05 is ten oh five.*

WATCH OUT! In some languages they tell the time with the twenty-four hour clock and say fourteen-thirty. Remind students that this is not usually the case in spoken or written English, although it is acceptable in written form.

1 three o'clock   2 five past three   3 ten past three
4 quarter past three   5 twenty past three
6 twenty-five past three   7 half past three
8 twenty-five to four   9 twenty to four
10 quarter to four   11 ten to four   12 five to four

Pronunciation saying the time

- Write *It's half past four* on the board. Say it and ask students which letters are not pronounced. Answer: the *l* in *half* and maybe the *r* in *four* depending on your accent. Then, ask students which words are stressed: *half* and *four*
- Ask students to read the Pronunciation box and check understanding.

Exercise 5a 2.9 🎧

- Play track 2.9 and ask students to listen and complete the exercise. For extra support play the track again and then check answers.

Exercise 5b 2.9 🎧

- Play track 2.9 again and tell students to repeat the phrases.

ANSWERS
1 half   2 to   3 to   4 five   5 past   6 twenty-five

AUDIOSCRIPT 2.9
1 half past eight
2 quarter to three
3 ten to ten
4 five to six
5 twenty past three
6 twenty-five to four

EXTRA ACTIVITY   Do a substitution drill. Offer a starter sentence and a cue word or words. Ask the students to put the cue word into the sentence. For example,
I get up at half past six. Cue (written) = 07.15.
Answer: I get up at quarter past seven.
Give different times and/or different verbs and students have to invent an appropriate time. For example,
I start work at nine o'clock. Cue = finish work
Answer: I finish work at six o'clock.

Exercise 6

- Ask students to read the phrases. Check their understanding of *sun rises* (= when the sun moves up in the sky in the early morning). Demonstrate the activity with your own examples.
- Put students into pairs to discuss the events.

EXTRA ACTIVITY   A day in space – writing.
Tell students to imagine they are Sanaa and they are now working in space. Tell them to write a description for their family back home about what they do every day.
Ask students to compare their ideas in pairs or post them around the room and then get everyone to walk around and read the texts choosing the most interesting, the funniest, the most normal, etc. day.

Reading & Grammar present simple negative

Exercise 7

- To lead in to this section, you could show images of the world from space and ask students what they think it feels like being in space. Tell students to imagine they are in space and are describing what they see and feel. Give them some sentence starters or categories to help them think of adjectives.
  It's (adjectives to describe it) dark, cold, scary, strange, different, amazing … .
  I feel scared, cold, strange, amazing and excited.
  The space ship is big, dark, light, cold, hot, fast.
  The sky is big, full of stars, light, dark, blue, black … .
  I can see stars, the earth, the sky, the moon, planets … .
- Tell students to work in pairs and tell their partner what they see and feel. Listen and write any new vocabulary on the board and check understanding.
- Tell students to read the instructions for the exercise.
- Ask for examples about *washing* from the class.
- Ask students to work in pairs and discuss the question. Listen and write examples on the board.

FEEDBACK FOCUS   If you hear examples of present simple positive and negative in this exercise, use them to lead in to the grammar focus. If students use the present simple correctly, use their sentences as models; if they make mistakes, add the sentences to the board and ask if the class can correct them.

Exercise 8a

> **Text summary:** This is an article about Chris Hadfield, who was the first Canadian to walk in space. It describes the differences between life on earth and life in space.

- As a lead-in, you could show or tell students some information about Chris Hadfield.
- Refer students to the photos. Ask them to think about how the images might affect their ideas in exercise 7. Would they change any of their ideas, or add any ideas?
- Ask students to read the text and compare the ideas in it with their ideas in exercise 7. Open a class discussion on the ideas.

POSSIBLE ANSWERS
Daytime and night-time: The sun rises every 45 minutes, so it is hard to know what time it is.
Washing: Astronauts wash with a cloth; they don't have showers.
Sleeping: They don't sleep in beds, they sleep in special sleeping bags on the walls.

Exercise 8b

- Write one of the students' sentences using present simple positive on the board, e.g. *I think they have showers.* Ask students to make the sentence negative. Ask them to read the text again and find and underline examples of negative present simple.
- Tell students to read and complete the Grammar focus box.

ANSWERS
doesn't have   don't have   don't sleep
doesn't rise   doesn't want

- Refer students to *Grammar reference* on p139. There are three more exercises here that students can do for homework.

Exercise 9a

EXTRA SUPPORT Write *I do not work* and *She does not play* on the board. Ask students to form the contractions (*don't* and *doesn't*). Ask students to give more examples of the negative form using *you, we, she* and *it*.

- Ask students to work individually and complete the exercise and then compare their answers in pairs.

EXTRA CHALLENGE You could ask the students how they think the sentences will be pronounced before they listen.

Exercise 9b 2.10 🎧

- Play track 2.10 and ask students to listen and check their answers, and then listen again and repeat the sentences.

ANSWERS/AUDIOSCRIPT 2.10

1 They don't have a lot of free time.
2 I don't go to classes in the evening.
3 Chris doesn't have a shower in the morning.
4 Sanaa doesn't sleep in a sleeping bag.
5 They don't speak to their families every day.
6 He doesn't work eight hours a day.

EXTRA ACTIVITY Ask students to imagine they are interviewing Chris or Sanaa about a normal day in space. Get students to work in pairs and think of five or six questions to ask. For extra support give them the questions, e.g.

1 When do you get up?
2 What do you have for breakfast?
3 How do you wash?
4 Can you cook in space?
5 Do you watch TV or listen to music?
6 How do you talk to your family?

Ask students to then role-play, taking turns to play the journalist and an astronaut. Students should use information from the text but use the 1st person to answer the questions.

Exercise 10a

- Ask students to read through the example conversation and think about their opinions and reasons for those opinions.
- Put students into pairs and ask them to discuss the six points. Listen and note good language and errors with the present simple.
- Open a class discussion to share and compare ideas. Encourage cross-class discussion.

Exercise 10b 2.11 🎧

- Play track 2.11 and ask students to listen to the sentences and compare them with their opinions.

FEEDBACK FOCUS Formative assessment: quickly assess listening comprehension by asking students to close their eyes and raise their left hands if they think they heard a negative sentence and right hands for a positive sentence. This helps you assess how successfully students have understood. Play the track again if there was a low level of comprehension.

- Go over good language and errors you collected in the speaking exercise.

ANSWERS/AUDIOSCRIPT 2.11

1 Most astronauts don't feel well when they first go into space. Space sickness is very common.
2 Astronauts don't wear special clothes in the space station. They only need a space suit when they go on a space walk.
3 Astronauts don't change their clothes every day. It isn't possible to wash clothes in space.
4 Astronauts usually exercise for two hours a day.
5 Usually, an astronaut doesn't go on a space walk more than once a week.
6 Most astronauts sleep for less time in space but they don't feel very tired.

Exercise 11a

- To lead in to this, ask if they think Chris's day is their idea of a perfect day.
- Ask students to read the instructions and write sentences. They can use the example for support and ideas.
- Monitor and check sentences and prompt self-correction.

Exercise 11b

- Ask students to work in pairs and compare their perfect days.

Exercise 11c

- Ask students to work with a different partner and explain the previous partner's ideas to practise using 3rd person positive and negative forms.

EXTRA ACTIVITY Ask students to imagine it is the future and people are going on holiday in space. Get them to work in groups of three or four and create a poster advertisement or a radio recording of an advertisement describing a typical tourist's day in space, e.g. *You get up at six o'clock and then you have a special breakfast of … at half past seven. The day starts with … .*

EXTRA ACTIVITY This would work well as homework. Ask students to do research to find out the typical working hours in different countries. When do people start and finish their working day? You could assign countries to different students or tell them to choose five or six countries they are interested in finding out about. Ask students to present their information at the start of the next class.

GRAMMAR REFERENCE ANSWERS

Exercise 1

1 doesn't 2 doesn't 3 close 4 don't 5 have
6 always eat 7 never go 8 doesn't often

Exercise 2

1 You don't need perfect eyesight.
2 He doesn't work hard.
3 She doesn't stop for a break at lunchtime.
4 They don't watch films on Fridays.
5 You don't agree with me.
6 I don't exercise a lot.
7 It doesn't rain every day.
8 We don't change our clothes every day.
9 She doesn't feel good in the morning.
10 They don't sleep for eight hours a night.

Exercise 3

1 don't 2 am 3 doesn't 4 don't 5 eat 6 like
7 likes 8 doesn't

2.3 Vocabulary and skills development

Goals

- Understand conjunctions in reading
- Use verb + preposition phrases

Lead-in

1 Closed book. To review present simple and time vocabulary.

- Before the lesson, write sentences using verbs from lesson 2.2 and times, either on the board or on strips of paper to distribute to groups. Add one error to each sentence. Adapt the errors to include your students' typical errors, e.g. *I get up at half to three, She starts work at twenty six, … .*
- Ask students to work in pairs to find errors and correct them. You could give a time limit.
- Check answers. You could use these sentences in exercise 1, asking students, *Are these good times to do things?*

2 Closed book. To review present simple verbs from lesson 2.2 and relate ideas to their own lives.

- Ask students what they remember about Sanaa and Chris from lesson 2.2.
- Put students into pairs and tell each pair to write two full sentences about the people they learnt about in lesson 2.2, e.g. *Sanaa studies Russian.* Set a time limit of four to five minutes.
- When the time is up, regroup students with other pairs and ask them to share and compare their sentences. Listen and correct any errors you hear and praise good sentences.
- Ask students to work with their partner and discuss if there are any similarities between their own lives and those of the astronauts.

Reading & Speaking understanding conjunctions

Exercise 1

- Put students into groups of three or four and tell them to discuss the questions. Encourage students to express reasons for their ideas to assess their use of connectors, e.g. *I think the best time to go to sleep is ten o'clock **because** you need eight hours' sleep.*
- Check ideas and encourage cross-class discussion.

Exercise 2a

- To lead in to this activity, you could write one of the sentences you heard students say in the previous exercise. Add a gap where the conjunction goes, e.g. *I think the best time to go to sleep is ten o'clock _____ you need eight hours sleep. (because)*
- Ask students what can go in the gap.
- Add an alternative ending and elicit the correct conjunction, e.g. *I think the best time to go to bed is ten o'clock _____ for some people this is very early. (but)*
- Tell students to work alone and complete the exercise and then compare their ideas in pairs before checking as a class.

EXTRA CHALLENGE Ask faster learners to change the meaning of the sentences by giving them different conjunctions to use. Get them to change verbs from positive to negative and from negative to positive, or use different verbs or nouns. Ask students to discuss how the meaning changes, e.g. *I usually sleep five or six hours a night but I sleep well. (and)* Answer: *I usually sleep five or six hours and I don't sleep well* OR *I usually sleep eight hours and I sleep well.*

ANSWERS

1 and   **2** but   **3** because   **4** or

Exercise 2b

- Ask students to read the Unlock the code box and check their ideas from 2a.

Exercise 3a

- Tell students to work alone and match the sentence halves to make complete sentences.

Exercise 3b   2.12 💿

- Play track 2.12 and ask students to listen and check answers. Ask them to listen again and repeat the sentences.

EXTRA CHALLENGE Ask students to complete the sentences with a different ending. Give an example of your own, e.g. *I wake up and get dressed.*

ANSWERS/AUDIOSCRIPT 2.12

1 I have lunch at one or two in the afternoon.
2 I wake up and have breakfast.
3 People eat because they're hungry.
4 I try to wake up early, but it's difficult!

Exercise 4a

- Ask students to read the sentences and then add the correct conjunction.
- Tell them to refer back to the Unlock the code box and to give reasons for their answers when you check the answers together. For example, number 2 is *or* because there are two choices – coffee or tea.

ANSWERS

1 but   **2** or   **3** and   **4** because

Exercise 4b

- Put students into pairs. Ask the class about sentence 1 to demonstrate the conversation. Encourage students to connect the ideas to their own life, e.g. *I agree with number 2 because if I drink coffee late at night, I don't sleep.*
- Ask students to work with a partner and discuss the questions.

WATCH OUT! Watch out for these typical problems with present simple:
*I **am not** agree …* (in some languages the verb *to be* is used with *agree*)
*I eat small meals because/and **is** better for me.* (omitting *it*)

- As a follow-up, ask students to write four sentences summarizing their partner's ideas, e.g. *Miriam eats small meals often because she doesn't like big meals.* Make sure students can use the conjunctions correctly.

Exercise 5a

> **Text summary:** This is an article about sleep and what is a good amount to have for a healthy life. Dr Howell is an expert on sleep and how it affects the brain.

- (Books closed) As a lead-in, write the headline *Know your body clock* on the board and ask students to discuss the meaning with a partner. Explain what it means (= something inside you that controls how you feel, for example when you feel hungry or feel sleepy, at different times of the day or year) and share ideas with the class.
- Tell students to read through the questions 1–5 and then read the text to find the answers. Check answers with the class and ask for evidence from the text. If you can, display the text so students can come to the front of the class and point to the answers.

ANSWERS

1 We can feel tired and hungry during the day.
2 No, because everyone's body clock is different.
3 He thinks six hours at night and two hours in the afternoon is best. This is often difficult because a lot of people are at work in the afternoon.
4 It is best to eat breakfast two hours after you wake up and eat dinner three hours before you go to sleep.
5 If you pay attention to your natural sleeping and eating patterns you will be happy and healthy.

Exercise 5b

- Put students into groups of three or four. Ask students to discuss the question.

CRITICAL THINKING Relate information from the reading to yourself. Encourage students to give reasons for their ideas by saying how they relate to their own lives, e.g. *I think it's true that we need to sleep in the afternoon because I'm always tired in the afternoon. I always want to sleep at four o'clock.*

EXTRA ACTIVITY Are you a *morning person* or a *night person*? Ask students what they think these words mean and teach the meanings to the class: *morning person* (= a person who finds it easy to get up in the morning); *night person* (= a person who likes staying up until late at night). Ask a student if they are a night or a morning person and why they think that. Get students to walk around the class asking the question, talking to at least five or six people. Put students in groups of four and ask them to discuss if they think the class are night or morning people.

Write on the board *Our class are morning people/night people because* _____.

Tell students they have to work together to finish the sentence. Groups present their sentences to the class. Based on these sentences, they agree on whether the class are morning or night people.

Vocabulary & Speaking verb + preposition

Exercise 6a

- Ask students to work alone and complete the sentences and then check with a partner.

ANSWERS

1 about   2 to

Exercise 6b

- Tell students to look at the article in exercise 5a to check their answers.

Exercise 6c

- Refer students to the Vocabulary box and ask them to read the information.

Exercise 7a

- As a lead-in, ask students to read sentences 1–8 and underline the verbs + prepositions to help them notice the verbs + prepositions in context.
- To make the activity more fun you could write these phrases on cards.
- Put students into pairs and tell them to complete the exercise.

ANSWERS

1 b   2 d   3 e   4 h   5 c   6 a   7 f   8 g

Exercise 7b 2.13 🔘

- Play track 2.13 and ask students to listen and check their answers.

AUDIOSCRIPT 2.13

1 A I watch the news on TV every morning.
   B I listen to it on the radio.
2 A It's a good idea.
   B I agree with you.
3 A Do you pay for tea and coffee at work?
   B No, they're free, but we buy sandwiches at lunchtime.
4 A Do people often wait for buses and trains in your city?
   B No, not often. They're usually on time.
5 A I'd like to talk to you before the meeting tomorrow.
   B OK, are you free after lunch?
6 A Do we have a reply from them?
   B No, they want more time to think about it.
7 A It's not nice to laugh at other people.
   B I know, my grandmother always says that!
8 A Do students often ask for a discount?
   B Yes, but they need to show their student card.

Exercise 7c

- Tell students to work with their partners and practise the mini conversations.

EXTENSION Ask students to choose one conversation, imagine the context and write four more lines of dialogue, including at least one verb and preposition.

Exercise 8a

- Check that students understand the meaning of *cash* (= money in notes and coins).
- Ask students to work in pairs and complete the exercise.

Exercise 8b 2.14 🔘

- Play track 2.14 and tell students to check their answers.

ANSWERS

1 talks to   2 laughs at   3 waits for   4 agree with
5 listens to   6 thinks about   7 pay for   8 asks for

AUDIOSCRIPT 2.14

1 Tarik talks to his family on the phone every day.
2 Kristofer never laughs at funny films. He doesn't enjoy them.
3 My sister never waits for people who are late.
4 I usually agree with my friends, but we sometimes have different ideas.
5 Gregorja listens to pop and classical music.
6 When he's alone, he thinks about his friends and family.
7 We always pay for our shopping with cash.
8 Intira always asks for help when she doesn't understand something in class.

EXTENSION Ask students to think of more nouns the verbs can go with, e.g. *pay for … a meal, a new bag, a drink; ask for … the bill, help*.

Put students in pairs and give them a time limit to think of at least two examples for each verb. Regroup students in groups of four and tell them to compare examples. Ask students to make a note of new examples they learn from the other pair.

STUDY TIP Discuss the benefits of making notes of new words with common collocations. Students could think of useful ways to do this in their notes – verbs and nouns, adjectives and nouns, etc.

EXTRA CHALLENGE Ask students to tell the class any other examples of verbs and prepositions they know. You could say some verbs to the class and ask them to add prepositions they know, e.g. *look (at/for), talk (about)*.

Exercise 9a

- To lead in, write the second sentence from exercise 8a on the board. Ask students how they could change it to make it true for them; what word(s) do they need to change? Elicit that they could change the adverb and the verbs, e.g. I **always/sometimes** laugh at funny films. I **enjoy** them.

- Ask students how they could make this into one sentence using a conjunction from the lesson, e.g. I always laugh at funny films **because** I enjoy them.

- For extra support, do another example on the board with the class.

- Ask students to work alone and change the sentences.

EXTRA SUPPORT Ask students to check their sentences for correct grammar and vocabulary with a partner (then put them into new pairs for the next exercise).

Exercise 9b

- Put students into pairs and ask them to tell each other their sentences. Encourage students to ask for more information.

- Listen and note examples of good language and mistakes to go over after students have finished speaking. Focus on conjunctions and prepositions in your corrections.

- Add the following to the board:
  (Student's name) and I _____ talk to our families on the phone every week.
  Ask students what can go in the gap; elicit *both*. Then show students how they can replace the two subjects and use the pronoun *we*, e.g. *We both talk to our families …* .

- To teach them how to say a difference, write this sentence on the board and ask students what word goes in the gap (*but*).
  I call my sister every day _____ Stefan talks to his family once a week.

- Ask faster learners to think of more examples before the class starts the exercise.

- Ask students to share their four sentences with the class.

- With larger groups, ask pairs to tell another pair instead of the whole class.

EXTRA ACTIVITY To use *and, but, because* and *or*. Put students into groups and ask them to say what they found out about their previous partners. Tell them to write four sentences using the conjunctions. When everyone has finished, ask them to read their sentences to the class. The people they write about can say if the sentences are correct or not.

2.4 Speaking and writing

Goals

- Make suggestions and arrangements
- Describe where you live

Lead-in

1 Closed book. To review verbs with prepositions from lesson 2.3.

- Write the following sentences on the board:
  We all/some of us
  – laugh at funny films.
  – ask for help when we don't understand something in class.
  – get enough sleep.
  – eat small meals.
  – have a sleep in the afternoon.

- Put students into groups of three or four and tell them to find out information about each other for each of the activities. Ask them to complete the sentences with the correct phrase – *we all*, or *some of us*. For an extra challenge, ask the groups to create three more sentences that are true for their group.

2 Closed book. A pair drill. To lead in to the context of making plans and talking about free time activities.

- Ask students what they usually do at the weekend. Add examples to the board. Drill the question *What do you usually do at the weekend?* Tell students to work in pairs and ask their partner the question ten times. Their partner can't repeat an answer. For example:
  What do you usually do at the weekend? I wake up late.
  What do you usually do at the weekend? I go shopping.

Listening & Speaking making suggestions and arrangements

Exercise 1

- Put students into groups of three or four. Ask them to discuss the questions.

- Compare ideas as a class and check definitions of *a 24-hour city* (= a city where many shops and businesses are open 24 hours a day, seven days a week).
  Write useful vocabulary on the board if it comes up, e.g. *The shops stay open all night, A 24-hour city doesn't stop.*

2 A 24-hour city is a city that never sleeps; where many businesses, shops and restaurants are open through the day and night.

Exercise 2a 2.15 🔘

> **Audio summary:** The audio is a conversation between a German and a Korean speaker. They are work colleagues. Karl Schmidt, the German speaker, is visiting Seoul in Korea for work. He meets with Bon Dae Kim, who is from Seoul.

- Refer students to the photo of Seoul. Ask them to describe it – do they think it is a 24-hour city? Why?
- Tell students to read the instructions. Check understanding with these questions: *Why is Karl in Seoul?* (for work); *Does Karl work with Bon Dae Kim?* (yes, it says they are colleagues)
- Tell students to read through questions 1–4. Play track 2.15 and ask them to listen and complete the exercise.

ANSWERS
1 c 2 b 3 b 4 a

Exercise 2b

- Ask students to check their answers with a partner.
- Check answers in class.

Exercise 2c

- Tell students to read through the questions and answers and guess the order of the answers (they may remember it from the recording).

Exercise 2d 2.15 🔘

- Play track 2.15 again and ask students to check their answers. You may need to play the recording twice.
- Check answers together.

EXTRA SUPPORT Pause the audio track every two or three phrases.

ANSWERS
1 e 2 c 3 a 4 d 5 b

AUDIOSCRIPT 2.15

BDK … So, welcome to Seoul, Mr Schmidt. Nice to meet you.
KS Thank you, Mr Kim. Nice to meet you, too.
BDK How was your journey?
KS It was fine, thanks.
BDK Good. I'd like to take you to dinner. Are you free tonight?
KS Um … yes, I am. But what time is our first meeting tomorrow?
BDK It's at nine thirty.
KS OK, that's fine, then.
BDK Great! Would you like to go for dinner at Jinju Jip? They do very good Korean soup there …
KS Yes, that sounds nice. What time do you want to eat?
BDK Well, I usually go at about midnight.
KS Er … I'm sorry, but I'm usually in bed at that time. Can we go a bit earlier?
BDK OK, no problem. It's open 24 hours. Let's go at half past nine.
KS Right …

BDK And do you want to do some shopping while you're here?
KS Yes, I'd love to.
BDK Great! Let's do that after dinner.
KS After dinner? What time do the shops close?
BDK Oh, very late! Some shops close at 5 a.m. People say that in Seoul, everything is open all the time!
KS 5 a.m.? Wow! OK, then. Where shall we meet?
BDK I'll pick you up from your hotel. It's not very far …

Exercise 3

- As a lead-in, ask students to suggest five to ten places to go in their current town or city.
- Demonstrate the dialogue with different students two or three times to show the class how to change the conversation each time using the prompts. Display the prompts on the board if you can.
- Put students into pairs and ask them to practise the dialogue, changing roles and activities/times, etc.

FEEDBACK FOCUS Focus on pronunciation to make sure students sound polite.

EXTENSION Write *Would you like to … ?* on the board. Elicit different endings, e.g. *go for dinner, go shopping*. Demonstrate with a faster learner, asking them to refuse politely and think of a reason, e.g.
Would you like to go for dinner?   I'm sorry but I have plans.
Would you like to go shopping?   I'm sorry but I'm busy.
Put students into pairs and tell them to finish the question *Would you like to … ?* to make a suggestion. Their partner either accepts (*Yes, I'd love to*), or refuses with a reason (*I'm sorry, but …*).

PRONUNCIATION To practise weak forms and intonation in questions. Ask students to listen to the questions again and mark which words are stressed, e.g.
Where shall we meet? OooO
Would you like to go for dinner? ooOoooOo
What time do you want to meet? oOooOoO
Are you free tonight? ooOoO?
Do you want to do some shopping? ooOoOoOo

Drill the questions, focusing on sentence and intonation. To help students you could add gestures to indicate rising and falling intonation. Make sure students repeat as a group and individually.

SMART COMMUNICATION It's important that students refuse invitations with polite intonation and give a reason why they cannot do the activity.
Focus on the way we often start with an apology: *I'm sorry, I'm afraid, + but …* and how the intonation goes up to show we are being polite.
You could extend the pronunciation exercise by including refusals to the drills.

A Are you free tonight?
B I'm sorry, but I am having dinner with my family.
A Are you free tomorrow night?
B Yes, I am.
A Would you like to go to the cinema?
B Yes, I'd love to. What time do you want to meet?
A Let's meet at half past seven.
B OK. Where shall we meet?
A Outside the cinema.
B Yes, that sounds good.

Exercise 4

- As an alternative, you could do this role-play using a map of your current location.
- As a lead-in, write *Lagos* and *Buenos Aires* on the board. Put students into pairs and tell them to think what kinds of things there are to do there and if they are 24-hour cities.
- Group the students into A and B and refer to p127 and p132. Students read their page instructions and check any vocabulary they don't know. Tell students to choose what things they would like to do and circle them.
- Demonstrate the conversation with a student.
- Group students A and B in pairs. Students make arrangements to meet. Tell students to make at least two arrangements.
- Students could repeat the exercise with a different partner for further practice.

EXTRA ACTIVITY Using real materials. Ask students to repeat the activity using real materials – brochures, website information, etc., from the place you are in. You could ask them to try and bring examples of these to class for homework. Encourage them to find English language examples.

EXTRA CHALLENGE The material may be in their first language so you could ask them to translate the activities if you think they are simple enough.

Reading & Writing describe where you live

Exercise 5

- As a lead-in, use images of cities and the countryside (small villages, etc.) to engage students in the topic. Display images on the board or on the walls around the room, or distribute images on paper. Put students into small groups of three or four.
- Ask students to think of at least five differences between life in the city and the country. Listen and add relevant vocabulary to the board.
- Regroup the students into pairs. Go over the vocabulary you noted.
- Ask students to read the instructions. Ask for some opinions and for reasons for them, to practise using conjunctions. Ask students to work in their pairs and discuss the questions.

FEEDBACK FOCUS Listen out for examples of conjunctions: *because, but, or, and*. Add good examples to the board and correct mistakes with the class.

POSSIBLE ANSWER
In the town: The buses and trains are frequent, so it's easy to get around. There are more jobs. There are lots of things to do. House prices are high. Life is expensive. There is often a lot of traffic and noise.
In the country: There is a lot of fresh air. There isn't a lot of traffic. There aren't a lot of jobs, so people often work in the town. The buses and trains don't come often and don't run late at night.

Exercise 6a

- Refer students to the three photos. Ask them to describe what they can see in each photo. Write useful vocabulary on the board.

- Ask students to read the texts and match them to the photos.
- Ask students to compare their ideas with a partner, giving reasons for their answers. Check answers with the class.

ANSWERS
1 c   2 b   3 a

Exercise 6b

- Ask students if they think these are good places to live. Get one or two ideas from the class, asking students for reasons. Put the students in pairs and ask them to discuss the questions.

EXTRA CHALLENGE Ask students to list the advantages and disadvantages for the places. Encourage dictionary use. Ask students to write ideas on the board. Go over new vocabulary with the class and encourage peer teaching. Ask students to connect the ideas using *and* or *but* to show similar ideas (two advantages) and contrasting ideas (one advantage and one disadvantage).

Exercise 7a

- Refer students to the Language for writing box.
- Check their understanding by asking these questions:
  1 Which word is used to give two or more choices? (*or*)
  2 Which word is used to show a reason? (*because*)
  3 Which word is used to give similar information? (*and*)
  4 Which word joins two different ideas? (*but*)

Exercise 7b

- Ask students to read the texts in exercise 6a again and write the correct conjunctions in the gaps.

ANSWERS
1 but   2 and   3 because   4 but   5 or   6 because
7 but   8 or   9 and

Exercise 8a

- As a lead-in, you could elicit things to do in the place you are in and write them on the board.
- Ask students to read the sentences and then complete them with their own ideas.

EXTRA SUPPORT Go through the sentences and ask for suggested answers to help students with ideas, e.g. 1 *I like the beach but I don't like all the tourists.*

Exercise 8b

- Put students into pairs and tell them to compare and discuss their sentences.
- Ask two or three students to share one similarity and one difference they found.

Exercise 9a

- Ask students to suggest a place they know well and write it on the board. Draw two columns below it and ask for good things and then bad things about it.
- Put students into pairs so they are working with someone from the same place or with someone they share a place they can talk about with.
- Give students a time limit of five to ten minutes. Ask them to make a similar list. Encourage them to use dictionaries to look up words or help them with words they don't know. Monitor and write any interesting new vocabulary on the board to go over later.

Exercise 9b

- Ask students to complete the exercise referring to exercise 6a as their model. Monitor and check texts are correct, and remind students to leave gaps for the conjunctions. You could ask students to check their texts with a partner if you have a large class.

Exercise 9c

- Tell pairs to swap their texts with another pair and complete the gaps.
- Get pairs to check each other's answers and discuss any mistakes. You can act as a referee on any disputed answers.

EXTENSION Regroup students in pairs so they are working with new partners. Ask them to tell their partner about the text they completed and the information about the place that was described. If everyone writes about the same place, they could try and discuss any similarities or differences.

Exercise 10

- This could be managed in two ways:
1 Students work in groups of four. Texts are distributed to the groups; make sure that no one has their own. Each student reads a text and then summarizes it to their group. Students then discuss the place or places they would like to live in and why.
2 Post the texts around the room so students can walk around and read them. Seat students in groups of four and get them to discuss the texts they read and what they remember of them, saying which place or places they would like to live in and say why.

EXTRA ACTIVITY To challenge students you could ask them to imagine they are going to live in one of these places for a year. They are travelling in pairs. They have to decide on one place with their partner and have three to five reasons why it is the place they chose.

EXTRA CHALLENGE Assign a place to each student and tell them they have to convince their partner their place is better. For example:
A Madrid is ok but in London we can practise English.
B Yes. Ok, in London we speak English but in Madrid we spend less money. It's cheap but London is very expensive.

2.5 Video

The Menna family

VIDEOSCRIPT

This is the Menna family. They live in Colegiales, a neighbourhood in Buenos Aires.
During the week they are very busy.
This is Roberto. He works as a reporter for Channel 9, an Argentinian television network. He reports on lots of different news stories. Every day is different, and there's a lot to do, but he loves his job.
This is Gabriela. She's always busy too. She works at a local radio station and she starts very early. She wakes up before the rest of the family and leaves the house at around 6.30 a.m.!

Milagros and Julieta are Roberto and Gabriela's daughters. Milagros is 11 and Julieta is 7. They go to the same school and they start at 8 a.m. So it's always a rush in the morning.
During the week the Menna family don't have a lot of free time so they really enjoy the weekend! On Saturday they usually get up around 9 or 10 a.m. and they all make breakfast together.
They eat toast with cheese and butter, but Julieta has cereal with chocolate milk. Roberto and Milagros drink *mate*, a typical Argentinian drink, and Gabriela drinks coffee.
Sometimes Roberto makes special omelettes. They're delicious!
After breakfast the family often play games. Sometimes they play board games but the girls often prefer to play video games.
In the afternoon they often go for a walk or go to the park near their house. It's a small park but it has swings and a slide so the girls have lots of fun.
In the evening they play music. Milagros plays the guitar and the rest of the family sing. Sometimes Roberto plays the bongos!
Sunday is a relaxing day too. In the morning they stay at home. Gabriela reads the paper, Roberto drinks more *mate* and the girls play on the computer.
In the afternoon they usually visit Gabriela's parents and have a large meal with them.
They all eat outside. They have barbecued meat with salad and bread. After the meal they have coffee and go home.
By the time they get home it's time for bed. On Sunday they go to bed early, so they have lots of energy for the week ahead!

VIDEO ANSWERS

Exercises 1 & 2
Students' own answers

Exercise 3
a Roberto works for a television network.
b Gabriela goes to work at 6.30 a.m.
c Milagros and Julieta go to the same school.
d The girls get up at 9 a.m. / 10 a.m. on Saturdays.
e Gabriela drinks *mate*.
f After breakfast the girls play board games / video games.
g They go to the park in the afternoon.
h The family usually visits the girls' grandparents on Sundays.
i They eat salad / bread with their barbecue.
j On Sundays they go to bed early.

Exercises 4a & b
Students' own answers

Review

Exercise 1a

1 like 2 go 3 works 4 study 5 have 6 lives

Exercises 2a & b 2.16 ◉

They never have fish for breakfast.
They are hardly ever late for meetings.
They sometimes go to a different city to study.
They often have more than one TV at home.
They usually eat lunch at work.
They always talk about the weather.

AUDIOSCRIPT 2.16

1 British people never have fish for breakfast. They usually have toast or cereal.
2 They are hardly ever late for meetings. They like to arrive on time.
3 British people sometimes go to a different city to study at university.
4 British people often have more than one TV at home: some people have three or four.
5 They usually eat lunch at work. They don't have time to go home.
6 And British people always, always talk about the weather!

Exercise 3a

get up, have a shower, go to work, have lunch, go home, have dinner, watch TV, go to bed

Exercise 3b

have/make breakfast, read a book, listen to music, play computer games, see/meet friends

Exercise 5a

1 e 2 c 3 f 4 a 5 d 6 b

Exercises 6a & b 2.17 ◉

1 free 2 busy 3 plans 4 like 5 love 6 shall
7 want 8 let's

AUDIOSCRIPT 2.17

A Are you free after class today?
B I'm sorry, but I'm busy this evening. But I don't have any plans tomorrow.
A Would you like to go out for a pizza?
B Yes, I'd love to. What time shall we meet?
A Eight o'clock at Gino's? Or do you want to meet at the station?
B Yes, let's meet there at 7.45.
A OK, see you then!

3

The world of work

Unit overview

Language input

***yes/no* questions** (CB p27)	• *Are you a nurse? Yes, I am.* • *Does he work outside? No, he doesn't.*
***Wh-* questions** (CB p29)	• *What, When, Where, Who, Why, How often*
Grammar reference (CB pp140–141)	

Vocabulary development

Jobs (CB p26)	• *chef, dentist, journalist, nurse, pilot …*
Work (CB p28)	• *Work for a big company/from home* • *Earn a good salary* • *Be retired/un-employed*
***er-* suffix** (CB p31)	• *baker, dancer, runner, worker …*

Skills development

Listening: the schwa /ə/ (CB p30)
Speaking: making requests (CB p32)
Writing: opening and closing an email (CB p33)

Video

Documentary: An Iranian doctor in the USA (CB p34)
Vox pops (Coursebook DVD & TG p260)

More materials

Workbook	• Language practice for vocabulary, grammar, pronunciation, speaking and writing
Photocopiable activities	• Grammar: Party talk (TG p204 & TSRD) • Vocabulary: Guess the job (TG p222 & TSRD) • Communication: Ask me something! (TG p238 & TSRD)
Tests	• Unit 3 test (TSRD) • Progress test: Units 1–3
Unit 3 wordlist (TSRD)	

3.1 Jobs

Goals
- Talk about jobs
- Ask *yes/no* questions

Lead-in

1 Open book. To recycle job title vocabulary from units 1 and 2.
- Put students into pairs. Give a time limit of two minutes.
- Ask students to look back and find as many jobs as they can from units 1 and 2.
- Ask students for the job titles and write them on the board. Check meaning and pronunciation by asking for examples, e.g. *astronaut – they work in space.*

2 Closed book. To elicit job title vocabulary and test *yes/no* present simple questions through a game.
- Tell students you are thinking of a job. Tell them they have twenty questions to guess the job. Write example questions on the board, e.g. *Do they work alone? Do they work in space? Do they work with animals? Do they write? Is it a hairdresser/journalist?*
- Tell students to ask questions to guess the job.
- Put students into pairs. Tell them to think of a job and play the game in their pairs. Listen and write job titles on the board as they guess them.
- Go over the vocabulary with the class and check meaning and pronunciation.

Vocabulary & Speaking jobs

Exercise 1a
- Put students into pairs. Tell them to match the job titles to the photos.

ANSWERS
See exercise 1c, track 3.2.

Exercise 1b 3.1 ⊚
- Play track 3.1 and tell students to listen and check their answers.

ANSWERS/AUDIOSCRIPT 3.1
1 She has her own company. She's a businesswoman.
2 My son fixes a lot of different machines. He's a mechanic.
3 Manu takes pictures with his camera. He's a photographer.
4 My brother flies planes for a Japanese airline. He's a pilot.
5 She washes hair, cuts it, and dries it. She's a hairdresser.
6 Ekaterina writes for the newspaper. She's a journalist.
7 Sameeha cleans and fixes people's teeth. She's a dentist.
8 My cousin sings and plays the guitar in a band. He's a musician.
9 He studies at university. He's a student.
10 She works in a hospital and helps sick people. She's a nurse.
11 Daniela cooks food in a restaurant. She's a chef.
12 My best friend cleans offices and people's houses. He's a cleaner.

EXTRA ACTIVITY Focus on verb and noun collocations. Ask students what the people in the photos do. Elicit verbs from the recording, e.g. *fix machines, take pictures*. Students make a note of the collocations in their notebooks. There are two alternatives for extending this:
1. Tell students to work in pairs and make a gap fill or verb/noun matching exercise for another pair.
2. Tell students to think of other nouns for as many of the verbs as they can, e.g. *fix a car, write for a magazine, play the saxophone.*

Exercise 1c 3.2 ⊚
- Write *businessman* on the board and ask students how many syllables it has. (Three) Ask a student to come to the board and underline the stressed syllable. (The first syllable.)

ANSWERS/AUDIOSCRIPT 3.2
1 businessman/businesswoman   2 mechanic
3 photographer   4 pilot   5 hairdresser   6 journalist
7 dentist   8 musician   9 student   10 nurse   11 chef
12 cleaner

PRONUNCIATION/DICTIONARY SKILLS Help students identify the number of syllables and where the main stress goes with stress bubbles, e.g. *businessman* Ooo, *pilot* Oo.

To help students' dictionary skills, show them how the main stress appears in dictionaries: 'businessman.

Discuss which method they prefer and encourage them to mark word stress when they learn new words.
- Play track 3.2 and ask students to mark the stressed syllables.
- Write answers on the board to show the stress clearly.

WATCH OUT! Many of these words are similar in Latin-based languages. This can cause problems with learning the correct pronunciation. To help with this, ask students to identify how the stress moves from the word in their language to the word in English.

Exercise 1d 3.2 ⊚
- Play the track again and tell students to listen and repeat.

EXTRA CHALLENGE Drill the words in a sentence, e.g. *I'd like to be a pilot. My brother's a journalist.* Drilling a word in a sentence can help improve word stress.

Exercise 2
- Ask students to work with their partners. Tell them to read the words in each box and discuss the meaning with their partner. Check meanings with the class. Ask for examples, e.g. *Who works outside?* (A farmer) *What words mean you get a lot of money?* (Well-paid) *What's the opposite of well-paid?* (Badly-paid)
- Tell students that jobs can go in more than one box, e.g. *dentist* can be *work inside* and *well-paid*. Students add the vocabulary to the correct boxes.
- Write answers in boxes on the board and add students' own examples. Explain that there are different possible answers for this exercise.

Work inside: businessman/businesswoman; photographer; hairdresser; dentist; mechanic; pilot; journalist; musician; student; nurse; cleaner
Work outside: photographer; mechanic; journalist;
Well-paid: businessman/businesswoman; dentist; pilot; musician
Badly-paid: hairdresser; nurse; cleaner
Work with a computer: businessman/businesswoman; student; journalist; photographer
Work with their hands: hairdresser; dentist; musician; nurse; cleaner; mechanic

EXTRA CHALLENGE Encourage students to give reasons for their answers, e.g. *Photographers can take photos outside and inside.*

Exercise 3

- Put students in small groups of three or four. Ask one student what they think the best job is and why. You could write their answer on the board for extra support, e.g. *Pilot. Reasons: Well-paid, interesting, travel.*
- Ask students to look at the jobs and think of their own ideas and reasons for one minute. Tell them to explain their opinions to the others in their group and give reasons for opinions. Encourage them to use vocabulary from exercise 2, e.g. *I think the best job is a photographer because you can work inside and outside and your job is different every day.*

FEEDBACK FOCUS Listen to pronunciation of job titles and correct problems with word stress.

Grammar & Listening *yes/no* questions

Exercise 4

Text summary: An advert for a television programme. They are looking for people with unusual jobs to appear on the programme.

- Pre-teach *unusual* to the class (= the opposite of usual; something that you don't often see). Ask students for examples of unusual jobs. Write them on the board.
- Check students understand the meaning of *advert* (= short for advertisement, a notice that tells people about a product, job or service).
- Ask students to work alone and read the advert to answer the questions. Students then compare their answers with a partner before you check answers as a class.

ANSWERS
1 It is for people with unusual jobs who want to be in a TV programme.
2 People with dangerous, surprising or difficult jobs will answer.

EXTENSION Ask students to work alone and think of jobs that are dangerous or difficult or make people happy. Put students into new pairs and tell them to share their ideas and explain why they chose those jobs.

Exercise 5

- Ask students to read the text again to complete both parts of the exercise.
- Check answers.

ANSWERS
<u>Do</u> you have … ? <u>Are</u> people surprised … ? <u>Does</u> your job … ? <u>Is</u> your job … ? <u>Do</u> you do … ?
1 Is 2 Does 3 Do

EXTENSION To practise *yes/no* questions. Write the question: *Is your job _____ ?* on the board. Write different adjectives on the board. Ask the students to suggest examples, e.g. *easy, fun, interesting, busy, well-paid, dangerous, relaxing, simple.*

- Ask students to choose a job from exercise 1, but not to tell anyone which job they have chosen. Ask them to walk around the room asking the question above and using the different adjectives on the board to guess each other's jobs.
- Refer students to *Grammar reference* on p140. There are three more exercises here that students can do for homework.

Exercise 6a

- Tell students to read the information about Máté and Dana. You could ask students if they know where Budapest and Santa Fé are (Budapest is the capital city of Hungary, in Eastern Europe; Santa Fé is the capital of the state of New Mexico in the United States) to help create interest in the recording.
- Tell students to work with their partners and complete the exercise, and then check their ideas with the class.

Exercise 6b 3.3

Audio summary: Máté and Dana describe their jobs. Dana works in a forest checking for fires; Máté plays the piano at a cinema.

EXTRA SUPPORT If you think your students might find it difficult to understand the listening, pre-teach *forest, tower, winds, silent movies.*

- Play track 3.3. Ask students to listen and check their answers to exercise 6a.

ANSWERS
Máté is a piano player in a local cinema. He plays live music to go with the scenes in silent movies.
Dana is a 'fire lookout'. It is her job to see if any fires have started in the forest. She works in a high tower so she can see very far. She checks the weather for strong winds.

AUDIOSCRIPT 3.3
M I work at a cinema in town, but I don't sell tickets, I'm the piano player! At my cinema they have a lot of old, silent movies so they need someone to play music. I watch the film and decide what type of music to play. If it's a sad part of the film, I play slow music; but if it's an exciting part, I play it fast.
D I am a 'fire lookout' and I work in a big forest. Fire can be very dangerous here, so my job is to make sure no fires start. I work in a very high tower, so I can see very far. I check the weather on the internet every morning because strong winds can be a big problem. I like my job because the forest is beautiful and quiet.

Exercise 6c

- Tell students to work with their partners and to discuss the questions. To help students explain reasons for their ideas, model your answer to the class before they start.

Encourage students to use adjectives from this lesson, e.g. *I would like to have Dana's job because you help other people. I wouldn't like to have Máté's job because he works inside.*

Exercise 7a

- Complete the first question with the class.
- Ask students to work alone and complete the exercise and then to check their answers with a partner.

1 Does; work; does   2 Does; play; doesn't   3 Is; isn't
4 Does; work; doesn't   5 Does; like; does
6 Do; have; do

Exercise 7b   3.4 🔘

- Play track 3.4 and ask students to listen to check their answers.
- Ask students to practise saying the sentences to each other.

AUDIOSCRIPT 3.4

1 Does Máté work at the cinema? Yes, he does.
2 Does he always play fast music? No, he doesn't.
3 Is Dana a police officer? No, she isn't.
4 Does she work in a big office? No, she doesn't.
5 Does she enjoy her job? Yes, she does.
6 Do Dana and Máté have unusual jobs? Yes, they do.

Pronunciation *do and does*

- Tell students to read the Pronunciation box.

Exercise 8   3.5 🔘

- Ask students which words are stressed in the example question in the box: *Do they like their jobs?* (*like* and *jobs*).
- Ask students what kind of verb *like* is (*a main verb*) and explain that we often stress main verbs but not auxiliary verbs in sentences and questions. In short answers, we stress the auxiliary because there is no main verb.
- Play track 3.5 and ask students to listen and repeat. Ask them to identify which words are stressed in the questions. (*like, jobs, play, piano, sell, tickets, have, job*)
- You could ask students to mark the stressed words as they listen.

Exercise 9

- Refer students to the example.
- Tell students to work in their pairs and practise asking questions and replying using short answers.

A Is Dana a police officer?
B No, she isn't.
A Does Dana check the weather every day?
B Yes, she does.
A Does Dana work from home?
B No, she doesn't.
A Is Máté a piano player?
B Yes, he is.
A Does Máté play slow music?
B Yes, he does.
A Does Máté work at the theatre?
B No, he doesn't.

Exercise 10a

- Tell students to work alone and read the words in the box. Check they understand *organized* (= with everything planned and in order), *busy* (= with a lot of things happening/to do), *calm* (= quiet, not excited/noisy/worried about things).
- Ask students to identify if the words and phrases in the box have adjectives or verbs in them. Explain that adjectives are used in questions with *to be,* and verbs need the auxiliary *do.*
- Ask for examples of a question with the verb *to be* and one of the words in the box. Write it on the board, e.g. *Are you organized?* Repeat this with a question with a main verb and auxiliary *do,* e.g. *Do you walk a lot?*
- Write *What's the best job for you?* on the board and ask a student to answer. Tell the class you are going to test if this is true by doing a quiz. Ask the student questions using the words in the box and tell students to listen to the answers carefully. For example, *Are you organized? Do you walk a lot? Do you get up early in the morning? Do you like children?*
- Ask the class to say if they agree with the student's original choice or to suggest another job based on the answers the student gave. They need to explain their ideas, e.g. *I think a nurse is the best job for you because you like to help people and you are calm. You don't like to work with computers,* etc.
- Put students into pairs and ask them to read the instructions and write questions. They should write four to six questions.

Are you a calm person? Are you an outdoor person? Do you enjoy helping people? Do you get up early? Do you like being busy? Do you like children? Do you like working alone? Do you like working with computers? Are you organized? Do you walk a lot?

Exercise 10b

FEEDBACK FOCUS This is a speaking activity but focus the feedback on accurate use of *yes/no* questions.

- Put students into new pairs. Students ask and answer their questions to discover *What's the best job for you?* You could set a time limit for this of four to five minutes for each interview. Students have to make a note of answers (*yes* or *no*).

Exercise 10c

- Ask students to read their results and to suggest a good job for their partner. Encourage them to say why they think so.

WATCH OUT! Students can find it hard to switch to using the third person. You may want to remind them to use the third person verbs in their explanations. For example, *I think* nurse *is the best job for Asha because she likes children, she likes being busy and she's calm.*

- Ask the students what they think about the suggestions made for them. Do they agree or do they think another job is better for them?

EXTRA ACTIVITY Students could research information about an unusual job and write a short description to bring to the next class.

Exercise 1

1 f 2 h 3 e 4 a 5 g 6 d 7 c 8 b

Exercise 2

1 Do; you do 2 Do; I don't 3 Is; she is 4 Is; he is
5 Does; it doesn't 6 Do; we don't 7 Do; they do
8 Do; they don't 9 Are; they are 10 Does; she doesn't

Exercise 3

1 Are 2 am 3 Do 4 Do 5 do 6 Are 7 'm
8 Do 9 Is 10 she's

3.2 What do you do?

Goals

- Talk about work
- Ask *Wh-* questions

Lead-in

1 Closed book. Jobs alphabet activity to review job title vocabulary.

- Put students in groups of three or four. Ask them to write the letters of the alphabet in a vertical list in their notebooks. Tell students to think of one job for as many letters of the alphabet as they can, e.g. *artist, builder, chef, dentist*, etc.

- Tell them the team with the most words after five minutes is the winner. After five minutes check answers and decide on the winner.

- Ask students what letters they could not think of a job for and encourage students to help each other to think of more examples. There aren't answers for every letter.

2 Open book. Create interest in the lesson and review language from lessons 2.1, 2.2 and 3.1.

- Put students into pairs. Tell them to look at the photo. Ask them what job it shows (photographer) and then ask students to discuss these points in their pairs:
  Describe a typical day in this job.
  How many years does it take to learn to do this job?
  Is this a difficult job?
  Who does this person work with?
  Would you like to do this job?

Vocabulary & Speaking work

Exercise 1

- Put students into groups of three or four.

- Write *nurse* on the board and ask students these questions:
  Where does a nurse work? (in a hospital)
  Do they make a lot of money? (No, they don't.)
  Who do they work with? (doctors and patients)
  How many hours do they work a day? (eight or nine)

- Tell students to read the instructions and discuss the questions.

  CRITICAL THINKING Reflect on a question. Ask students to think about different jobs and if the answers to exercise 1 are different for people in different jobs, e.g. some people might think that money is less important to a musician than to a businessman/woman. Encourage them to give reasons for their opinions.

Exercise 2

> **Text summary:** A blog post. A blog is a website where people can write about their own ideas or experiences. In this post a photographer talks about his work and what jobs his family do.

- Pre-teach vocabulary to help students: *freelance* (= an adjective to describe someone who does not work for just one company, they earn money by selling their services to different companies); *salary* (= money that people get paid every month for doing a job); *retired* (= an adjective to describe someone who does not work anymore, usually because they are older than the legal age to work).

- Students work alone and read the text and answer the questions.

  ANSWERS
  1 Pierre 2 Pierre's father 3 Pierre's mother
  4 Pierre's sister

  EXTENSION Ask students to work with their group and discuss the jobs Pierre's family do. They can discuss these questions:
  1 Do you know anyone who does these jobs?
  2 Which jobs do you think are good and why?

Exercise 3a

- Refer students to the diagrams on the right-hand side of the page.

- Do one example with the class. Ask them which category *work from home* goes in (place).

- Ask students to work alone and complete the exercise.

  EXTRA CHALLENGE Put fast finishers into pairs and ask them to compare answers and then add more examples if they can to each category. Ask them to share their words with the class when everyone is finished. Encourage them to teach the meaning and give examples.

Exercise 3b 3.6 ⊚

- Play track 3.6 and ask students to listen and check their answers.

  ANSWERS/AUDIOSCRIPT 3.6
  1 *company/no company*: work for a big company, work freelance, work for a fashion magazine
  2 *place*: work in a hospital, work from home, work in a factory, work in a big office
  3 *money*: salary, earn
  4 *hours*: work full-time, work part-time, work long hours
  5 *no job*: retired, unemployed
  6 *people*: colleagues, manager/boss

Exercise 3c 3.6 ⊚

- Play the track again and ask students to listen and repeat.

  PRONUNCIATION Ask students to mark the stress on words and phrases:
  company **free**lance **fac**tory **sa**lary **off**ice **full**-time, **part**-time re**tired** em**ployed** unem**ployed man**ager **coll**eagues

  EXTENSION Ask students to write four to six sentences using the vocabulary. Tell them to focus on vocabulary that is new for them. The sentences should show the meaning clearly, so encourage them to think of real examples, e.g. *Nurses work full-time. My uncle is retired because he's sixty-eight now.*

Exercise 4

- Put students into pairs. Refer them to the example dialogue.
- Demonstrate the activity by asking a student questions using the phrases in the diagram.

EXTRA SUPPORT   If you think students will have problems completing the questions, ask them to listen again to your questions and write them down.

- Ask a more confident student to ask you two questions using the words to check they understand the exercise. Write these questions on the board to give extra support for the task.
- Tell students to ask and answer each other's questions.

POSSIBLE QUESTIONS

Do you/Does anyone you know have nice colleagues?
Do you/Does anyone you know earn a high salary?
Do you/Does anyone you know work in an office?
Are you/Is anyone you know retired?
Do you/Does anyone you know wear a uniform?
Do you/Does anyone you know work for a big company?
Do you/Does anyone you know work long hours?

FEEDBACK FOCUS   Listen to the students' use of the vocabulary from exercise 3 and their *yes/no* question forms. Write examples of good language and errors on the board and ask students to work in their pairs to identify good examples and correct mistakes.

EXTRA ACTIVITY   Ask students to work with their partners and write definitions of jobs for other teams to guess. They should write three definitions for each job and then test another pair to guess the jobs, e.g. *This person works in a hospital. He isn't a nurse. He studied for many years for this job.* (doctor)

Reading & Grammar *Wh- questions*

Exercise 5a

> **Text summary:** An online article of FAQs (frequently asked questions) about stand-up meetings. In these meetings people stand instead of sitting. The article explains what these meetings are and what happens in them.

- Put students into pairs. Tell them to look at the photo and discuss the questions. Ask students to share their ideas with the class. There are no right or wrong answers here. Students are predicting the content of the article.

Exercise 5b

- Pre-teach vocabulary: *software companies* (= companies that work with/make computer programs).
- Ask students to work alone and read the article quickly to check the class predictions. Give a time limit of two to three minutes.
- Ask if any of their predictions were correct. Tell students to work with their partners and ask them to discuss their opinions of stand-up meetings. Ask students to share their ideas with the class.

Exercise 6

- Tell students to read through questions a–g.
- Put students into new pairs and tell them to complete the exercise.
- Go through the answers together.

ANSWERS

1 e   2 b   3 g   4 c   5 a   6 f   7 d

Exercise 7

- Refer students to the Grammar focus box and ask them to complete the rules. Ask them to compare their answers in pairs.

ANSWERS

1 What   2 Who   3 When   4 Where   5 Why
6 How often

- Refer students to *Grammar reference* on p141. There are three more exercises here that students can do for homework

Exercise 8a

- Do the first question with the class. (Answer: *Where* because it's a place)
- Put students into pairs and tell them to complete the exercise. You may need to check the meaning of *take breaks* (= stop working for a short time).

ANSWERS

1 Where   2 What   3 Why   4 What time   5 When
6 Who   7 What   8 How often

Exercise 8b   3.7 🔘

- Play track 3.7 and tell students to listen and check their answers.

AUDIOSCRIPT 3.7

1 Where do you live?
2 What do you usually wear to work?
3 Why do you want to learn English?
4 What time do you start work or class?
5 When do you take breaks?
6 Who do you live with?
7 What do you do when you're bored?
8 How often do you check your emails?

EXTRA SUPPORT   If you think your students need to review the rules, ask them to say why each answer is correct. For example, question 2 is *what* because the question is about things, question 3 is *why* because the question is asking for a reason.

Pronunciation *Wh- questions*

Exercise 9   3.8 🔘

WATCH OUT!   Students sometimes find it hard to hear intonation, even in their own language. You could discuss this as part of the activity and explain that this exercise is to try and help them get better at recognizing intonation.

- Play track 3.8 and tell students to listen to the intonation and repeat the questions.

PRONUNCIATION Sentence stress. To help students to produce correct intonation we can show them where to place emphasis. In *wh-* questions, the stress is usually placed on the question words (*where, when, why* …) and the main verbs and nouns. In the last question, *how often* go together and the *how* and *of-* in *often* are stressed.

e.g. **Where** *do you* **live**?

What *do you* **usually wear** *to* **work**?

How *often do you* **check** *your* **emails**?

Read out the questions in exercise 8a and ask students to mark which words are stressed. To practise you can do the following drill activity: Say only the question word, verb and noun, e.g.

Where/live

What/usually wear/work

How often/work/home

Tell students to repeat. You can clap a rhythm to help. After two or three repetitions add in the grammar words to say the complete sentence but try and keep the same rhythm. This will help students notice they have to stress the main words and de-stress the grammar words.

Exercise 10

EXTRA SUPPORT Tell students to read through the questions in exercise 8a and think about how they would answer the questions.

- Ask a more confident student two or three of the questions to demonstrate the exercise and model the intonation. Ask follow-up questions to make the exercise more communicative. For example:

Teacher: Where do you live?

Student: In the city centre.

Teacher: Oh. OK. In a flat or a house?

Student: In a flat.

Teacher: Do you like living in a flat?

Student: Yes, but sometimes I would like a garden. And you?

Teacher: I live in a flat too. I like it because I am in the centre of town and near all the shops and cafes.

- Put students in groups of three or four. Tell them to stand up and imagine they are having a stand-up meeting.
- Tell them to practise asking and answering the questions in their groups.

FEEDBACK FOCUS If you think your students need some correction then you could try a sandwich correction activity. This is where you stop a speaking activity, do some quick correction and then tell the students to continue without making the same errors.

In this case, stop the speaking activity and drill the correct intonation. Drill chorally and individually. Start the speaking activity again and listen for improved intonation.

Exercise 11a

This activity gets the students to use *wh-* questions in the third person. It's primarily a speaking activity but you should also focus on correct grammar.

- Ask students to read the instructions and to suggest other questions they could ask.

EXTRA SUPPORT If you think students will find it difficult to think of questions, ask them to write questions in their notebooks before they start.

- Put students into pairs. Explain the activity and tell students they need to make notes so they remember the

answers. They will have to tell someone else in the class about their partner later.

- Tell students to ask each other questions and make notes.

Exercise 11b

- Refer students to the example sentence with the gap. Tell them to write similar sentences about their partner's family and their jobs.

Exercise 11c

- Put students into groups of four. Make sure they are with people they have not just written about. Tell them to take turns reading the sentences they have written and guessing who the people are. For example, one student reads their sentences about their previous partner's family. The others listen and guess the family members.
- Demonstrate this exercise to make sure students are clear on what to do.

EXTENSION You could ask students to work in new groups and repeat the exercise.

EXTRA ACTIVITY Students use the information they have just heard in the group activity and check it's correct. This will work especially well if you have done the extension above.

Tell students to walk around the room and find people they know something about. They say what they remember from the group activity. Ask students to listen and confirm if the information is correct. For example:

Student A: Hello! OK. I think you have got two brothers. One is called Ivon. He's a businessman and he works in a big company. Your other brother is a doctor.

Student B: Yes! That's right.

GRAMMAR REFERENCE ANSWERS

Exercise 1

1 Why 2 How (often) do 3 Where 4 time 5 Who

6 Why 7 do 8 does

Exercise 2

1 How often does his brother work outside?

2 When do the students use the internet?

3 Who does your friend work for?

4 Why are the children bored?

5 Where does their team play?

6 What do you usually wear to work?

7 How often are you late for class?

Exercise 3

1 What does 2 Why do 3 Who does

4 When/What time do 5 How often do 6 What do

7 Where do 8 Who do 9 Why does 10 When does

3.3 Vocabulary and skills development

Goals

- Recognize the schwa sound
- Use the suffix *-er*

Lead-in

1 Closed book. Vocabulary revision and recycling.

- Write the anagrams below on the board and tell students they are words from the last lesson. Put students into

pairs. They have to order the letters to make words from this unit. If students find this difficult, write the first letter and perhaps one or two other letters of each word (separated by blanks) on the board. You could add the part of speech as well, for further support.
ecrfenlae yslaar rteider nrea dareshsirre
(Answers: freelance salary retired earn hairdresser)

- You could then ask the pairs to create their own anagrams and test another pair. Ask them to choose words from previous lessons.

2 Closed book. To introduce the topic of happiness and work.

- Ask students to work with a partner and discuss these questions.
  1 What makes people happy?
  2 Can your job make you happy?
- Ask students to share their ideas with the class.

Listening & Speaking the schwa /ə/

Exercise 1

- Put students into pairs. Ask them what jobs they can see in the photos (author, pilot, mechanic, teacher).
- Tell students to discuss the questions with their partners and then share their ideas with the class.
- Encourage students to give reasons for their opinions. Ask them what it is about jobs that makes people happy, e.g. *I think the author is happy because she doesn't have a boss and her job is interesting.*

EXTENSION Ask students to discuss with their partner if any of these jobs would make them happy. Ask two or three students to tell the class if they heard anything interesting from their partner.

Exercise 2a 3.9

- Write *doctor* on the board and say it with the stress on different syllables: **doc** tor / doc **tor**. Ask students which is the correct pronunciation. Ask which syllable is **un**stressed in the correct pronunciation and circle it on the board. doctor
- Play track 3.9 and tell students to circle the unstressed syllables.

ANSWERS/AUDIOSCRIPT 3.9
author mechanic pilot teacher

Exercise 2b 3.9

- Play track 3.9 again and tell students to listen and repeat the words.

EXTENSION Ask students to use these words in a sentence, e.g. *I'd like to be an author. A pilot flies around the world.* Saying the word in a sentence helps to practise the word stress in context.

Exercise 3 3.10

- Refer students to the Unlock the code (1) box. Play track 3.10 and ask students to read and listen.
- To help them understand the schwa sound, ask them to say *pilot* and focus on the movement of their mouth. Show them that when we say the second syllable with the schwa, our mouth is totally relaxed. You could mime a relaxed position with your body to help them feel this.

- You could try drilling these sounds to help them feel the difference in their tongue and jaw position. /iː/ and /ə/. Drill these sounds together quickly. They should feel their tongues relaxing and moving to the middle, neutral position on the schwa.
- Explain that this sound is important to English pronunciation. It will help them to listen and speak better if they can hear and say it.

Exercise 4 3.11

EXTRA CHALLENGE Ask students to say these words to themselves quietly and see if they can identify the schwa before they listen.

- Ask students to work alone and listen and circle the schwa sounds. Play track 3.11.
- Check answers and ask students to repeat the words. Help them by getting them to focus on the position of their mouths (lips, tongue and jaw).

ANSWERS/AUDIOSCRIPT 3.11
address after again answer breakfast clever daughter forget internet later

Exercise 5 3.12

- Ask students to look at the Unlock the code (2) box. Play track 3.12 and ask students to read and listen.
- Explain that the words *a, to* and *and* are grammar words; they don't carry meaning. Explain that in English the stress is usually on the content words – nouns, verbs, adjectives, etc. Grammar words – articles, determiners, conjunctions and prepositions – are usually not stressed and so have the schwa.

EXTENSION Ask students to say the phrases in the box to practise saying the schwa.

PRONUNCIATION Sentence clap drill to practise using the schwa. Write ONE TWO THREE FOUR on the board. Clap your hands as you say each word, and get students to clap with you. Get a rhythm going. Then stop and write *and* between the numbers and drill *one and two and three and four,* clapping at the same speed as before. On each clap the students say a number. This forces the students to use the schwa on *and.* Now add *and then* between the numbers and do the drill again, clapping at the same speed.

Exercise 6a 3.13

- Ask students to work alone and read the sentences and think about what word or words can go in the spaces. You could tell them how many words are in each space to give extra support.
- Play track 3.13. and ask students to complete the exercise. Check answers.

ANSWERS
1 a 2 that 3 are 4 for a 5 of

AUDIOSCRIPT 3.13
1 a recent report
2 one job that makes people very happy
3 there are three reasons
4 work for a company
5 a lot of different people

Exercise 6b 3.13 🔊

- Play the track again and ask students to listen and repeat. Tell them to focus on producing the schwa in the grammar words *a, for, that,* etc.

  PRONUNCIATION English is a stress-timed language. This means the rhythm of the language is more irregular and open to variation in stress and intonation. Some words appear to be 'eaten' and this can make it difficult to listen to English when it's spoken quickly. Other languages are syllable-timed. This means the rhythm is more regular and even. Find out if your students' first language is stress- or syllable-timed. If their first language is syllable-timed, it can make it harder to produce a natural rhythm when they speak English as they can tend to put equal stress on all syllables.

Exercise 7 3.14 🔊

> **Audio summary:** A radio programme about a new book. The book is written by a mechanic and is about how work can make you happy.

- Ask students to work alone and read through the questions and think about what information they need to listen for, e.g. in question 1 they are listening for the names of jobs.
- Play track 3.14 and ask students to listen and make a note of their answers. Tell them to talk to their partner and answer the questions.
- You may have to play the track twice or three times. For extra support, pause the recording after each answer.
- Check answers with the class.

ANSWERS
1 He is an author and a mechanic.
2 He believes:
   a, people who work with their hands are happy in their jobs because they see results very quickly, and,
   b, that office workers are unhappy in their jobs because they have to wait a long time to be successful.
3 Because office workers work as part of a team. Working as part of a team can help people be happy.
4 Hairdressers.
5 Hairdressers are happy because they don't have a boss, they work with a lot of different people, and they make their customers look and feel good. They see a lot of happy people and that makes them happy.

AUDIOSCRIPT 3.14
A new book by author and mechanic Matthew Crawford says that people who work with their hands are often happy in their jobs. The great thing about working with your hands is that you can see the result very quickly – you fix a bike and it works … or it doesn't! It's not the same for people in office jobs. For them, success often comes after weeks or months of hard work, which can make them feel unhappy.
Not everyone agrees with the author. They say that office workers are happy because they usually work as part of a team, and that spending time with other people can help them to be happy. But people who work with their hands, like cleaners, mechanics, farmers and artists, often work on their own and can have a lonely life.

A recent report says that there is one job that makes people very happy. And who are these lucky people? Hairdressers! Researchers say that when they ask people in different jobs how happy they are, hairdressers usually answer they're 'very happy'. The report says there are three reasons why hairdressers are so happy. They don't usually work for a company, so they don't have a boss. They see a lot of different people every day. And they make their customers look good and feel good. So, because they see a lot of happy people every day, they're happy, too.

Exercise 8

- Put students into groups of three and ask them to discuss the questions.
- Get feedback from some groups and encourage students to give reasons for their opinions. Encourage students to speak to each other and listen to each other's ideas. You could help this to happen by putting students in a circle so they can see each other.

  EXTENSION Ask students to write a list of things about a job that create happiness, e.g.
  work with people
  make other people happy
  As a class make a list of the five most important things about a job that make people happy.

  EXTRA ACTIVITY Ask students to work with a partner and think of other jobs where:
  people work with their hands
  people don't have a boss
  people speak to lots of different people.
  Set a time limit of four or five minutes. After this ask pairs to compare their ideas. Ask students to tell the class some of their ideas.

Vocabulary & Writing *-er* suffix

Exercise 9

- Put students into pairs and ask them to discuss the questions. Tell them to practise saying the words to help them decide the answer to question 2.
- The final *r* is often not pronounced. For example, *cleaner* is pronounced /kliːnə/.

  WATCH OUT! Some English accents are rhotic. This means the speakers pronounce the letter *r* in these words. Accents which are not rhotic do not pronounce the letter *r* at the ends of words. American English is the most common rhotic accent. You could ask students to try and notice this the next time they hear an American accent. Be aware of your own accent when teaching this suffix *-er*.

- Tell students that *-er* is a *suffix* (= a letter or letters that are added to the end of a word to make a different word). Ask them what happens to the words if we take off the *-er*. (We have a verb.)
- Tell students to think of other words that end in *-er*. Ask them to look back to previous pages in their books.

ANSWERS
1 *-er*
2 The letters are pronounced schwa /ə/

Exercise 10a

- Draw students' attention to the Vocabulary focus box. Ask them to read the information.
- Ask *CCQs* (= concept checking questions): *How do we make a noun?* (add *-er*), *What do we change in the verb* begin *when we make a noun?* (We double the last consonant.)

STUDY TIP Tell students that knowing the suffixes can help them recognize and form nouns and other word types. Tell them it's useful to add the class of a word when they are making notes and adding other forms of the word to these notes. For example, from this lesson they can make notes of verbs and nouns: *clean/cleaner*.

Exercise 10b

- Put students into pairs and tell them to complete the exercise. Check answers.

ANSWERS

Verb	Noun
teach	a teacher
paint	1 a painter
2 dance	a dancer
build	3 a builder
4 sing	a singer
write	5 a writer
6 begin	a beginner
run	7 a runner
8 bake	a baker
play a DVD	9 a DVD player
work	10 a worker

Exercise 11

- Pre-teach *heat* (v) (= to make something warm); *heater* (n) (= machine that makes something warm).
- Ask students to work with their partners to complete the exercise.
- Go through the answers.

ANSWERS

1 baker   2 manager   3 writer   4 beginner   5 driver
6 farmer   7 winner   8 heater

EXTRA ACTIVITY: Ask students to choose five to seven of the words from the exercise that they want to remember and practise. Tell them to write sentences about their life similar to the sentences in exercise 11.

Put students into pairs and ask them to tell each other about their sentences. Monitor and help students with vocabulary. Focus on correct use of the words with *-er* and not other grammar in their sentences.

Exercise 12a

- As a lead-in, you could play a game called 'back to the board'. Ask one student to sit/stand in front of the board facing the class. Draw or display an image of one of the nouns from exercise 10b on the board, e.g. *dancer*. Tell the students to describe the word to the student without saying the word, or any part of the word, e.g. *This person*

moves their body to music. Students take turns guessing the words and describing them.

- Put students into pairs. Give them a time limit of eight to ten minutes to write their definitions. Tell them that both students in each pair must write the definitions down.
- Remind students they can't use the verb that the noun is formed from in their definitions, e.g. *This person bakes bread*. This would make the activity too easy.
- Move around the class and read their sentences. If you see any errors, show the students and encourage self-correction.

Exercise 12b

- Put students into new pairs to do the activity.

FEEDBACK FOCUS Listen to their pronunciation of the nouns and drill the correct word stress if necessary.

3.4 Speaking and writing

Goals

- Make requests
- Use opening and closing phrases in an email

Lead-in

1 Closed book. Discuss taking courses and students' experiences and future expectations.

- Ask students to work in pairs. Tell them to discuss these questions:
  Do you like taking courses? Why?
  What types of courses would you like to take?
- As you listen, write types of courses students mention on the board: *art, painting, language, sports, computer, work related, marketing, internet*, etc.

2 Closed book. Test before you teach email writing.

- Put students into pairs. Tell them to imagine they want to start a new course in English and want more information about it. To help create interest you could bring in or display some advertisements of local courses that are on offer. Ask students what types of courses they might do (e.g. a ten-week evening course, a full-time course, a four-week course in England). Tell students they now have to write a short email asking for one or two pieces of information about the course. Give them a time limit of two or three minutes.
- Tell students to swap emails with their partner, and to now imagine they work for the school offering the courses.
- Tell them to write a short reply answering the questions in the email.
- As they are writing, look at their work and write useful language on the board. Assess what language they already know and adapt the lesson to this.

Listening & Speaking   making requests

Exercise 1

- Ask students to remember the first day of their English course. What do they remember? What things did they need to do to join the class? What did they ask the teacher?

- Put students into pairs. Ask them to give an example of a request people ask the teacher on day one of a computer course and write it on the board. To direct them to the idea of requests and not questions in general, write the word *requests* on the board and teach them the meaning (= to ask for something in a polite way). Tell them to discuss the question and make their lists.

Exercise 2 3.15 ◉

> **Audio summary:** A conversation between a teacher and students on the first day of a course. The teacher is giving information and answering students' questions.

- Play track 3.15 and tell students to listen to the requests they hear. Encourage them to make notes.
- You could pause the recording to give students time to make notes.

EXTRA CHALLENGE Ask students to write the questions that they hear in full.

- Focus on the question words they heard: *can* and *could*.

AUDIOSCRIPT 3.15

A Hello and welcome, everyone. Before we begin, I'd like to tell you a few things about the course.

B Excuse me. Could I open the window?

A Yes, of course. It's really hot in here, isn't it? So … class is at 2 p.m. every Thursday and Friday in the room next door. You can use the computers there … Yes, do you have a question?

C … Er, yes … Can we use the computers after class?

A Yes, of course, but you need a password. It's 'student451'.

C Sorry, can you repeat that, please?

B Sure. It's student451. That's S-T-U-D-E-N-T-4-5-1.

B And can we leave our books and bags in the computer room?

A I'm afraid not. There are evening classes in that room from 6 p.m. Now, if there's nothing else … Oh, before you leave today, could you give your personal details to the administrator, including your bank details, please?

C Sorry, but I don't have them with me today. Could I send them by email later?

A That's fine. Just tell the administrator before you leave. OK, our first lesson is …

Exercise 3a

- Ask students to work alone to do the matching exercise.
- Ask students to underline the parts of the answers which show a positive or negative response, and to write + for positive or – for negative next to these words.
- Tell students to check their answers with a partner.

SMART COMMUNICATION Tell students that it is common to start with an apology when you give a negative reply to a request. We say, *I'm sorry, but …* or *I'm afraid …* .

ANSWERS
1 b+ 2 a– 3 c+ 4 f+ 5 e+ 6 d –

Exercise 3b 3.16 ◉

- Play track 3.16 and tell students to listen and check their answers.

AUDIOSCRIPT 3.16

1
A Could I open the window?
B Yes, of course. It's really hot in here, isn't it?
2
A Could you give your bank details to the administrator?
B Sorry, but I don't have them with me today.
3
A Could I send them by email later?
B That's fine. Just tell the administrator before you leave.
4
A Can you repeat that, please?
B Sure. It's student451. That's S-T-U-D-E-N-T-4-5-1.
5
A Can we use the computers after class?
B Yes, of course, but you need a password.
6
A Can we leave our books and bags in the computer room?
B I'm afraid not. There are evening classes in that room from 6 p.m.

Exercise 3c

- Put students into pairs. Ask students to take turns asking and answering the questions in exercise 3a.

EXTENSION With their partners, students write other requests using *can* and *could*. They can then either give the requests to another pair to use for further practice or work with another pair to ask and answer their questions. Students invent a positive or negative response.

Exercise 4a 3.17 ◉

- Before students read the information in exercise 4a, raise their awareness of intonation by playing track 3.17 and asking students to read and listen. What do they notice about how the voices rise and fall at the end of each sentence? Ask for ideas from the class about what they hear.
- Tell students to read the information in exercise 4a and then play the track again.

Exercise 4b 3.17 ◉

- Play the track again. Ask students to listen and repeat.
- Check the intonation rules: What type of questions have a rising intonation? (*Yes/no*). When does our voice fall? (At the end of answers/statements.)

SMART COMMUNICATION *Can* and *could* – when do we use them? *Can* and *could* can be used in the same situations but you should make students aware that there is a difference. *Can* is more direct and *could* is more formal and polite. For example, if you call an office and you know the person you are speaking to it is fine to use *can*; if you don't know the person, it is more polite to use *could* – *Could I speak to Mr Fox, please?*

- Tell students they should also add *please* to their requests to sound polite.

Exercise 5

- Put students into pairs and ask them to complete the exercise.

Pre-teach the meaning of *lend* (= to give somebody something for a short time), *park* (= to leave your car somewhere for a time) and *bring* (= to take someone/ something with you to a place).

- Go through the answers together.

ANSWERS

1 bring   2 call   3 use   4 lend   5 leave   6 park
7 tell   8 pay

EXTENSION   Highlight the collocations in this exercise. Write the verbs below on the board and ask students to suggest other examples of nouns, using the examples in these sentences to help. For example:
Bring: a friend/something to eat or drink/an object (pen, pencil etc.) … to a place.
Lend: money, a pen/pencil/other object … to someone.
Leave: a bag/coat/object … in a place.
Students use this to make more requests.

Exercise 6

- Demonstrate the exercise with a student. Refer the class to the Language for speaking box to help with their answers.
- Tell students to work with their partners to complete the exercise, taking turns to make and answer requests.

EXTRA SUPPORT   If you think your students need help with this activity, ask them to read the Language for speaking box alone first and to silently or quietly rehearse making requests and answering them.

Exercise 7

- Put students into different pairs. Tell them to read the three situations and think of requests they might make in these situations.

EXTRA SUPPORT   Tell students to write their requests out in full if you think they will find it difficult to do this exercise.

- Ask students to take turns making requests and answering.

POSSIBLE ANSWERS

1
A Can you wake me up at 7.00 a.m., please?
B Yes, of course.
A Can I have a shower, please?
B Yes, that's fine.
A Can you show me where the bus stop is, please?
B Sure.
A Could you show me the area, please?
B No, I'm afraid not. I am really busy today. Maybe tomorrow.
A Could you tell me how to get to the city centre, please?
B Yes, of course.
2
A Could I join the library, please?
B Yes, of course.
A Can I borrow this book?
B Yes, of course.
3
A Could you help me with my luggage, please?
B Of course, just leave it here and I will bring it to your room.
A Could you tell me what time dinner is served?
B Yes, of course, from 8.00 p.m. to 10.30 p.m.

A Can I smoke in my room?
B No, I'm sorry but smoking is not allowed in the hotel. There is a smoking area outside.
A Could I have an alarm call at 6.30 a.m.?
B Yes, of course.

FEEDBACK FOCUS   Listen for how the students use the language in the Language for speaking box. Write errors on strips of paper and hand them out to students to correct in their pairs. Go over corrections with the class.

- Tell students to repeat one of the situations without making the same errors.

EXTENSION   Ask students to think about their English class and three requests they might make in it. Ask students to take turns making and answering requests. They can work in pairs or make their requests to you.

Reading & Writing   opening and closing an email

Exercise 8

- As a lead-in, ask students to think about the emails they write in their own language and/or in English. Put students into pairs. Ask them to describe and discuss what they write about and how well they know the people they write to. You could ask them to discuss how the emails are different depending on who they are writing to.
- Ask students to work alone and read the emails. Then tell them to complete the exercise in their pairs.
- Check answers.

ANSWERS

1 b   2 c   3 a

EXTENSION   Ask students to look at the use of *can* and *could* in the emails. Tell them to underline the requests. Ask students to look for other useful phrases they would like to use when they write their emails later in the lesson. Tell them to underline them. Ask students what phrases they underlined and check understanding with the class.

Exercise 9a

- Ask students to work in the same pairs and discuss the question. The answer should focus on the use of formal and informal language.

ANSWERS

Emails 1 & b: Tanit and Ricardo are colleagues. They may know each other well, but the email is formal in style as it is for business purposes.
Emails 2 & c: Eliza Zammit and Takashi Itou do not know each other.
Emails 3 & a: Roz and Sally know each other well. They are probably friends as the email is informal and they sign off their emails with *Love*.

Exercise 9b

WATCH OUT!   Different cultures have different ways of addressing each other. In English-speaking cultures, people use first names a lot more frequently than in many other cultures. For example, employees and bosses – in some other cultures you wouldn't call your boss by their first name, whereas nowadays for many English-speaking cultures this is OK. You could ask students to discuss this.

- Tell students to work alone and complete the gaps in the emails, referring to the Language for writing box if necessary. Go through the answers together.

1 Sally 2 Love 3 Roz 4 Dear Tanit 5 Ricardo
6 Dear Takashi 7 Yours sincerely 8 Zammit

Exercise 10a

- Ask students to read the instructions and choose one of the requests 1–3. Ask them to decide how well they know the person they are writing to. Check ideas with the class. Answers here may vary depending on the students' choices.
- Tell them to write their emails, using the emails in exercise 8 to help them. They can also find useful phrases in the Language for writing box.

Exercise 10b

- Ask students to swap their emails with a partner, read the email and write a reply.
- Tell them to use the correct phrases depending on how well they know the person who is writing to them.
- Ask students to work together to improve the emails. Are there any errors in grammar or spelling and punctuation, for example?

Exercise 10c

- Tell students to swap emails back again and read the replies their partners wrote. Ask them to tell their partner if they think the language is correct. Is it correct for the level of formality?

EXTENSION Ask students to write another email for one of the other situations in exercise 10a, swap with a different partner and repeat the swapping activity. Encourage each student to write one formal, and one informal, email.

EXTRA ACTIVITY Speed email writing activity. This activity focuses on fluency but gives students an opportunity to practise question forms and opening and closing phrases for email writing. The objective is to create a written conversation. This activity is useful for analysing language errors and assessing progress.

Put students into pairs or groups of three. Students decide on a situation: they are old friends, work colleagues or themselves (classmates). Tell them they all need a piece of paper; they shouldn't write in their books. Tell them to write an email to the other people in their group to say hello, find out how they are and ask a question about doing something together (going out for dinner, having a work meeting, etc.). They only have one minute to write. They must write neatly at the top of the page. When one minute is finished, tell them to pass on the paper to someone else in their group.

Students then have one minute to read the email and write a reply. They must include at least one question in their reply. Ask them to stop writing again after one minute, pass on the paper and repeat the process. Each time they pass on the paper they should reply and ask at least one question.

When they have finished, they can read the emails and compare their conversations. Ask groups what their plans are. You can then ask them to find examples of good language and errors and to try and correct their errors together.

3.5 Video

An Iranian doctor in the USA

VIDEOSCRIPT

Arash Fazl is a doctor in neurology at Mount Sinai Hospital. He's from Iran but now he lives in New York City. Mount Sinai is a huge hospital with over a thousand beds and about 3,500 doctors and student doctors.
Around 36,000 people work in its 32 departments.
Dr. Fazl is a final year resident. That means he is a student doctor in his last year. He has a degree in medicine from a medical school in Tehran, Iran's capital.
He moved to the USA in 2001 because he wanted to study. He now has a PhD from Boston University.
So, what does he do each day?
He usually gets up at 6.30 and leaves home at 7. He arrives at around 7.30. He checks the new patient list and talks to other doctors.
Then he visits his patients. He discusses their illnesses and the medicine they need.
He usually has lunch during his midday meeting, but he doesn't eat a lot because he doesn't have a lot of time.
In the afternoon Dr Fazl usually visits his patients and with the nurses he checks that they are OK and have the right medicine.
He does this once, twice, even three times a day, so he can make sure that everybody has what they need. His days are always very busy and he often stays late. He sometimes works until 9 p.m.
Mount Sinai is an excellent hospital and is famous all over the world.
For Dr Fazl it's very different from hospitals in Iran which were usually small and not very modern.
But both in America and Iran patients need the same help and care. Dr Fazl enjoys this part of his job. He works hard but every day he helps people and can really change their lives for the better.

Exercise 1a
Students' own answers

Exercise 1b
bed ☑ degree ☐ doctor ☑ hospital ☑ laptop ☐
medicine ☑ nurse ☑ patient ☑ phone ☑
pillow ☑ reception ☑ university ☐

Exercise 1c
Students' own answers

Exercise 2
1 1,000 number of beds
2 36,000 total working in hospital
3 2001 Dr Fazl moved to USA
4 6.30 a.m. Dr Fazl gets up
5 7.30 a.m. Dr Fazl arrives at work
6 midday Dr Fazl has a meeting
7 three times a day Dr Fazl visits his patients
8 9 p.m. Dr Fazl often works until this time.

Exercise 3

a Arash Fazl is a doctor in neurology at Mount Sinai Hospital.

b He is from Iran but he lives in New York now.

c He is a student doctor in his last year.

d He moved to the USA in 2001 because he wanted to study.

e Arash Fazl has a PhD from Boston University.

f When he visits his patients he discusses their illness and the medicine they need.

g At lunchtime he doesn't eat a lot because he doesn't have a lot of time.

h His days are always very busy.

i Mount Sinai is an excellent hospital and is famous all over the world.

j He enjoys his job because every day he helps people and can really change their lives.

Exercises 4a & b

Students' own answers

Review

ANSWERS

Exercise 1a

1 office   2 meetings   3 student   4 uniform   5 hours
6 retired

Exercise 1b

POSSIBLE ANSWERS

1 Do you work in an office?
2 Do you have a lot of meetings?
3 Are you a student?
4 Do you wear a uniform?
5 Do you work long hours?
6 Are you retired?

Exercise 2a

1 c   2 e   3 a   4 f   5 b   6 d

Exercise 4a 3.18

1 teacher   2 painter   3 singer   4 DVD player
5 builder   6 baker

AUDIOSCRIPT 3.18

1 She teaches in a school or university.
2 He paints people's houses.
3 Her job is to sing songs.
4 You use this thing to play DVDs.
5 He builds houses.
6 She makes bread.

Exercise 5a

1 you   2 I   3 you   4 you   5 I   6 I

4 Places and things

Unit overview

Language input

there is/there are (CB p37)	• There's a theatre in the town.
	• Are there any museums near the centre?
Articles *a/an*, *the*, – (CB p39)	• I'm not a student.
	• She's an English teacher.
	• Lima is the capital of Peru.
Grammar reference (CB pp142–143)	

Vocabulary development

Places in a town (CB p36)	• chemist, cinema, hairdresser's, hospital, library …
Rooms, furniture and prepositions of place (CB p38)	• bathroom, bedroom, kitchen, living room …
Opposite adjectives (CB p41)	• messy/tidy, cheap/expensive, old/new …

Skills development

Reading: pronoun referencing (CB p40)
Speaking: asking for and giving directions (CB p42)
Writing: imperatives (CB p43)

Video

Documentary: Almas Tower (CB p44)
Vox pops (Coursebook DVD & TG p256)

More materials

Workbook	• Language practice for vocabulary, grammar, pronunciation, speaking and writing
	• Reading for pleasure
	• Review: Units 3 & 4
Photocopiable activities	• Grammar: World cities (TG p204 & TSRD)
	• Vocabulary: Design dictation (TG p222 & TSRD)
	• Communication: Which hotel? (TG p239 & TSRD)
Tests	• Unit 4 test (TSRD)
Unit 4 wordlist (TSRD)	

4.1 Underground towns

Goals

- Talk about places in towns and cities
- Use *There is/There are*

Lead-in

1 Closed book. To make the lesson relevant to the students and elicit relevant vocabulary.

- Ask students to think of a place in their country where tourists like to go. Ask them to work in pairs and discuss why tourists go there. What do they do there?

2 Closed book. To activate students' knowledge of the topic.

- Write the title of the lesson on the board and ask students to discuss what they think an underground town is and what it has in it. You could ask one student to come to the board and write ideas for what is in these places. They can compare their ideas with the text in exercise 2 of the lesson after they check their answers for exercise 1.
- After students finish discussing it, tell them they are going to read about an underground town in the lesson today.

Vocabulary & Reading places in a town

Exercise 1

- Put students into pairs. Refer students to the photos and ask them what they can see (a living room with some sofas, a sign with a kangaroo on it and some earrings). Write useful vocabulary on the board and make sure students understand the meaning of *underground*. You could draw a picture to help clarify this.
- Tell students to discuss the statements. Encourage them to give reasons for their ideas, e.g. *I don't think this is in the USA because there's a picture of a kangaroo. It's in Australia.*
- Discuss ideas with the class. Check they understand the meaning of *opals* (= a type of precious stone). It will help them to understand the reading exercise.

Exercise 2

> **Text summary:** An article about Coober Pedy, an underground town in Australia connected to an opal mine. It's a popular place for tourists to visit.

- Ask students to work alone.
- Give them plenty of time to read the text and find the answers.
- Ask students to compare their ideas with a partner before you go over answers with the class.

ANSWERS

1 F – Coober Pedy is in Australia.
2 T – People work in mines under the ground.
3 F – The houses are underground, so they don't have windows or gardens.
4 T – A lot of people visit the underground buildings. There are four or five hotels, a campsite, a museum and a big tourist information centre.

EXTRA CHALLENGE Ask students for more information about the text with these questions:
1 *Why do people live underground?* (Because it's cool.)
2 *Is it a new town?* (No, it's more than 100 years old.)
3 *Where do most people work?* (In the opal mines.)

EXTENSION Students work in pairs and discuss if they would like to visit Coober Pedy and why/why not.

Exercise 3

- Refer students to the article and tell them to complete the exercise. Ask them to work with the same partner and compare answers.

ANSWERS

1 eat: restaurants
2 buy things: shops
3 stay: hotels, campsite
4 visit: underground buildings, museum, tourist information centre
5 go in your free time: shops, restaurants, swimming pool, museum
6 find information: tourist information centre
7 travel to/from: airport, roads

Exercise 4a

- Ask students to work in pairs and complete the matching exercise. Check answers.

WATCH OUT! In some varieties of English they say *pharmacy* instead of *chemist*. They also use *movie theatre* instead of *cinema*.

ANSWERS

1 library 2 cinema 3 hospital 4 hairdresser's
5 chemist 6 theatre

Exercise 4b

- Put students into pairs and ask them to think of more places in a town. You could also ask them to work as a class and brainstorm vocabulary together, with one student writing on the board.
- Tell students to record new vocabulary in their notebooks.

POSSIBLE ANSWERS

supermarket, offices, restaurants, butcher's, bus station, railway station, museum, shops, dentist's, hotel, swimming pool, sports centre, café, bank

Pronunciation word stress

Exercise 5a

- Students looked at word stress in the last unit so should be familiar with concepts such as the schwa and stressed syllables. Instead of giving them a model, this exercise is asking them to try out the word stress and feel the correct pronunciation themselves.
- Write *hospital* on the board but don't say it. Ask students to tell you the correct pronunciation (**ho**spital). Use students as good examples of correct pronunciation and ask other students to listen to them. Tell a student to come to the board and circle the stressed syllable.

WATCH OUT! Note that in the last unit they had to circle the unstressed syllable so make sure they are clear on the change in instruction here.

- Ask students to work with a partner. Tell them to say the words aloud to each other and decide on the stressed syllables. To help them decide on the correct stress, encourage them to experiment by saying the words with the stress on different syllables. Ask them to think about what sounds or feels right, e.g. **li**brary, lib**ra**ry, libra**ry**.

Exercise 5b 4.1 🔘

- Play track 4.1 and ask students to listen and check their answers.

ANSWERS/AUDIOSCRIPT 4.1

airport campsite chemist hairdresser's hospital hotel library museum railway station restaurant swimming pool theatre

- Play the track again and ask students to repeat the words.
- Encourage students to act as good models of pronunciation again here instead of modelling the pronunciation yourself.

PRONUNCIATION Word stress in compound nouns. *Swimming pool* and *railway station* are compound nouns (two nouns that come together to form one noun). The first noun is usually stressed in compound nouns. So, the strongest sound will be the stressed syllable in that word, e.g. **swim**ming pool.

Exercise 6a

- Ask students if an airport is an important place in a town. Ask them if a campsite is important. Ask for reasons. Tell them to work alone and put the places from exercise 5a into the three categories. To clarify the exercise, write three columns on the board with the headings *very important/quite important/not important* and ask a student to add a place to each column.
- Tell students to think of reasons for placing the words into those categories.

EXTRA SUPPORT Tell students to make notes to help them explain their reasons. Encourage them not to write full sentences because this is primarily a speaking exercise.

Exercise 6b

- Put students into pairs.
- Refer students to the example dialogue. Demonstrate the conversation with one or two students.
- Tell students to work with their partner and compare their choices.

FEEDBACK FOCUS Listen for errors in word stress. Drill the correct pronunciation after the speaking activity. You may want to stop the drill if you hear an error, do a quick correction and then let students continue if there are lots of errors.

Listening & Grammar *there is/there are*

Exercise 7 4.2 🔘

Audio summary: A conversation between a hotel receptionist and two tourists visiting Coober Pedy. The tourists are asking for more information about the hotel and the town.

- Ask students to read the instructions for the listening exercise.

- Play track 4.2 and tell students to complete the exercise.

ANSWERS

1 shop ☐   2 museum ✓   3 cinema ✓   4 chemist ☐
5 tourist information centre ☐   6 theatre ✓
7 restaurant ✓   8 swimming pool ✓

AUDIOSCRIPT 4.2

F I'm so hot! I'm so happy to be at the hotel at last. Is there a swimming pool? I'd like to have a swim.

R No, I'm sorry, there isn't. It doesn't rain a lot here, so there aren't many swimming pools.

F You mean there aren't any swimming pools at all?

R No, don't worry! There's a big swimming pool in the town centre if you want to go swimming. There just isn't one at the hotel.

F Are there any museums near the centre?

R Yes, there are. There's the opal mine museum. Look, here's some information about it.

A Thank you. That looks interesting. And are there any underground buildings we can visit?

R Yes, there are lots of beautiful underground buildings in Coober Pedy. They aren't very far from the hotel, so you can walk up to most of them. I'll show you on the map.

A OK, I see. And is there a theatre in Coober Pedy?

R No, there aren't any theatres here, I'm afraid. But there is a cinema just near the hotel.

A Great, thank you very much. Well, I'm really hungry, so I think we should find a restaurant and have lunch.

R There are some really nice restaurants in the town centre. And they're quite cheap, too.

F Great! And after lunch we could go to the swimming pool.

Exercise 8a

- Tell students that these mini dialogues are from the recording in exercise 7.
- Ask students to cover the words in the box and try to guess what words will go in the gaps. Then, ask them to refer to the words in the box and see if they match their ideas.
- Put students into pairs and ask them to complete the sentences with the words from the box.

ANSWERS

1 Is there; there isn't; there aren't
2 Are there; there are
3 Is there; there aren't

Exercise 8b 4.3 🔘

- Play track 4.3 and tell students to listen and check their answers.

AUDIOSCRIPT 4.3

1 Is there a swimming pool?
  No, I'm sorry, there isn't. We don't have much rain here, so there aren't many swimming pools.
2 Are there any museums near the centre?
  Yes, there are. There's the opal mine museum.
3 Is there a theatre in Coober Pedy?
  No, there aren't any theatres here.

Exercise 8c

- Ask students to work with their partners. Refer them to the conversations in exercise 8a and tell them to take turns being the receptionist and one of the guests (Amir or Farah).

Exercise 9

- Tell students to read the Grammar focus box.
- Check their understanding with these concept check questions (CCQs):
  a. Is *cinema* a singular or plural noun? (singular)
  b. Do we use *there is* or *there are* with *cinema*? (*There is* because it's singular)
  c. Can we use *any* with positive sentences? (No)
  d. Can we use *any* with questions? (Yes)
  e. Can we use *any* with negative sentences? (Yes)
- Tell students to work alone and match the examples 1–6 with the correct form in the Grammar focus box. Explain that they should write the number of the correct example in the bracket after each form in the box.
- Tell students to compare their answers with a partner.
- Check answers together.

ANSWERS

There's a/an + (singular noun) (**6**)
There are + *some* + (plural noun) (**3**)
There isn't a/an + (singular noun) (**2**)
There aren't + *any* + (plural noun) (**1**)
Is there a/an + (singular noun)? (**4**)
Are there + *any* + (plural noun)? (**5**)

EXTRA SUPPORT Ask students to write six sentences and questions using items in the classroom or places in the school for each form: positive, negative and question form. Example: *There's a black/white board.*

- Refer students to *Grammar reference* on p142. There are three more exercises here that students can do for homework.

Exercise 10

- Ask students to look at the photo of RÉSO. Tell them to work in pairs and describe what they see. How is it similar or different to Coober Pedy?
- Refer students to the first example which is done for them. Do number 2 with the class. Make sure they remember to look at the symbol to help them complete the exercise with a positive, negative or question form. Get students to work alone and complete the exercise.

ANSWERS

1 There are   2 There are   3 There isn't   4 there are
5 There aren't   6 there are   7 Is there   8 there isn't
9 there are   10 there is

Exercise 11

- Write the name of the city/town you are in on the board. Tell students to work with a partner and list as many places and things to do in the town as they can. Give a time limit of two minutes.
- Ask the class questions about the place using *Is/Are there … ?* e.g. *Is there a campsite? Are there cheap hotels? Are there hostels?*

EXTRA SUPPORT If you think students need more practice asking and answering questions before they begin the activity, then get them to work in pairs and to ask each other about a different place. They can use their town or another place they know well.

- Put students into pairs and tell them to decide who is Student A and who is Student B. Tell them they are going on holiday together but need to decide between Bruges and Krakow. To create further interest in the exercise, show images from these places and ask students what they know about the cities.
- Refer them to p127 and p132.
- Tell students to read the information about their places in part one of the exercise and check they understand the vocabulary.
- Explain that they are going to ask their partners questions using the things in part one – the list of things they want to do. You could demonstrate the exercise with a student if you think the class needs extra support. Refer students to the short example dialogue in part two also.
- Tell students that they have to agree on which place they are going to go to and to be ready to explain to the class why they chose that place.
- Get students to work in their pairs and complete the speaking exercise.
- Ask students to explain their choices to the class.

FEEDBACK FOCUS This is primarily a speaking activity so accept different question types but focus on practising *Is/Are there … ?* Listen to examples of *There is/There are* in their explanations and correct errors after everyone has spoken.

EXTENSION Ask students to write a postcard or email from their chosen city describing it. Give example sentences for extra support, E.g.
Hi Anna, We're in Bruges. It's good. There are lots of … but there aren't any … . There's a … .
I hope you're well.
Lots of love
Sherry

EXTRA ACTIVITY Tell students to find out information about a place they would like to visit and write a short description for homework. They should bring it to the next class. In the next class, students compare their places and decide which places they would like to visit. They could work in groups and read each other's texts and discuss where they would like to visit and why.

GRAMMAR REFERENCE ANSWERS

Exercise 1
1 Is there   2 There are   3 Is there   4 Are there
5 There is   6 There aren't   7 There is   8 Are there
9 There isn't   10 There is

Exercise 2
1 Yes, there is.   2 No, there aren't.   3 Yes, there are.
4 No, there isn't.   5 Yes, there are.   6 Yes, there is.
7 No, there aren't.   8 Yes, there are.

Exercise 3
1 there is   2 There aren't   3 There are   4 There is
5 There are   6 there is   7 there are   8 There aren't
9 There aren't   10 there is

4.2 Where I live

Goals

- Talk about rooms and furniture
- Use prepositions of place
- Use articles

Lead-in

1 Closed book. To recycle *there is/there are* and assess students' current use of prepositions.

- Tell students to look around them and describe the room they are in, and what they can see in it, with a partner.

2 Closed book. To test before you teach.

- Show an image of a street from the town you are in or from the places in the last lesson.

- Ask students *What's next to … ? What's under the ground? What's opposite the … ?* etc. to elicit vocabulary of places from the last lesson. As the students give you answers, write the vocabulary on the board.

- Ask students where other places are from lesson 4.1, e.g. *Where's the library?* If students use prepositions, you could make a note of them and go over this later in exercise 2 after the matching exercise.

Vocabulary & Speaking rooms, furniture and prepositions of place

Exercise 1a

- As a lead-in, describe your house or flat to the students using a photo or image if possible. Use the language in exercise 1a to check understanding of vocabulary, e.g. *I live in a flat. I live with my sister. In my flat there is a living room and a kitchen and there are three bedrooms. There isn't a dining room.*

- Mention to students that in American English they use *apartment*. Students may be more familiar with this word.

- Tell students to work alone and to complete the sentences in their notebooks. Monitor their work closely and help students where necessary.

Exercise 1b

- Put students into pairs. Ask them to use their sentences to help them describe their flat or house to their partner.

  EXTENSION Put students into small groups. Ask students to discuss these two questions:

  1 Do people usually live in flats or houses in your country or town/city?

  2 What is good or bad about living in a house or flat? e.g. *It's good living in a flat because there are lots of neighbours. It isn't good because there isn't a garden.*

Exercise 2

- If students used prepositions of place in the second lead-in, you could go over these and ask them to demonstrate the prepositions showing the position of a book compared to their hand or similar objects.

- Demonstrate the prepositions using objects in the class. For example, place a book *above, behind, between,* etc. a table or other object. Check understanding by asking

volunteers to do the same with their book and table. Instruct them where to put the book, e.g. *Put your book under your table.*

- Ask students to work alone and complete the matching exercise.

- Check answers together.

ANSWERS

1 under 2 behind 3 on 4 between 5 opposite
6 next to 7 above 8 in front of

WATCH OUT! Students can get confused with *opposite* and *in front of*. To show the difference, ask two students to stand up. Tell them to face each other to demonstrate *opposite,* and then tell one to stand with their back to the other to show *in front of*. Tell them we stand in front of someone in a queue in the supermarket, not opposite them.

EXTRA ACTIVITY To practise prepositions. Tell students to make four to six sentences using prepositions about the room you are in, e.g. *Samantha sits next to Brenda.*

Exercise 3 4.4 🔘

Audio summary: This recording is about someone living in a studio flat in New York. It is common to live in a small one-room flat because the city is expensive. Often the people living in these flats have to use services like a launderette because they don't have space for a washing machine in the flat.

- Tell students they are going to listen to Claire talking about her flat. Ask them to look at the illustrations and guess where the flat is. Tell them to discuss their ideas with a partner.

- Play track 4.4 and tell students to listen for the answers to the questions.

- Ask students to compare their answers with a partner, and then check answers with the class. You may need to teach them the meaning of *studio flat* (= a one-room flat).

ANSWERS

1 The flat is in New York City in the Lower East Side District.
2 There is one room.

AUDIOSCRIPT 4.4

I live in New York City, in the Lower East Side District. My flat is very small, but the rent is $800 a month. It's a studio flat. There isn't a kitchen, dining room, living room, or bedroom. I cook, eat, relax and sleep in one room.

Exercise 4a

- Pre-teach:
  shelf (show an image, draw a picture on the board or show them an example in the classroom)
  launderette (= a shop where you can pay to wash your clothes)

- Ask students to work alone and read the description of the flat and complete the gaps with a preposition.

- Tell students to compare their answers with a partner.

ANSWERS

1 on 2 between 3 opposite 4 next to 5 above
6 under 7 In front of 8 behind

Exercise 4b 4.5 🔘

- Play track 4.5 and tell students to read and listen and correct their answers. You may need to play the recording twice.

AUDIOSCRIPT 4.5

The flat's on the 4th floor of a building between Delancey Street and Grand Street. The building is opposite a 24-hour garage and next to an Indian restaurant, so there are always lots of cars and people in the street. The cars are quite noisy. It's a studio flat with only one room. My bed is on a shelf above the kitchen. The toilet and shower are under the shelf. In the kitchen there's a sink, a fridge and a cooker, but there isn't a dishwasher or a washing machine – I go to the launderette on Grand Street to wash clothes. In front of the window, there's a red carpet on the floor and there's an armchair and table with a television on it. From the window, I can see the East River. It's behind the building.

Exercise 5

- Do the first example together with the class. (bed)
- Ask students to work alone and complete the exercise, using the illustrations to help them.
- Put students into pairs, and tell them to compare their answers and help each other complete the exercise.
- Check answers together.

ANSWERS

1 a bed 2 an armchair 3 a sink 4 a fridge
5 a washing machine 6 a cooker 7 a red carpet
8 a shower

EXTENSION Students work in pairs to think of more furniture vocabulary. You could show them some photos or ask them to think of a house or flat they have been in which they remember well, e.g. when visiting a palace or famous building while on holiday.

Exercise 6

- Tell students to work with their partners. Explain the game *Spot the difference*. Ask students if they have played this game before. It is common in many children's activity books.
- Tell students to decide who is Student A and who is Student B and refer them to p127 and p132.
- Demonstrate the game with a more confident student.
- Ask the pairs to complete the activity.

ANSWERS

A: no washing machine
B: washing machine next to fridge
A: picture above sink
B: picture above washing machine
A: lamp behind armchair
B: lamp next to armchair
A: shelf above armchair
B: shelf above bed
A: plant next to table
B: plant in front of bed
A: magazine on table
B: magazine under table
A: dishwasher next to sink
B: no dishwasher

EXTRA CHALLENGE There may be fast finishers in this activity. Ask them to discuss these questions.
1 Which flat would you prefer to live in? Why?
2 Could you live in a small flat like this?
3 Do people live in flats like this where you are from?

Grammar & Speaking articles *a/an, the, –*

Exercise 7a

- Focus students' attention on the highlighted words and phrases in Claire's description in exercise 4a. Write *a/an* and *the* on the board and ask students what kind of words they are (articles – some students will be more accustomed to describing grammar than others so you may need to teach your class what this means).
- Ask students to look at the words and tell you what kind of word comes after the articles (nouns).
- Tell students to work alone and read the Grammar focus box and complete the exercise.
- Check answers together.

ANSWERS

1 a 2 an 3 a 4 an 5 – 6 the 7 –

- Refer students to *Grammar Reference* on p143. There are three more exercises here that students can do for homework.

Exercise 7b

- Ask students to work with a partner. Tell them to go through all the highlighted words in exercise 4a and add them to the Grammar focus box.

ANSWERS

With *a*: building, shelf
With *an*: armchair
With *the*: building, cars, kitchen, shelf, launderette
With – (no article): Grand Street

Exercise 8a

- Tell students to read the text first and ask them:
  What are two good things about the flat? (Possible answer: It's in the centre of the city and it's near a theatre.)
  Does Claire use the bus or the subway? How do you know? (Answer: She uses the bus because she says unfortunately her flat is not near the subway station but there is a bus stop opposite her building.)
- Pre-teach *district* (= a noun that means the same as an area of a town or city).
- Do numbers 1 and 2 with the class. Make sure they are clear that – means 'no article'. Tell students to read the text again and complete the exercise. Refer them to the rules in the Grammar focus box for help.
- Tell them to compare their answers with a partner.

ANSWERS

1 a 2 – 3 the 4 – 5 the 6 a 7 a 8 an 9 a
10 the

Exercise 8b 4.6 🔘

- Play track 4.6 and tell students to listen and check their answers.

AUDIOSCRIPT 4.6

It's very difficult to find a flat in New York. I'm very lucky. I like my flat because it's in the centre of the city. There are shops and restaurants all around me. The Lower East Side isn't the best district in the city but my flat is near a theatre and it's also near the East River and a small park. One of the things I don't like about my flat is that there isn't a lift. Also, unfortunately, I'm not near the underground station, but there's a bus stop opposite the door of my building.

WATCH OUT! In other varieties of English they use different vocabulary for some of the words in this text.

lift = elevator

subway = metro/underground/Tube (London only)

EXTRA ACTIVITY Ask students to write a similar text about their own town and house/flat. This will practise articles and also help students with exercises 10 and 11. Ask them these questions as a lead-in:

1 *Is it difficult or easy to find a flat here?*
2 *Do you like your house or flat? Why/Why not?*
3 *Are there shops and parks around your house/flat?*
4 *What is near your flat/house?*

- Tell them to use the answers to write their texts. Ask them to use the correct articles and refer to the Grammar focus box for help.

Pronunciation the schwa /ə/

Exercise 9a 4.7 🔘

- Play track 4.7 and tell students to read and listen to the sentences. Ask them to listen in particular to the stressed words and the schwa sounds.
- Play the track again and pause after each sentence. Tell students to listen again and repeat.

Exercise 9b 4.8 🔘

- Play track 4.8 and tell students to listen and underline the schwa on *a/an* and *the*.

ANSWERS

1 I live in <u>a</u> flat.
2 My flat is on th<u>e</u> 5th floor.
3 There's <u>a</u> supermarket opposite my house.

Exercise 9c 4.8 🔘

- Play the track again and ask students to listen and repeat.

Exercise 10a

- Do the example sentence with the class, to make sure they remember how to form questions correctly.
- Tell students to work alone and complete the exercise.
- Put students into pairs and tell them to compare answers and help each other.
- Check answers together.

FEEDBACK FOCUS Check students have remembered the change in verb/noun word order and that they have used *do* correctly to make questions.

- You could walk around and prompt self correction as the students are working, or you could make a note of common errors and write them on the board and go over them with the whole class after they've made their questions. If you choose the second option, ask them to check and correct their questions before the next exercise.

ANSWERS

1 Do you live in a house or a flat?
2 Which floor do you live on?
3 How many rooms are there in your house/flat?
4 What is opposite your house/flat?
5 Which is your favourite room?
6 Why do you like it?

- For extra support, drill the sentences using the back-chaining method. Drill the last word in the question, then the last two words, the last three and so on until you are drilling the whole sentence.

Exercise 10b

- Ask a more confident student the questions to demonstrate the activity.
- Put students into pairs and tell them to complete the exercise.

Exercise 11

- To support this task, you could ask your students to take a photo of their room if they have a smartphone or digital camera and bring it to class.
- As a lead-in, describe your favourite room and ask students to listen and guess which room it is – living room, kitchen, bedroom, office, etc.
- Tell students to work alone and think of their favourite room and make notes to help them describe it. Tell them not to write full sentences as this is primarily a speaking activity.
- Put students into pairs and ask them to describe their rooms to each other.

EXTRA CHALLENGE To focus on prepositions as well as vocabulary, you could do a picture dictation activity where students sit back to back and describe their rooms to each other. Ask students to listen and draw what they hear. They don't have to sit back to back. If they can see what their partner is drawing it can also be useful, as they can correct it and adapt their description to support their partner.

EXTRA ACTIVITY To appeal to the more creative students, ask them to design a new house, or a new working space.

- Put students into groups of three. If you have access to Cuisenaire rods then give each group a set. These are pieces of wood of different colours and lengths. They are used in maths teaching and language teaching. If you don't have these, tell students to choose one person to be the artist for the group. Tell them to decide if they want to design a home or a work space. Give a time limit.
- Tell students they have to design the space and get ready to explain it to another group.
- If you have a small class, then ask students to present their space to the class. If you have a large group, put two groups together and ask them to present to each other.
- As a class discuss the designs people liked and why.

GRAMMAR REFERENCE ANSWERS

Exercise 1

1 an 2 a 3 an 4 the 5 the 6 the 7 –; the 8 –
9 a 10 a

Exercise 2

1 There isn't a museum in my town.
2 There are twenty noisy children in the garden.
3 Is there a tourist information centre here?
4 Meet me in the city centre at eight o'clock.
5 There are a lot of shops open in the evening.
6 There's a swimming pool in my friend's house.
7 Is there a toilet at the railway station?
8 There isn't a bathroom in my hotel room.

Exercise 3

1 a 2 the 3 the 4 – 5 a 6 a 7 a 8 a 9 the
10 –

4.3 Vocabulary and skills development

Goals

- Understand pronoun referencing
- Use opposite adjectives

Lead-in

1 Closed book. Students describe the space they work in.

- Put students into pairs. Tell them to discuss these questions:
  1 Where do you usually work/study?
  2 What can you see from that work space? Do you have an interesting view?
  3 How important is it to have a good work/study space?

2 Closed book. To review vocabulary for describing places to live and prepositions, ask students to describe a view they know well.

- You could use the view from the classroom if you have one. You could also ask students to take a picture with their smartphones if they have one and bring it to this class.

- Put students into pairs or small groups and ask them to describe a view by talking about these questions:
  1 Where is the view from?
  2 What kind of houses or flats can they see?
  3 What else can they see?
  4 Do they like the view? Why? Why not?

Reading & Speaking pronoun referencing

Exercise 1

- Put students into groups of three or four.
- Refer them to the photos and tell them they have three minutes to write down as many objects as they can from the images.
- After three minutes, tell them to close their books. Ask each group how many items they have written down. You could make this into a competition.
- Ask students to write the items on the board and check spelling and pronunciation. Encourage students to teach each other any unknown vocabulary.

EXTRA CHALLENGE Ask students to write the words on the board in alphabetical order. Nominate one or two students to write.

- Tell students to work in their groups and discuss question 2. Get some ideas from the group after they have finished speaking. Write useful adjectives on the board and check meaning with the class. Make sure students are clear on the meaning of *messy* and *tidy* because they need to know this later in exercise 4.

Exercise 2

- As a lead-in, write the sentences *Where's my phone? I can't find _____* on the board and ask students what word or words can go in the space. Write their suggestions on the board.
- Tell students to read the Unlock the code box and check whether their ideas were correct.

EXTRA SUPPORT Help students understand and practise this grammar point with a substitution drill. Write *Where is/are my _____ ? I can't find _____* on the board. Ask students to suggest words that can go in the first space, e.g. *bag, keys, sister, brother, friends, car,* etc. Say the sentence and stop before the second space. Ask students what words go in the space for each noun.
Example: *Where are my **keys***? I can't find **them**.
 *Where's my **brother***? I can't find **him**.

- Write two lists with the nouns and pronouns on the board. Drill the sentences: insert different nouns, pause before the last word and let students say the correct pronoun. Do choral, individual and small group drills.

Exercise 3

- Make sure students understand that a pronoun (*I, me, she, her, him,* etc.) is a word that takes the place of a noun. In the sentence *Aisha helps Anna with maths homework and she teaches her English*, the pronouns *she* and *her* take the place of *Aisha* and *Anna* respectively. There are two types of pronouns here: subject (*she*) and object (*her*). Subject pronouns are used when the pronoun refers to the subject of the sentence (the person doing the action). Object pronouns are used if the pronoun takes the place of the object of the sentence (the person receiving the action). Most sentences in English follow the pattern Subject Verb Object SVO.

- Write some simple rules on the board:
  – *it* (object or subject) refers to singular nouns
  – *she* (subject) and *her* (object) refer to female names and singular nouns
  – *he* (subject) and *him* (object) refer to male names and singular nouns
  – *they* (subject) and *them* (object) refer to plural nouns

- Ask students to work alone and complete the exercise.
- Ask students to compare their answers with a partner.
- Check answers. As you check, ask students to explain their answers, e.g. *Number one is* bedroom, *because* **it** *has replaced* **my bedroom**.

ANSWERS
1 My bedroom is very big but I share it with my sister.
2 His things are all on the floor. He never tidies them.
3 We've got two big armchairs in the living room – they're really comfortable.
4 That's a beautiful picture. Where did you get it?
5 Our house is quite small, but I really like it.
6 **A** Are those keys yours? **B** No, they're yours.

Exercise 4

> **Text summary:** These two short texts are forum posts. A forum is an online conversation where people leave comments and respond to other posts. The posts here are from people at work discussing tidy and messy work spaces.

- Ask students to read the texts quickly to have a general understanding of them. Ask them where they might read texts like this (online in a forum). (If necessary, explain that a forum here refers to an internet site where people discuss a topic.) Ask them how they know this. (The texts have invented names, there are *share*, *delete* and *tick* buttons at the top right of each forum post.) Teach students the words *forum post*. Ask them to tell you which person is messy to check understanding. (Officegirl94 is messy; Netguy is tidy.)
- Tell students to read the forum posts again and complete the exercise, and then to work with a partner and check their answers.
- Check answers together. Focus on numbers four and five. Ask students why there are different pronouns referring to the same objects (*they* is a subject pronoun and *them* is an object pronoun).

ANSWERS
1 my colleagues   2 my desk   3 the things (on my desk)
4 a computer and a printer   5 the computer and printer

Exercise 5

> **Background note:** In many cities and towns it is expensive to live alone so young people share a house or flat. This is common with both students and people who are working. People advertise in local newspapers and websites to look for flatmates or advertise rooms in a flat. They share the costs of the flat or house. You could ask students to discuss if it is common for people to share a flat in their country.

> **Text summary:** Another forum post. This time it is written by someone living in a shared flat. They are describing the good things and bad things about it.

- Explain to the class that they are going to read another reply from the website. The writer is talking about living in a shared house. Refer students to the name Homeworker 77. What does this tell you about the writer? (They work from home.) Ask students to think about why this is important for the topic of being messy or tidy (because if someone works from home in a shared flat it might be important to live with tidy people).
- Tell students to work alone and read the reply and complete the exercise. Tell them to use the pronouns to find the answers.
- Ask students to compare their answers with a partner and then check answers with the class. You may need to teach them *laptop* (= a small computer that you can carry around). Question 7 talks about a computer but the text has the word *laptop*.

ANSWERS
1 The kitchen and the bathroom are never clean.
2 Her housemates never do any cleaning.
3 Her friends don't want to come and see her.
4 The shared house isn't expensive.
5 Her housemates are good fun.
6 There's nothing on Mala's desk.
7 She keeps her books in the cupboard with her computer.

Exercise 6

- Ask students to put up their hands if they are like Mala. Then ask them to put their hands up if they are more like her housemates.
- Tell students to work alone and think about their office, house or flat and how they will describe how messy or tidy it is.
- Put students into pairs and ask them to describe their office, flat or house to each other, using pronouns so that they don't repeat nouns.

EXTENSION Ask students to walk around the room and talk to classmates to try and find someone who is as messy or tidy as them. Alternatively they could work in different pairs. Change pairs two or three times and ask them to discuss who is most similar to them.

CRITICAL THINKING Discuss advantages and disadvantages. This activity is similar to a previous discussion. It gives students extra practice in using the vocabulary and grammar from this lesson and previous ones.

Ask students to work in groups of three or four and discuss the advantages and disadvantages of sharing a house or flat. If they have shared, tell them to talk about their experience. After students have finished speaking, you could write the advantages and disadvantages on the board and look at useful vocabulary that came up.

EXTRA ACTIVITY To consolidate the language, ask students to work alone and write a short description of their work space. Give a clear word limit of fifty to seventy words.

After they have written the texts, you could ask students to swap with a partner and tell them to find similarities and differences in the descriptions. They could also peer correct the use of pronoun referencing.

EXTRA CHALLENGE Review articles by asking students to read their text again and check that the articles are used correctly. Help them to correct any errors. They can refer to the Grammar focus box in lesson 4.2.

Vocabulary & Speaking opposite adjectives

Exercise 7

- Ask students what kind of words *messy* and *tidy* are. (adjectives)
- Ask students to work in pairs. Tell them to refer to the example in exercise 7 and then to read the forum posts in exercise 4 and complete the exercise.
- Check answers together.

Officegirl94: I'm a very <u>messy</u> person. My colleagues think my desk's really <u>terrible</u>: …
Netguy: … For me a <u>messy</u> place is <u>difficult</u> to work in. I need a <u>big</u> desk to work on. … They're both <u>new</u> and <u>expensive</u> so I like to keep them very <u>clean</u>.

Exercise 8a

• Ask students to read the Vocabulary focus box.

DICTIONARY SKILLS If your students have dictionaries, you could ask them to check whether their dictionaries give the opposite to some of the adjectives in exercise 4. Ask them to look up one or more of the adjectives in this lesson.

Exercise 8b

• Tell students to work alone and complete the matching exercise. Then ask them to compare their answers with a partner.

ANSWERS

1 h   2 f   3 b   4 c   5 j   6 a   7 d   8 i   9 g   10 e

Exercise 8c   4.9

• Play track 4.9 and ask students to listen and check their answers.
• Play the recording again and ask students to listen and repeat the words.

PRONUNCIATION Ask students to identify the word stress in longer words, e.g. **di**fficult ex**pe**nsive **hea**vy **qui**et **old**-fashioned **mo**dern **beau**tiful **ea**sy **noi**sy **dir**ty

AUDIOSCRIPT 4.9

1	difficult	h	easy
2	big	f	small
3	new	b	old
4	good	c	bad
5	clean	j	dirty
6	long	a	short
7	heavy	d	light
8	quiet	i	noisy
9	ugly	g	beautiful
10	old-fashioned	e	modern

Exercise 9

WATCH OUT! Some students may have problems with word order when using adjectives. They may put the adjective after the noun. This is because this is the order in some languages. You could ask students what the word order is in their language so you are more aware of this potential problem.

• Put students into groups of three.
• Ask the class to give an example answer for a bag (*big, small, new, heavy*).
• Tell students to work together and make a list of adjectives for each item, using adjectives from exercise 8b.
• Discuss answers with the class.

POSSIBLE ANSWERS

1 **a bag:** old/new; big/small; heavy/light
2 **a building:** tall; big/small; new or modern/old
3 **a person:** short; old; ugly/beautiful; old-fashioned/modern
4 **a restaurant:** big/small; new/old; good/bad; clean/dirty; quiet/noisy; old-fashioned/modern

EXTRA ACTIVITY Ask students to talk about their preferences using some of the items, e.g.
Do you prefer noisy or quiet restaurants?
Do you prefer old-fashioned or modern restaurants?

Exercise 10a

• Ask students what the opposite of *big* is (small). Tell them to complete the exercise writing the opposite adjective in the gap. Do numbers 1 and 2 together for extra support.
• Ask students to compare their answers with a partner.

ANSWERS

1 small   2 old-fashioned   3 old   4 messy   5 noisy
6 expensive   7 long; short

EXTENSION Ask students to think of other words that could be used in each number. For example, we could use *quiet* or *noisy* with *part of town*. They could also think of two more questions to ask using the adjectives from the lesson.

Exercise 10b

• Demonstrate the speaking activity with a student. Tell students to look at the example dialogue and listen to your conversation.
• If you think your students need more support to have a well-developed conversation, ask two confident students to model the activity for the class.
• Put students into groups of three and tell them to complete the exercise.

FEEDBACK FOCUS Listen for correct pronunciation of the adjectives. Add any mispronounced words to the board and ask students to work in pairs and practise the correct pronunciation. Check pronunciation with the class.

STUDY TIP Remind students how to record pronunciation using phonemic script. Ask students if they use any other methods of recording pronunciation. Share methods with the class and encourage students to choose a method they like and to use it when they record new vocabulary in their notebooks.

EXTRA ACTIVITY Write a forum post. Tell students they are going to write a forum post. Ask them to think about the topics in exercise 10a and which one they found most interesting.

Ask students to get a piece of paper (they will be passing the paper to another student so shouldn't write in their notebooks). Tell them to write a short forum post about the topic they chose from exercise 10a. Tell them to use ideas they spoke about in exercise 10b. Set a time limit of three to five minutes.

Tell them to pass their papers to the person sitting to their left. They should read the post and write a reply, adding their own ideas and opinion. Carry on passing papers round the class until students have written four to six replies.

Ask them to give the papers back to the person who wrote the first post so that they can read their replies.

4.4 Speaking and writing

Goals

- Ask for and give directions
- Use the imperative to give instructions

Lead-in

1 Closed book. To recycle prepositions, play a spot-the-mistake game.

- Write ten sentences about the classroom on pieces of paper or sticky notes and stick them around the room. Some of the sentences should be correct and some should have an incorrect preposition, e.g *The board is above the teacher's desk*.
- Ask students to walk around the room and read the notes. They have to decide if they are correct or not.
- Give students a time limit to read all the sentences and then tell them to sit down and remember the correct sentences with a partner.
- Go over the sentences with the class. You could ask them to correct the sentences which are wrong by changing the prepositions, e.g. *The board is next to the teacher's desk*.

2 Closed book. To create interest in the topic, ask students if they have ever asked for or been asked for directions in English. What happened? You could do this as a class discussion or ask students to work in pairs and discuss their experiences.

Listening & Speaking asking for and giving directions

Exercise 1

- As a lead-in, you could show images of Bali and ask students to describe it and discuss if they would like to visit it. Tell students to read the instructions about Susan Melba to help set the context for the exercise. You could refer them to the photo of her.
- Put students into pairs and ask them to look at the map of Ubud and complete the exercise.
- Go through the answers together. Check that students can pronounce the words correctly.

  PRONUNCIATION Ask students to circle the stressed syllables. Remember that in compound nouns the first noun is stressed. The second noun will also have word stress (secondary stress) but the main stress is on the first noun. (bank **book**shop **che**mist **in**ternet **ca**fè **mar**ket **pa**lace po**lice sta**tion **po**st **o**ffice **su**permarket Susan's hot**el**)

Exercise 2

- Refer students to the table and ask them to read the information in it and the example sentences. Ask the class to make one or two more example sentences. Write them on the board.
- Put students into pairs and tell them to complete the exercise.

  EXTRA CHALLENGE You could give them a time limit and make it a race to make as many sentences as possible. You could also give them a minimum number of sentences to create.

- Check answers together.

FEEDBACK FOCUS To check all students' sentences are correct, you could ask them to write their sentences on a piece of paper and then tell them to swap the paper with another pair to correct. Tell students to check that the prepositions are correct and all the place names are spelt correctly.

POSSIBLE ANSWERS

The bank is on Ubud Main Road.
There is an internet café opposite the bookshop.
The supermarket is opposite the police station and next to the chemist.
The palace is next to Susan's hotel.

Exercise 3

- Test before you teach. Ask students to tell you how to get from one point on the map to another (e.g. from the post office to the supermarket). You could write good language they use on the board to build their confidence about what they already know.
- Tell students to work alone to read though the directions and complete the matching exercise.
- Ask them to compare answers with the person sitting next to them.
- Check answers together.

ANSWERS
1 d 2 h 3 e 4 a 5 i 6 f 7 c 8 j 9 g 10 b

Exercise 4a 4.10 🔊

SMART COMMUNICATION It's polite to say *Excuse me* when we approach people in the street to ask them a question. You could tell students to listen and notice what Susan says to be polite when she approaches the person.

- Ask students to find Susan's hotel on the map.
- Play track 4.10 and ask them to complete the exercise.
- You may need to play the recording twice.
- Check answers.

ANSWERS
bank ☐ bookshop ☐ chemist ✓ internet café ☐
market ☐ palace ✓ police station ☐ post office ☐
supermarket ☐ Susan's hotel ☐

AUDIOSCRIPT 4.10
S Excuse me, could you give me some directions, please?
A Yes, of course! How can I help you?
S Thanks! So is there a chemist near here?
A Yes, there is. It's in the town centre.
S How do I get there?
A OK, well go out of the main door and turn left. Then go to the end of the road and turn left again.
S OK.
A Go straight on for about five minutes. Go past the internet café and the bank, and then turn left into Raya Andong. It's on the left next to the supermarket.
S OK, thanks. Oh, and where's the palace?
A That's easy. It's at the end of this road on the corner. Here, take one of these maps. It has all the important places on it.
S Good idea!
A And we are just here.

Exercise 4b 4.10 🔘

- For extra practice, ask students to read through the sentences before they listen again and guess the answers. Ask them what might go in the gaps. You could ask them to cover the words in the box to make it more challenging.
- Play track 4.10 again and tell students to listen and complete the exercise. You could do the first example with the class to offer extra support.

ANSWERS
1 Excuse 2 near 3 get 4 end
5 straight; past; left; on 6 where's 7 corner

Exercise 4c

- Ask students to work with their partner to check they have the same answers.

EXTENSION Ask students to find the audioscript in their books (pp163-4) and practise reading the dialogue to each other, taking turns to be the receptionist and Susan. Listen and help them with their pronunciation. You could encourage them to try and do the dialogue without looking at the book after they have practised it a couple of times.

Exercise 5a

- Do question 1 together on the board.
- Put students into pairs and ask them to complete the exercise: they should write the questions in their notebooks.

EXTRA CHALLENGE If your students enjoy competitive activities, you could make this a race. Tell students they will lose points if their sentences are wrong, to encourage them to do the exercise properly and check their answers before they say they are finished. You could ask the winners to write the answers on the board while the other students finish the activity.

STUDY TIP Encourage students to create sections in their notebooks: grammar, vocabulary (and pronunciation), etc. Discuss how they might best organize their notes and the benefits of having all notes in one book.
One section could be practical phrases or survival English (they can add more practical English phrases that they might use when they meet a tourist or when they are travelling to an English-speaking country).

Exercise 5b 4.11 🔘

- Play track 4.11 and ask students to check their answers.
- Play the track again, pause it after each sentence and tell students to repeat the sentences,.

ANSWERS/AUDIOSCRIPT 4.11
1 Excuse me, is there a bank near here?
2 Excuse me, where's the library?
3 Excuse me, how do I get to the post office?
4 Go past the café.
5 It's on the left.
6 Turn right into Albert Street.
7 Take the second right.
8 Go straight on for about ten minutes.
9 Go to the end of this street.
10 It's on the corner.

PRONUNCIATION Sentence stress. To help students with their pronunciation you could ask them to circle the stressed syllables in the phrases as they listen one more time, e.g. *It's on the left*. Then, play the track again and ask them to repeat.

Exercise 6a

- Ask students to look at the map of Ubud. Choose a confident student and ask them for directions from the police station to another point on the map.
- Tell students to choose three places on the map they want to visit.

Exercise 6b

- Explain that students are standing outside the police station. To check this is clear, ask them what is on their left and right.
- Refer them to the Language for speaking box. Tell them to use it for extra support.
- Tell students to work with a partner to ask for and give directions to the three places each student chose.
- Listen and go over any problems with the language after they have finished speaking.

Exercise 7

- Put students into new pairs. Refer Student A to p128 and Student B to p133.
- Ask students to read the instructions and the sample dialogue. Check that they are clear on what to do. Demonstrate the task with a student.
- Tell students to complete the exercise.

EXTRA CHALLENGE You may have students finishing this task at different speeds. Ask fast finishers to:
– do more examples, choosing a starting point and asking for directions to places they want to visit.
– write a short description of where things are to revise prepositions, e.g. *In Denpasar there's a good restaurant. It's opposite the …* etc.

EXTRA ACTIVITY If you have students who have travelled a lot, you could ask them to bring a map of a town or city they have been to in the past and use this to do a similar activity. Before they practise giving directions, they can tell their partner some information about what places there are to visit in the town/city. This will help revise vocabulary from the lessons in Unit 4. Alternatively, you could use a map of the place you are in.

Reading & Writing imperatives

Exercise 8

> **Text summary:** This is an email from a tour organizer to a customer going on one of their tours. It's giving instructions for the tour, and it's quite informal in tone. It uses imperatives which will be focused on later in the lesson.

- As a lead-in, ask students if they like to go on tours when they are on holiday. How do they usually arrange to go on the tour? Elicit ideas – in the hotel, by email, calling the tour company.

- Tell students to read the information in exercise 8. Check that students understand *to book* a tour (= to ask for a place on a tour).
- Tell students to work alone to complete the exercise and then to check their ideas with a partner. You may need to teach the meaning of *to tip* someone (= to give a small amount of extra money for a service).

ANSWERS
1 The tour bus leaves from in front of the Ubud Village Hotel in the city centre.
2 It leaves at 10 a.m.
3 Her booking form; her passport; a hat or a scarf to wear in the temples; a tip for the bus driver.

EXTRA ACTIVITY Use the email to start a discussion on tipping. Ask students to work in groups of three or four and share experiences and opinions on how tipping works in different countries. You could ask them to suggest what an appropriate amount to tip would be for this tour.

Exercise 9

- Tell students to work alone and read the email and the Language for writing box.
- Ask students where else they might read imperatives, e.g. instructions on how to use something and recipes.
- Ask for some examples of when you might use imperatives in the classroom, e.g. when the teacher gives instructions: *open your books, work with a partner*, etc.
- Check students are clear on the form and meaning before you go on with the lesson. You could ask them for more examples of imperatives to check this.

Exercise 10

- Put students into pairs and ask them to complete the exercise. You may need to teach the meaning of *tap* (= where water comes from in the kitchen and bathroom).
- Check answers together.

ANSWERS
1 Bring   2 Smile   3 Learn   4 Do not use
5 Don't drink; Drink   6 Leave

EXTENSION Ask students to think of advice they could give a tourist (either in their country or other countries they know about). Ask them to write four or five sentences. Put students into pairs and ask them to give their advice to their partner. Encourage students to ask for more information about the place if they haven't been there before.

You could ask students to tell the class about new places they got advice about and what they found out about that place from their partner.

Exercise 11a

- Refer students to p128 and tell them to read the instructions.
- Give clear guidelines including a time limit and suggested word count. Refer them to the example in exercise 8 to help them.
- Tell students to choose their situation and write the email. After they finish writing, encourage them to check for correct use of imperatives, spelling and other punctuation.

Exercise 11b

- Put students into pairs. Tell them to swap their emails with their partners.
- Students read the emails and check for the information in questions 1 and 2. Tell them to give feedback to their partners.
- You could ask them to underline any errors they spot in the use of imperatives. Students can then correct their errors.

EXTENSION Ask students to write a follow-up email in reply, which says thank you for the information and asks one or two questions about the information.

EXTRA ACTIVITY Put students into groups of four and tell them they are going to plan a tour of the place where they are studying. Tell them to share information about the places they know which tourists might want to visit. Students plan the tour and write an email to a tourist with a description of the tour and instructions on what to bring.

EXTRA ACTIVITY Students write an email to a new student coming to their English class. This could be done for homework. They must write a short email and include:
a A description of the class (where it is, how many people are in the class, what kinds of things they study)
b What to bring to class.

4.5 Video

Almas Tower

VIDEOSCRIPT
Dubai in the United Arab Emirates is a city of skyscrapers. There's the Burj Khalifa, the Burj al Arab and the Almas Tower.
The Almas Tower is the tallest business tower in the Middle East. It's 360 metres tall and has 68 floors.
It's in the Jumeirah Lakes Towers Free Zone, a large business area in the centre of Dubai. There are 66 skyscrapers here and they are all near the beautiful Jumeirah lake.
The Almas Tower is on its own island in the middle of the lake.
It is the centrepiece of the Free Zone and famous for its amazing structure. The tower is actually two connected towers that stand next to each other.
The surface of the tower is glass so it sparkles in the hot Dubai sun. In fact, Al Mas means 'the diamond' in Arabic.
The Almas Tower is the home of Dubai's jewellery trade, and the Dubai Diamond Exchange and the Dubai Pearl Exchange are here. There are lots of very expensive jewels here! They are in the basement for security reasons.
The Dubai Multi Commodities Centre – the authority for the entire Free Zone – is on the ground floor.
Above this, there are floors full of offices, and there are lots of big businesses here. This is the headquarters of Harley Davidson for the Middle East and North Africa. It's on the 48th floor.
The Almas Tower is an office building but there aren't just offices here. There are lots of other facilities, too. There are shops and restaurants and a huge car park with 1,700 spaces.

At the top of the tower there's a viewing point, with wonderful views of Dubai.
The Almas Tower is only one of Dubai's many incredible skyscrapers. But its height, its structure and its location make it one of the city's iconic buildings.

Exercise 1
basement ☐   car park ☐   diamond ✓   facilities ☐
glass ✓   gold ☐   ground floor ✓   jewellery ✓
lake ✓   pearl ✓   shops ☐   skyscraper ✓   tower ✓
wonderful view ✓

Exercise 2
1 The Almas Tower is the tallest business tower in the Middle East.
2 The Almas Tower is on an island / in a lake.
3 The Almas Tower is 2 towers joined together.
4 The Almas Tower is covered with glass.
5 Dubai's pearl / diamond exchange is in the Almas Tower.
6 Harley Davidson has its head office in the building.
8 The Almas Tower contains offices / restaurants.
9 At the top of the tower there is a viewing area.

Exercise 3
a 360 metres tall
b 68 floors
c 66 number of skyscrapers in the Jumeirah Lakes area
d 48 Harley Davidson offices on 48th floor
e 1,700 number of spaces in the car park

Exercise 4a & b
Students' own answers

Review

Exercises 1a & b 4.12 ◉
1 There are   2 there are   3 Are there   4 There are
5 there's   6 Is there   7 there's   8 there isn't
9 there aren't

AUDIOSCRIPT 4.12
A What's special about Neft Daşhlari?
B It's a town on an oil platform in the Caspian Sea.
A A town in the sea? Is it very small?
B No, not really. There are 300 km of streets and 2,000 people. And there are lots of things to do.
A Really? Are there any restaurants?
B Of course! There are some nice restaurants and hotels, and there's a cinema and a park, too.
A What about education? Is there a school?
B Yes, there's a school, but there isn't a university.
A So can people visit the place?
B No, there aren't any tourists. Only people who work on Neft Daşhlari can go there.

Exercise 2a
1 –   2 the   3 –   4 a   5 the   6 a   7 an   8 an

Exercise 3a 4.13 ◉
1 hospital   2 library   3 cinema   4 airport   5 hotel
6 restaurant   7 swimming pool

AUDIOSCRIPT 4.13
1 You go here when you are ill.
2 You can study here or take books home.
3 You can see a film here.
4 You usually need your passport to travel from here.
5 You can sleep here on holiday.
6 You can go here to have dinner.
7 There's lots of water and you can swim here.

Exercise 4
living room: armchair; television; DVD player
bedroom: bed; wardrobe; drawers
kitchen: dishwasher; sink; fridge
bathroom: shower; toilet; bath

Exercise 5a 4.14 ◉
1 old-fashioned   2 expensive   3 beautiful   4 difficult
5 noisy   6 short   7 small   8 dirty

AUDIOSCRIPT 4.14
1 modern   5 quiet
2 cheap   6 long
3 ugly   7 big
4 easy   8 clean

Exercise 6a
chemist

5 Clothes and shopping

Unit overview

Language input

can/can't/could/couldn't (CB p47)	• *You can buy clothes on the internet.* • *Can you use euros in Sweden?* • *I couldn't swim when I was four.*
Present continuous (CB p48)	• *They're wearing hoodies.* • *She isn't working today.* • *Where are you going?*
Present continuous or present simple (CB p49)	• *I'm wearing a jacket today. I often wear a jacket.*
Grammar reference (CB pp144–145)	

Vocabulary development

Shopping (CB p46)	• *baker's, cash, newsagent's, online, sales …*
Clothes and accessories (CB p48)	• *He's wearing a suit and tie.*
Adjectives and adverbs (CB p51)	• *He's a quick worker. He works quickly.*

Skills development

Listening: understanding similar vowel sounds (CB p50)
Speaking: in a shop (CB p52)
Writing: a product review (CB p53)

Video

Documentary: Camden Market (CB p54)
Vox pops (Coursebook DVD & TG p257)

More materials

Workbook	• Language practice for vocabulary, grammar, pronunciation, speaking and writing
Photocopiable activities	• Grammar: Find someone who can … (TG p205 & TSRD) • Vocabulary: Who is it? (TG p222 & TSRD) • Communication: High-street shopping (TG p239 & TSRD)
Tests	• Unit 5 test (TSRD)
Unit 5 wordlist (TSRD)	

5.1 Shopping

Goals
- Talk about shopping
- Use *can* and *could* to talk about possibility and ability

Lead-in

1 Closed book. Vocabulary-focused introduction to the topic.
- Write these words on the board: *shop shopping centre*
- Put students into pairs and ask them to discuss the differences between the words. (A shop is a building and there is usually one owner. A shopping centre is a large building with lots of shops in it.) Ask students to think of examples of these things in their town.

2 Closed book. Discussion about shopping and making suggestions about where to shop. This will also revise giving directions and prepositions from the previous unit.
- Tell students you have a friend visiting town who loves shopping. Ask students to suggest where they can go shopping. Encourage students to ask you questions about your friend (either invent the information or base it on a real friend) to find out what things they want to buy.
- Put students into pairs and get them to plan a perfect shopping day in your town/city. Tell students they have to write a set of instructions that you can give to your friend.
- Students explain their instructions and suggestions to the class.
- Choose the day that is best for your friend.
- Go over shop-related vocabulary from the activity.

Vocabulary & Speaking shopping

Exercise 1
- Put students into groups of three or four. Tell them to read the sentences and discuss the question. Encourage them to give reasons and examples for their choices.
- Ask groups to summarize their discussion. You could get feedback on the exercise by asking students to hold up their hands to show which sentence describes them.

Exercise 2a
- You may need to pre-teach *cash* (= paper and metal money), and it would be useful to also explain *credit card*, which appears later in the lesson (= plastic card that lets you pay later for things you buy) and *debit card* (= plastic card that lets you pay immediately for things you buy). Make sure students understand the difference.
- Put students into pairs.
- Tell students to work together and complete the exercise.

WATCH OUT! Students may wonder why there are apostrophes in some of the shop names. We use apostrophes to indicate the word *shop* would follow – *a butcher's shop*. The word *butcher's* is describing a type of shop.

ANSWERS
1 baker's 2 spend 3 newsagent's 4 butcher's
5 online 6 discount 7 shopping centre 8 return
9 sales 10 cash

Exercise 2b 5.1
- Play track 5.1 and ask students to check their answers.
- Play the track again, pausing after each sentence. Tell students to listen and check their answers.

AUDIOSCRIPT 5.1
1 I buy bread from the baker's.
2 I spend a lot of money at the weekends.
3 I buy magazines and newspapers from the newsagent's.
4 I buy meat from the butcher's.
5 I do a lot of my shopping online.
6 I get a discount because I'm a student.
7 I go shopping to a shopping centre. I prefer them to small shops.
8 When I buy something I don't like, I return it to the shop.
9 I stand outside and wait for the shops to open on the first day of the sales.
10 I pay for small things with cash.

Exercise 3a
- Ask students if the sentences in exercise 2a are true for them. Ask a student to change the first sentence using *never*, *sometimes*, *usually*, *often* or *always*. Write the sentence on the board, e.g. I **usually** buy bread from *the baker's.*
- Remind students about word order with adverbs of frequency. (Adverb goes before a main verb and after the verb *to be*.)
- Tell students to change the sentences in exercise 2a. Refer them to the adverbs in the instructions. Tell them to write the sentences in their notebooks.
- Demonstrate the exercise with a more confident student. For example:
  Teacher: Where do you buy bread?
  Student: I usually buy it from the baker's.
  Teacher: I never buy it from the baker's. I always buy it in a supermarket.
- Put students into pairs and ask them to discuss their sentences and compare them.
- Tell pairs to make a note of the similarities and differences between their sentences.

Exercise 3b
- Put students into new pairs. Tell them to complete the exercise. Refer students to the examples in the instructions and for extra support give more examples using two students in the class.

EXTENSION Find similarities in the group. Write *Some of us, Lots of us, Nobody* on the board. Ask students to work in groups of four to six. Ask them to complete the sentences using the information they have about each other, e.g. *Some of us shop online.*

Listening & Grammar *can/can't/could/couldn't*

Exercise 4a

Background note: The photo shows a typical street in the UK in the 1970s. It was common for towns and parts of cities to have one main street with small shops on it. This is called a *high* or *main* street. However, this has changed and now there are fewer small shops on these streets because supermarkets and chains of shops (= shops with the same name, owned by the same company, which you see in every city or town) have opened. These companies usually have more money, are bigger and can sell things more cheaply. Small shops cannot compete, so many of them have closed.

Audio summary: A woman talking about the difference in shopping on a typical British high street iin the 1970s and nowadays.

- Put students into pairs and tell them to look at the photo for one minute and discuss what they can see.

Exercise 4b 5.2 🔘

- Play track 5.2 and ask students to listen and check their ideas from exercise 4a.
- Go through the answers together.

ANSWERS

In the 1970s, you went to different shops to buy different things. Shopping took a long time. There were shopping assistants to help you and to chat to. There was no internet shopping. There were no cafes on the high street. Today, you can buy everything in a supermarket and in a shopping centre. But you can't chat to a shopping assistant or ask for help in the same way. You can buy almost anything on the internet. There are a lot of cafes on the high street now.

AUDIOSCRIPT 5.2

Today the typical town centre is very different from in the 1970s. Then, you couldn't buy everything from one shop. People needed to go to different shops: the butcher's for meat, the baker's for bread, and the newsagent's for their newspapers. Shopping took a long time! But there were good things. You could TALK to the people in the shops. Now it's easy to buy everything in the supermarket and in the shopping centre. But customers can't ask for information and chat to the shop assistant like they could in the past. In the 1970s you couldn't go shopping on the internet, but now you can buy almost everything online. Online shopping is cheap and easy, so it's difficult for the high street shops. Lots of them closed. I can't buy my bread and meat in the town centre now. But there are some things customers can't buy online. The internet can't cut your hair, for example, and it can't give you a cup of coffee. In the 1970s you couldn't get a cup of coffee on the high street, but there are five cafés here now – and three hairdresser's!

Exercise 5 5.2 🔘

- Ask students to read the instructions and the information in the table.

- Play track 5.2 again and tell students to complete the exercise individually.
- Check answers in pairs and then as a class.

ANSWERS

	1970s	Now
Possible	*talk to people in shops* buy bread at a baker's, meat at a butcher's, newspapers at a newsagent's	*shop online* buy everything at a supermarket or in a shopping centre buy everything in one shop
Impossible	buy everything in one shop have a cup of coffee on the high street	ask for information chat to the shop assistant

CRITICAL THINKING   Relate information from the listening to yourself. Put students into groups of three or four and ask them to discuss these questions:
1 Do you think the information in the listening is true for all high streets in the UK? What information do you think might be different in some places? (Here students could say that in some places you can probably ask for information and talk to people in shops – the speaker in the recording may be talking about her experience only and not things generally, in all parts of the UK.)
2 Are things the same or different in your country?

Exercise 6

- Put students into pairs. Refer them to the Grammar focus box and tell them to work together and complete the exercise.

WATCH OUT!   Some students tend to insert *to* after *can/could* and before the main verb, e.g. *we can ~~to~~ buy things online*. When you are checking answers, tell students we don't use *to* after modal verbs (except in *have to/don't have to*).

- Check answers. If you think your students might have problems writing the apostrophe in *can't* and *couldn't*, tell them how to form the contraction: by adding the apostrophe before the final *t* and taking out the *o*. When changing *cannot* to *can't*, we also drop one *n*.

ANSWERS
1 can
2 can't (cannot)
3 could
4 couldn't (could not)
5 infinitive
- Refer students to *Grammar reference* on p144. There are three more exercises here students can do for homework.

Exercise 7a

Background note: This quiz asks about shopping in the past and present. Tell students they will hear the answers to the quiz later in the lesson.

- Put students into pairs and tell them to read the questions and check any vocabulary they don't understand. Refer students to the definition of *vending machines* to help them with vocabulary.

- Tell students to complete the exercise. To make this more fun and interesting, you could try one of these ideas for doing gap fills:
  1 Make it a speed activity. When you say *go* they have to do the exercise in one minute.
  2 Do a beep dictation of the sentences. Tell the students to close their books. Read the questions and say *beep* when there is a space. Students have to listen carefully and say *can* or *could*. When you have finished, tell them to open their books and read the questions. Tell them to work with a partner and decide if their answers were correct or not.
- Check answers together.

1 Could   2 could   3 Can   4 Can   5 Can   6 Could
7 could   8 Can

Exercise 7b

- Tell students to work alone and complete the exercise by writing a tick if they think the answer is yes and a cross if they think it is no.
- The ask them to compare their answers with their partners.

Pronunciation *can*   5.3 💿

- Refer students to the pronunciation explanation, play track 5.3 and ask students to listen and read.

Exercise 8a   5.4 💿

- Explain that the listening exercise is to help students hear the pronunciation of *can* in the strong and weak forms.
- Play track 5.4 and tell students to listen to the pronunciation.

Exercise 8b   5.4 💿

- Play track 5.4 again and ask students to listen and repeat. Pause the recording after each sentence.

PRONUNCIATION Do a transformation drill to practise the strong and weak form of the verb. Write these verbs on the board: *dance sing swim read speak drive act draw paint*
Drill the question *Can you … + verb?*, making sure you use the weak form of *can*. Repeat the question using different verbs from the board and direct different students to reply *Yes, I can* or *No, I can't* to say the true answer. For example:
Teacher: Can you draw?
Student A: Yes, I can. Student B: No, I can't.
Put students into pairs and tell them to take turns asking and answering questions to practise pronunciation.

Exercise 9a

- Ask the class question 1 from exercise 7a. Ask them to explain their answers.
- Put students into groups of three or four.
- Tell students to complete the exercise. Tell them they have to give reasons for their answers and be prepared to tell the class their reasons.
- Check ideas with the class when they have finished speaking.

EXTRA CHALLENGE Ask fast finishers to write sentences on the board to explain their answers, e.g. *People couldn't buy things online in 1994 because they didn't have the internet.*

- Don't focus too much on errors with past simple; focus on the ideas and content in their answers. When everyone has finished you could discuss if the class agrees with the given reasons.

Exercise 9b   5.5 💿

- Play track 5.5 and tell students to listen and check if their answers were correct.
- If you think your students will find the listening difficult, pre-teach these terms:
  Dennis Tito (= a person), *kroner* (= a type of money used in some countries), *postcards* (= small cards you send to people when you are on holiday), *Chanel* (= a famous fashion label)
- You could pause after each question is answered to help students follow the information.
- Ask students which answers surprised them.

1 People could buy things online in 1994. The first thing they could buy was pizza.
2 In the 1990s, rich people couldn't buy trips into space. But in 2001 Dennis Tito paid to visit the International Space Station.
3 Today you can buy eggs from vending machines in Japan. And you can also buy flowers, fruit and umbrellas and many other things.
4 You can buy a bottle of rainwater for $11 these days. The water comes from the sky, into a bottle and then you drink it. It never touches the ground.
5 You can't use euros in Norway and Sweden. They use the Norwegian Krone and the Swedish Krona.
6 People could buy things from machines in 1890. The first vending machines were in London in the 1880s and they sold postcards.
7 In the 1960s, you couldn't buy petrol at supermarkets. They started to sell petrol in the 1970s.
8 You can't buy clothes online from all the big fashion companies. For example, Chanel don't sell their clothes online because they believe customers need to try everything on.

Exercise 10

- Tell students to work alone and read the ideas in the list. Tell them to think about how these things were different or similar in the past. How have things changed?
- Put students into pairs.
- Refer students to the example conversation and demonstrate the speaking exercise with a student.
- Tell students to complete the exercise.

FEEDBACK FOCUS Check that students are pronouncing *can* /kæn/ and *can't* /kɑːnt/ correctly. If necessary, explain the different vowel sounds and the importance of pronouncing the *t* so the distinction is clear.

- Discuss ideas with the class.

EXTENSION Ask fast finishers to think of other ideas and discuss how things have changed using *can* and *could*. Encourage them to think of examples from their own lives.

EXTRA ACTIVITY Ask students to write a short article about changes using their ideas from the speaking exercise. They should work in the same pairs and use their ideas to write about two or three of the points they discussed. For each point, get them to write about their reasons. Ask students to swap articles with another pair and discuss if they agree or disagree:

A *I agree with their article because …*
B *Yes, I agree too. It has the same ideas as our article, I think./ I don't agree. I don't think things are different now.*

Exercise 1

1 I can't.   2 Can; you can   3 Can; I can't
4 Could; I couldn't   5 Could; I could   6 Can; she can
7 Can; they can't   8 Could; they couldn't

Exercise 2

1 Could … send   2 couldn't buy   3 can download
4 Can … swim   5 Could … use   6 can't live
7 couldn't play

Exercise 3

1 couldn't   2 could   3 Could   4 talk   5 travel
6 could   7 can   8 could   9 can't   10 pay

5.2 What is he wearing?

Goals

- Talk about clothes
- Use the present continuous to talk about actions at the moment

Lead-in

1 Closed book. Talk about shopping for clothes to elicit vocabulary for this lesson and review vocabulary from lesson 5.1.

- Put students into pairs and ask them what they remember about the last lesson. Ask students to discuss buying clothes.
  What clothes do you like buying? Where do you buy them? Online? In a shop? Do you pay by cash or credit card?

- Write useful clothes and shopping vocabulary on the board. Check meaning and pronunciation.

2 Open book. Elicit useful clothes vocabulary.

- Refer students to the illustrations on p48.

- Put students into pairs and ask them to discuss these questions:
  What's happening in the illustrations? Are you often in similar situations? Do you have similar clothes? Do you like the clothes they are wearing? Do you wear clothes like picture c at home?

- Write useful vocabulary on the board and check meaning and pronunciation.

Vocabulary & Speaking clothes and accessories

Exercise 1a

- Put students into pairs and tell them to complete the exercise. You could give students big pieces of paper and big pens to write with so you can display the vocabulary later. You could set a time limit of one minute.

Exercise 1b

- Put pairs together to make groups of four. Encourage peer teaching of new vocabulary.

- You could tell students to write their vocabulary on the board. If you used big pieces of paper, stick the papers on the walls so students can read them.

- Check meaning and pronunciation. Encourage students to make a note of new vocabulary in their notebooks.

STUDY TIP To help students record vocabulary using translation. There are usually direct translations for clothes vocabulary, so recording vocabulary with the word in a student's first language makes sense. Encourage students to write translations for the words they learn in this lesson. You could also remind them to write the pronunciation of words they find difficult to pronounce.

Exercise 2

> **Background note:** The clothes here are examples of clothes worn in different situations in western culture.
>
> A suit is worn at formal occasions and for work. Both women and men wear suits.
>
> At western weddings it is typical for women to wear a dress and sometimes a hat. Men wear suits but don't usually wear hats.
>
> It's typical to wear more comfortable clothes when you are at home.

- Make sure students understand the word *hoodie* (= a top with a hood on it, usually worn for sport or in casual situations).

- Tell students to work alone and complete the exercise.

ANSWERS

1 b   2 d   3 a   4 c

EXTRA ACTIVITY Ask students which of the plural clothing words can't be used in the singular – trousers, jeans, glasses (in this sense), shorts – and which ones can – trainers, socks, gloves, shoes.

Exercise 3

- Put students into pairs and tell them to discuss possible answers for each number.

WATCH OUT! The term *top* refers to most types of clothes you can wear on the top half of your body. You can use it for men or women.

ANSWERS

1 on feet/hands: socks, gloves
2 outside only: a coat, a hat, a scarf, gloves
3 to do sport: shorts, socks, trainers, a T-shirt, a hoodie
4 in cold weather: a hat, a coat, a scarf, gloves
5 in hot weather: a hat, a dress, shorts, a T-shirt, a skirt
6 to a job interview: a suit, a jacket and trousers, a tie, a skirt and a top, a dress, shoes
7 to exercise: shorts, a T-shirt, socks and trainers, a hoodie
8 to relax: a T-shirt, shorts, jeans, a hoodie, trainers

PRONUNCIATION Students often forget the pronunciation of *suit*. The spelling is unusual. To help them, show them the word in phonemic script /suːt/ and show them that it rhymes with *boot*. The /uː/ sound can have different spellings.

EXTENSION Ask students to talk about their own culture and what types of clothes people wear for different situations. They could also talk about other places they have visited where people wear different clothes to work, relax or celebrate an event, or when it's cold.

Grammar & Speaking present continuous

Exercise 4a

- Tell students to work in pairs and refer them to the Grammar focus box.
- Ask them to read the information and complete the exercise.
- Check answers together.

ANSWERS
1 are **2** is **3** aren't **4** is

- Refer students to *Grammar reference* on p145.

Exercise 4b 5.6 🔊

- Play track 5.6 (sentences 1–3 in exercise 4a) and ask students to read and listen. Play the track again and pause after each sentence. Tell students to repeat what they heard. You could ask small groups and individuals to repeat to make sure all students have the correct pronunciation.

PRONUNCIATION In these examples, the auxiliary verb is not stressed in the positive forms. It is stressed more in the negative sentence. Explain this rule to students and help them produce it when they repeat the sentences. You could ask them to listen and mark the stressed words.

Exercise 5

- Put students into pairs and tell them to complete the exercise.
- You could ask them to repeat the sentences to each other to practise pronunciation.
- Check answers together.

POSSIBLE ANSWERS
1 is … wearing **2** she's carrying **3** Anita and Paul are having **4** Leila and Mike are relaxing; they aren't working

Exercise 6a

- Ask students to describe your clothes. Write this sentence on the board. *(Your name) is wearing …*
- Ask the class to complete the sentence in as many ways and as much detail as they can. You could ask one student to write on the board.
- Tell students to work alone and complete the exercise.
- Refer students to the Grammar focus box for support.

Exercise 6b

- Put students into pairs and ask them to read their sentences without telling their partner who they are describing. Ask students to listen and guess the person their partner is describing.

EXTRA CHALLENGE: Ask students to find someone wearing the same item of clothing as them. Tell them to work together and practise writing sentences describing what they're wearing in the plural form, e.g. *We're wearing trainers/ Pavlos and I are wearing hoodies.*

EXTRA ACTIVITY Before the lesson, prepare some photos of people – one photo for each student. Put students into pairs

and give each student a photo. Tell them to describe their photo but not to show it to their partner.

Collect all the photos and post them around the room or on the board. Tell students to look at the photos and find the one their partner described to them. Tell them to find their partner and check if they are correct.

Grammar & Listening present continuous or present simple

Exercise 7a

- Refer students to the podcast title and photos and tell them to work with a partner to discuss the question. Explain that there are no right or wrong answers here.
- Students label the photos with words in the box.

ANSWERS
a strong **b** tidy **c** fun **d** peaceful **e** serious

Exercise 7b 5.7 🔊

> **Audio summary:** This recording is a podcast. A podcast is a recording online which people can download and put on a phone, MP3 player or computer to listen to. It may be helpful to discuss what a podcast is with your students, and to tell them that there are lots of podcasts available online that they can use to listen to English out of the classroom. This podcast is about what information the colour of a person's clothes tells us about them.

- Play track 5.7 and ask students to listen and see if their predictions were correct.

AUDIOSCRIPT 5.7

… And, of course, we don't all wear the same clothes every day. But most of us have a colour, or two colours, that we wear more than others. And the colours you choose to wear can say a lot about you as a person. Let's start with a very common colour: are you wearing black? People who often wear black like to be the boss. It can make you look serious and important. But what about the opposite? I'm wearing white today. If you often wear white clothes, there's a good chance that you like things to be tidy and clean, and you enjoy a simple life. Yes, that's true – I am a tidy person.
Another popular colour is blue. This means you are a peaceful person and you don't like change … Now, how about some less common colours? Are you wearing red today? Do you often wear red? Well, the good news is that you are probably a strong person and you always try hard at everything you do.
Finally, who is wearing yellow? You are the good students because you love learning … and – this is important – you are a lot of fun! So, does any of this sound true to you? …

Exercise 8 5.7 🔊

- Ask students to read through the sentences they have to complete.
- Play track 5.7 again. Tell students to complete the exercise. You may need to play the track twice.
- Ask students to work in pairs to check their answers.

1 boss   2 important   3 clean   4 change   5 a strong
6 try   7 learning   8 fun

Exercise 9

- Put students into pairs and refer them to the Grammar focus box.

- Tell them to read the information and discuss the questions.

- To give more support, ask students to read audioscript 5.7 on p164 and find more examples of present continuous and present simple in positive and question forms.

- Refer students to *Grammar reference* on p145. There are three more exercises here that students can do for homework.

1   sentence b   2   sentence a

Exercise 10

- Put students into groups of four.

- Tell them to discuss the questions, giving reasons for their opinions where appropriate.

EXTRA CHALLENGE   Ask students to work in their groups and suggest alternative ideas for what each colour could mean about a person. Ask them to take turns to present their ideas to the class.

Exercise 11a

- Tell students to read the dialogue quickly to understand the story. Ask these questions to check understanding.
    1 Where's Mike? (At home)
    2 Why's he calling Leila? (He wants her help)
    3 How is Mike feeling? (He's stressed)
    4 What does Leila say she'll do? (She says she will come home soon)

- Tell students to read the dialogue again and underline the correct verbs. You could do the first example together with the class.

Exercise 11b 5.8 💿

- Play track 5.8 and tell students to listen and check their answers.

1 are you doing   2 am I doing   3 do people usually do
4 'm buying   5 'm trying   6 are making   7 's running
8 go   9 's raining   10 never play   11 'm paying

AUDIOSCRIPT 5.8
L Hello?
M Where are you?
L I'm in a clothes shop. Why?
M Because I need your help. What are you doing?
L What am I doing? What do people usually do in clothes shops? I'm buying clothes, of course.
M Well, are you nearly finished? I'm trying to cook a meal for six people, and the kids are making a lot of noise and the dog's running around and …
L Why are the kids there? They go to tennis practice on Thursdays.
M Not today because it's raining. They never play in the rain.
L OK, I'm paying now. I'll be back in an hour.
M An hour? Why …

Exercise 12

- Put students into pairs. Explain they are going to do a spot-the-difference activity. They have done this kind of activity before. There are similar activities in previous lessons.

- Ask students to decide who is Student A and who is Student B.

- Refer students to their pages at the back of the Coursebook and tell them to read the information.

- Demonstrate the activity with a more confident student.

EXTRA SUPPORT   If you think your students will find it difficult to form the questions, then tell them to write out the questions from the prompts before they begin.

- Tell students to complete the exercise.

Student A
1 Is the shop assistant standing?   **B** Yes, she is. **A** No, she isn't.
   NOT Does the shop assistant stand?
2 What time does the shop open?   **B** At 10. **A** At 9.
   NOT What time is the shop opening?
3 Does the shop take credit cards?   **B** No, it doesn't. **A** Yes, it does.
   NOT Is the shop taking credit cards?
4 What's the young man holding?
   B He's holding some jeans. **A** He's holding a white shirt.
   NOT What does the young man hold?
5 What's the old man wearing?   **B + A** Black jacket, orange shirt and grey trousers.
   NOT What does the old man wear?
6 What's the shop assistant wearing?   **B + A** A red top and blue trousers.
   NOT What does the shop assistant wear?
Student B
1 What time does the shop close?   **A + B** At 5.
   NOT What time is the shop closing?
2 What's the old man doing?
   A He's talking to the shop assistant. **B** He's trying on hats.
   NOT What does the old man do?
3 What languages do the shop assistants speak?
   A + B They speak English and French.
   NOT What languages are the shop assistants speaking?
4 What's the young man holding?
   A He's holding a white shirt. **B** He's holding some jeans.
   NOT What does the young woman hold?
5 What's the young woman wearing?   **A + B** A red top/T-shirt and a green skirt.
   NOT What does the young woman wear?
6 What's the young man wearing?
   A He's wearing jeans and a red hoodie. **B** He's wearing jeans and a red top/T-shirt.

EXTRA ACTIVITY   Students invent a dialogue of two people speaking on the phone.

- Put students into pairs. Tell them to think of their relationships – friends, colleagues, family. Ask them to choose a situation, e.g. *they are calling because they are late for a meeting, they need help with something, they are angry about something, they have some good news, they are giving information about a project and how it's progressing*, etc.

- Tell students they have to write a ten to twenty line dialogue using the present simple and present continuous at least twice each. They should not say who they are. Tell them to practise their dialogues. When they have finished, put them together in groups of four and tell them to act out their dialogues for the other pair. The listeners have to listen to identify the relationship and what the call is about.

Exercise 1
1 Are; Yes, I am.   2 Am; No, you aren't.
3 Are; No, they aren't.   4 Does; Yes, he does.
5 Do; No, I don't.   6 Is; Yes, she is.   7 Are; Yes, we are.
8 Is; No, it isn't.   9 Do; Yes, they do.   10 Does; Yes, he does.

Exercise 2
1 's wearing   2 walk   3 'm working   4 aren't taking
5 never play   6 are you running   7 do you watch
8 Is he having   9 dancing   10 does your brother do
11 's starting   12 are sleeping

Exercise 3
1 are you doing   2 am visiting   3 lives   4 am staying
5 does your sister do   6 works   7 are you doing
8 am learning   9 are you learning   10 am waiting
11 is wearing   12 (is) talking

5.3 Vocabulary and skills development

Goals
- Understand similar vowel sounds
- Use adjectives and adverbs

Lead-in

1 Closed book. To identify the number of syllables and sounds in words.

- Write some clothes items on the board, e.g. *trousers, suit, t-shirt, skirt*.

- Put students into pairs and tell them to say the words to each other and work out answers to these questions:
  1 What does the word mean?
  2 How many syllables are there in the word?
  3 How many sounds are in the word?

- Do an example to help demonstrate the task: *suit* – draw a suit on the board to show the meaning; it has one syllable and three sounds /s/uː/t/.

- Go over the answers together.

2 Closed book. To discuss making decisions about what to wear.

- Put students into pairs and tell them to discuss these questions:
  1 Do you find it easy to decide what to wear?
  2 What helps you decide?
  3 What events have you been to recently and what did you wear?

- Go over their answers with the class.

Listening & Speaking   understanding similar vowel sounds

Exercise 1

> **Background note:** The listening is about a virtual mirror. This is an idea for a special mirror that will show people what they look like with a clothing item from a shop. The mirrors will be in shops so that people won't need to try on clothes. They can check how they will look and decide to buy the clothes or not.

- Put students into pairs. Refer them to the photos and tell them to discuss the question. Check they understand what *virtual* means (= created by computers; made to look real by computers).

- Ask pairs to explain their ideas to the class and encourage discussion.

EXTENSION   Ask students to discuss any other technology they know about that helps shoppers make decisions. For example, some shops have cameras in the changing rooms that are activated by an app on your smartphone. They take a photo when you have tried on some clothes and you can then share the image with friends. Your friends can comment and give you advice on whether to buy the item. Ask students to discuss if they have heard of this and what other technology they know about.

Exercise 2   5.9

> **Background note:** Learning the sounds of English and being able to hear them in words can help students to understand better when they listen. We can help them tell the difference between the vowel sounds in English by looking at minimal pairs. This is when two words have only one sound that is different, e.g. *cut* and *cat*.

- To introduce what a vowel sound is, you could refer to a phonemic chart if you have one. You could also write the word *cheap* on the board and ask students how many sounds are in the word. /tʃ/iː/p/. (Answer: three sounds) Ask students which sound is the vowel sound. (Answer: /iː/)

- Play track 5.9 and ask students to notice if the vowel sounds in the words are the same or different.

- Check answers together, pointing out to students the different vowel phonemes (hat/hate = æ/eɪ; not/note = ɒ/əʊ; man/main = æ/eɪ).

ANSWERS
1 D   2 D   3 D

AUDIOSCRIPT 5.9
hat   hate
not   note
man   main

PRONUNCIATION   There is a spelling rule in English that says that if we add the letter *e* to the end of a word with a vowel and consonant ending, the vowel is pronounced as it is when we read the alphabet. The first two examples in the recording illustrate this: *hat* – *hate*. In *hat* the vowel sound is /æ/. When we add the letter *e*, the *a* is pronounced as it is when we say the letter A of the alphabet /heɪt/.

Exercise 3 5.10 🔊

• Refer students to the Unlock the code box.

• Play track 5.10 and tell them to listen and read.

EXTENSION To help students hear the vowel sounds in isolation, write the vowel symbols from the Unlock the code box on the board. Ask a volunteer to come to the board. Say the sounds and ask them to point to the sound you are saying. Tell the class to say if they are correct, then repeat this with all the sounds. Ask students to look at your mouth position as you say the sounds. Ask what happens to your mouth when you say the sounds. Tell students to copy the shape of your mouth.

Ask two different students to come to the board. One says the sounds and the other points to the word they think their partner is saying, and the class confirms if they are correct. Put students into pairs and ask them to do the same using the symbols in the Unlock the code box.

Exercise 4 5.11 🔊

EXTRA SUPPORT If you think your students will find this difficult, ask them to work with a partner and try saying the words to each other before they listen. They could also think of sentences for the words so they focus on meaning and potential contexts. Monitor and help them with the pronunciation. They may not get all the sounds 100% correct but it will help to prepare them to listen.

• Play track 5.11 and tell students to underline the words they hear.

• Check answers together.

ANSWERS

1 man 2 sit 3 not 4 met 5 red 6 coat

AUDIOSCRIPT 5.11

1 That man is her husband.
2 Can I sit here?
3 He's not a teacher, he's a student.
4 I met my wife at university.
5 I have a red jacket.
6 Take off your coat, it's hot in here.

Exercise 5a 5.12 🔊

• Ask students to read the words and think what vowel sound is in each word.

• Refer students to the lines where they should write the words. Play track 5.12 and ask them to listen to each word and write it next to the correct sound.

• Make sure students have enough time after they hear each word to choose the correct category and write the word. Pause the recording between words if necessary.

Exercise 5b 5.13 🔊

• Play track 5.13 and ask students to listen and check their answers. Play the recording again and pause after each word so the students can repeat.

ANSWERS/AUDIOSCRIPT 5.13

1 /æ/ hat, man, stand
2 /eɪ/ play, hate, main, take, sales, page
3 /ɒ/ lot, shop, long, not
4 /ʌ/ cut, shut, one

5 /əʊ/ home, boat, note, coat
6 /e/ set, text, press, sells
7 /ɪ/ sit, live, tin, thing
8 /iː/ seat, cheap, eat, jeans

Exercise 6a 5.14 🔊

Audio summary: A radio presenter talking about how a virtual mirror helps him when he goes shopping. Virtual mirrors were covered in the first background note in the lesson. You could remind students about them as a lead-in to the listening.

• Play track 5.14 and ask students to listen and complete the exercise.

• Tell them to check their answers with a partner.

ANSWERS

Words spoken: hate, man, shop, cheap, main, long, jeans, take, stand, press, sells, one, thing, page, not, note, coat

Exercise 6b 5.14 🔊

• Tell students to work alone and read the phrases.

• Play track 5.14 again and ask them to complete the exercise.

ANSWERS

2 presses a button to see all the jeans in the shop
3 presses a button to choose a pair of jeans
5 sends a picture to Facebook
6 makes a note of the best jeans
7 pays for the jeans

Exercise 6c

• Put students into pairs.

• Tell them to compare their answers. Then check answers together as a class.

AUDIOSCRIPT 5.14

I hate shopping. Maybe it's because I'm a man, but I usually walk into a shop, choose something cheap, pay for it and leave quickly. The main problem is that it takes such a long time. But I'm here today to try the 'virtual mirror'. It's a new way to shop and it might change my life! I'm in a clothes shop and I need some jeans. But I don't need to take five pairs of jeans to the changing rooms. Instead, I just stand in front of this 'virtual mirror', press a button and it shows me in every pair of jeans the shop sells. I choose a pair, press a button and the mirror shows me wearing them! I press another button and the next pair appears. I can see myself in ten pairs in just one minute! And another thing: if I'm not sure, I press a button and a picture of me wearing the jeans goes to my Facebook page and my friends can say what they think. It's not difficult to use, and I can find the right jeans easily. So I make a note of the jeans I like, pay for them and go home!
The company behind the virtual mirror plans to put them in shops all around the world. So next time you need a new hat, top or coat, go to a shop with a virtual mirror!

Exercise 7

• Put students into small groups and tell them to discuss the questions.

• Discuss ideas with the class.

EXTRA ACTIVITY If students like the idea of the virtual mirror, they could create an advert for it. This would recycle *can* and *could* for ability (present/past). For example:
In the past you couldn't shop quickly on a busy Saturday. Now you can walk into a shop and have a new pair of jeans in less than five minutes! With a virtual mirror you can … .

Vocabulary & Speaking adjectives and adverbs

Exercise 8a

- To start the focus on adjectives and adverbs, refer students to the two sentences from the radio programme so that they can see the language in context.
- Put students into pairs and ask them to work together and complete the exercise.

ANSWERS

1 The highlighted words are adverbs. They describe an action.
2 We usually form adverbs with an adjective + -*ly*.

Exercise 8b

- Refer students to the Vocabulary focus box and ask them to read it.
- Ask students to work alone and check their answers.
- As this is the first time students have looked at adverbs, go through the answers to exercise 8a with the class and make sure everyone understands these grammar rules. Ask students to look at the position of the adjectives and adverbs in the sentences. Ask them these questions to check they are clear on word order.
  1 *Do adjectives go before or after the noun? Answer: they go before.*
  2 *Do adverbs go before or after verbs? Answer: they go after.*

Exercise 9

- Ask students to work with their partners and complete the exercise.
- Check answers together.

ANSWERS

1 adj 2 adv 3 adv 4 adj 5 adj 6 adv 7 adv

Exercise 10

- Ask students to work with their partner and complete the exercise.

WATCH OUT! In *carefully* we need to double the letter *l*. It follows the rule that if we have a word with a consonant + vowel + consonant at the end of the word, the final consonant is doubled.

ANSWERS

quietly, carefully, clearly, dangerously, well, correctly, late

Exercise 11a

- Put students into different pairs and ask them to complete the conversations.
- Check answers together.

ANSWERS

1 carefully 2 dangerously 3 quietly 4 late
5 clearly 6 correctly 7 well

Exercise 11b 5.15 🎧

- Play track 5.15 and ask students to listen and check their answers.
- Then ask them to practise saying the conversations together.

AUDIOSCRIPT 5.15

1
A How much money do you earn?
B Not much, so I try to spend it carefully.
2
A What's the matter? Why do you look so scared?
B Because you're driving dangerously! Be careful!
3
A Why are you talking so quietly?
B Shhhh! Because we're in the library!
4
A I always get up late at weekends.
B Me too, at about ten o'clock!
5
A I can't see the television clearly.
B I think you need glasses.
6
A Maria answers every question correctly.
B I know. She's the best student in the class.
7
A Did you do well in your exam?
B I got an 'A'.

EXTRA ACTIVITY Ask students to find the opposites to the adverbs in exercise 10, e.g. *quietly = loudly*. Tell them to create mini conversations using these adverbs. For example:
A What's the matter? You look angry.
B Yes! My neighbours are playing their music really loudly and I can't relax.
They could perform their conversations for other pairs. Ask listeners to check if the adverbs are being used correctly.

EXTRA CHALLENGE Ask students to work with their partner and think of three more adjectives/adverbs and write pairs of sentences for each.

Exercise 12a

- Ask a more confident student if they know someone who can play a musical instrument. Ask them if they play it well. What instrument is it?
- Tell students to read the instructions and think for one minute about people they know (including themselves) who do things in these ways.
- Put students into pairs and ask them to tell their partner about the people they thought about. Encourage students to ask follow-up questions as you did when you demonstrated the exercise.

FEEDBACK FOCUS Walk around the class and check students are using adjectives and adverbs correctly. Also, listen to how they form questions. Write examples of good language on the board and some errors. Ask the class to correct them.

Exercise 12b

- Put students into different pairs and tell them to compare what they spoke about. Refer them to the example conversation.
- You could ask them to find things they have in common.

5.4 Speaking and writing

Goals

- Buy things in a shop
- Write a product review

Lead-in

1 Closed book. To revise clothes and shopping vocabulary.

- Write the questions below on the board before the lesson starts.
- Put students into small groups and ask them to discuss at least three of these questions. Tell students to choose the questions they think are most interesting.
  Do you love shopping or hate it?
  What kinds of shops do you enjoy the most?
  Do you like shopping in a shopping centre, in small local shops or online?
  What clothes are you most comfortable in?
  What clothes do you like/hate buying?

2 Closed book. To revise adverbs and adjectives from lesson 5.3.

- Write these sentences on the board.
  1 She walks home.
  2 He speaks English.
  3 They've got a car.
- Remind students that we use adjectives and adverbs to make sentences more interesting and to give more details. Examples: *She walks home slowly. They've got a red car.*
- Ask students to work in their groups and think of adjectives and adverbs they could add to these sentences to give more information. You could set a time limit of four or five minutes.
- Ask one person from each group to come up to tell you one idea for each sentence and to write it on the board. You could ask the class to vote on the most interesting examples.

Listening & Speaking in a shop

Exercise 1

- Refer students to the photos.
- Put students into pairs and ask them to discuss the question and complete the task.

ANSWERS
a clothes shop: changing rooms, shop assistant, customer
b sandwich shop: shop assistant, customer, till
c newsagent: customer, shop assistant

EXTRA ACTIVITY Ask students to discuss what the people in the photos are saying. Tell them to write the conversation in their notebooks and then compare their conversations with another pair. You could ask pairs to act out their conversations for the class. They can then compare their conversations with the recording in exercise 2.

Exercise 2a 5.16

> **Audio summary:** Three different conversations that take place in shops. The first is in a newsagent, the second in a clothes shop and the third in a sandwich shop.

- Play track 5.16 and ask students to complete the exercise.

- Check answers together.

ANSWERS
1 c 2 a 3 b

Exercise 2b 5.16

- Play the track again and ask students to listen and write the items the people buy.
- Check answers.

ANSWERS
1 a magazine and some batteries
2 a hoodie
3 two egg and tomato sandwiches and two coffees

AUDIOSCRIPT 5.16

Conversation one
C Excuse me?
SA Yes? How can I help?
C How much is this magazine?
SA It's £4.99.
C Right … and do you offer a student discount?
SA Yes, we do. You get 20% off.
C Oh, that's good. Do you sell batteries?
SA: Yes, we do. What kind do you need?
C Erm … AA please. Just one packet.
Conversation two
SA Can I help you?
C No, thanks. I'm just looking.
SA Well if you need anything, just ask.
C Can I try this hoodie on, please?
SA Yes, of course. The changing rooms are over there.
Conversation three
C Two egg and tomato sandwiches and two coffees.
SA That's £10.98, please.
C Can I pay by card?
SA No, I'm afraid we only take cash.
C OK, that's fine.
SA Would you like a bag?
C Yes, please. Just a small one.
SA And would you like a receipt?
C Yes, please. Just put it in the bag.

Exercise 3a

- Tell students to work alone and match the questions and answers.
- Tell them to compare their answers with the person next to them.

ANSWERS
1 e 2 f 3 h 4 a 5 b 6 c 7 i 8 g 9 d

Exercise 3b 5.17

- Play track 5.17 and tell students to listen and check their answers.

AUDIOSCRIPT 5.17

1
A Can I help you?
B No, thanks. I'm just looking.
2
A Do you need a bag?
B Yes, please. Just a small one.

3

A Can I try this on, please?

B Of course. The changing rooms are over there.

4

A Can I pay by card?

B No, I'm afraid we only take cash.

5

A How much is this magazine?

B It's £4.99.

6

A Do you offer a student discount?

B Yes, we do. You get 20% off.

7

A Would you like a receipt?

B Yes, please. Just put it in the bag.

8

A Do you sell batteries?

B Yes, we do. What kind do you need?

9

A What time do you close?

B At eight o'clock.

Exercise 3c

- Working alone, students go through each line and write C or SA.
- Tell them to compare their answers with the person next to them.

ANSWERS

1 SA 2 SA 3 C 4 C 5 C 6 C 7 SA 8 C 9 C

a SA b SA c SA d SA e C f C g SA h SA i C

Exercise 3d

- Ask students to work with a partner and practise the conversations.

SMART COMMUNICATION Polite intonation. Students usually need a lot of help to improve their intonation. Remind them that when we are asking someone we don't know questions, we often raise the pitch of our voices to sound polite. Usually in *Wh-* questions our voice goes down at the end of the question but in these situations it can go up to help us sound more polite.

Play the recording again and ask students to identify the rising and falling intonation at the ends of questions and sentences.

Exercise 4

- As a lead-in, ask students if they like buying gifts. Do they find it easy/difficult to buy gifts for people?
- Ask students to read the instructions and think of what type of gift they could buy.
- Tell students to read the information in the Language for speaking box.
- Tell them to work with their partners and to role-play conversations between a shop assistant and a customer.

EXTRA SUPPORT If you think your students will find this difficult, tell them to write out the conversations first and then practise them.

FEEDBACK FOCUS Listen to students' pronunciation. How polite do they sound? You could ask students to record themselves and listen with their partner. Ask them if they think they sound polite.

Reading & Writing a product review

Exercise 5

> **Background note:** There are lots of websites that have product reviews to help people choose the product that is right for them. Customers usually write about products they buy online. The reviews often describe the good and bad things about the product and recommend whether to buy it or not. They also mention if the service is good or not. There are some very famous sites like Amazon, where you can find lots of reviews. You could mention local examples of online retailers to your students to help them understand the concept if you think they need a reference point.

- Tell students to close their books so they don't see the reviews. Put students into groups of three or four. Tell them to imagine they want to buy something online, e.g. *a bike*. Tell them to think about all the things they need to know before they can decide which bike to buy and where to buy it.
- Ask students to tell you their ideas, and write key words on the board, e.g. *price, delivery, size, weight, type of bike* etc. You might need to explain *delivery* (= how the product gets to your house) and *weight* (= how many kilograms something is).

POSSIBLE ANSWERS

the price, the size, the make or brand, the look, customer reviews, availability, delivery times and cost

Exercise 6a

- Tell students to open their books and look at the reviews. Ask students where they might find these reviews. (Answer = online, on websites where you can buy products.)
- Ask students what the different buttons and stars represent. The stars show how good the product/service is. Explain the meaning of *recommend* (= say that a thing is good or useful) and that the *Recommend* button shows how many people would recommend the product. *Report* (= tell the website owners something) is a button people can press to report a problem with the review — sometimes people write incorrect or unpleasant information and the website allows readers to report the problem so they can delete the post.
- Tell students to read the reviews and match them to the photos. Then put students into pairs and tell them to discuss the questions, giving reasons for their answers. They should mention the star ratings, the language in the text and how many people recommended the products.
- Ask students also to discuss who the reviews are for. They will have to consider this when they write their reviews later in the lesson.

ANSWERS

1 A 2 B

Exercise 6b

- Tell students to read the categories a–f and make sure they understand all of the vocabulary. You may need to teach *value for money* (= how expensive or cheap something is), *look* (= what something looks like) and *user-friendliness* (= how easy the product is to use).

- Put students into pairs and tell them to complete the exercise.
- Check answers together.

a cost: 2
b value for money: 5, 10
c look: 3, 4, 7
d user-friendliness: 8, 9
e delivery: 6, 11
f writer's opinion/advice: 1, 12

Exercise 7a

- Tell students to read the Language for writing (1) box and complete the exercise.

ANSWER

It's big, awful and very heavy …

Exercise 7b

- Ask students to work in pairs.
- For extra support, do the first question together with the class.
- Tell students to complete the exercise. Remind them to take out *and* where they add a comma.
- Check answers together. You could ask fast finishers to write the answers on the board.

ANSWERS

1 My job is to open the shop, sell products and answer customers' questions.
2 I use it for the internet, sending emails, doing homework and playing games.
3 If you are looking for a machine that's fast, cheap and easy to use, then this is for you.

EXTENSION Ask students to suggest items you can buy online, e.g. *music systems, computers, toys, books, furniture, clothes*. Tell them to work in pairs and choose two items to write a sentence about. They have to include three adjectives or descriptions as in exercise 7b.

Give them a time limit of five minutes to write their sentences but tell them they can't include the name of the item.

Tell them to swap sentences with another pair who have to read the sentences and guess which item they are writing about. Encourage them to peer correct sentences also.

Exercise 8

- Tell students to read the sentences in the Language for writing (2) box.

Exercise 9a

- Put students into pairs.
- Tell the pairs to choose a product to write about. Give them a word limit and a time limit for writing. About fifty to sixty words is a good length.
- Tell students to decide on a good or bad review and look for useful vocabulary in the Language for writing (2) box.
- Tell students to plan the content of their review. Refer them to step 2 and the texts they read earlier for support and ideas.

Exercise 9b

- Tell students to write their reviews together on a piece of paper, making sure they include a list and commas where appropriate.
- Encourage them to check their reviews for grammar and spelling errors when they have finished.

Exercise 9c

- Ask students to swap texts with another pair and discuss the questions.

CRITICAL THINKING Ask students if they've ever written a review online, what it was for and whether they recommended the product. Also ask them whether they find reviews helpful or not (*there may be too many to read, they may say opposite things*, etc.). They could discuss this in pairs or you could have a class discussion.

EXTRA ACTIVITY Role-play a complaint. Students can use some of the language for writing a bad review to have a conversation where they complain in a shop.

- Ask students if they have ever returned something that they bought and why. Write useful vocabulary on the board, e.g. *it doesn't work, it's too small/big, it's broken, it's not worth the money, it's poor value*.
- Tell them to work in pairs. One person is a shop assistant and the other is a customer. Tell them to role-play returning an item they bought. Tell them to think about the language they will need before they start. You could group shop assistants and customers together before they start to help them prepare.
- Ask students to practise their role-plays. Less confident students could work in pairs (two customers and/or two assistants together).
- You could ask them to repeat the problem with different shop assistants and then tell the class who was the most helpful in solving the problem.
- Praise students for fluency and using the expressions rather than focusing on grammatical correctness.

5.5 Video

Camden Market

VIDEOSCRIPT

The high street is an important part of British life. Shoppers can buy everything here – food, music and, of course, clothes.
In fact, people often call popular fashion 'high street fashion'.
This is because a lot of large clothes shops are here. People can buy all kinds of clothes in these shops and they are usually cheap. But a lot of these clothes look the same, and they are often poor quality. This is why some shoppers prefer old, vintage clothes that they can't find on the high street.
These people come to Camden.
Camden is an area of London in the centre of the city. It's famous for its five markets, including Camden Lock Market and Stables Market.
Camden Lock is beside the Regent's Canal. It's over forty years old. At first people could buy art and furniture here,

but today it has a large indoor market and several outdoor stalls that sell all kinds of clothes.
The Stables Market is the largest part of Camden Market. It has famous clothes shops, like Cyberdog, and lots of different stalls selling vintage and hand-made clothes.
Shoppers can find all kinds of clothes in Camden that they can't buy anywhere else.
These people aren't all looking for the same thing but they're all hoping to find something for their own special style.
You can see many different styles in Camden.
Walker: *I'm wearing a green overcoat, grey jacket, black trousers, white shirt, tie, waistcoat.*
Elizabeth: *I'm wearing a red jacket, a black and white dress, and gold shoes.*
Alfie: *I'm wearing a black overcoat with a black scarf, grey cardigan, dark blue tie, black shirt, black skinny jeans and black shoes.*
At Camden Market clothes are very important. But there are other things here too.
Shoppers can buy books, jewellery and music. In fact, these shoppers are looking for old music records in a vintage music shop.
There are lots of food stalls too and they sell food from all over the world.
Camden Market is most famous for its style. The shoppers are stylish, the clothes are stylish, even the food is stylish!

VIDEO ANSWERS

Exercise 1

Students' own answers

Exercise 2

1 A stall is a small shop or table in a public place where things are sold, often in a market.
2 Something that is old, but high quality is called vintage. e.g. an old car, a black and white film or a book that people still like nowadays, even though it was made a long time ago.
3 A style that is popular, e.g. fashion magazines, show what styles of clothes or hair are popular at the moment.
4 People make home-made products in their houses to sell, .e.g. I prefer to make my own homemade bread so I know what ingredients the bread has in it.
5 The high street is the street where the most important shops, banks and businesses are.
6 Something that is stylish is something that is attractive and of good quality.

Exercise 3

street café, umbrella, flag, hat, double-decker bus, sunglasses, shoes
Distractors
a red telephone box, somebody swimming, a red letter box

Exercise 4

a Popular fashion in the UK is called street fashion / high street fashion / popular clothes.
b People prefer shopping in Camden Market because they can find cheaper clothes / clothes they can't find on the high street / the latest fashion.
c In the past Camden Lock sold art and furniture / clothes/ bread and cakes.

d All the speakers are wearing something hand-made / white shoes / something black.
e At Camden Market you can also buy international food / holidays / old cars.

Exercise 5a & b

Students' own answers

Review

ANSWERS

Exercise 1a

POSSIBLE ANSWERS

Can you drive a car?
Could you drive a car when you were a child?
Can you play a musical instrument?
Could you play a musical instrument when you were a child?
Can you run for half an hour?
Could you run for half an hour when you were a child?
Can you speak English?
Could you speak English when you were a child?
Can you stay up late?
Could you stay up late when you were a child?
Can you use credit cards in most shops?
Could you use credit cards in most shops when you were a child?

Exercise 3a 5.18 🔊
1 b   2 a   3 f   4 d   5 e   6 c

AUDIOSCRIPT 5.18
1 I'm a student. Do I pay less?
2 Could I have a small chocolate cake, please? And what types of bread do you have?
3 I don't think we need to go to any other shops. This place has everything we need.
4 Excuse me, but these jeans are too small for me. Could you give me my money back, please?
5 Do you sell a magazine called 'Garden World'?
6 Look at this. It's half-price. Everything is so cheap!

Exercises 4a & b
1 hat   2 jacket   3 jewellery   4 dress

Exercise 5a
1 d   2 f   3 b   4 a   5 e   6 c

Exercise 5b
1 They're talking quietly.
2 She's singing badly.
3 He's driving slowly.
4 She's running quickly.
5 They're dancing well.
6 He's carrying the plates carefully.

Exercise 6a

POSSIBLE ANSWERS
1 Can I … pay by card/try this on/have a receipt, please?
2 How much … are these/are those shoes?
3 Do you … offer a student discount/have a sale on?
4 What time do you … open/close on Sundays?

The past

Unit overview

Language input

was and **were** (CB p56)	• *We were in Rome last month.* • *Was she in class yesterday? No, she wasn't.*
Past simple regular verbs (CB p58)	• *play – played; marry – married; stop – stopped*
Grammar reference (CB pp146–147)	

Vocabulary development

Time expressions (CB p57)	• *three weeks ago, in the 19th century, at night …*
Common regular verb collocations (CB p59)	• *wait for a long time/for a friend* • *visit a museum/a relative*
Adverbs of degree (CB p61)	• *a bit, quite, very, really …*

Skills development

Listening: understanding present and past simple verbs (CB p60)

Speaking: showing interest as a listener (CB p62)

Writing: write a tweet or text message (CB p63)

Video

Documentary: Istanbul (CB p64)

Vox pops (Coursebook DVD & TG p257)

More materials

Workbook	• Language practice for grammar, pronunciation, vocabulary, speaking and writing • Listening for pleasure • Review: Units 5 & 6
Photocopiable activities	• Grammar: Three in a row (TG p205 & TSRD) • Vocabulary: Memories (TG p223 & TSRD) • Communication: The right response (TG p240 & TSRD)
Tests	• Unit 6 test (TSRD) • Progress test: Units 4–6
Unit 6 wordlist (TSRD)	

6.1 Don't give up!

Goals
- Use *was/were* to talk about the past
- Use past time expressions

Lead-in

1 Open book. To speculate about the content of the lesson and learn the meaning of *Don't give up!*
- Put students into small groups of three or four and ask them to discuss these questions:
  What does *Don't give up* mean? When do we say it?
- Check ideas with the class. Answer: *Don't give up* means don't stop trying; keep going even when things get difficult. We might say it to someone who is training to do something difficult like a race or sports event.
- Tell students to think of a person they know that they could say this to. Ask them to tell their group what they would say to the person. For example: *My sister is working hard but her company doesn't say thank you and they pay her badly. She wants to work for a better company.*

2 Closed book. To understand the meaning of success and relate it to your own experience.
- Write *success (noun)* on the board and ask students if this is a positive or negative word. Tell students what it means (= to do or have something that you really wanted to do or have).

DICTIONARY SKILLS If students have a dictionary, get them to practise their dictionary skills by asking them to look up the adjective and verb of this noun (= successful; succeed). Show them that most words are found by looking up the root form of the word (noun or verb) and then searching through the definition for other forms of the word. Check the pronunciation of all forms of the word.

Reading & Grammar *was* and *were*

Exercise 1
- Ask students to work in their groups and give an example of someone who is successful, e.g. a famous sports person, a business person who has done very well, a student who has passed exams. Ask students to think about the sentence *To be successful a person needs …*
- Tell them to think of different ways to finish the sentence. Tell them to read the instructions in exercise 1 and create their lists.
- Ask students to write their ideas on the board. Have a class discussion to find out if people agree on ideas.

Exercise 2
- Put students into pairs. Ask them if they have heard of Vera Wang or Akio Morita.
- Pre-teach:
  fail (v) (= the opposite of *succeed* or *pass*, e.g. *She failed the exam. Her mark was below 50%.*)
  ice skater (n)/*to skate* (v) (= a person who skates on ice – draw a pair of ice skates to define this)
  founder (n) (= a person who starts a company)
- Ask students to decide who is Student A and who is Student B. Tell students to complete the exercise.

- Check answers together.

ANSWERS

	Vera Wang	Akio Morita
Born (when?)	1949	1921
First job	at Vogue magazine	businessman
Problems	She wasn't in the US Olympic ice skating team in 1968. This made her very unhappy.	They developed an electric rice cooker that didn't sell well and burnt the rice.
Famous for … (what?)	Her own Vera Wang fashion label	Founder of Sony

Exercise 3
- Tell students to summarize their stories for each other, then complete the table and discuss the questions.
- Ask the class for some feedback on which story was more interesting and why.

EXTRA CHALLENGE Ask students to say why these people were successful, e.g. *They were successful because they had lots of problems but they didn't give up.*

EXTRA ACTIVITY Ask students to write a short biography of a person they think is successful, using these texts as a model. They could research the people in class if they have access to the internet or they could do this for homework.

Exercise 4

At this level students will probably have seen the past simple forms *was* and *were* before. The Grammar focus here will revise and consolidate this grammar for them.
- Ask students to read the instructions and underline the verbs *was* and *were* in the article.
- Refer students to the Grammar focus box and ask them to complete the exercise.
- Check answers.

ANSWERS
1 was 2 wasn't 3 were 4 weren't

EXTENSION Use two of the categories from the reading to practise *was* and *were*. Write these words on the board: *born* and *first job*. Ask students to help you make questions. Write these questions on the board:
Where/When were you born? What was your first job? Tell students to walk around the class and ask and answer these questions.

Refer students to *Grammar reference* on p146. There are four more exercises here that students can do for homework.

Exercise 5a

> **Text summary:** The article is about a Jamaican bobsleigh team who competed at the 1988 Winter Olympics although they had no ice to practise on in Jamaica.

- Refer students to the text about the bobsleigh team. Teach the meaning of *bobsleigh* (= a type of sledge for racing down an icy track).

- Ask them to read the text and discuss what's unusual about the bobsleigh team (the team is from Jamaica and there is no snow in Jamaica).
- Tell students to complete the exercise.

Exercise 5b 6.1 💿

- Play track 6.1 and tell students to listen and check their answers.
- Ask students if they have seen the film. Was it good?

ANSWERS

1 were   2 wasn't   3 was   4 were   5 weren't   6 were
7 was   8 was

AUDIOSCRIPT 6.1

People were surprised to see a bobsleigh team from Jamaica at the 1988 Winter Olympics in Canada. It wasn't very easy for the team to practise in Jamaica before the Olympics because there was no ice and there were no bobsleighs for them to use. They weren't successful in their races, but they were very popular with the people watching because they tried so hard. There was a film telling their story in 1993 called *Cool Runnings* and it was a huge success, making $150,000,000 around the world.

Pronunciation   the past of *to be*

Exercise 6a 6.2 💿

PRONUNCIATION   *Was* and *were* have strong and weak forms. /wɒz/ and /wəz/ and /wɜː/ and /wə/. Usually they are weak in questions and positive sentences, but strong in short answers.

- Play track 6.2 and ask students to listen and complete the exercise.

ANSWERS

Was/were/wasn't/weren't are stressed in the answers.

Exercise 6b 6.2 💿

- Play track 6.2 again and ask students to listen and repeat. Pause the track after each sentence.

Exercise 7a

- Refer students to the example.
- Tell students to work in pairs. Ask them to work together and write the questions.

ANSWERS

1 Were you hungry this morning?
2 Were you a good student at school?
3 Was your partner late for class today?
4 Was your teacher at work yesterday?
5 Were your school friends from the same town as you?
6 Were you at home at seven o'clock last night?

Exercise 7b

- Tell students to take turns asking and answering the questions.

FEEDBACK FOCUS   Listen to the pronunciation of *was* and *were*. Drill the correct pronunciation again if necessary and ask students to repeat.

WATCH OUT!   Some students confuse the pronunciation of *were*, *we're* and *where*. Write these on the board and drill them. Ask students to come to the board and write sentences using the words. Drill the sentences.

Vocabulary & Speaking   time expressions

Exercise 8a

- Refer students to the photo. Ask students what it shows and refer them to questions 1–6 for the answer. Answer: it shows the first football World Cup.
- Put students into pairs and tell them to complete the exercise.
- Ask students to compare their answers with another pair. Encourage them to give reasons, e.g. *The first Olympics were 2,800 years ago. The other dates are too late. The Olympics were in Ancient Greece.*

Exercise 8b 6.3 💿

- Play track 6.3 and ask students to listen and check their answers.

ANSWERS

1 d   2 e   3 b   4 f   5 c   6 a

AUDIOSCRIPT 6.3

1 The first football World Cup was in the last century, in 1930.
2 The first Olympic Games were about 2,800 years ago, in 776 BCE.
3 The first dishwasher was in the 19th century.
4 The first Sony Walkman was in 1979.
5 The first talking film was in 1927.
6 The first Oscars ceremony was in 1929.

FEEDBACK FOCUS   Listen for correct use of *was* and *were* in grammar and pronunciation. Write errors on the board and ask students to work in pairs and correct the pronunciation and grammar.

Exercise 9

- Write _____ 1929 and 2,800 years _____ on the board and ask students to say what goes in the spaces. (*In* and *ago*).
- Refer students to the time expressions in the box and tell them to complete the exercise. Ask them to compare their answers with a partner. Tell students the expressions must refer to the past. For example, *in three weeks* is possible but it refers to the future – we are focusing on past time references.
- Check pronunciation of the vocabulary.

ANSWERS

in	last	ago
1999	night	a long time
the 18th century	year	three weeks
2001	week	six months
	summer	

Exercise 10a

- Tell students to work alone and complete the exercise.
- To make this a more active exercise, you could write the expressions on large pieces of card and ask students to arrange the cards on the board or wall.

Exercise 10b

- Ask students to work in pairs and compare their answers.

a long time ago   in the 18th century   in 1999   in 2001

last year   last summer   three weeks ago

last week   last night

EXTENSION To practise writing sentences with *I was ...* .
Write the time expressions on the board or use the cards you
created. Point to one of the times and ask a student to say
where they were. Do this with different times and different
students. You could also ask students to come to the board
and do this or ask them to practise this in pairs pointing to
the times in their book.

Exercise 11a

- Ask a student: *Where were you at 10 a.m. yesterday?* Write
  their answer on the board and ask the class to help you
  write the correct grammar. *I was at home*, for example.
- Ask students to read the time phrases and complete the
  exercise.

EXTRA SUPPORT If you think students might find it difficult to
write the sentences, add some examples of your own to the
board to help them with vocabulary.
For example: *I was in bed/at home/on the train/in my car/at
the cinema/in a restaurant/on the beach/on holiday/at school/
at work.*

EXTRA CHALLENGE Point out to students that time
expressions can also go at the start of the sentence, e.g.
Last Tuesday I was on the beach.

- Ask fast finishers to change some of their sentences so the
  time expression is at the beginning.

Exercise 11b

- Refer students to the sample dialogue.
- Demonstrate the exercise with a confident student.
- Ask the students to ask you questions to guess where you
  were at the times.
- Tell students to work in pairs and complete the exercise.

EXTRA ACTIVITY To give extra practice with *was* and *were*,
ask students to choose a time word/expression. Teach the
question *Where were you* + time expression? and write it on
the board, e.g. *Where were you yesterday afternoon/last night/
last summer/last Saturday, etc?*

Tell them to walk around the class asking different people
their question. After they have spoken to at least four
different people, you could ask them to sit with a partner
and tell them what they remember, e.g. *Joan was at work
yesterday afternoon. Sara was at the cinema last night.*

GRAMMAR REFERENCE ANSWERS

Exercise 1
1 were   2 Were; weren't   3 was   4 Was; was   5 were
6 Was; wasn't   7 Were; were   8 were

Exercises 2 & 3
1 Where were; f   2 Who was; b   3 When was; e
4 What was; j   5 Why were; d   6 Was the film; a
7 Were they; g   8 Where were; i   9 Why was; h
10 Why was; c

Exercise 4
1 was   2 was   3 was   4 was   5 were   6 were
7 were   8 was   9 was   10 weren't

6.2 Stories

Goals
- Use regular verbs to talk about what happened in the past
- Use common collocations

Lead-in

1 Open book. To create interest in the topic and assess
  vocabulary use.

- Put students into pairs. Students take turns to describe the
  photos to their partners. Encourage them to ask questions
  about the photos their partner is describing, e.g.
  *A There is a photo of some snakes. I think they're made of
  metal. They're old, I think.
  B How old are they? How many are there?
  A I think they're very old. There are eight.*

- Students then look at the photos their partner was
  describing and tell them how good their description was.

2 Closed book. To assess vocabulary use.

- Ask students to get out some money from their pocket or
  purse/wallet.
- Ask the class this question and write money vocabulary
  on the board as you discuss the answers:
  What do you call your money? (Possible answers = *cent,
  dollar, pound, pence, coin, note* etc.). Teach the meanings
  of *coin* (= metal money), *note* (= paper money) and
  currency (= the money of a country, e.g. *pounds, dollars*) if
  necessary.

Listening & Grammar   past simple regular verbs

Exercise 1a

- Put students into groups of three or four. Give them a time
  limit of one or two minutes and tell them to make a list of
  as many different currencies as they can.
- Ask one student from each group to write their answers
  on the board.
- Check pronunciation.

POSSIBLE ANSWERS

euro, peso, dinar, real, franc, peso, forint, yen, dirham,
rupee, zloty, riyal, krone

Exercise 1b

- Refer students to the photos and ask them to read the
  words in the box. Check they understand the vocabulary.
- Ask students to label the photos in their books and
  compare their answers with a partner.

Background note: The ancient Chinese had coins with
holes in the middle. They used string to join a lot of coins
together (the usual amount was 1000 coins). They did this
because single coins had very little value on their own,
so people had to carry a lot of coins to pay for things.
The string made it easier to carry the large number of
coins. People would carry these strings of coins over their
shoulders, as they were very heavy.

EXTENSION Ask students to guess which country the currencies came from, e.g. *Maybe the Egyptians gave rings to buy things.* Tell them they'll find out the answers later in the lesson.

ANSWERS

a metal snakes   **b** coins   **c** rings   **d** salt

Exercise 2   6.4 🔊

> **Audio summary:** A radio programme with some factual information about the history of money. It talks about how money was used in Egypt, Turkey, China, countries in the Roman Empire and Ancient Ghana.

- Play track 6.4 and tell students to put the photos in order.
- Check answers together.

ANSWERS

c 1   **b** 2   **d** 3   **a** 4

AUDIOSCRIPT 6.4

Welcome to *The Money Programme*. Today we're talking about the history of money. These days most people use notes, coins and credit cards to buy things. But people in the past used different ways of paying for things.

The Ancient Egyptians liked wearing their money on their fingers as rings. The rings were made of gold. When they wanted to pay for something they pulled a ring or two off their fingers.

People in ancient Turkey were some of the first to use coins as money in the 7th century BCE. The Romans also used coins but added pictures of their emperors to them in the first century BCE. The Chinese put their coins on a piece of string to make them more valuable.

For hundreds of years, people around the world paid for things with salt. In fact, the word 'salary' comes from a Latin word that means 'money used to buy salt'. This is because the Romans sometimes paid their soldiers with salt.

The Lobi people of Ancient Ghana in Africa lived as farmers. Because they worked in the fields and there were a lot of snakes, they decided to make metal snakes and use them as money. They believed their snake money helped them to stay safe.

Exercise 3   6.4 🔊

- Tell students to read through the sentences.
- Play track 6.4 again and tell students to complete the exercise.
- Check answers together.
- Finally, write *salary* on the board and ask students what they think it means (= money somebody earns every month).

ANSWERS

1 The **Egyptians** used jewellery as money.
2 The **Romans** copied a Turkish idea in the first century BCE.
3 The **Romans** earned something you can eat.
4 The **Lobi** believed their money was lucky.

EXTRA CHALLENGE Ask students to discuss these questions about the recording.

1 Why did people use salt as currency? (Answer: salt was important for keeping food fresh in those times, so it was worth a lot.)
2 Do you think the systems were better than ours?

CRITICAL THINKING To reflect on a question. Ask students to work in small groups and discuss if they think money is a good or bad thing. You could ask them to think of two good things and two bad things.

Exercise 4a

- Refer students back to the sentences in exercise 3 and direct this question to the whole class. (Answer: before now.)

Exercise 4b

- Still referring to the sentences in exercise 3, tell students to find the verbs in the past and then complete the Grammar focus box.
- Put students into pairs and ask them to compare answers, and then check answers with the class.
- Test students by asking them to think of one or two more verbs for each rule. Write them on the board.

ANSWERS

Verbs in exercise 3:
1 used   **2** copied   **3** earned   **4** believed
Grammar focus box:
1 *-ed*   **2** *-d*   **3** *-ied*

- Refer students to *Grammar reference* on p147. There are three more exercises here that students can do for homework.

Pronunciation *-ed* ending in past simple verbs

Exercise 5a   6.5 🔊

- Write *started planned cooked* on the board and tell students that the *-ed* ending is pronounced differently in each word. Ask students to say the words to each other to discover how the pronunciation is different.
- Play track 6.5 and tell students to listen to the recording and read the text.
- Refer students to the phonemes at the beginning of each line and drill these sounds.
- Play the track again, pause after each line and ask students to repeat.

PRONUNCIATION Verbs that end in /t/ or /d/ have an extra syllable on the end when we add *-ed* to form the past simple. Other verbs will not have an extra syllable. They will have the /t/ or /d/ sound at the end of the verb. Students can find this difficult because they have to pronounce two consonant sounds together. This is called a consonant cluster.

Exercise 5b   6.6 🔊

- Ask students to read through the verbs and check they understand the meaning. Tell them to try saying them quietly to themselves and decide which line they might go on.
- Play track 6.6 and tell students to add the words to the correct line.
- If your students like to move around in class and work as a team, you could add the words in exercises 5a and 5b to large cards and ask students to stick them in three columns on the board to distinguish the pronunciation.

Exercise 5c 6.7 🔘

- Play track 6.7 and ask students to check their answers.
- Pause the recording after each word and tell students to repeat.

/d/ believed, copied, loved, moved, prepared, received, used

/t/ liked, noticed, worked

/id/ posted, shouted, waited, wanted

EXTRA ACTIVITY To check students understand the meaning of the verbs in exercises 5a and 5b, put students into pairs. Divide the verbs secretly among the pairs. You could do this by writing the verbs on small pieces of paper and giving them to the pairs.

Tell them to write sentences using their verbs but to leave a space where the verb should go. Tell pairs to swap sentences and try to fill the spaces with the correct verb.

Exercise 6

- This exercise involves intensive listening and forces students to focus on their pronunciation. You could tell the class that this activity is to help them improve their speaking and listening skills.

EXTRA SUPPORT If you think your students will find this difficult or if you have different levels in your class, you could ask students to work together on their sentences; so two As work together and two Bs work together. Regroup them into A and B pairs to complete the story exercise.

- Put students into pairs: one Student A and one Student B. Explain they are going to work together to create a story from sentences.
- Refer them to the correct pages and tell them to read the instructions.
- You might need to pre-teach: *owner* (= a person who has their own company, house or object, e.g. *Jana is the owner of this bag. It's her bag*); *amount* (= quantity); *cab* (= a taxi).

WATCH OUT! In Student A's text they use *taxi* and in Student B's text they use *cab*. Tell students that British English uses *taxi* and American English uses *cab*.

- Monitor closely and check answers as students fill in the gaps. Write the answers on the board.
- Demonstrate the second part of the activity with a stronger student and explain that they will have to listen carefully to each other's sentences and then order the sentences to create the story. You may want to tell them to write down each other's sentences as they listen to make the ordering activity clearer.
- Tell students to read and listen to each other's sentences. Students will have to repeat their sentences a few times so their partner understands everything.
- Ask students to work together to create a story from the sentences.
- Ask students to work with another pair and compare their stories.

EXTENSION Ask the class to work together and recreate the story on the board so everyone can check their answers. Discuss this as a class. Did they all make similar mistakes (if any)?

Student A

a 1 returned 2 called

b 3 worked

c 4 looked 5 noticed

d 6 thanked

Student B

a 1 opened

b 2 decided

c 3 collected

d 4 finished 5 started

A b B d A c B a A a B c A d B b

EXTENSION Ask students if they know any similar stories, and if so, to tell the class what happened.

Vocabulary & Speaking common regular verb collocations

Exercise 7a

- Remind students what collocations are (= words that are regularly used together).
- Put students into pairs and ask them to underline the words that form collocations with the verbs on the left.
- Check answers.

1 wait: for a long time, for a friend

2 post: a letter, a comment on a web page

3 enter: a race, a competition

4 move: jobs, to the countryside, house

5 visit: a museum, a relative

6 shout: at your dog, at someone

7 prepare: a meal, for an exam

8 receive: an email, a phone call

9 call: a taxi, an old friend

10 use: a dictionary, a tablet

Exercise 7b 6.8 🔘

- Play track 6.8 and ask students to check their answers. Then play the track again so they can repeat.

AUDIOSCRIPT 6.8

1 wait for a long time, wait for a friend

2 post a letter, post a comment on a webpage

3 enter a race, enter a competition

4 move to the countryside, move house

5 visit a museum, visit a relative

6 shout at your dog, shout at someone

7 prepare a meal, prepare for an exam

8 receive an email, receive a phone call

9 call a taxi, call an old friend

10 use a dictionary, use a tablet

EXTENSION Ask students to think of the correct pronunciation of these verbs in the past simple. Put students into pairs and ask them to practise saying the verbs with the *-ed* ending. Check their pronunciation and drill any problem words.

Exercise 8a

- Ask students to work alone to read the questions and match them to the correct answers.
- Ask them to compare their answers with the person next to them.

Exercise 8b 6.9 🔘

- Play track 6.9 and tell students to listen and check their answers.

ANSWERS

1 f   2 j   3 g   4 a   5 d   6 b   7 e   8 c   9 h   10 i

AUDIOSCRIPT 6.9

1
A When was the last time you moved house?
B In 2010. From an apartment to a house.
2
A When was the last time you received an email?
B This morning. It was from my boss.
3
A When was the last time you prepared a meal?
B Last night. I cooked spaghetti for my housemate.
4
A When was the last time you posted a letter?
B A month ago. It was to my friend in Australia.
5
A When was the last time you shouted at someone?
B About a week ago. My son was very naughty.
6
A When was the last time you visited a relative?
B Last summer. I travelled to Kenya to see my grandmother.
7
A When was the last time you called a taxi?
B Yesterday. I was late for work.
8
A When was the last time you entered a competition?
B When I was a child. I was in a swimming race.
9
A When was the last time you used a dictionary?
B Last week. I checked the meaning of 'coin'.
10
A When was the last time you waited for a long time?
B Two hours ago. My bus was very late.

Exercise 8c 6.10 🔘

- Play track 6.10 and ask students to repeat the questions.
- You could ask them to focus on the stressed words and the intonation for an extra challenge. Remember, in *wh-*questions the intonation usually goes down or stays flat at the end.

STUDY TIP Encourage students to write down the collocations in exercise 8. Tell them that collocations are a good way to remember vocabulary. You could tell them to write the verbs and think of other nouns for some of the verbs. For example:
To move: house, from one city/country to another
To receive: an email, a present/gift
To post: a letter, a postcard, something on a website, blog or forum

AUDIOSCRIPT 6.10

1 When was the last time you moved house?
2 When was the last time you received an email?
3 When was the last time you prepared a meal?
4 When was the last time you posted a letter?
5 When was the last time you shouted at someone?
6 When was the last time you visited a relative?
7 When was the last time you called a taxi?

8 When was the last time you entered a competition?
9 When was the last time you used a dictionary?
10 When was the last time you waited for a long time?

Exercise 9a

- Tell students to work alone and think about their answers.
- Make sure they know to write their answers in the wrong order. To clarify, you could demonstrate the activity on the board.

Exercise 9b

- Put students into pairs and ask them to read the instructions and sample dialogue.
- Demonstrate the activity with a student so the class are clear on what to do.
- Ask students to work in their pairs and complete the exercise.

EXTRA CHALLENGE If you have fast finishers, you could extend their range of vocabulary with this activity. Put students into groups of three and ask them to think of four or five more verbs. Tell them to ask and answer questions using *When was the last time you* (+ verb) … ?

Ask students to work together and write five or six sentences about the information they discussed, e.g. *Miriam started her English classes last year.*

GRAMMAR REFERENCE ANSWERS

Exercise 1
1 The hotel room included breakfast yesterday.
2 I posted our letters last Monday.
3 We waited for twenty minutes for my sister.
4 I wanted a new laptop last week.
5 They visited my uncle (once) in May 2013.
6 People used money to buy things 500 years ago.
7 He shouted at his brother for an hour.
8 I liked dancing in the 1980s.

Exercise 2
1 chatted   2 enjoyed   3 listened   4 carried
5 changed   6 started   7 called   8 stopped

Exercise 3
1 worked   2 happened   3 noticed   4 waited
5 walked   6 asked   7 showed   8 stayed   9 shouted
10 wanted   11 looked   12 opened   13 changed
14 closed   15 walked

6.3 Vocabulary and skills development

Goals

- Understand present and past simple verbs
- Use adverbs of degree

Lead-in

1 Closed book. To review verbs learnt in lesson 6.2.

- Put students into pairs and give them one or two minutes to write down all the verbs they can remember from the last lesson.
- Ask students to count how many verbs they remembered. Ask them to write them on the board. As they write them on the board, you could elicit nouns the verbs collocate with and write them on the board.

- Check pronunciation of the verbs in the present and then ask students to say the verbs in the past. Elicit the rule for pronouncing -ed endings. (The main rule to focus on is that after /t/ or /d/ we add a syllable.)
2 Closed book. To create interest in the topic of art galleries and visiting museums.
- Tell students that a friend is coming to visit you who loves art and visiting galleries.
- Put students into pairs and ask them to think of places you can tell your friend to visit.
- Ask students to discuss galleries and museums they know in the city or town you are in and if they like visiting them.
- Listen to their conversations and write useful vocabulary that emerges on the board. Go over the meaning and pronunciation after they have finished and encourage them to record it in their notebooks.

Listening & Speaking understanding present and past simple verbs

Exercise 1
- Put students into groups of three or four. Tell them to read the statements and discuss their opinions in their groups.
- Ask some students to report what people in their group said.

Exercise 2 6.11 💿
- Play track 6.11 and ask students to listen and tell you what is different about the two sentences. If they don't identify the past and present verbs tell them to listen again and to identify which is past and which is present.
- Check the answer.

ANSWER
Sentence 1 is in the past. *visited* is a past simple verb form and *last* is an adverb used with *week/day/year* to talk about a time in the past.
Sentence 2 is in the present. *visit* is a present simple verb form and *every* is an adverb used with *morning/day/ Monday, etc.* to talk about a fact or a habit that is always true.

AUDIOSCRIPT 6.11
1 Five thousand people visited this gallery last month.
2 Fifty thousand people visit this gallery every year.

Exercise 3 6.12 💿
- Ask students if all verbs are as easy to hear in the past. They should realize that the answer is no. Most verbs don't have an extra syllable and it can be hard to hear the -ed ending.
- Refer students to the Unlock the code box. Play track 6.12 and tell students to read and listen.
- You could tell students that we can also usually understand if someone is talking about the past or present from the context of the conversation or situation.

Exercise 4a 6.13 💿
- Tell students you are going to test their listening skills.
- Play track 6.13 and ask them to identify if they hear a present or past verb. You may need to play the recording twice.

- Ask students to compare their answers with the person sitting next to them.
- Check answers together.

ANSWERS/AUDIOSCRIPT 6.13
1 cooked   2 carried   3 change   4 helped   5 wait
6 listened   7 chatted   8 dance   9 enjoyed

Exercise 4b 6.13 💿
- Play track 6.13 again and ask students to listen and repeat.
WATCH OUT! There may be some consonant sounds that students don't have in their first language. This will make the pronunciation difficult for them. It may distract from focusing on the -ed endings. For example, some students find it difficult to say the sound /dʒ/ in *change*, while others find the /r/ in *carried* difficult. You could use this opportunity to help students who have problems with sounds in this exercise by showing them how to make the sounds with their mouths.

Exercise 5a 6.14 💿
- Play track 6.14 and ask students to listen and complete the exercise. Tell them to focus on the verbs and listen for any time references. You may need to repeat the track.
- Check answers together. Ask students how they decided on their answers.
- Play the track again and ask students to repeat the sentences.

ANSWERS
1 past   2 present   3 past   4 present   5 past   6 past

AUDIOSCRIPT 6.14
1 My friends cooked a great meal for me last night.
2 A lot of people at work listen to the radio these days.
3 I helped my parents a lot when I was a child.
4 We dance a lot when we go out.
5 I waited a long time for the bus last Monday.
6 I washed the car carefully, it was really dirty.

Exercise 5b
- Ask students to compare their answers with a partner.
- Check the answers together as a class.
EXTENSION Ask students to work in pairs. Ask them to refer to the audioscript and take turns to say the sentences to each other. Drilling in pairs can help students to feel less worried about making mistakes.

Exercise 6a

Audio summary: Inhotim is a garden space in Brazil which is famous for the art in its grounds. You can find out more about it here: http://www.inhotim.org.br/en/

- Refer students to the photos and ask them to read the questions and try to guess the answers.
- Put students into pairs and ask them to discuss the questions. Get some ideas from the group.

Exercise 6b 6.15 💿
- Pre-teach vocabulary and place names if you think your students will find this recording difficult.
fields (= land where farmers grow plants and keep animals)

billionaire (= a person who is worth one billion dollars or pounds)
Bernardo Paz (= a man's name)
Disneyland (= an amusement park for children)
sculpture (= a form of art where people create solid objects, often made from marble or bronze – translate this if you know it in the learners' first language for quick understanding)

- Play track 6.15 and ask students to check their answers.

ANSWERS

1 Before the 1990s, Inhotim was a farm in the Brazilian countryside.
2 Now it is a 'Disneyland for art lovers', an 'outdoor museum' which displays thousands of works by Brazilian and international artists with approximately 250,000 visitors a year.
3 It is important culturally but also for the 1,000 local people who work in its museums, gardens and restaurants.

AUDIOSCRIPT 6.15

From a distance, Inhotim looks like typical Brazilian countryside, but as you get closer, you notice something a bit unusual. There are hundreds of tourists walking through the fields and gardens! This beautiful place started as a farm and for many years only farmers lived here. They worked in the fields and looked after the animals. But that all changed in the 1990s when billionaire Bernardo Paz decided to use the space for something very different. He created a 'Disneyland for art lovers'! Today, people travel from around the world and they look at the art. The spaces of Inhotim include more than 500 sculptures by Brazilian and international artists. As well as being important culturally, it is really important for the local area because Inhotim creates a lot of jobs – 1,000 people work here in the museum, gardens and restaurant. Although it is quite far from the usual tourist spots of Brazil, it is now a very successful and popular 'outdoor museum'. In 2011, nearly a quarter of a million people visited Inhotim. Mr Paz believes there will soon be a million visitors a year.

Exercise 7a 6.15 🎵

- Ask students to read the verbs.
- Play track 6.15 again and ask them to mark the verbs that they hear in the past and leave the verbs that they hear in the present.
- You may need to play the recording twice or more. For extra support isolate sentences that students find difficult. Encourage them to listen for time references.
- Check answers together.

ANSWERS

present: notice, travel, look, include, work
past simple: start(ed), live(d), work(ed), look(ed), change(d), decide(d), visit(ed)

EXTRA CHALLENGE Ask students to work in pairs and discuss if they would like to visit Inhotim and why. Ask them to talk about similar places they know of and when they went there.

Exercise 7b

- Ask students to change the present verbs into the past.
- Check answers together.
- Check the pronunciation of all the verbs.

WATCH OUT! Draw attention to the fact that in British English we double consonants that end in consonant-vowel-consonant patterns when we form the past simple. This applies in verbs like *travel*. You could tell students that in American English the consonant is not doubled.

ANSWERS

noticed   started   lived   worked   looked   changed
decided   travelled   looked   included   worked
visited

PRONUNCIATION Remind students that we only pronounce the -ed ending if the infinitive form of the verb ends in /t/ or /d/. Ask them to identify which verbs end in these sounds in exercise 7a (*start, decide, include, visit*).

Exercise 8

- As a lead-in to this exercise, you could demonstrate the conversation with a student. Make sentences about yourself using the verbs in the past and the present. Try to include some time references to help the listener.
- Ask the student to identify if you are talking about the past or present.
- Refer students to the example dialogue as well. Put students into pairs and tell them to take turns making sentences and identifying if the sentences they hear are in the past or present.

EXTRA SUPPORT If you think your learners will find it difficult to make sentences spontaneously, then tell them to write sentences first in the past and the present.

EXTRA ACTIVITY Ask students to remember what their partner told them and to write a sentence about them using past simple and a time reference on a small piece of paper. Tell them to write their partner's name on the paper. Collect all the papers and give them out to different students. Ask students to walk around and read their sentence to other students (not saying the name). Listeners have to guess who the sentence is about. If they can't guess, ask students to say who it's about. After five minutes, ask them to sit with a partner and talk about what they can remember about different people in the class.

Vocabulary & Listening adverbs of degree

Exercise 9a

- As a lead-in, write this sentence on the board and ask students what could go in the gap to make the sentence more specific:
  The painting was _____ beautiful.
- Elicit adverbs. Possible answers: *really, very, quite,* etc.
- Refer students to the sentences and the Vocabulary focus box and tell them to read about adverbs of degree.
- Check grammar by asking about word order, e.g. *Do we put the adverb before or after the adjective?* (Answer: before) Then ask them which has a stronger meaning, *a bit* or *really*? (Answer: really)

Exercise 9b

- Refer students to the line from 0% to 100% and ask them to place the adverbs on it.
- Check answers together.
- To check understanding you could ask some questions, e.g.
  Teacher: How warm is it today?
  Students: It's really warm/It's quite warm.
  Teacher: How big is this room?
  Students: It's quite small.

ANSWERS
1 a bit 2 quite 3 very 4 really

WATCH OUT! We often use *a bit* to indicate that there might be a problem, e.g.
Can I walk to the park from here? Not really. It's a bit far.
It's a bit hot to wear those jeans today.

- You could ask students to think of more examples.

EXTENSION Tell students about the use of *a bit* + adj (in the Watch out! feature above). Ask students to complete these sentences with their own ideas to consolidate understanding. Encourage them to add information before and after the sentence. Examples:
_____ is very cold. (*Winter is very cold here. It can be −20°.*)
_____ is quite easy.
_____ is a bit difficult.
_____ is really beautiful.

Exercise 10a 6.16

- To practise adverbs, ask students again if they would like to visit Inhotim. Why? Elicit use of the adverbs, e.g. *I think it is really interesting.*
- Play track 6.16 and ask students to complete the exercise. Tell them to compare answers with a partner. You may need to play the recording again so students can check their answers.

ANSWERS
1 Speaker 1 is more positive about the sculptures.
2 Speaker 2 is more positive about the gardens.
3 Speaker 2 is more positive about the food and restaurants.
4 Speaker 1 is more positive about the journey.

Exercise 10b 6.16

- Play the recording again and tell students to listen for the phrases that helped them decide who is more positive. For extra support pause the recording after each phrase they should write.
- Tell students to compare their answers with a partner before going through the answers with the class.

ANSWERS
1 very interesting (a bit boring) 2 really beautiful (quite nice) 3 quite good (really expensive) 4 quite long (really long)

AUDIOSCRIPT 6.16

S1 I visited Inhotim last week. My main reason for going was the art, and the sculptures were very interesting. The gardens were quite nice, too. However, the restaurants were really expensive. It was a bit difficult to find, too, and the journey was quite long.

S2 I travelled to Inhotim a couple of months ago. I thought the sculptures in the park were a bit boring, actually, but the gardens were really beautiful. The food was quite good at the restaurants. Oh, and the journey to the park was really long and I was very tired when I arrived.

Pronunciation sentence stress

Exercise 11 6.17

- Play track 6.17 and ask students to read the sentences and listen to the pronunciation. Ask them to identify which adverb is stressed most. (Answer: *really* is stressed most clearly.)
- Explain that we often stress *really* to show we feel strongly about something. With other adverbs we don't put as much stress on them because we don't feel as strongly.
- Ask students to practise saying the sentences to each other with appropriate stress.

PRONUNCIATION Encourage them to exaggerate with *really*, e.g. *It was **really** good!* Some students find it difficult and a little uncomfortable adding stress, as their first language doesn't vary stress as much as English. If they exaggerate, it can help them reach the correct levels of emphasis. Tell students to work with a partner and practise saying the sentence to each other.

Exercise 12

CRITICAL THINKING Express your likes and preferences. As a lead-in to this exercise, you could show some photos of modern art and ask students to describe the images and give their opinions. Respond to their descriptions to show agreement or disagreement.

- Refer students to the sentences and ask them to read them and think about their opinion and circle an adjective.
- Put students into pairs and refer them to the sample dialogue. Ask them to discuss their opinions, using the adjectives and adverbs of degree. Tell them to respond to each other and agree or disagree.

POSSIBLE ANSWERS
2
A Clothes in this country are really expensive.
B No, they aren't! They're really cheap.
3
A The classroom is quite hot today.
B No, it isn't! It's very cold.
4
A Trains and buses are quite slow in this country.
B No, they aren't! They're quite fast.
5
A Cars are really dangerous.
B No they aren't. They're quite safe.

Exercise 13a

- As a lead-in, tell students about a place you have visited in the last two years. You could take in photos or leaflets from the place if you have some. Model the language used in this lesson. Encourage students to ask you questions about your story.
- Refer students to the questions and ask them to discuss if you spoke about all these areas in your story.

- Tell students to think about a place or event they went to in the last two years to get ready to tell a story. Remind them to use two to three adverbs of degree.
- Monitor and help students with language. Encourage them to make notes about their story and not to write it out in full.

Exercise 13b

- Put students into groups of three or four. Tell them to tell their stories and to ask each other questions.
- Tell the listeners to write down the adjectives and adverbs of degree.
- Ask one student to report on what their group talked about and how well they used adverbs.

EXTRA ACTIVITY To consolidate adverbs of degree. Tell students to write an email to a friend describing a visit to a place and using at least three adverbs of degree. This could be done for homework.

6.4 Speaking and writing

Goals

- Tell a story
- Show interest
- Write a tweet or text message

Lead-in

1 Closed book. To listen to a story and discuss the aims of the lesson.

- Think of a funny/strange/scary story you can tell the class and prepare it before the lesson.
- Tell students your story and ask them to think about when they hear or tell stories to friends in their own language. Do they listen silently or do they respond (say things to show interest and that they are listening)? Hopefully students will say they respond. Ask them to think of typical things they might say in English to find out what they already know. If they can't think of any language ask them to think about what they say in their own language.
- Tell students they are going to learn to respond to stories in the lesson so they can show interest.

2 Closed book. To review language from lesson 6.3. To model the language from this lesson.

- Put students into pairs and ask them to remember the stories they spoke about in the last lesson and to tell their partner.
- Ask a volunteer to tell you their story. Respond and use the language from this lesson to show interest.
- Ask students to think about what you said and did while you listened.

Speaking & Listening showing interest as a listener

Exercise 1

- Put students into pairs and refer them to the photos. Ask them to describe the first photo.
- Ask students to work with their partner and complete the exercise.

- There are no right or wrong answers at this point. Ask some pairs to describe their ideas about the story. Encourage students to listen to what other pairs say and agree or disagree.
- Write any useful vocabulary on the board as you listen and check meaning and pronunciation with the group.

EXTRA SUPPORT The collocation *miss the bus/train/plane* can be a difficult concept for some students. Draw attention to the use of *miss* in this context. If you miss a class dinner, you don't go because it is not possible – usually something happens that means you can't go.

Exercise 2 6.18 🔘

- Tell students they are going to hear the story related to the photos.
- Play track 6.18 and ask them to listen and see how similar their ideas were to the story. They also have to listen for why Oscar missed the dinner.
- Check answers together.

ANSWERS
1 a 2 c 3 f 4 b 5 d 6 e
Oscar missed his Business Management class dinner because he couldn't find his shoes, the bus was late, it started to rain, and then the taxi didn't come.

AUDIOSCRIPT 6.18
A … It was my Business Management class dinner on Saturday.
B That's great! How was it?
A I don't know. I didn't go.
B Oh no! Why not?
A Well, first I couldn't find my shoes.
B Really?
A Yeah … I looked everywhere. In the end I used my ordinary shoes. Then the bus was late. I waited for half an hour, but it never arrived!
B Oh no! That's awful!
A I know. After that it started to rain … so I called a taxi. And I waited and I waited … . In the end I decided to walk home. I was just so wet by the time I got home.
B What a nightmare! Poor you!
A I know. I was really angry about it …

Exercise 3 6.18 🔘

- Tell students to read through the expressions.
- Play track 6.18 again and ask students to tick the expressions they hear.
- Check answers together.
- Ask students how these phrases help the conversation. A possible answer is that the listener shows they are listening and following the story and they sounds interested. This makes the speaker continue with the story.

WATCH OUT! Draw attention to the meaning of *nightmare* (= a bad dream; used to mean a terrible situation) to help students understand this phrase. It's idiomatic.

ANSWERS
That's terrible! ☐   Really? ✓   That's brilliant! ☐
Poor you! ✓   What a nightmare! ✓   That's interesting! ☐
Oh no! ✓   That's great! ✓   That's awful! ✓
The expressions help the conversation by showing the listener is interested.

Exercise 4a

- Put students into pairs and ask them to decide which expressions are best for each type of news.

a good news: That's brilliant!, That's great!
b bad news: That's terrible!, Poor you!, What a nightmare!, Oh no!, That's awful!
c interesting news: Really?, That's interesting!

Exercise 4b

- Refer students to the Language for speaking box and ask them to read it and check their answers.

Exercise 5a   6.19

- Play track 6.19 and ask students to listen to the intonation. You could ask them to draw lines on the phrases to show the voice going up or down.

Exercise 5b   6.19

- Play the track again and ask students to repeat after each phrase. Check by asking the whole group, pairs and individuals to repeat.

PRONUNCIATION   To practise intonation to show emotion. Write the word *hello* on the board. Hum it to the students in different ways with your voice going up and up-down to show specific emotions. Ask students to say what you are feeling. For example, you could say it in an angry, happy, sad, excited or tired way.

- Tell students to hum *hello* to each other and guess the emotion. Tell them to repeat the word with different emotions.

Exercise 6

SMART COMMUNICATION   Some students may sound flat and uninterested when they speak English because their first language does not have as wide a pitch range as English. This makes it hard for them to hear and produce intonation with a wide enough pitch range. This speaking activity should focus on helping them to widen this pitch range to sound interested.

- Put students into pairs and tell them to decide who is Student A and who is Student B.
- Refer them to the communication pages and tell them to read the instructions on their page and ask you about any words they don't understand.
- Tell them to use the phrases from exercise 3 to respond to each other's news. You could write these phrases on strips of paper. Have enough for a set of phrases for each pair. Students can grab or discard the phrases as they use them.

FEEDBACK FOCUS   Sometimes students use the same phrases and avoid using new ones. As you listen check they are using a wide range of expressions. If you think there were moments when they could have used some of the new expressions, draw their attention to this.

EXTENSION   For an extra challenge they could expand on the story. Their partner can use the phrases to respond and show interest. For example:
Student A *I've got a new job!*
Student B *That's brilliant!*
Student A *It's in a big company. I'm very happy.*
Student B *That's great!*

EXTRA ACTIVITY   To practise responding in a more personalized way. Tell students to think of some real news they have. If they don't want to share real news, tell them to invent news. Tell them to walk around the room telling each other their news and responding.

EXTRA SUPPORT   Write the phrases on the board if you think students still need to refer to them.

POSSIBLE ANSWERS
Student A
a We moved house three times last year.
   That's terrible!/Poor you!/What a nightmare!/Oh no!/
   That's awful! It is really stressful, isn't it?
b Someone shouted at me in the street yesterday.
   That's terrible!/Poor you!/What a nightmare!/Oh no!/
   That's awful! What did you do?
c I've got a new job!
   Really?/That's brilliant/great! Congratulations!
d I walked ten miles on Sunday.
   Really?/That's brilliant/great! You are really fit!
e I've got too much work at the moment.
   That's terrible!/Poor you!/What a nightmare!/Oh no!/
   That's awful! Try to get an early night.
Student B
a I booked a holiday to Australia.
   Really?/That's brilliant/great! When do you go?
b I couldn't sleep last night.
   That's terrible!/Poor you!/What a nightmare!/Oh no!/
   That's awful! Did you sleep at all?
c I was on TV when I was a child.
   Really?/That's interesting! What were you in?
d I've got a cold.
   That's terrible!/Poor you!/What a nightmare!/Oh no!/
   That's awful! Take an aspirin.
e I watched a great film on TV last night.
   Really? What was it called?

Reading & Writing   write a tweet or text message

Exercise 7

> **Background note:** Some students may not have access to social media or they may use local social media sites. If you are teaching students from a different culture to your own or one that you do not know much about, then research local attitudes to social media and local social media sites.

CRITICAL THINKING   Discuss advantages and disadvantages. The third question encourages students to think about whether social media are useful or not. You could extend this and ask them to make a list of the advantages and disadvantages.

- Put students into groups of three or four and ask them to discuss the questions.
- Ask one student from each group to report on what their group talked about.
- Write any useful vocabulary that the students use on the board.

Exercise 8a

- Ask students to work alone and read the tweets and match them to the functions.

- Check! answers together.

1 tweet 3   **2** tweet 1   **3** tweet 2

Exercise 8b

- Tell students to read the responses and match them to the tweets.
- You might need to pre-teach *still* (= an adverb that describes a time period from the past up to and including now).
- Check answers together.
- Ask students what they notice about the language. Is it formal or informal? (Informal) Are they using full sentences? (No)

a 3   **b** 1   **c** 2

Exercise 9

- Refer students back to the first tweet and ask them to read it again.
- Put students into pairs and ask them to discuss the questions. Refer them to the Language for writing box to check their answers.

WATCH OUT! Some students wrongly say *Anyone know where …?* because they don't realize that in *Anyone know where …?* the *Does* is missed out. Point this out to the students.

1 Does anyone know where I can dance salsa? I really want to learn.
2 The tweets are informal and written quickly. We can leave out auxiliary verbs and subject pronouns to keep them brief.

SMART COMMUNICATION When we write tweets, forum posts and SMS messages we use informal language and we use an ellipsis (this is when we leave out parts of a sentence). Students at this level will be exposed to language in different registers and it is important to make them aware of how to adapt their register to the means of communication.

EXTENSION Ask students to work in small groups and discuss how they write tweets and SMS messages in their own language. Do they use similar methods to shorten language? They could discuss *abbreviations* (= shorter forms) and *emoticons* (= little faces or symbols showing emotions) if you feel it is appropriate for your group. Some common abbreviations are LOL – laugh out loud and Thx – Thanks.

Exercise 10

- Refer students to the tweet replies and ask them to find more examples of ellipses. You could ask them to write the tweets out in full sentences to consolidate their understanding.

a Really? I saw it years ago and I hated it. **It was** boring!
b Try Café Sol. I think they have classes on Mondays.
c Ha ha! **Are** you still at work? Don't wake her up. Then you can go home!

Exercise 11

- Ask students to work alone and to read the tweets and complete the exercise. Do the first tweet together.

- Ask students to work with a partner and check their answers. You could ask fast finishers to write the tweets (without the unnecessary words) on the board.

SUGGESTED ANSWERS
1 ~~I~~ tried explaining Twitter to ~~my~~ Dad. ~~It~~ wasn't easy!
2 Francis! ~~Do you~~ want to go out tonight?
3 ~~Is~~ anyone watching the programme on Channel 6? ~~Does~~ anyone understand it?
4 ~~I~~ just missed the bus again! ~~It's the~~ third time this week!

EXTENSION: Ask students to write a reply to the tweets in exercise 11. Students could work alone or in pairs.

Exercise 12a

- Ask students to get a piece of paper. Tell them to think about something that they have done today or yesterday and write a tweet about it. Tell them to leave out subject pronouns and auxiliary verbs and use appropriate language – not too formal. Tell students that tweets have a 140-*character* limit. Explain the word *character* (= a character is a letter, symbol or space).

Exercise 12b

- Tell students to swap tweets with another student and write a response to the tweet they read. Tell students to pass their paper to another student, who then adds their own tweet to the latest reply. Repeat this until each original tweet has three responses below it.
- You could post the papers around the room and ask students to walk around and read the tweets and replies and vote for the tweet with the best replies.

CRITICAL THINKING Ask students why the winning tweet got the best replies. This could encourage them to analyse the content of social media. You could widen the discussion to what people write about on social media and how students feel about that. Do they like reading about people's lives and opinions or not? Why?

6.5 Video

Istanbul

VIDEOSCRIPT

Istanbul is the largest city in Turkey.
It sits on two continents – Europe and Asia and it has a population of over 10 million people.
It's an ancient city and its first name was Byzantium.
In the year 324 CE, the Roman Emperor Constantine created a new city to replace Byzantium. He called it Constantinople.
When the Republic of Turkey was born in 1923, the city's name changed to Istanbul.
Today it is still one of the world's major cities and visitors can see its fascinating history everywhere.
This is the Hagia Sophia. It's over 1,500 years old.
At first it was a church, then it was a mosque and now it's a beautiful museum.
Today this magnificent building with its large dome is a symbol of the city and its history.
Istanbul is also famous for the Bosphorus Strait.
This is the border between Europe and Asia, and stretches from Istanbul to the Black Sea.

Because of its location, the Bosphorus was important in Ancient Greece, Ancient Persia and Ancient Rome. In those times, many people visited the city, and boats used the Bosphorus to travel between Europe and Asia.

The strait is still a part of Istanbul life today. The public transport on the Bosphorus is very popular with local people, and ferries are a great way for tourists to see the city.

It's useful for industry too. It's one of the busiest waterways in the world. A lot of the ships travelling to the Middle East pass through here.

And it is here that the local fishermen catch their famously fresh seafood.

They sell it – here – at the city's Grand Bazaar.

This market is over 560 years old. There isn't much of the original structure, but some of these buildings are from the 18th century. At that time it was one of the most important markets in the world.

Today it's still really busy. The market covers 60 streets and has over 3,000 shops.

Around 300,000 people come here every day. They buy lots of different things and enjoy the aroma of herbs, spices, coffee and cooking food.

Byzantium, Constantinople, Istanbul – this city was the centre of civilizations for centuries. These civilizations ended and the city changed.

But Istanbul is always full of life.

Here, where the east meets the west and the ancient meets the modern, you can discover the past and enjoy the present.

VIDEO ANSWERS

Exercise 1
ancient buildings ✓   buses ☐   busy market ✓
dome ✓   fishermen ☐   gardens ✓   herbs ☐
modern buildings ✓   mosque ✓   public transport ✓
residents ✓   ships and ferries ✓   souvenirs ✓
spices ☐   strait ✓   tourists ✓

Exercise 2 & 3
Students' own answers.

Exercise 4
a Istanbul is the second largest city in Turkey.
b In ancient times the city was first called Byzantium.
c The city's name was changed to Istanbul in 1923.
d Today the Hagia Sophia is a museum.
e The sea that divides Istanbul is called the Bosphorous. ✓
f Local people and tourists can use the ferries on the Bosphorous.
g Istanbul is famous for its fresh seafood. ✓
h The Grand Bazaar was first built over 560 years ago.
i There are 60 streets in the market.
j The market sells fresh seafood, herbs, spices, coffee, cooked food.
k The city is different now to how it was in ancient times. 'These civilizations ended and the city changed.'

Exercise 5a & b
Students' own answers

Review
ANSWERS

Exercise 1a
1 was   2 Was   3 Were   4 Were   5 Was   6 were

Exercise 1b 6.20
1 He was 18.
2 No, it wasn't. It was on a Friday.
3 No, they weren't. It was completely dark.
4 Yes, they were.
5 Yes, there was.
6 They were behind the sofa.

AUDIOSCRIPT 6.20
I remember my eighteenth birthday very well. It was on a Friday and I was really excited when I got home from college. I called out 'Mum? Dad?' But there was no answer. I walked into the living room. It was completely dark – I couldn't see anything! Then suddenly the lights came on and everyone was there! All my family and friends! And there was a huge birthday cake. I was really happy, but I couldn't see any presents. Then my dad told me to look behind the sofa and there they were – all my presents. A new tablet and a new suit – for my first job interview!

Exercise 2a
1 yesterday   2 last year/a year ago
3 last week/a week ago   4 five years ago
5 five minutes ago   6 half an hour ago/30 minutes ago

Exercise 3a
1 died   2 was   3 decided   4 love   5 pay   6 wanted
7 was   8 painted   9 's/is   10 travel

Exercise 4a
1 e   2 g   3 h   4 c   5 b   6 d   7 a   8 f

Exercise 6a 6.21
POSSIBLE ANSWERS
1 Really? That's brilliant! That's amazing! That's great!
2 Really? Poor you!
3 That's terrible! What a nightmare! Oh, no! That's awful!

AUDIOSCRIPT 6.21
1 I passed my driving test!
2 I don't have a television.
3 My brother goes to a lot of job interviews, but he can't find a job.

Health and fitness

Unit overview

Language input

Past simple irregular verbs (CB p67)	• *chose, sat, put, took, wrote ...*
Past simple negative (CB p69)	• *He didn't walk before the age of five.*
Grammar reference (CB pp148–149)	

Vocabulary development

A healthy lifestyle (CB p66)	• *Eat lots of fruit and vegetables.* • *Ride a bicycle.*
Sports and fitness (CB p68)	• *Do athletics/judo/yoga* • *Play basketball/football/tennis* • *Swim/ski/job/run*
Easily confused words (CB p71)	• *lend/borrow; take/bring; come/go*

Skills development

Reading: time sequencers (CB p70)
Speaking: opinions, agreeing and disagreeing (CB p72)
Writing: post a website comment (CB p73)

Video

Documentary: Health and fitness in New York (CB p74)
Vox pops (Coursebook DVD & TG p257)

More materials

Workbook	• Language practice for vocabulary, grammar, speaking and writing
Photocopiable activities	• Grammar: What's the question? (TG p206 & TSRD) • Vocabulary: A sporting chance (TG p223 & TSRD) • Communication: What do you think? (TG p240 & TSRD)
Tests	• Unit 7 test (TSRD)
Unit 7 wordlist (TSRD)	

7.1 My health, my business

Goals

- Use collocations for a healthy lifestyle
- Use past simple irregular verbs

Lead-in

1 Open book. To practise word formation and create interest in the topic.

- Write *health* on the board and check the meaning and form (= noun, the general condition of the body or mind). Explain that we can talk about mental health (to do with the mind) or physical health (to do with the body).
- Put students into pairs and ask them to think of or look up a positive and negative adjective formed from *health* (healthy, unhealthy).
- Ask them to complete the sentences below in their notebooks and ask you for help or look in a dictionary for any unknown words:
  A healthy person ... .
  An unhealthy person ... .
- Put students into groups of four and tell them to compare their sentences.
- Write some examples on the board and go over the meaning of any new words the students discovered during the exercise.

2 Open book. To think about the title of the lesson.

- Write *It's my business* and *It's none of your business* on the board.
- Put students into different pairs and ask them to discuss the meaning of the sentences. You could ask them to think about how they might say this in their own language. Do they have similar phrases?
- Discuss the meaning as a group and clarify any doubts with the class. (Answer: I can make my own decisions, you cannot tell me what to do; I don't want your opinion; I don't want you to know about this.)
- Ask students to read the title of the lesson and discuss with their partner what they think it means. Open this out to a class discussion.

Vocabulary & Speaking a healthy lifestyle

Exercise 1

> **Background note:** This question focuses on the connection between physical and mental health. Some people think that they are closely connected. They think that if you keep fit and do exercise, you are more likely to have good mental health. Some people also say that you can actually control physical illness through positive thinking and that the saying could be the other way around: *healthy mind, healthy body*.

- Put students into pairs and ask them to discuss the questions. You may need to prompt the discussion using the points in the background note.
- Ask some pairs to report back to the class.

1 *Healthy body, healthy mind* means that if you look after your diet and fitness, you will have good mental health. The health of the mind and the body are connected.
2 Students' own answers

Exercise 2a

- Ask students to work with their partner and tell them to complete the exercise.

Exercise 2b 7.1 🔘

- Play track 7.1 and tell students to listen and check their answers.

1 eat   2 take   3 walk   4 ride   5 drink   6 do
7 sleep   8 go   9 do

AUDIOSCRIPT 7.1

1 eat lots of fruit and vegetables
2 take the stairs, not the lift
3 walk to work
4 ride a bicycle
5 drink eight glasses of water a day
6 do an hour of exercise each day
7 sleep seven to eight hours a night
8 go to the gym or an evening class
9 do physical jobs around the house

Exercise 2c

- Ask students for an example of a type of exercise from the list in exercise 2a. Ask a student if they do this type of exercise and, if so, how often.
- Put students into pairs and tell them to discuss questions 1–3.
- Ask two or three students to report back to the class what their partner said. Ask the class if they think they are a healthy group in general.

1 Exercise: 2, 3, 4, 6, 8, 9 Not exercise: 1, 5, 7
2 Students' own answers
3 Don't smoke or drink unhealthy drinks, eat healthy food with less fat and sugar, use the car less

EXTENSION To encourage deeper thinking about the topic. Ask students to choose the top three activities for a healthy lifestyle, and to put all the items in exercise 2a into order of importance. Ask the class to report back and agree on the most important activities. Encourage them to give reasons for their ideas.

Reading & Grammar past simple irregular verbs

Exercise 3

> **Background note:** This menu leads into the text in exercise 4. The mayor of New York introduced a law in which restaurants had to write the number of calories on menus as part of a healthy-living project.

- As a lead-in, you could bring some menus from local restaurants into class. Ask students to work in small groups and compare how healthy the menus are. They could also discuss which menu they prefer.

- Put students into pairs and tell them to look at the menu and discuss the questions.
- Ask students to share their ideas with the group.

Exercise 4a

> **Background note:** This text is about a famous mayor of New York who started a healthy lifestyle campaign in the city because he thought the citizens were unhealthy. You could search for more information on the internet to support this part of the lesson.

- Put students into pairs and refer them to the title of the article and the photo. Ask them to guess what the mayor did.
- Ask students to share their ideas with the class.

Exercise 4b

- Tell students the article is about the mayor of New York. Ask them what they know about New York.
- Refer students to the glossary below the article before they read.
- Ask students to read the article and see if their ideas were correct. Tell them to discuss their ideas with a partner.

ANSWERS
The mayor tried to change people's habits. He had restaurant menus include calories, not just prices. He banned smoking in public places. He tried to reduce the size of sweet drinks. He encouraged healthy lifestyles with more exercise.

Exercise 5

- Tell students to read questions 1–4 and think about what the answers might be. Ask them to read the article again and find the answers.

STUDY TIP Reading strategies. Help students to think about how they read a text to find specific information. Explain they should first read the questions and think about the information they are looking for, e.g. are they looking for actions, places, names, other nouns? In question 1 they are asked to look for *four things New Yorkers* **did**. That tells them they need to look for verbs. Ask students what information the other questions are looking for.

- Check answers together.

ANSWERS
1 They ate the wrong food, smoked, drove everywhere, and did little or no exercise.
2 He added information about calories on restaurant menus and banned smoking in public places.
3 He tried to reduce the size of sweet drinks.
4 Leave your car at home, walk or ride a bicycle, and take the stairs not the lift.

Exercise 6

- Put students into groups of three or four and ask them to discuss the questions. Encourage students to give reasons for their ideas and speculate about how they would feel if they lived in New York.
- Ask some students to report back to the class on what their groups said.

CRITICAL THINKING Relate a reading to your own experience and opinions. Ask students if rules like this apply in their home town/country, and if so, what they think about them.

FEEDBACK FOCUS Focus on content rather than accurate language here. You could help students to form their opinions by showing them how to express opinions and give reasons. Listen to students' discussions and help them re-form their language to express themselves better, e.g. *I think/I reckon he was right because it costs the government lots of money when people are unhealthy.*

Exercise 7

- Write *Bloomberg starts to change people's lifestyles* on the board and ask students to change this to the past. Tell students the verb *start* is regular so we add -*ed*. Ask them if they know any irregular verbs. They will know the verb *to be* is irregular and will probably have come across past simple irregular verbs before, e.g. *went*.
- Put students into pairs and tell them to read the extract from the text and discuss the question.
- Ask students what the present of *chose* is (choose).

ANSWER
wanted

Exercise 8a

- Refer students to the Grammar focus box and ask them to read it.
- Refer students to *Grammar reference* on p148. There are four more exercises here that students can do for homework.

Exercise 8b

- Tell students to complete the exercise and then check their ideas with a partner.

Exercise 8c 7.2 🔊

- Play track 7.2 and tell students to check their answers.
- Play the track again and ask them to listen and repeat.

PRONUNCIATION Some students will find the spelling of *thought* confusing and want to pronounce the *gh* as /x/, a guttural sound. Tell them the *gh* is usually silent in English words. *Done* and *took* may also cause problems as the pronunciation is different from the spelling. *Done* is pronounced /dʌn/ and *took* is pronounced /tʊk/.

ANSWERS

present	past
come	came
make	made
do	did
eat	ate
drive	drove
give	gave
write	wrote
have	had
tell	told
take	took
think	thought

AUDIOSCRIPT 7.2

come	came
make	made
do	did
eat	ate
drive	drove
give	gave
write	wrote
have	had
tell	told
take	took
think	thought

Pronunciation past simple irregular verbs

Exercise 9a 7.3

- Ask students if they can find two verbs in exercise 8 that have the same vowel sound, e.g. *make/take/came/made*.
- Play track 7.3 and ask students to put a letter S next to the groups of words which have the same sound in all the words and put a letter D next to the groups of words which have different sounds. You may need to play the track twice. You could do the first example together with the class.
- Check answers.

WATCH OUT! For some accents, e.g. Scottish English, the words in group number 5 have the same sounds.

1 same 2 different 3 different 4 same 5 different 6 same

Exercise 9b 7.3

- Play the track again and ask students to identify the different vowel sounds in examples 2, 3 and 5.
- If you use phonemic script with your students, show them the vowel sound symbols. (2 *chose* and *wrote* are the same [əʊ], *got* is different – it's a short vowel [ɒ]. 3 *sat* and *had* are the same [æ], *went* is different [ɜ]. 5 *flew* is different [uː], *took* and *put* are shorter sounds [ʊ].)
- Repeat the track and tell students to listen and repeat the words.

EXTRA ACTIVITY Students might find it difficult to remember the spelling of some of these verbs as the verbs are not pronounced as they are written. Put students into pairs and tell them to close their books. Read out the verbs you think they will have trouble with and tell them to write them down on a piece of paper. Tell students to swap their papers with another pair and check answers.

Exercise 10a

- Check that students understand what a *survey* is (= a set of questions, usually asked to a group of people, to find out what they think about something or how they behave).
- Students work alone. Tell them they are going to read about a survey on health.
- Tell them to use past tense verbs to complete the sentences.

WATCH OUT! Some verbs are regular and some are irregular.

ANSWERS
1 ate 2 played; did 3 slept 4 watched 5 took 6 said 7 sat 8 thought; had

Exercise 10b

- Put students into pairs and ask them to check their answers, and discuss the question in their pairs. Open this out to a class discussion.

EXTENSION Ask students to think if these results would be the same for their class. What would be similar or different, in their opinion?

EXTRA ACTIVITY Conduct a class survey. Give each student one of the survey results from exercise 10a, e.g. *85% ate snacks between meals*. Ask them to turn their sentence into a question, e.g.
1 Do you eat snacks between meals?
2 Do you play sport or do exercise every week?
Tell students to walk around and ask everyone their question and make a note of the answers. When they have asked everyone their question, put them into groups of three or four and tell them to tell each other their results. Teach them how to say the phrases *XX out of XX eat snacks*, e.g. *5 out of 10 people eat snacks*.

Ask each group to prepare a mini presentation to share their results with the class. The class can then compare their results with the survey in the book.

Exercise 11a

- Tell students to think about habits they had in the past and to write some sentences to describe these habits with regard to a healthy lifestyle. All students have to write sentences.

Exercise 11b

- You can ask students to share their sentences with the whole class or you could put students into groups and tell them to share their sentences with each other.
- Ask them to compare their past habits with the results from the survey (the one in the book or their own if you did the extra activity) and think about how things were the same or different at that time, e.g. *When we were children we ate more healthy food.*
- Ask one or two students to share any interesting things they heard with the class.

EXTENSION A general discussion about habits in the past. Tell students to work in pairs and write five sentences describing people's healthy and unhealthy habits ten to twenty years ago using the information they heard in the last exercise.

Put pairs together and tell them to share their sentences with each other. Ask listeners to say if they agree or not with the ideas they hear. Encourage them to give reasons for their responses. For example: *I don't agree because I think people in the past were more active. We watch more TV now and kids play more video games.*

GRAMMAR REFERENCE ANSWERS
Exercise 1
1 slept 2 drank 3 went 4 rode 5 ate 6 gave 7 chose 8 ran 9 left 10 told 11 did 12 swam 13 lent 14 kept 15 lost 16 was 17 felt 18 wrote

Exercise 2
1 came 2 thought 3 wrote 4 left 5 drank 6 had
7 rode 8 gave

Exercise 3
1 ran 2 went 3 chose 4 swam 5 won 6 did
7 had 8 met

Exercise 4
1 got 2 drank 3 drove 4 took 5 ate 6 sat
7 went 8 watched 9 was 10 started 11 swam
12 rode/ran 13 went 14 lost

7.2 Sporting heroes

Goals
- Talk about sports and fitness
- Use the past simple negative

Lead-in
1 Closed book. To revise regular and irregular past simple verbs.
- Ask students to think about what healthy activities they did yesterday/last week and last month.
- Put students into pairs and ask them to tell each other what they did.
- Listen and write correct examples of past tense verbs on the board to reinforce the rules and pronunciation.

2 Closed book. To explore the theme of modern heroes.
- Put students into small groups.
- Write *heroes* (= people who have done something good or brave) on the board and elicit words that students think about when they think of heroes. Create a mind map on the board.
- Ask students to discuss the ideas elicited and think about these questions.
  1 Who are the modern heroes?
  2 Do you think they are good role models for children? Why? (A role model is someone who behaves in a positive way and is a good example for children.)
- Ask students to report what their groups said to the class.

Vocabulary & Speaking sports and fitness

Exercise 1a
- Tell students to look at the illustrations and think about the activities they can see. Put them into pairs and tell them to complete the exercise.

Exercise 1b 7.4 ⊙
- Play track 7.4 and tell students to check their answers and listen to the pronunciation.
- Play the recording again and tell them to listen and repeat.

ANSWERS/AUDIOSCRIPT 7.4
1 jog/run 2 go fishing 3 play football 4 play tennis
5 ski 6 swim 7 do yoga 8 go to the gym
9 do athletics 10 play basketball 11 cycle
12 do judo

EXTENSION Extend vocabulary and practise saying sports that take the verbs *play*, *do* and *go*. Ask students to think of other sports that you can do, play or go (to). (Suggested answers: do karate, play baseball, badminton, go horse riding, skiing) Ask students to write their ideas on the board. Check meaning and pronunciation.

Exercise 2
- Put students into pairs and tell them to discuss the question.
- Write some examples on the board as the students talk so you can refer to them in the feedback.

FEEDBACK FOCUS Students sometimes confuse the verbs *do* and *play* and might even use *make*. Listen and check they are using the correct verbs.
- Ask some students to report back to the class on what they spoke about.

Exercise 3a
- You might have to pre-teach *keep fit* (= do exercise to stay healthy), *win* (= be the first or best in a game or match) and *lose weight* (= become less heavy or thinner).
- Tell students to work alone and complete the exercise.

EXTRA SUPPORT To help students complete the exercise teach them the phrases *individual* and *team sports*, e.g. *Football is a team sport so it's good for meeting friends*.

Exercise 3b
- Put students into pairs and tell them to compare answers.
- Ask some students to share their ideas with the group.

Exercise 4
- Tell students what you do to demonstrate the exercise.

EXTRA SUPPORT Teach or revise time phrases and adverbs to help students explain how often they do sports, e.g. *every week, once/twice/three times a week, now and then, sometimes, never*.
- Put students into pairs. Refer them to the example dialogue and tell them to answer the questions.
- Ask some students to report back to the class on what their partner told them.

FEEDBACK FOCUS Students sometimes forget to use the third person -*s*. Listen for this in the reporting stage and help students correct themselves by repeating the mistake with rising intonation or by using metalanguage – *third person*.

Listening & Grammar past simple negative

Exercise 5
- As a lead-in, ask students to work with a partner and list four or five famous sports people.
- Check ideas and ask students to write the names on the board.
- To support this exercise, teach students the phrase *a good role model* (= someone who behaves in a positive way and is a good example for children).
- Tell students to work with their partners and discuss the questions.

CRITICAL THINKING To reflect on a question. Encourage students to give reasons for their opinions. You could also ask them to give examples from their own lives, e.g. *When I was young I thought (name of sports person) was a hero. He was a good role model for me. He seemed a good person; he was strong and worked hard.*

- Ask some students to report to the class what their partner said.

Exercise 6

> **Background note:** The recording is about Fauja Singh. It's a true story of a man who had a sad life but managed to feel more positive by starting to run marathons. He was the first person to run a marathon aged 100.

- Refer students to the photo.
- Put students into pairs and ask them to discuss the questions.

Exercise 7a 7.5 🔊

- Pre-teach *Toronto* and *Punjab,* as these places may be unknown to students and may distract them while listening.
- Play track 7.5 and ask students to listen and see if their ideas were correct. You may need to play the track twice. You could encourage students to make notes to help them in exercise 7b.

ANSWERS
1 He celebrated his 100th birthday in April 2011.
2 He is a runner.
3 He runs to be happy and to forget his problems.

CRITICAL THINKING Relate a recording to their own ideas. There are no right or wrong answers here. Students can reflect on each other's opinions.

- Put students into pairs and ask them to discuss the questions. You could remind students of the phrase *don't give up* from a previous lesson as it is relevant here.
- Ask students to report back to the class and encourage them to give reasons for their ideas. For example: *I think he's a sporting hero because he had lots of problems and he didn't give up. He had a sad life and sport helped him.*

Exercise 7b 7.5 🔊

- Ask students to read through the sentences before they listen.
- Play the recording again and ask students to complete the exercise.
- Tell them to compare their answers with a partner before you go over answers with the class.

ANSWERS
1 ✗ 2 ✓ 3 ✗ 4 ✗ 5 ✓ 6 ✗

AUDIOSCRIPT 7.5
In April 2011, Fauja Singh celebrated his 100th birthday. In October 2011, he ran the Toronto marathon and became the first person aged 100 years old to finish a marathon. But Fauja didn't run his first marathon until the year 2000. Why not? This is his story.

Fauja was born in Punjab in India. He wasn't a strong child and he had problems with his legs. He didn't walk before he was five years old. But he grew up on the family farm with his parents and brothers and sisters. He was happy and life was good after he learnt to walk. Later Fauja got married and had six children. But his happy life didn't continue. Unfortunately, his wife and two of his children – a daughter and a son – died.

Fauja then moved to London to live with another son, but he wasn't happy. It wasn't easy to forget about his life in India. So he started to go running. When he ran, he didn't think about the past and didn't feel sad. Then in 2000, at the age of 89, he ran his first London Marathon in a time of 6 hours and 54 minutes. And he didn't stop then. From 2000 to 2011 he ran eight marathons. He said marathons changed his life and helped him feel happy again.

EXTENSION Discuss why Fauja found running helpful. Put students into pairs or small groups and ask them to discuss why they think running helped him. Share the ideas with the class.

CRITICAL THINKING Relating a text to your own experience. Ask students to work in small groups. Allow them to choose one of these questions to discuss. In feedback ask someone from each group to say which question they chose and one or two things they spoke about.
1 Do you know anyone who has run a marathon? Would you like to run a marathon? Why/Why not?
2 Do you know anyone who has used sport to help them through a difficult situation? What happened?

Exercise 8

- Refer students to the Grammar focus box and ask them to read and complete it.
- To practise this, you could do a substitution drill. Examples:
  Teacher: I walked to school.
  Students: I didn't walk to school.
  Teacher: I ran to school.
  Students: I didn't run to school.
- Repeat with different verbs from the lesson.
- Put students into pairs and ask them to repeat the drill with each other, taking turns to invent sentences in past simple positive and then making them negative.

ANSWER
didn't

EXTRA CHALLENGE Tell students to continue the drill but to reply with the negative and then a different positive to say how they did things differently. For example:
A: I played football.
B: I didn't play football. I played basketball.

- Refer students to *Grammar reference* on p149. There are three more exercises here that students can do for homework.

Pronunciation past simple negative

Exercise 9a 7.6 🔊

- Play track 7.6 and ask students to listen and notice where the stress falls in the sentences.
- Play the track again and ask students to listen and repeat.

Exercise 9b

- Do the example in the book with the class. Focus on the pronunciation and drill the correct stress. If you did the extension exercise, you could repeat sentences students created for that to work on the stress.
- Put students into pairs and ask them to complete the exercise.

Exercise 9c 7.7 ⊚

- Play track 7.7 and tell students to listen and repeat.

ANSWERS/AUDIOSCRIPT 7.7

1 Fauja didn't run marathons when he was young.
2 He didn't have a lot of problems when he lived on his family's farm.
3 His happy life didn't continue after he had a family.
4 He didn't stop after his first marathon.

Exercise 10a

> **Background note:** Usain Bolt is a world champion runner. He won the 100m race in the 2012 Olympics as well as many other competitions. He also runs 200m races.

- Refer students to the photo of Usain Bolt. Ask them to tell a partner what they know about him.
- Pre-teach *thunderstorm* (= bad weather with loud noises and lights in the sky – thunder and lightning) and *lightning* (= the light in the sky when there is a thunderstorm).
- Tell students to read the sentences about him and compare this information with what they spoke about.
- Tell them to complete the exercise, reminding them that some verbs might be negative.

ANSWERS

1 didn't do   2 slowed; broke   3 didn't show   4 didn't hit

Exercise 10b 7.8 ⊚

- Play track 7.8 and tell students to listen and check their answers.
- Ask them to work with a partner and discuss the question.

AUDIOSCRIPT 7.8

1 When he was a young boy, Usain Bolt didn't do athletics all the time. He played cricket and football.
2 In 2008, when he won the Olympic 100m final, he slowed down at the end and he broke the world record. His time was 9.96 seconds.
3 When he won the 100m final at the 2012 London Olympic Games, two billion people watched him on TV. American TV didn't show the race when it happened. They showed it later in the evening.
4 There was a thunderstorm during the 100m World Championship final in 2013. Lightning didn't hit him, but there was lightning in the sky.

Exercise 11a

- Ask students to think about the sports and activities they did when they were children.
- Say four sentences of your own and ask students to guess which one is false. Examples:
  I swam in competitions when I was young.
  I played chess when I was six.
  I rode horses when I was ten.
  I started judo when I was twenty-one.
- Tell students to work alone and complete the exercise. Remind them that two sentences must be false.

Exercise 11b

- Ask three students to act out the example conversation in the book.
- Put students into small groups and tell them to read their sentences to each other and guess which are the false sentences. Encourage students to give more information about the sentences.

FEEDBACK FOCUS Listen for the correct form (grammar and pronunciation) of the verbs in the positive and negative. You could write good and incorrect examples on the board afterwards for students to identify and correct.

EXTRA ACTIVITY Ask students to research information about a sports person from their country (or one they like). Tell them to write a description with four sentences using the Usain Bolt text as an example. They should focus on using past simple correctly. This could be done for homework.

GRAMMAR REFERENCE ANSWERS

Exercise 1

1 didn't think   2 didn't look   3 didn't make
4 didn't put   5 didn't say   6 didn't look   7 didn't bring
8 didn't pay   9 didn't wait   10 didn't sit

Exercise 2

1 No, I didn't go shopping two days ago, I went swimming.
2 She didn't do yoga last Friday, she did judo.
3 He didn't lose his mobile phone yesterday morning, he lost his wallet.
4 They didn't think the lesson was easy, they thought the homework was easy.
5 We didn't sleep at our aunt's house last night, we slept at our niece's house.
6 I didn't borrow some money from him last week, I borrowed some (money) from him last month.
7 She didn't lend him a book yesterday, she lent him a pen.
8 I didn't take the bus to work last week, I took the train.
9 My mother didn't make a cake for my birthday last year, she made a cake (for my birthday) two years ago.
10 He didn't buy lots of vegetables at the market, he bought lots of fruit.

Exercise 3

1 won   2 didn't win   3 didn't stay   4 moved   5 lived
6 didn't work   7 didn't earn   8 visited   9 brought
10 came   11 didn't live   12 didn't come
13 didn't have   14 went   15 didn't speak   16 said

7.3 Vocabulary and skills development

Goals

- Understand time sequencers in a text
- Understand easily confused words

Lead-in

1 Open book. To discuss the difference between *stay* and *be healthy* and recycle vocabulary from lesson 7.2.

- Ask students how they stay healthy. Recycle vocabulary from the previous lesson, e.g. *go to the gym, play tennis*.
- Write *BE v STAY healthy* on the board. Put students into pairs and ask them to discuss how these ideas are different.
- Check ideas with the group. (Possible answers: *Be healthy is a state; people are healthy or not. Stay healthy is an action, you do things to remain healthy. It's the act of keeping healthy, like keeping fit.*)

2 Open book. Predict content of the lesson.

- Write *technology* and *health* on the board. Ask students for examples of technology and go over the meaning of these words if necessary: *app* (= a program or game on a smartphone or tablet), *website, mp3, smartphone, laptop, computer,* etc.
- Put students into pairs and ask them to discuss the possible connection between technology and health.
- Ask some students to report their ideas to the class. Their ideas can be confirmed later in the lesson.

Reading & Speaking   time sequencers

Exercise 1

- Tell students to read through the sentences. You may need to pre-teach *set a goal* (= make a plan).
- Put students into pairs and ask them to discuss the exercise.
- Ask some students to report their ideas to the class. Ask listeners to say if they agree with the order or not. (Possible answers: Choose an activity you enjoy. Set a goal for yourself. Find a friend to exercise with you. Make a timetable. Repeat the exercise twice a day.)

Exercise 2a

- Refer students to the Unlock the code box. Tell them to read the information.
- To check understanding, ask students when writers might use these sequencers in a text and why. (Possible answers: When they are listing instructions, when they are describing a list of events in someone's life, when they are explaining things that happened in a story. They do it to show what events happened first, next, last, etc.)

Exercise 2b

- Ask students to complete the exercise and compare their answers with the person next to them.
- Check answers together.

1 First/Firstly
2 Next; Then; After that
3 Finally; Lastly

Exercise 2c

- Refer students back to the sentences in exercise 1 and tell them to order them using the sequencers. You could do the first example with the group, e.g. *Firstly find an activity you enjoy, then find a friend …*

SUGGESTED ANSWERS
First, choose an activity you enjoy. Then, set a goal for yourself. After that, find a friend to exercise with you. Next, make a timetable. Finally, repeat the exercise twice a day.

EXTRA ACTIVITY Ask students to think about what they did earlier today. Put them into pairs and ask them to take turns telling each other about their day, putting the events in order. You could model this with your own example, e.g. *First, I got up early because I had a doctor's appointment. Then, I went for breakfast in a café. After that, I met a friend.*

Exercise 3a

- Pre-teach *to take steps* (= demonstrate this by walking in the classroom – ask students how many steps you take).
- Ask students if walking helps you stay healthy and how much they think you have to walk every day to stay healthy.
- Put students into pairs and ask them to complete the exercise.
- Ask them to discuss their answers.
- Ask some students to report what their partner said to the class.

Exercise 3b

- Refer students to the TV review and ask them to work with the same partner as before.
- You may need to pre-teach *gadget* (= a small mechanical tool/object).
- Ask students to read the title of the review, guess what the text is about and answer the question. Ask two or three students to share their ideas and ask the class to say if they agree or disagree.

Exercise 3c

- Tell students to read the review and check whether their ideas were correct.

ANSWERS
Technology can make you healthier because there are apps and gadgets that check health and daily exercise, i.e. the number of steps a person takes and how long and how deeply they sleep.

Exercise 4a

- Ask students to work alone first.
- Refer them to sentences a–d and tell them to order them without reading the review again.
- You may need to teach *equipment* (= the necessary items for a special activity).
- Put students into new pairs and tell them to discuss and then to check their answers by referring to the text again.

ANSWERS

1 d 2 b 3 c 4 a

Exercise 4b

- Tell students to work with their partners and take turns to describe each part of the story, using as many time sequencers as they can.

EXTRA SUPPORT Write the time sequencers on the board in order, so students have visual support for the exercise.

- Ask a volunteer pair to retell the story for the class.

Exercise 5

- Put students into pairs or groups of three and ask them to discuss the questions.

EXTRA SUPPORT Help students express their ideas with these useful phrases:

I like/don't like the idea because …
I think/don't think it can change your routine because …
I think that it's a great/good/bad/awful idea because …

CRITICAL THINKING Reflect on a question. Ask students to work in their groups and discuss this question:

- What types of technology do you think are good or bad for us? (Tell students that by *technology* we mean computers, electronic gadgets, mobile phones, computer games: things people use every day.)
- Give an example to help demonstrate what you want them to think about, e.g. *I think computers are bad for our eyes. We sometimes look at them for several hours a day.*

Vocabulary & Speaking easily confused words

Exercise 6

- As a lead-in, write these sentences on the board:
Can you lend me a pen?
Can I borrow a pen?
- Ask students what is different about the sentences. You can demonstrate the meaning with a student. (Answer: The difference is the direction of the action as well as the grammar. The meaning is the same.)
- Make sure that students understand what they have to do, and then ask them to complete the exercise.
- Put students into pairs and ask them to compare answers.
- Check answers together.

ANSWERS

1 b 2 a 3 a 4 b 5 b 6 a 7 b 8 a 9 a 10 b

Exercise 7a

- Ask students to read the Vocabulary focus box.

EXTENSION Practise the meaning of the verbs with TPR. TPR stands for Total Physical Response and it's a method of learning English that combines language with physical movement. As students learn the words, they associate them with a particular action.

- Prepare some instructions for students in order to help them practise these words by acting them out. You can assess their understanding by observing them doing the actions. For example:
lend Maria a pen
borrow some money
take a book to Juan

bring me a pencil
come to the board
go to the window/door
look at the door
watch the teacher writing on the board

- Ask students to give each other instructions using the verbs.

Exercise 7b

- Refer students to the example in the book.
- Ask students to work alone and complete the exercise. Point out that they will need to use some different tenses.

ANSWERS

1 lend 2 watched 3 Come 4 told 5 take 6 said
7 looked 8 borrowed 9 bring 10 go

Exercise 7c 7.9 🎧

- Play track 7.9 and ask students to check their answers.

AUDIOSCRIPT 7.9

1 Can you lend me your car for the weekend?
2 They watched basketball on TV last night.
3 Come here! I want to speak to you.
4 My colleague told me about a new restaurant in town.
5 Can you take this book to the library for me?
6 'I'm lost,' he said.
7 When Jacek looked at his phone during the meeting, I got very angry.
8 I didn't have a pen, so I borrowed one from my friend.
9 When you come to the party, can you bring something to drink?
10 Let's go to the beach tomorrow.

STUDY TIP Collocations. Show the students how these verbs have common collocations. Discuss how making notes of common collocations can help them learn chunks of language and make their notes more meaningful and easy to remember.

Ask students to read the sentences in exercise 7b and underline the verbs and nouns, e.g. *lend a car, watch basketball, come here*, etc. Ask them to think of other nouns for each verb.

Tell them to write their ideas on the board and then to write the collocations in their notebooks.

Possible answers:

Lend money, a pen/pencil/rubber, bike, DVDs, CDs, books
Borrow (same as lend)
Watch a film, a play, sport, people in the street, out!
Tell someone something, a lie, a story
Say something to someone
Look at me!, yourself in the mirror, a view
Take something somewhere, medicine, a photo
Bring food/drinks to a party, books to class, something to someone
Go to the gym, the cinema, the theatre, the swimming pool, class, school

WATCH OUT! Students may have problems when using pronouns after *lend, tell, bring*, e.g. *Can you lend **me/her/him/them** a pen?* They sometimes miss out the pronoun or use a subject pronoun instead of an object pronoun. Go over this with the class and check they are using pronouns correctly.

EXTRA ACTIVITY Practise *lend* and *borrow*. Students often get confused about how to use these words.

Ask the class to think of one question to ask with *lend* and one with *borrow*, and to write them down. Check students are clear on the structure, e.g. *Can I borrow … ? Can you lend me … ?*

Then ask them to walk around the class asking and answering questions using these verbs. Encourage peer correction as they do the activity.

Exercise 8a

- Ask students to read the questions and decide which have errors.
- Put students into pairs and ask them to compare ideas and correct the errors.
- Check answers together.

ANSWERS

Questions 2–5 are incorrect.
2 ~~look at~~ watch   3 ~~looking at~~ watching   4 ~~say~~ tell
5 ~~lend~~ borrow

EXTRA ACTIVITY Further error correction to practise *lend*, *bring* and *tell/say* and the use of pronouns. Write five sentences on the board with errors in them. For example:
1 *Can you lend to me a pen?*
2 *He said her to go home.*
3 *Did you bring she a book?*
4 *You have to tell to him!*
5 *Did you lend their some money?*

Ask students to correct the sentences.

Exercise 8b

- Put students into groups of three.
- Ask students to ask you a question from exercise 8a. Demonstrate an answer. Explain your answer and encourage follow-up questions from the students.
- Refer students to the sample dialogue.
- Tell students to complete the exercise in their groups.

FEEDBACK FOCUS Listen to collocations and write examples of good language and errors on the board. Ask students to identify good language and correct errors in their groups.

EXTENSION Ask students to write their own questions using the easily confused words.

- Put students into pairs and refer them to exercise 7. Tell them to write between five and eight questions using the verbs. For example:
  Can you tell me the way to the bank?
  How do you say 'house' in Spanish?
  How often do you go to the cinema?
- Encourage them to use different nouns.

EXTRA ACTIVITY Revise past regular and irregular verbs and vocabulary from this lesson. Tell the class some examples of what you have done recently using the verbs from this lesson. For example:
I borrowed money from a friend to buy lunch.
I watched a good film.
I went to the gym.
My aunt came to visit me.

Ask students to ask you questions if appropriate, e.g. *Did you return the money?*

Tell students to write at least five sentences about themselves. Put students into pairs or small groups and ask them to tell each other their sentences and ask each other questions.

7.4 Speaking and writing

Goals

- Ask for and give opinions
- Agree and disagree
- Post a website comment

Lead-in

1 Closed book. To revise commonly confused words from lesson 7.3.

- Write the sentences below on the board before the lesson starts.
- Ask students to try and correct them alone.
- Put students into pairs and ask them to compare their answers. Go over answers with the class.
  Can you borrow me your pen? (Can you lend me your pen?)
  Can you go to my house for dinner tomorrow? (Can you come to my house for dinner tomorrow?)
  I looked at the television last night. (I watched the television last night.)
  He heard a noise and watched the door. (He heard a noise and looked at the door.)
  Can you take me a cake from the shop please? (Can you bring me a cake from the shop, please?)

2 Open book. To predict the topic of the lesson.

- Ask the class to look at the photo on p72.
- Put the students into pairs and ask them to predict the topic of the lesson. For extra support, write this on the board: *We think it's about … because … .*
- Ask two or three students to report their ideas to the class.
- Listen and write relevant vocabulary on the board. Go over meaning and pronunciation.

Listening & Speaking   opinions, agreeing and disagreeing

Exercise 1a

- Put students into pairs.
- Confirm that the people in the photo are playing a video game.
- Pre-teach *violent*, which students may want to use (= an adjective to describe a person or thing that hurts or damages someone or something).
- Refer students to the questions and ask them to discuss them with their partner. Ask one or two students to share their ideas with the class.

FEEDBACK FOCUS Encourage students to use the connector *but*. Help students reform their ideas by asking for examples and rewriting their ideas in full on the board, e.g. *Video games are fun but they can be violent.*

Exercise 1b

- Group pairs together to make groups of four and tell them to compare ideas.

CRITICAL THINKING Discuss advantages and disadvantages. Ask groups to make two lists: advantages and disadvantages of video games. Ask fast finishers to write their lists on the board, and then discuss ideas with the class. Ask other groups to say if they agree or disagree. Add ideas from other groups to the lists on the board.

As an alternative, you could ask students to make lists on large pieces of paper and stick the pieces of paper round the room. Then, ask students to walk around, read the lists and draw ticks or crosses to indicate whether they agree or not.

After that, ask some students to sit in pairs and explain what they think of the ideas they read. Ask two or three volunteers to explain why they drew a tick or a cross.

- If you don't do the critical thinking ideas above, ask two or three students to report what their group said to the class.

Exercise 2 7.10

> **Audio summary:** A radio programme about some research into the effects of video games on children in the USA.

- Refer students to the questions and ask them to read them before they listen.
- Play track 7.10 and tell students to listen for the answers.
- Put students into pairs and ask them to discuss the questions.
- Check answers together.

ANSWERS
1 People usually think video games are bad for children's health.
2 The research showed that perhaps this isn't true.
3 Children played video games like *Just Dance* and surfing on *Wii Sports Resorts* in their gym class every week.
4 The children started to enjoy the classes.

AUDIOSCRIPT 7.10
People usually think that video games are bad for children's health. But new research says that perhaps this isn't true. At a school in Hedgesville, West Virginia, in the USA, students played video games in their gym class every week. Some children didn't enjoy exercise before, but with games like *Just Dance* and surfing on *Wii Sports Resorts*, they started to enjoy their gym classes. Jan Hamilton and Sarah White, two local parents, are in the studio with me to discuss this.

Exercise 3a 7.11

> **Audio summary:** Two parents discuss the research from the previous recording. They give their opinions about it.

- Tell students to think back to the ideas they spoke about in exercise 1a.
- Play track 7.11 and ask students to listen to hear if the people mention similar ideas. Encourage students to make notes. If students made lists on pieces of paper, you could ask them to refer to these as they listen. You may need to play the recording twice.

EXTRA SUPPORT Pause the recording regularly to help students understand what they hear.

- Tell students to put their hands up when they hear an idea similar to those discussed in exercise 1a. Ask them to say what idea they heard.
- Tell students to discuss what they heard with their partners, then check ideas with the class.

ANSWERS
Jan thinks exercise games are a fun way to do exercise, and that children then want to be like their heroes. Sarah says it depends whether the video games are violent or not. Sometimes children try to do things they see in *FIFA Soccer* when they play football, which is a good thing.

AUDIOSCRIPT 7.11
P: Jan and Sara, you're both parents, what do you think of this idea?
J: I think it's great. And it's a fun way to do exercise, too.
S: Hmm … I don't know about that. Some video games aren't OK for children because they're very violent.
J: Yes, but they didn't use violent games like that at the school. They were exercise games, like *Just Dance*.
S: Well, for me, it depends on the game. But you're right, some games can be good. My son plays the football video game *FIFA* for hours and hours sometimes. But then he goes out to the park and plays football with his friends, and they try to do things they see on the video game.
P: Yes, my son is the same. What's your opinion, Jan?
J: Well, they want to be like their heroes.
S: I agree with that. They certainly do. But do we want our children to be like their heroes?
P: Well, an interesting discussion but I'm afraid that's all we have time for today. [fades out]

FEEDBACK FOCUS Listen and make a note of any language students use for giving opinion, agreeing and disagreeing. You can use your notes for exercises 4 and 5 when students practise these types of phrases.

Exercise 3b

- Ask students to read through the sentences and complete the exercise with a partner.

ANSWERS
1 What, of   2 think   3 don't, that   4 but   5 for
6 right   7 opinion   8 agree

Exercise 3c 7.12

- Play track 7.12 and ask students to check their answers.
- Repeat the track and ask students to listen and repeat.

PRONUNCIATION Focus on emphasis and weak forms. Help students to improve their listening and speaking skills by practising listening to which words are stressed and where there are weak forms.

Write *what/think/idea?* on the board. Ask students if they understand the question with these words only. Tell them to listen to the sentence again and notice how these words are stressed and how the other grammar words are unstressed. Ask them to listen to the other sentences and underline words that are stressed. Drill the phrases with the correct stress.

AUDIOSCRIPT 7.12
1 **What** do you think **of** this idea?
2 I **think** it's great.
3 I **don't** know about **that**.
4 Yes, **but** they didn't use games like that at the school.
5 Well, **for** me, it depends on the game.
6 You're **right.**
7 What's your **opinion**?
8 Yes, I **agree** with that.

Exercise 4

- Refer students to the four questions and do number 1 together.
- Put students into pairs and tell them to complete the exercise.
- Check answers together.

ANSWERS
1 ask for an opinion: 1, 7
2 give an opinion: 2, 5
3 show the speaker agrees: 6, 8
4 show the speaker disagrees: 3, 4

Exercise 5

- To demonstrate this exercise, ask a student to ask you the question: *What do you think about using video games at school?* Model a reply using the language from exercise 3b.

EXTRA SUPPORT Allow students to rehearse. Tell students to think about their opinion and consider how they might describe their opinion using the phrases. Tell them to silently rehearse what they will say. To model the responding phrases, ask a student to tell you their opinion and model a reply. Encourage students to have conversations and ask questions about each other's opinions.

- Put students into pairs and ask them to discuss the question.

Exercise 6

- Tell students to read the statement.
- Ask them to suggest an example of how a company might help its employees stay fit and healthy, e.g. *build a gym in the office.*
- Elicit one argument for and one against the statement and write them on the board. Encourage students to explain their ideas.
- Tell students to work in pairs to complete the exercise.

EXTRA SUPPORT Feed in some of the suggested answers below if students find it difficult to come up with ideas.

POSSIBLE ANSWERS

Arguments for:	Arguments against:
People will be off sick less. Learning how to live a healthy life is part of a good education. Healthier, happier people create a better working environment. Exercise improves concentration.	Being healthy doesn't protect you against all illness and stress. Lifestyle is an individual's responsibility/choice. It cannot be proved that exercise improves concentration.

Exercise 7

- Refer students to the Language for speaking box and ask them to read the examples.
- Put pairs together to make groups of four.
- Ask them to share their ideas and tell each other if they agree or disagree.
- Ask some students to report back to the class about their discussions.

WATCH OUT! Some students tend to say *I am agree* and *I am not agree*. This is probably from their first language.

Reading & Writing post a website comment

Exercise 8a

- As a lead-in, refer students to the photo next to the text and tell them the photo shows paper clips in a bucket of ice. Tell students the text is about an experiment. Ask them to work in pairs and discuss what the experiment might be about.
- Tell students to read the text and compare it with their ideas. To help them describe the text, tell them to read it again and try to remember as much as they can in one minute. After one minute, tell them to cover the text and work with their partner to describe the experiment.
- You could ask fast finishers to write key words on the board to summarize the experiment.

Exercise 8b

- Tell students to read the text again.
- Ask them to discuss the questions with their partner.
- Check answers together.

ANSWERS
1 The writer says the experiment shows that gamers live in a virtual world, not the real world.
2 Students' own answers

Exercise 9

- Refer students to the comments and put them into pairs.
- Tell them to read the comments and discuss the questions.

ANSWERS
Agree: FT, Firos
Disagree: Haruki, Jeff

EXTENSION: Ask students to work in small groups and discuss who they agree with most and why.

Exercise 10

- Ask students to work alone and complete the exercise.
- Ask them to compare answers with a partner.

ANSWERS
I agree That's right I'm afraid I don't (really) agree That's true

SMART COMMUNICATION Being polite when you disagree. Refer students to the disagreeing phrase in exercise 10. Ask them how polite it is and what makes it polite. Answer: *I'm afraid.* Explain to students we often use *Sorry* or *I'm afraid* to introduce a disagreement phrase. We usually use *I'm afraid* in writing and *Sorry* in speaking.

Exercise 11a

- Refer students to the Language for writing box and tell them to read it.
- Ask students to read the website comments and find examples of *too* and *also*.

Exercise 11b

- Tell students that *too* or *also* can be added to each sentence. Do number 1 with the class to show this: *He played for his local team and also played for his national team./He played for his local team and for his national team, too.*
- Put students into pairs and tell them to complete the exercise.
- Check answers.

ANSWERS

1 He played for his local team and also played for his national team.
  He played for his local team and for his national team, too.
2 She goes swimming every day and also goes to the gym twice a week.
  She goes swimming every day and she goes to the gym twice a week, too.
3 He likes watching football on TV and he also likes playing it.
  He likes watching football on TV and he likes playing it, too.
4 My cousin is a black belt in judo and (she's) also (a black belt) in karate.
  My cousin is a black belt in judo and she's a black belt in karate, too.

Exercise 12a

- Put students into pairs and ask them to write down the ideas they talked about in exercise 8b.
- Ask a student to give you two ideas agreeing with the article. Write a sentence using *also* or *too* to demonstrate the exercise. For example: *Sahel thinks video games make people lazy and also stop them talking to each other.*
- Tell students to use their notes to write a comment.

EXTRA SUPPORT Help students with ideas before they write. Ask students to report the ideas they discussed with their partners. Write them on the board and organize them into *agree* and *disagree* columns before students write their comments.

Exercise 12b

- Ask pairs to swap their comments with another pair.
- Tell students to tell the other pair if they agree or disagree with the ideas they read about.

FEEDBACK FOCUS Listen to how students use the phrases for agreeing and disagreeing and praise them for good use and encourage them to correct errors on the spot.

Exercise 13a

- Refer students to the activity on p129. Tell them to read the information and think about their opinions.
- Do the first example together with the class to demonstrate the exercise. Ask a more confident student their opinion. Write it on the board and ask the class to add in *too* or *also*, e.g.

I disagree that all students need to go to the gym because it's difficult to find time and it's expensive, too.

- Tell students to choose one of the ideas and write their own comment.

Exercise 13b

- Ask students to work in groups of four. Tell them to read each other's comments and discuss if they agree or disagree.
- Encourage students to give reasons for their opinions and to write replies.
- Ask some students to report what their group discussed to the class.

EXTRA ACTIVITY Write a forum comment. Put students in groups of four or five. Write *Children need more freedom* on the board. Ask students to think about their opinion and reasons why they think that.

Tell one student from each group to take a piece of paper and write their comment at the top of the page. You could make this a timed activity to focus students and add some challenge.

Tell students to pass their comment to the person on their left. The person on their left has to read the comment and write their response below it, as if it were in an online forum. Students repeat this until they have their original paper back. Tell them to read the comments and discuss who agrees and disagrees in the group, e.g. *I think Darius agrees because he says that children don't play in the street now. Sunniva wrote that, too.*

7.5 Video

Health and fitness in New York

VIDEOSCRIPT

New York is the 'city that never sleeps'. It is very busy and it runs for 24 hours.
The most famous part of New York is Manhattan. Every day two and a half million people travel into Manhattan for work and every year about fifty million tourists come here to visit.
Because the city is so busy it's difficult to get around. For many years, people didn't walk very far because the sidewalks were so crowded. They didn't cycle either because the traffic was so dangerous. They always took the subway or drove their own cars.
So, for many years a lot of people in New York didn't get much exercise. Because they were very busy, they ate a lot of bad food too. It isn't a surprise that a lot of New Yorkers were unhealthy.
But in 2002, the mayor of New York City, Michael Bloomberg, decided to try and change things. He told New Yorkers to take more exercise, leave their cars at home and eat better food.
So what changed? Well, New Yorkers take more exercise now. Even in winter, there are lots of runners and joggers in Central Park. And now they can also run and walk here – on the High Line. The High Line was an overhead railway on Manhattan's West Side. In 2006, it re-opened as a park. It is now a great place to jog, walk or relax.

In May 2013, New York finally got a bike scheme. With Citi Bikes, you can rent a bike anywhere in the city for nearly ten dollars a day. Now forty-two thousand people use these bikes in the city every day.

New Yorkers also eat better now. You can still eat every kind of food in the city, but the restaurant menus tell you how many calories are in your meal, so you know more about the food you're eating.

Of course, you can't change everything. Some people here still don't take enough exercise, and many people still enjoy a slice of real New York pizza! But more and more New Yorkers now enjoy a happier, healthier lifestyle.

VIDEO ANSWERS

Exercises 1 & 2
Students' own answers

Exercise 3
1 g   2 d   3 a   4 h   5 e   6 c   7 f   8 b

Exercise 4
Students' own answers

Exercise 5
Students' own answers

Exercises 6a & b
Students' own answers

Review

ANSWERS

Exercise 1a
1 d   2 c   3 e   4 f   5 b   6 a

Exercise 2a
1 I **didn't drive**. I **came** to work on foot.
2 I **didn't cook** chips or fried food. I **made** a healthy salad for lunch.
3 I **went** to the gym. I **didn't watch** TV.
4 I **went** to bed early. I **had** eight hours' sleep last night.
5 I **had** an apple for dessert. I **didn't eat** ice cream or cake.
6 I **took** the stairs. I **didn't use** the lift.

Exercise 3a
1 go   2 lend   3 tell   4 look at   5 bring

Exercises 4a & b   7.13 ⊙
1 football   2 Basketball   3 Tennis   4 ski   5 jog
6 go to the gym

AUDIOSCRIPT 7.13

The most popular sport in Argentina is football. People like playing it, going to games and watching it on TV. The Argentinian team won the World Cup in 1978 and 1986, and came second in 2014.

Basketball is also very popular, especially after Argentina won the semi-finals against the NBA players in 2004, and then took the Olympic gold home.

Tennis was a sport for rich people in the past, but now lots of people play it. The best Argentinian player, Juan Martín del Potro is world number 8.

Winter sports are also very popular in Argentina, people often ski in the Andes Mountains. And of course lots of people jog in local parks or go to the gym to keep fit!

Exercise 5a
1 asking for an opinion   2 giving an opinion
3 disagreeing and giving an opinion
4 asking for an opinion   5 giving an opinion
6 agreeing

8 Travel and transport

Unit overview

Language input

Past simple questions (CB p77)	• *Did you go with a friend? Yes, I did.*
should, shouldn't, have to, don't have to (CB p79)	• *You should have a map. You don't have to pay.*
Grammar reference (CB pp150–151)	

Vocabulary development

Talking about holidays (CB p76)	• *staying in your own country/in the countryside* • *going to another country/on a city break/on a beach holiday*
Transport (CB p78)	• *car, bike, train, on foot, taxi, bus …*
Expressions with *get*, *take* and *have* (CB p80)	• *How many emails do you get a day?* • *Where do you usually have lunch?*

Skills development

Listening: present simple and past simple questions (CB p81)
Speaking: asking for information at the train station (CB p82)
Writing: an email: your perfect holiday (CB p83)

Video

Documentary: Adventure holidays (CB p84)
Vox pops (Coursebook DVD & TG p257)

More materials

Workbook	• Language practice for vocabulary, grammar, pronunciation, speaking and writing • Reading for pleasure • Review: Units 7 & 8
Photocopiable activities	• Grammar: Rules and advice (TG p206 & TSRD) • Vocabulary: Parakeet Island (TG p223 & TSRD) • Communication: South Port to North End (TG p241 & TSRD)
Tests	• Unit 8 test (TSRD)
Unit 8 wordlist (TSRD)	

8.1 I went to …

Goals

- Talk about holidays
- Ask questions using the past simple

Lead-in

1 Closed book. Test before you teach.

- Ask students to work in pairs or groups of three and tell each other about their last holiday. You could model this with a student to demonstrate the conversation. Make sure you ask them questions and encourage them to ask you questions.
- Listen and write relevant vocabulary on the board. When students have finished, check understanding and teach pronunciation.
- Listen to students' grammar use and assess their production of the past simple and question forms. This will help you adapt the grammar focus exercises in this lesson.

2 Open book. Describing photos and eliciting vocabulary.

- Put students into pairs.
- Refer the students to the photo next to the backpacking text. Teach the word *backpacking* (= a type of holiday where people travel to different places carrying their bags on their back). Ask students to describe the photo to their partner. Ask them to discuss if they would like this type of holiday, and, if not, what holidays they like.
- Listen and write useful, relevant vocabulary on the board. Go over this with students and teach meaning and pronunciation. Try to elicit *city break* and *countryside* as this vocabulary is in exercise 1.

Vocabulary & Speaking talking about holidays

Exercise 1a

- Ask students to read the items and complete the exercise. You may need to pre-teach *city break* (= a short holiday in a city) and *countryside* (= the land away from cities with very few buildings).

Exercise 1b

- Put students into pairs and ask them to compare their ideas. Encourage them to give reasons for their choices, e.g. *I like going to other countries so I can learn about new cultures and try new food.*

Exercise 2a

- Ask students to read the texts first. You could give them a time limit of two minutes to skim them for general understanding.
- Check the meaning of unknown vocabulary. Students may need clarification on the meaning of *sightseeing* (= going to see the important monuments and tourist attractions in a place) and *trek* (= to walk in the hills and mountains).
- Tell students to work in pairs and complete the texts.

STUDY TIP Encourage them to make guesses with unknown vocabulary by reading the surrounding text and identifying the type of word that is needed in the gap, e.g. a verb, noun or adjective.

ANSWERS
1 an apartment   2 the beach   3 swimming
4 museums/art galleries   5 art galleries/museums
6 a tour   7 the town   8 lost   9 cheap hotels
10 local people   11 sightseeing   12 trek

Exercise 2b 8.1 🔘

- Play track 8.1 and ask students to listen and check their answers.

AUDIOSCRIPT 8.1

1 I love lazy holidays. I normally rent an apartment by the sea with my family. We lie on the beach most of the day and go swimming in the sea. For me, the most important thing to do on holidays is to relax and have fun.
2 For me, holidays are about culture, and I enjoy visiting all the art galleries and museums. Sometimes I go on a tour with a guide because it's a great way to learn about a place and its history. I also like going out on my own and looking around the town without a map. I always get lost, but I think it's the best way to find interesting places.
3 We stay in cheap hotels and guest houses, and travel by public transport so we can meet local people. We don't go sightseeing. We prefer to trek in the mountains and visit places that tourists don't often see.

Exercise 2c

- Put students into different pairs and ask them to discuss the questions. Encourage them to give reasons for their choices, e.g. *I am like the backpacker. I like visiting places other people don't usually go to. I don't like sightseeing.*

FEEDBACK FOCUS Listen to the pronunciation of vocabulary and correct any errors after students have spoken. Try and find a student who has good pronunciation and use them as a model.

Exercise 3a

- Ask students to work in their pairs and complete the exercise.

ANSWERS
1 d   2 f   3 b   4 a   5 c   6 e

Exercise 3b 8.2 🔘

- Play track 8.2 and ask them to check their answers.
- Play the track again and ask them to repeat the phrases.

PRONUNCIATION Intonation and drilling in pairs. Some students tend to make their voices go up at the end of questions. This can make them sound unsure and unnatural. By asking students to identify the intonation in questions, we can help them hear how to sound more natural. Asking students to drill language in pairs can help build confidence as it is a more private form of drilling.

Play the recording again and ask students to mark rising or falling intonation by drawing arrows going up or down at the end of the questions.

Tell them to work with a partner and practise saying the questions together.

1 Do you like lying on the beach?
2 Do you visit art galleries and museums?
3 Do you usually take a map or do you get lost?
4 Do you like going on a tour of places you visit?
5 Do you prefer to stay in a hotel or rent an apartment?
6 Do you ever stay in expensive hotels?

Exercise 3c

- Demonstrate the conversation with a student. Tell them to ask you the questions and model how to answer and give extra information. Encourage the students to ask follow-up questions.
- Put students into pairs and ask them to ask and answer the questions.

FEEDBACK FOCUS Listen to the pronunciation of sentence stress and intonation in the questions. You could practise the correct pronunciation by back-chaining. See lesson 1.3 for instructions on how to do this.

EXTENSION You could ask students to work with a new partner and repeat the activity.

EXTRA CHALLENGE You could tell students to choose one or two of the questions and memorize them. Ask them to walk around the class asking other students. When they have spoken to at least four students, tell them to sit with a partner and explain what they heard.

EXTRA ACTIVITY Write a blog post. Ask students to use the information from their conversations to write a blog post about their own or their partner's travel preferences. Refer them to the texts as an example. Give a word limit of sixty to seventy words.

Grammar & Listening past simple questions

Exercise 4

- Put students into pairs. Refer them to the map and photos. Ask them to discuss the questions.
- Listen and write useful language on the board. Focus on language they will hear in the listening, e.g. *temples, mountains, lakes, ruins*.
- Ask two or three students to report what they spoke about to the class.

Exercise 5a 8.3 ⊚

- Ask students to read through the list of items. Check understanding by asking students to point to the photos as you say an item that is pictured.
- Play track 8.3 and ask students to complete the exercise.
- Check answers.

ANSWERS

ruined temples ✓   Pacaya volcano ☐   trekking ✓
Lake Atitlán ✓   Antigua ✓   a Mayan city ✓
the mountains ✓   lying on the beach ☐

K Hey Tom, so you went to Guatemala on holiday this time? Where is it exactly?
T It's in Central America, just below Mexico.

K Why did you go there?
T Because it's a really interesting country. I wanted to go sightseeing and visit some of the famous ruined Mayan cities and temples.
K I see, and whereabouts in Guatemala did you go?
T I visited the whole country. I started in Antigua, it's the historic capital and then I went to Lake Atitlán, a beautiful lake in the mountains.
K So what did you do and see?
T I went on lots of tours and I went trekking in the rain forest. My favourite thing was the ruins of a Mayan city in Tikal. They're in the middle of the rain forest and they're really beautiful. I climbed to the top of a temple at sunrise.
K Wow! It sounds fantastic.
T It was. I took a lot of pictures!
K And how long did you stay?
T About six weeks.
K Did you stay in hotels?
T No, mostly guest houses and I also stayed with a Guatemalan family. They were lovely and it really helped me with my Spanish.
K Did you go on your own?
T Yes, I did, but I met lots of local people and I made lots of new friends.

CRITICAL THINKING Express your likes and preferences. Ask students to work in pairs and discuss if they would like to visit Guatemala and if they have done any of these activities (visiting ruins, etc.) in other places.

Exercise 5b

- Ask students to work alone and complete the exercise.

WATCH OUT! Clarify that *whereabouts* is the same as *where*.

ANSWERS
1 f   2 c   3 e   4 a   5 d   6 b

Exercise 5c 8.4 ⊚

- Play track 8.4 and ask students to listen and check their answers.

1
K Why did you go there?
T Because it's a really interesting country.
2
K Whereabouts in Guatemala did you go?
T I visited the whole country.
3
K What did you do and see?
T I went on lots of tours and I went trekking.
4
K How long did you stay?
T About six weeks.
5
K Did you stay in hotels?
T No, mostly guest houses.
6
K Did you go on your own?
T Yes, I did, but I met lots of local people.

Exercise 6

- Put students into pairs and refer them to the Grammar focus box. Tell them to complete the information.
- Check answers together.

1 did   2 Did   3 subject

- Refer students to *Grammar reference* on p150. There are four more exercises here students can do for homework.

EXTRA SUPPORT If you think your students will find this difficult, ask them to notice the patterns in the examples in exercise 5b. Tell them to read the questions and identify and label the parts of speech, e.g. question word, subject, *did* and main verb. You may need to go over the parts of speech: subject, object, auxiliary verb, main verb, infinitive verb and question word.

Exercise 7a

- Refer students to the first completed example. You could do the second question with the class to give extra support.
- Ask students to work with their partners and complete the exercise.

Exercise 7b   8.5 💿

- Play track 8.5 and tell students to listen and check answers.

ANSWERS/AUDIOSCRIPT 8.5

1 Where did you go on your last holiday?
2 Did you go with a friend?
3 What did you do?
4 Did you have a good time?
5 How long did you stay?
6 Where did you stay?
7 Did you like the food?

Pronunciation *did* in past simple questions

- Play track 8.6. Ask students to listen and read the information in the Pronunciation box. If your students are not familiar with phonemic symbols, this is a good opportunity to focus on them. If you have a phonemic chart in your class, refer to that. If not, write the symbols on the board and drill them in isolation. Focus on how we make the sounds with our mouths if your students find them difficult.

Exercise 8   8.7 💿

- Refer students to the three questions and tell them to read them before they listen.
- Play track 8.7 and ask students to listen.
- Repeat the track and ask students to listen and repeat.

PRONUNCIATION Drilling stress in two different ways: back-chaining and humming. Look at lesson 1.3 for instructions on back-chaining. Another way to help students notice and feel the stress is by asking them to hum the questions. This way, they forget about individual sounds and focus on stress and intonation. Hum the first question and then ask students to hum question two or three to a partner. You could do this for the questions in exercise 7a.

Exercise 9a

- Demonstrate the exercise by telling a student to ask you the questions. Expand on your answers and give extra information. You could also ask questions back to the student to make it more of a natural conversation, e.g.
Student Where did you go on your last holiday?

Teacher I went to Malaysia. How about you?
Student I went to New York.
Teacher Really? Did you have a good time?
Student Yes. What did you do in Malaysia?
Teacher I went to the beach and visited temples and the countryside.

- Put students into pairs and tell them to complete the exercise.

FEEDBACK FOCUS Listen to how students pronounce the questions. You may need to do more drilling to help them produce natural-sounding stress patterns.

Exercise 9b

- For this stage you could ask students to work in new pairs and tell their partner how similar and different the holidays with the previous partner were.

EXTRA CHALLENGE Ask students to write three more questions in the past simple about holiday experiences, e.g.
Did you do any sightseeing?
How did you travel there?
Did anything strange happen?
Ask students to work with a new partner and repeat the activity with their new partner.

EXTRA ACTIVITY Create a poster/web page for Guatemala or another destination. This activity recycles language and extends the topic.

Ask students to work with a partner and write down all the things you can do and see in Guatemala (or the destination they have chosen). Tell students to discuss how they could sell the destination to different tourists – backpackers, city breakers and people who want to relax.

Tell students they have to create a poster or web page to give information about the destination. Students can present their information to another group or the class.

GRAMMAR REFERENCE ANSWERS

Exercise 1

1 g   2 c   3 f   4 b   5 e   6 d   7 a   8 h

Exercise 2

SUGGESTED ANSWERS

1 What did Marco eat?
2 Where did John go?
3 Who did she meet?
4 Why did he leave?
5 When did we/you start?
6 How many art galleries did he go to?
7 How far did she trek?
8 How often did we/you travel by public transport?

Exercise 3

1 Did she get up early? Yes, she did.
2 Did you lose your map? No, I didn't.
3 Did they go on holiday? No, they didn't.
4 Did he have fun? Yes, he did.
5 Did you like the food? No, I didn't.

Exercise 4

1 did   2 did   3 see   4 Did   5 What   6 Why   7 have
8 didn't

8.2 Journeys

Goals

- Talk about transport
- Use *should, shouldn't, have to, don't have to*

Lead-in

1 Closed book. Recycle holiday vocabulary from lesson 8.1 and introduce new travel vocabulary.

- Write these questions on the board:
  Where did you go last summer?
  Did you take _____ ?
  Did you lie _____ ?
  Did you stay _____ ?
  Did you meet _____ ?
  How did you travel there?

- Put students into small groups of three or four.
- Ask them to complete the questions trying to remember vocabulary from lesson 8.1.
- Tell them to ask and answer the questions in their groups.
- Go through answers and ask students how people in their group responded.

2 Closed book. Test before you teach.

- Tell the class you have to go to a place far from the school after class and you can't use a car. (Choose a specific place where you could travel in different ways.)
- Ask students for the best way to get there.
- Put students into small groups of three and ask them to plan your journey.
- Ask for suggested routes. Respond with questions such as:
  Is that a fast way to travel?
  Are taxis expensive?

Vocabulary & Listening transport

Exercise 1

- Put students into pairs and refer them to the photos. Ask them to discuss the questions.

  EXTRA CHALLENGE Set a two-minute time limit for students to think of other modes of transport.

- Write students' ideas for other ways of travelling on the board. Correct any problems with pronunciation.

  ANSWERS
  a taxi **b** bicycle **c** car **d** on foot/walking **e** bus
  Other ways to travel include: by motorbike, by plane, by boat/ship, by coach, by train, on a skateboard or roller skates, on horseback, etc.

Exercise 2a 8.8 ◎

- Play track 8.8 and ask students to listen and complete the exercise.
- Check answers together.

  ANSWERS
  1 e **2** d **3** c **4** b **5** a

AUDIOSCRIPT 8.8
1
M I get the bus and the underground to work. It takes about forty minutes.

2
W Most of the time, I go to work on foot. But if it's raining, I drive.

3
M I go to work by car and it takes about an hour because there's a lot of traffic. I listen to music during the journey or I sometimes listen to CDs in English.

4
W I go by bike to work. It's great exercise! But when it rains, I take the bus.

5
M I usually take the train. Sometimes I get up late and I miss my train, so I have to get a taxi. I should get up earlier!

Exercise 2b 8.8 ◎

- Refer students to the diagrams. Check students understand the meaning of *miss* (a train/bus, etc.).
- Play track 8.8 again and ask students to listen and complete the exercise, then compare their answers in pairs.

Exercise 2c 8.9 ◎

- Play track 8.9 and ask students to check their answers.

  ANSWERS
  take/get: **1** taxi **2** bus
  miss: **3** train
  go on: **4** foot
  go by: **5** car/bike **6** bike/car

AUDIOSCRIPT 8.9
1 You take or get the train, the Underground, a taxi or the bus.
2 You can miss the bus, your plane or your train.
3 You go on foot.
4 You go by public transport, by bike or by car.

EXTENSION Ask students to test each other on vocabulary. Put students into pairs and ask one student from each pair to close their books. Tell the other students to test their partners by saying the verbs. Their partner has to list the types of travel for that verb. For extra practice, they can swap roles.

EXTRA CHALLENGE Ask students to describe their journey to the English lesson today. Put students into groups of four. Tell them to think about their journey to the lesson that morning. Check the form of the verbs from exercise 2b in the past simple. Tell students to ask each other this question: *How did you get to the lesson today?*

Exercise 3a

- As a lead-in, you could describe your own journey to give an example, e.g. *I often take this transport to work. Sometimes I miss it and I take a taxi. I never do this because work is far from my home.*
- Ask students to guess the ways of travelling you're talking about as they listen.
- Ask students to read through the sentences and circle the options that are true for them, or use their own ideas.

Exercise 3b

- Put students into groups of three.

- Demonstrate the exercise with two students to show how to ask follow-up questions, e.g.
  Teacher Tell me about the transport you take, Ana.
  Ana I often take the bus.
  Teacher Do you? Why?
  Ana Because I haven't got a car and the bus is cheap.
- You can also refer students to the sample dialogue.
- Tell students to complete the exercise. Ask two or three students to report what their groups spoke about to the class.

EXTRA ACTIVITY Ask students to write a short report in their groups describing travel habits of the whole class. Give them the following subheadings:
A description of our class (age, where we live, size of class, etc.)
Travel habits (how we travel and where to)
Summary (the most popular way to travel)

Ask students to join another group of three and compare how they travel. Tell them to take notes of answers. They should write how many people use different types of transport. If you have a large class, repeat this stage so they speak to as many other people in the class as possible.

When they have all their information, tell them to write the report. Help them write information for travel habits. Write an example or two on the board, e.g. *Eight people take the bus every day. Everyone walks every day.*

You could ask them to swap reports with other groups and read them to compare results and find examples of good language. You could also ask them to suggest corrections to grammar, vocabulary and spelling.

Reading & Grammar *should, shouldn't, have to, don't have to*

> **Text summary:** A magazine article about ways to travel in Hanoi, the capital of Vietnam. It makes suggestions and is aimed at tourists coming to the city.

Exercise 4
- As a lead-in, ask students where Hanoi is. Ask the class if anyone has been there and, if so, what type of transport they used. Refer them to the photos and ask students to name or describe each type of transport.
- Put students into pairs and refer them to the language in the box. Ask them to complete the example sentence, e.g.
  Photo 1 (the motorbike) could be dangerous because there are lots of bikes together.
- Ask students to complete the exercise, using the other photos and the words in the box.

FEEDBACK FOCUS Ask students to explain their ideas to the class. Ask listeners to respond and say if they agree or not. You could write sentences on the board to focus on relevant language and correct errors.

POSSIBLE ANSWERS
Photo 1 (motorbike taxi) could be dangerous because you could fall off. It could be uncomfortable because the seat isn't very big. It could be wet or cold in bad weather. It could be quick in heavy traffic.
Photo 2 (taxi) could be comfortable and safe, giving protection from the weather and the street. It could be expensive. It could be quick in light traffic, but slow in heavy traffic.

Photo 3 (cyclo) looks quite comfortable. It could be cold or wet in bad weather. I think it is a quick way to travel short distances.
Photo 4 (pedestrians) is the healthy way to travel. It is free, but slow unless the journey is short or the traffic is bad. It is quite safe.

Exercise 5a
- You may need to pre-teach these words:
  show (= this is a verb we use to indicate or demonstrate something. You could demonstrate the meaning in this context by showing the class something on a page of the book.)
  hold (this is a verb and the best way to demonstrate this is by miming holding a door or the back of a chair)
  helmet (draw a picture of a helmet or mime putting one on to teach the meaning)
  be against the law (= this is a phrase we use to describe something that is not legal)
- Ask students to read the article, then write the kind of transport under photos 1–4 and compare their answers with a partner.

ANSWERS
1 *Xe om* 2 Taxi 3 Cyclo 4 On foot
EXTRA CHALLENGE A jigsaw reading. Put students into groups of four. Tell each student to read about a different mode of transport from exercise 5a. Give them a time limit of two minutes to read and prepare to summarize what they've read. Ask each student to tell their group about that way of travelling.

Exercise 5b
- Ask students to work with a partner and discuss the question.
- Ask two or three students to share their results with the class.

CRITICAL THINKING Relate ideas in a text to your own experience. Put students into groups of three or four. Ask them to compare the ways of travelling in the article with their own town or city.

Exercise 6
- Ask students to read the highlighted words in the text in exercise 5. Refer students to the Grammar focus box. Ask them to read it and complete the matching exercise.
- Tell students to compare their answers.
- Check answers together.

ANSWERS
1 c 2 b 3 a 4 d
EXTRA SUPPORT Ask students to find more examples of the grammar points in the article. This will help them understand the meaning.

WATCH OUT! Some students tend to put *to* before the main verb, e.g. ~~You should to do that~~. If you think your students will have problems with the form of the grammar, highlight it on the board and ask them to make a note of the structure in positive and negative forms. See the *Grammar reference* section for ideas on how to present this on the board.

WATCH OUT! Some students tend to find it difficult to understand the meaning of *don't have to*. They think it means the same as *mustn't*. Ask students to give examples to clarify meaning, e.g. *In this school you don't have to … . In my job I don't have to …* (*wear a uniform, for example*).

- Refer students to *Grammar reference* on p151. There are three more exercises here that students can do for homework.

Pronunciation sentence stress

Exercise 7a 8.10 🔊
- Play track 8.10 and tell students to listen and notice the stress.

Exercise 7b 8.10 🔊
- Play the track again and ask students to listen and repeat.

Exercise 8a
- Ask students to work in pairs and complete the sentences.
- Encourage students to extend the answers with reasons, e.g. *You should wear your seatbelt for the whole journey on a plane. You don't have to wear it all the time but it's safer.*

POSSIBLE ANSWERS
1 shouldn't 2 have to 3 don't have to 4 should
5 should

Exercise 8b
- Put pairs together to make groups of four and tell them to compare their answers.
- Ask them to report back to the class what they said for each answer. Discuss any different answers as a class.

PRONUNCIATION *Have to* /hæftə/. When we say *have to* in a sentence, we pronounce the /v/ as /f/ and we use the schwa in the *to*. You could show students this by saying some sentences from this lesson using *have to*. Ask the class for three more sentences using *have to* and write them on the board. Tell them to work in their pairs and practise saying the sentences to each other.

Exercise 9a
- Encourage students to relate the task to their own knowledge and context. As a lead-in, ask students to discuss their own transport system in their town or city.
- Put students into pairs and ask them to complete the exercise.

POSSIBLE ANSWERS
You shouldn't listen to music on a bicycle, it isn't safe.
You shouldn't eat hot, smelly food on public transport.
You shouldn't play loud music on public transport.
You don't have to give up your seat to old people, pregnant women or small children, but it is a kind thing to do.
You have to buy a ticket to travel on public transport.
You shouldn't put your feet on the seats.
You have to wear a seatbelt in the front and the back of a car.
You shouldn't leave your bags in everyone's way on trains, buses, or planes.
You should stand in a queue at the bus stop.

Exercise 9b
- Put pairs together and ask them to tell each other their sentences to find similarities and differences. Ask some pairs to tell the class what their similarities were.

EXTRA ACTIVITY Ask students to write rules and advice for other situations. Ask students to work in groups and think of situations where they might give advice to a tourist in their town or city, e.g. good places to visit and places to avoid. Tell students they are going to write a short article, similar to the text about Hanoi, about their town. Ask them to brainstorm ideas and make a note of them in their groups.

You could set this as homework or make it a collaborative writing activity in class.

GRAMMAR REFERENCE ANSWERS
Exercise 1
1 have to 2 don't have to 3 has to 4 have to
5 don't have to 6 should 7 shouldn't
Exercise 2
1 You should drink bottled water in Vietnam.
2 We have to show our passports to immigration.
3 I think children shouldn't eat lots of sweets.
4 He doesn't have to buy a ticket.
5 Her teacher says she should read every day.
6 She doesn't have to wear a coat (today).
7 Drivers shouldn't drive fast in the rain.
8 I have to study mathematics at school.
Exercise 3
1 has to 2 have to 3 have to 4 doesn't have to
5 have to 6 shouldn't 7 should

8.3 Vocabulary and skills development

Goals
- Use expressions with *get, take,* and *have*
- Understand present and past questions

Lead-in
1 Closed book. Revise transport collocations with *get* and *take*.
- Write the verbs on the board and ask the class to remember types of transport from lesson 8.2, e.g. *take/get a taxi.* Write the transport words on the board.
- Ask students if they know any other nouns that can go after these verbs. Ask for one or two examples only and write them on the board. Tell students they will learn more words that go with these verbs in this lesson.
2 Open book. Discussing an illustration.
- Refer students to the image. Ask the class to describe what they can see. Teach related vocabulary such as *(set of) scales, balance.* (Possible answer: The illustration has two images on a set of scales; one is about holidays and relaxing, the other is about work.)
- Put students into pairs and ask them to discuss what they think the image is representing, e.g. *It is about the life/work balance and what people spend time on.*
- Ask some students to share their ideas with the class.
- Group the students into bigger groups of four and ask them to discuss their own life/work balance. Do they work and relax in equal amounts or do they have more work or relaxation time?

Vocabulary & Speaking expressions with *get, take,* and *have*

Exercise 1

- As a lead-in, ask a more confident student the first question. Encourage them to expand their answer by asking them follow-up questions, and then refer students to the sample dialogue.
- Ask students to read through the rest of the questions. Tell them to think about their answers as they read.

EXTRA SUPPORT If you think your students will find it hard to ask questions spontaneously, ask them to write follow-up questions before they start the exercise for each question.

- Put students into pairs and tell them to ask and answer the questions with their partner.
- Ask two or three students to report a few things that their partner said to the class.

FEEDBACK FOCUS Listen to the students' follow-up questions and write good examples on the board. Go over them after the students have finished the exercise.

POSSIBLE FOLLOW-UP QUESTIONS

1 Who are they usually from? Are they business or personal? Do you read, and reply to, them all? How many are junk-mail?
2 Do you eat alone? What do you usually have? Is it expensive? Is it busy?
3 What do you take photos of? Do you post them online? Do you have a camera or do you use a phone or tablet?
4 Why do you think that? Would you be happy poor?
5 How do you decide? Do you always use the same company?
6 Do you read them straight away? Do you always reply? Are you quick at texting?
7 What time do you eat? Who cooks? Is he/she a good cook? What's your favourite dish/meal?
8 Why do you take the bus, not the train or a taxi? Are buses expensive in your country? Do they run on time?
9 Do you have a short sleep? Why/Why not? Do you sleep on the sofa or go to bed?
10 How long does it take you? Does anyone help you? Have you done your homework for today?

Exercise 2

- Refer students to the Vocabulary focus box. Ask them to read the information.

STUDY TIP You could discuss note-taking with your students and explain how students can help develop their vocabulary by writing down common collocations, e.g. verbs and nouns that commonly go together, verbs and prepositions, adjectives and nouns, etc.

- You could ask students to discuss the verbs and how they are different in their own language and which verbs they find difficult to remember and use.

Exercise 3

- Refer students to the box and the table, and tell them that most of these verbs and nouns appeared in exercise 1.
- Ask them to complete the exercise and compare their answers with a partner. Remind them to add other things they know.

- Check answers together.
- You could ask fast finishers to write the answers on the board.

WATCH OUT! You can *get* or *take a taxi and a bus*. You can *take* or *have a shower*. Teach students that both are acceptable.

PRONUNCIATION Weak forms. You could revise weak forms by showing students how the articles are not stressed when we say these phrases, e.g. *have a shower, take a taxi*. The article is pronounced as a schwa [ə].

Ask students to repeat these phrases after you and check the pronunciation chorally and individually.

ANSWERS

get	take	have
a bus	a bus	a good time
a taxi	a long time	a shower
a text message	a taxi	a sleep
emails	photos	dinner
lunch		fun
dinner		lunch
something to eat		something to eat

Exercise 4

- Ask students to complete the exercise. Tell them they have to change the form of the verb to the third person or past in some examples.
- Check answers together.

ANSWERS

1 has/takes 2 have 3 get 4 had 5 take
6 takes/gets 7 got/took 8 takes

Exercise 5

- Put students into pairs and ask them to discuss their daily routines.
- Ask some students to report what their partner does to the class.

EXTRA CHALLENGE Ask students to describe what they did this week using the verbs in the past.

EXTENSION Put students into new pairs and tell them to describe their previous partner's routine so they can practise using the third person.

Listening & Speaking present simple and past simple questions

Exercise 6a 8.11 🎧

- As a lead-in you could elicit two questions from the class about your life – one in the present and one in the past simple. Write them on the board.
- Play track 8.11 and tell students to complete the exercise.
- Check answers together.

ANSWERS

1 past 2 present 3 present 4 present 5 past
6 past

AUDIOSCRIPT 8.11

1 Did you have fun there?
2 How often do you have a sleep in the afternoons?
3 How many text messages do you get?
4 Do you want to get something to eat now?
5 Did he get a taxi last night?
6 Did it take her a long time to learn English?

Exercise 6b 8.12

- Refer students to the Unlock the code box.
- Play track 8.12 and ask them to read and listen to the information.
- Check understanding by asking students to summarize the information.
- You could also test their understanding of the phonemic script by writing the phonemes from the box on the board and asking students to say them.
- Further test understanding by asking for more examples of time references to indicate present and past.

Exercise 6c 8.13

- Play track 8.13 and ask students to complete the exercise.
- You will need to repeat the recording. Pause between sentences to allow time for writing.

EXTRA SUPPORT If you think your students will find this difficult, you could give them extra help by writing the questions or parts of questions on cards and asking them to listen and order the cards.

EXTENSION You could write some additional questions containing errors on cards and ask students to identify and correct the errors. To do this, put students into pairs or small groups and give each group one or two cards. Tell them to correct the question and write it in their notebooks. After a set time, tell them to pass the card(s) to another pair/group. Repeat this until they have written all the questions in their notebooks.

- Check answers together.

ANSWERS/AUDIOSCRIPT 8.13

1 Where did you have lunch?
2 Does he get lots of emails every day?
3 Why did you take the stairs?
4 Did he take photos last week?
5 How often do you get a taxi?
6 Did you take the bus on Sunday?

Exercise 7a 8.14

- As a lead-in, refer students to the photo. Ask them what they think it is. Tell students the information below if they don't know what it is. Ask them to discuss with a partner what they know about Moscow.

> **Background note:** The photo is of Komsomolskaya station in Moscow. It is part of the metro system in the city. This famous station was opened in the 1950s and is known for its beautiful decoration. The design is based on the theme of independence. You can find short videos in English on the internet if you wish to show your students some visuals of the station.

- Ask students to read through the information and questions before they listen.
- Play track 8.14 and ask students to complete the exercise.

- Check answers together.

ANSWERS

1 George is going to live there next month.
2 She thinks: the underground is fantastic and cheap; buses are often full; taxis get you around quicker; some days the transport is good, other days it is not so good.
3 You can wave down any car and get a lift from anyone, for money – it doesn't have to be a taxi.

AUDIOSCRIPT 8.14

G Guess what? I'm going to Moscow for two months.
H Really? Is it for fun or do you have to work?
G Well, a bit of both. You went to Moscow a few years ago, didn't you?
H Yes, I did. I even lived there for a while.
G How long did you live there?
H Three years.
G Oh, wow! And do you speak the language?
H Yes, a little. I can buy things in shops and order food in restaurants.
G And did you like the city?
H Yes, it's great. I had a really good time.
G What about things like accommodation and transport? What did you think of the transport system?
H Well, the Underground is just … fantastic! It's really famous! It was built in the 1930s, and every station is a work of art.
G But is it a good way to travel around Moscow?
H Well, local people complain about it a lot, but I always thought it was very good. And it's quite cheap.
G What about the buses? Do the local people use the buses?
H Oh yes, the buses are usually full. But to be honest, I got taxis quite a lot to my lessons. I taught in companies and local businesses, so I didn't want to be late! You know, Moscow's like lots of other big cities: lots of traffic, really busy, sometimes the transport is good, other days not so good. But there is one great thing: you can simply stand in the street and stop any car, like a taxi, and they give you a lift for money.
G Oh wow, that's cool! OK, so moving on to accommodation …

Exercise 7b 8.14

- Ask students to read through the questions.
- Play track 8.14 again and ask students to complete the exercise.
- Tell them to compare answers with a partner.

ANSWERS

1 present   2 past   3 present   4 past   5 past
6 present

Exercise 7c 8.15

- Ask students to listen and check their answers.

EXTENSION Ask students to change all the questions into the other tense, i.e. past to present and present to past.

AUDIOSCRIPT 8.15

1 Do you have to work? (present)
2 How long did you live there? (past)
3 Do you speak the language? (present)
4 Did you like the city? (past)
5 What did you think of the transport system? (past)
6 Do the local people use buses? (present)

EXTENSION Put students into pairs. Ask them to discuss if they would like to visit Moscow and why.

Exercise 8a

- Tell students to list the types of topics talked about in the lesson. (Possible answers: travel, routines, transport.)
- Ask students to work alone and write questions. Monitor them closely and check their grammar. Correct any errors on the spot.

EXTRA CHALLENGE Tell students who finish fast to write extra questions. You could give a time limit and ask students to try and use as many different question words as they can. When time is up, see who has the most different question words.

Exercise 8b

- Put students into pairs. Tell them to ask and answer their questions.

FEEDBACK FOCUS Listen to the pronunciation of weak forms in questions. If you hear errors, give students extra support by stopping the exercise and drilling the correct pronunciation. Then, tell students to continue while focusing on their pronunciation.

EXTRA SUPPORT Do a class brainstorm of questions students could ask each other. Write the questions on the board and ask students to correct any errors.

EXTRA CHALLENGE Tell students to invent the rest of the conversation from the recording by thinking of questions about accommodation first and then other topics we might ask about in this situation.

Tell them to write another eight to ten lines. They could then compare their conversations with a partner and/or act them out together.

8.4 Going places

Goals

- Ask for information at the train station
- Write an email about your perfect holiday

Lead-in

1 Closed book. Revise language from this unit.

- Put students into groups of three and ask them to look through the last two lessons and write five questions to test another group on vocabulary or grammar.
- Monitor and help them make questions. Suggest question types, e.g.
  What's the opposite of … ? How do you spell … ? Give me a word that means the same as … . Put … into a sentence or question.
- Put students into groups of six and tell the groups to test each other.
- Go over any common problems with the class.

2 Open book. Discuss a photo.

- Put students into pairs and refer them to the photos on page 82. Ask them to describe the photos. They should realize they show India from the reading beside the photos. Ask them to compare the transport they see with the transportation in their own city or town.

Listening & Speaking at the train station

Exercise 1

EXTRA SUPPORT If you think your students will find it difficult to talk about this straight away, then give them one minute to think about it and make some notes before they start. Refer to the prompts in the Coursebook and ask students to make full questions. For extra support you could ask them to write the questions out in full before they speak.

- Put students into pairs and ask them to ask and answer questions together.
- Listen and make a note of the language they use and whether their questions are accurate.

FEEDBACK FOCUS This lesson revises past simple questions. If your students make lots of errors with this grammar, spend some time going over the structure and meaning. Refer to the *Grammar reference* pages for ideas.

ANSWERS
Where did you go?
When did you go?
Why did you go?
What kind of transport did you take?
How long was the journey?
Did you enjoy the journey? Why/Why not?

Exercise 2a

> **Background note:** The recording is a conversation between Marcel and a ticket officer in Howrah station, Kolkata, India. Rail travel is very popular in India and the country is famous for its railways.

- As a lead-in, ask students what they know about India and its railways. After discussing this, refer them to the text next to the photos and tell them to read it.
- After reading, ask students what they found most surprising and interesting.
- Put students into pairs and ask them to read the questions and complete the matching activity before they listen.
- You may need to pre-teach:
  platform (= the thing people stand on to wait for the train before they get on)
  sleeper ticket (= a ticket that allows you to sleep on the train)
  a single/return ticket (= a one-way ticket; a there and back ticket)
  rupees (= they are Indian currency)

Exercise 2b 8.16

- Play track 8.16 and ask students to listen and check their answers.

ANSWERS
1 d 2 a 3 g 4 c 5 f 6 b 7 e

AUDIOSCRIPT 8.16
T Hello. Can I help you?
M Yes, please. I need to get to New Delhi.
T OK. When would you like to travel?
M Later today or tomorrow. When's the next train?
T The next one leaves at 18.40 p.m.
M OK, and how long does it take?
T About seventeen hours. It arrives at 11.25 a.m. tomorrow.

M Right. How much is a sleeper ticket?
T Would you like a single or a return?
M Just a single, please.
T OK, then. That's 775 rupees.
M 775 rupees … OK. Which platform does it leave from?
T Platform 7.
M Thank you.

Exercise 2c 8.17 📀

• Play track 8.17 and ask students to listen and repeat.

EXTRA ACTIVITY Focus on pronunciation of numbers. Draw two columns, A and B, on the board. In the A column write 13, 14, 15, 16, 17, 18, 19 and in the B column write 30, 40, 50, 60, 70, 80, 90. Tell students you will say a number from column A or B. Students have to listen and then put their left hand up for A and their right hand up for B.

Shout out numbers in a random order. Assess students' ability and extend this activity to give sufficient practice. Elicit the fact that in teen numbers the stress is on the last syllable.

Ask students to continue the activity in pairs taking turns to say the numbers to each other. The listener says A or B.

AUDIOSCRIPT 8.17

1 Can I help you?
2 When would you like to travel?
3 When's the next train?
4 How long does it take?
5 How much is a sleeper ticket?
6 Would you like a single or a return?
7 Which platform does it leave from?

Exercise 3a

• Refer students to the questions in exercise 2a and ask students to complete the exercise.

ANSWERS
1 Hello. Can I help you? T
2 When would you like to travel? T
3 When's the next train? M
4 How long does it take? M
5 And how much is a sleeper ticket? M
6 Would you like a single or a return? T
7 Which platform does it leave from? M

Exercise 3b

• Refer students to the Language for speaking box and ask students to read the information and to check the answers they wrote in exercise 3a.

• Check understanding of first- and second-class tickets. (First class is a luxury service and second class is a normal service. First class is more expensive. In British English second class is also called standard class).

Exercise 3c

• Put students into pairs and ask them to take turns asking and answering the questions. Encourage them to experiment by using the questions in the Language for speaking box.

FEEDBACK FOCUS Correct on the spot. This is a controlled practice activity so students need instant feedback to focus on their accuracy. Listen to the pronunciation of numbers and correct errors. Also listen to the questions and correct errors with grammar.

Exercise 4

• Put students into pairs and ask them to decide who is Student A and who is Student B.

• Refer students to their pages and tell them to read their information.

• Demonstrate the activity with a more confident student.

• Ask students to role-play the conversations.

Reading & Writing email: a perfect holiday

Exercise 5

• As a lead-in, put students into pairs and ask them to discuss what they see in the two photos on page 83.

• Listen and write any useful vocabulary on the board. Check meaning and pronunciation with the class.

• Refer students to the emails. Ask them to read them quickly. You could give a time limit for this.

EXTRA CHALLENGE A jigsaw reading to get a general understanding of the emails. Divide pairs into Students A and B. Tell Students A to read the first email and Students B to read the second email. Students should then summarize their email to their partner.

• Tell students to work together to insert the phrases into the emails.

• Check answers together.

ANSWERS
1 a 2 d 3 b 4 c

EXTENSION Discussion. Put students into groups of three or four and ask them to discuss whether they would like to visit India and why or why not.

Exercise 6a

• Refer students to the Language for writing box. Ask them to read the information.

• Check that students are clear that they need to add a pronoun and verb after the linking word.

EXTRA SUPPORT Use these sentence beginnings to elicit possible complete sentences using *so* and *because*. Write the students' examples on the board and correct any errors with grammar.
I was tired so/because …
It was an easy exercise so/because …
We woke up early so/because …

Exercise 6b

• Do the first question on the board with the class so they know what to do.

• Put students into pairs and ask them to complete the exercise.

• Check answers together.

ANSWERS
1 I'm taking lots of photos because everywhere is really colourful and interesting.
2 There's just so much to do and see, so I decided to stay for another week.
3 I got lost because I forgot my map.
4 We stayed in the hotel because the weather was bad.
5 We went to the beach because we love swimming.
6 The food was really good, so we ate at a local restaurant every night.

Exercise 7a

- As a lead-in, you could ask students to ask you the questions about your perfect holiday. Give clear, extended answers, e.g.
  Student A Where are you?
  Teacher I'm in the south of France.
  Student A How did you travel?
  Teacher I travelled by plane because it's so quick and easy. The train is very slow!
  Student B How long are you staying?
  Teacher I'm staying for two weeks, so I've got lots of time to explore the country.
  Student C What did you do on the first day?
  Teacher I arrived late at night, so I didn't do much. I arrived at my hotel and went to bed!
- Check comprehension by asking students to work in pairs and summarize what you said with their partner.
- Go over the answers you gave with the class.
- Ask students to think of their own perfect holiday. Tell them to use the questions to develop their ideas.

Exercise 7b

- Put students into pairs and ask them to take turns asking and answering questions about their perfect holiday.
- Remind them to use *so* and *because*.

EXTENSION Ask students to summarize what they spoke about. Put students into new pairs and ask them to tell their partner what their previous partner talked about, e.g.
Helene talked about a holiday in … . It was great because … She travelled by train. She had delicious food, etc.

To extend this further, ask students to repeat the original discussion with their new partner.

EXTRA ACTIVITY Do this fun activity to repeat and extend the language. Ask students to imagine their worst holiday. They can repeat the task using the questions but with different prompts for the last question: *What do you dislike about the place where you are?*

FEEDBACK FOCUS Pronunciation of weak forms. In the previous lessons, students practised using weak forms in questions. Listen to their pronunciation of the questions in this exercise and go over any problems with weak forms after they have finished speaking. If you think they are having lots of problems, stop them and do a sandwich correction slot. This is where you stop a speaking exercise, do some corrective work and then restart the exercise so students can try and implement what they have corrected in their speech in the rest of the exercise.

Exercise 8a

SMART COMMUNICATION Informal writing. Some students have trouble writing informally. To help them, we can focus on standard expressions that are regularly used, e.g. when opening and closing emails to friends instead of writing emails to work colleagues or people we don't know. This exercise focuses on informal writing.

- Refer students to the emails on page 83. Tell them they are going to write similar emails.
- Ask them how the emails start (*Hi …/Dear …*).
- Ask students how many words the texts have (around 50–70). They should write an email of a similar length.

- Ask students how the emails end. Tell them to use similar language in their emails.
- Tell students to use their ideas from the previous exercise to write the email.

Exercise 8b

- Tell students to swap emails with a partner and read the questions.
- Ask them to check the emails and discuss the questions with the person who wrote the email.

EXTRA CHALLENGE Use correction codes. Correction codes are used to correct written work. They help the writer to self-correct their work. Show students a simple correction code on the board, e.g.
GR – Grammar error
V – Vocabulary error
WO – Word order
P – Punctuation error

Adapt this to your students' needs. Ask students to read the emails they are given and try and use the codes to show errors.

Tell them to give the email back to the writer and ask writers to try and correct their errors before giving the email back to the 'editor'. The editor can then give more focused feedback on the three questions in exercise 8b.

EXTRA ACTIVITY Gallery reading and speaking. Post the corrected emails around the room. Ask students to walk around and read all the emails, and choose one or two to describe which places they would like to visit. Tell them to sit with a partner and explain which destinations they chose and why.

To further extend this, tell students to work with a new partner and repeat the conversation.

You could end the lesson by asking students to vote on the most popular destination.

8.5 Video

Adventure holidays

VIDEOSCRIPT

Holidays are a great way to see new places. But while some people want to go sightseeing or relax on the beach, others prefer exciting adventure holidays.
They hike through mountains, go trekking across the desert, or ride boats through dangerous waters.
Sarah Darby is one of these people.
Sarah is from Oxford in the United Kingdom. She took three months holiday from work and went on a cycling trip in South America.
I journeyed to Patagonia starting off in Ushuaia which is the southernmost city on earth.
I flew my bicycle out from Britain to Ushuaia and I wanted to cycle the Carretera Austral.
The Carretera Austral is a 1,240 kilometre long highway. It runs through Patagonia and Chile and goes through some of the most remote areas in the world. So, why did Sarah decide to go there?
I decided to go to Patagonia because it was an opportunity to go to a different continent, and I just thought well, you know, Patagonia is a dream place to go to if you like remote and wild places.

One of Sarah's favourite things about the journey was the scenery. The landscape was amazing and the colours changed all the time from red to orange, yellow, green and even grey.

But that wasn't the only thing she liked about the journey. *The other thing that amazed me about the place was the people. They're really, really generous and, you know, they often buy you coffee or a bowl of chips or even lunch … you know, after a whole day of cycling they kind of want to help you out and, yeah, the people are amazing.*

But cycling through this beautiful but empty landscape wasn't easy.

I read a lot of horror stories before I went about the Carretera Austral. It's a very lonely, empty road. There's hardly any traffic on it.

The road was in a very bad condition and she fell off her bike a lot of times. She sometimes had to push the bike, which wasn't easy.

The whole bike weighed 46 kilograms, so it was heavy. And I'm, you know, quite a fit, strong person I think but it was – yeah – it was difficult.

Sarah wanted to cycle the entire highway but she only had three months and she wanted to see a lot of places. So what other kind of transport did she use?

Chile is a very, very long country and I really wanted to get to the very northern tip and see the Atacama Desert as well so after cycling I left my bike in Santiago and I used overnight buses. I did use pickup trucks when I needed to. I also used boats and I took a flight to Easter Island as the very last thing.

Sarah travelled from the southern tip of Patagonia to the Atacama Desert in northern Chile. It was an incredible journey with lots of amazing things to do and see.

VIDEO ANSWERS

Exercise 1a
Students' own answers

Exercise 1b
Where did she go? She went to South America.
What did she do? She rode her bike.
What did she find difficult? She wanted to see lots of things during her trip.

Exercise 3a
1 Sarah prefers **exciting / adventure** holidays.
2 Sarah went to South America on a **cycling** trip.
3 She travelled around South America for **three** months.
4 Sarah wanted to go to Patagonia in Chile because it's **a different continent / a dream place / remote and wild**.
5 Her favourite thing about the journey was **the scenery / amazing landscape / changing colours.**
6 She thinks that the people of Chile are **amazing / generous / helpful.**
7 Cycling on the Carretera Austral wasn't easy because **it's empty / lonely / she fell off / difficult road in bad condition / bike was heavy.**
8 The bike was quite heavy, it weighed **forty-six** kilograms.
9 Sarah also used other forms of transport, for example, **overnight buses / pickup trucks / boats / aeroplane.**

Exercise 3b
Students' own answers

Exercise 4a & b
Students' own answers

Review

ANSWERS

Exercise 1a
1 Where did you go?
2 What did you do?
3 How long did you stay?
4 When did you go?
5 Did you travel alone?
6 Did you stay in a hotel?

Exercises 2a & b 8.18
1 You don't have to leave a tip in restaurants.
2 You shouldn't forget your umbrella.
3 Australians don't have to have a visa to visit.
4 You shouldn't go to Myers Park at night.
5 You have to get a student visa to study for more than three months.
6 You should visit the islands in the Hauraki Gulf.

Exercise 3
1 beach holiday, city break
2 apartment, hotel
3 go on a tour, go sightseeing, go trekking, lie on the beach, visit museums
4 backpacker, beach lover

Exercise 5a
1 take/get   2 get   3 have   4 take   5 have   6 have

Exercises 6a & b 8.19
A Hello. Can I **help** you?
B Yes. When's the next bus **to** Manchester?
A There's one at 4.00 p.m.
B How **much** does it cost?
A Do you want a single or **return** ticket?
B A return, please.
A And when would you like to come **back**?
B Next Sunday.
A OK, that's £32, please.
B How **long** does it take?
A Two hours 45 minutes. Here's your ticket.
B Where does it **leave** from?
A Bay six. It's just over there.

9 Cooking and eating

Unit overview

Language input

Countable and uncountable nouns (CB p86)	• *I had a pear for breakfast.* • *I often have rice for lunch.*
Quantifiers (CB p88)	• *How much time do you spend in the kitchen? A lot.* • *I don't have many cookbooks.*
Grammar reference (CB pp152–153)	

Vocabulary development

Food and drink (CB p86)	• *a bottle of lemondade, bread, chicken, jam, lemons, noodles …*
In the kitchen (CB p89)	• *bowls, fork, frying pan, kettle, oven …*
Say numbers (CB p91)	• *three thousand, four hundred and twenty*

Skills development

Listening: understanding numbers (CB p90)	
Writing: asking about and recommending a place (CB p92)	
Speaking: in a restaurant (CB p93)	

Video

Documentary: Making a pizza (CB p94)	
Vox pops (Coursebook DVD & TG p258)	

More materials

Workbook	• Language practice for vocabulary, grammar, pronunciation, speaking and writing
Photocopiable activities	• Grammar: Perfect pairs (TG p207 & TSRD) • Vocabulary: Let's cook (TG p224 & TSRD) • Communication: Ten conversations (TG p241 & TSRD)
Tests	• Unit 9 test (TSRD) • Progress test: Units 7–9
Unit 9 wordlist (TSRD)	

9.1 Food and drink

Goals

- Talk about food and drink
- Use countable/uncountable nouns with *some/any*

Lead-in

1 Open book. Review countries and test knowledge of food vocabulary.

- Put students into small groups and ask them to look back at Unit 8 and find at least three different countries that are mentioned.
- Ask them to think about what food they think people eat in those countries. Set a time limit of three minutes. Encourage them to help each other with vocabulary.
- Ask each group to tell the class about one country and the food they thought of. Listen and write relevant vocabulary on the board.
- Go over vocabulary after students have finished speaking. Encourage students to write the vocabulary in their notebooks.

2 Closed book. Describing food preferences.

- Prepare three images of different types of food, e.g. a piece of cake, a salad and some fish.
- Put students into groups and ask them to think of as many words as they can to describe each food. Listen and make a note of useful language. You could write it on the board and go over it after the activity has finished.
- Ask students to choose which dish they prefer and say why.

Vocabulary & Speaking food and drink

Exercise 1a

- Put students into pairs and ask them to complete the exercise.
- Check answers, and go over any unknown vocabulary together.

Exercise 1b 9.1 🎧

- Play track 9.1 and ask students to listen and check their answers.
- Play the track again and ask students to repeat the items.

ANSWERS/AUDIOSCRIPT 9.1

1 yoghurt   2 bread   3 a bottle of lemonade
4 salad   5 jam   6 chicken   7 honey   8 noodles
9 lemons   10 beef   11 rice   12 olives   13 sweetcorn
14 pasta   15 mushrooms   16 a pear

PRONUNCIATION Ask students to mark the word stress on words with more than one syllable. Check their answers together and drill any problem words.

Exercise 2a

- Ask students to read questions 1–6. They should know the meaning of all the terms but check they understand *healthy, sweet* and *unhealthy*. Tell students to work alone and complete the exercise.

ANSWERS

1 **meat:** beef, chicken
2 **vegetables:** mushrooms, salad, sweetcorn
3 **fruit:** lemons, olives, pears
4 **sweet:** a bottle of lemonade, honey, jam
5 **healthy:** students' own answers
6 **unhealthy:** students' own answers

Exercise 2b

- Put students into pairs and ask them to compare answers.
- Check answers. Students may have different ideas for questions 5 and 6. Ask them to justify and explain their choices.

FEEDBACK FOCUS Listen to students' pronunciation during this exercise and correct any errors with the vocabulary.

Grammar & Listening countable and uncountable nouns

Exercise 3a

- As a lead-in, you could test your students' knowledge of this grammar point. They should have come across it before.
- Write *lemons* and *rice* on the board and ask them what is different about the grammar of these items. Elicit that lemons can be counted; you can say *two lemons*. Rice on the other hand cannot be counted; you can't say *two rices*. Ask students to expand on their knowledge of the grammar if you think they can, e.g. we use *a* with singular countable nouns, but we can't say *a rice*.
- Refer students to the Grammar focus box and ask them to read it.
- Refer students to exercises 1–3 in *Grammar reference* on p152. Students can do these for homework.

Exercise 3b

- Refer students to the table and the example. You could ask for one more example for each column to clarify the exercise.
- Put students into pairs and ask them to complete the exercise.

WATCH OUT! There are some items which may confuse students. Chicken can be countable if we are talking about a whole chicken but usually we buy chicken breasts/legs/wings, etc. and ask for these by number. We usually talk about chicken in a more general way using the uncountable noun, e.g. *I like chicken/ I'd like some chicken*.

- Check answers together.

ANSWERS

Singular countable nouns: a bottle of lemonade, a pear
Plural countable nouns: lemons, mushrooms, noodles, olives
Uncountable nouns: beef, bread, chicken, honey, jam, pasta, rice, sweetcorn, yoghurt , salad

Exercise 4a

- As a lead-in, ask a more confident student about the food from exercise 1a that they like/don't like/often have.
- Refer students to the list and ask them to read the phrases to explain their ideas.
- Put students into pairs and ask them to talk about the food and drink in exercise 1a and other food and drink that they know.

Write the new words that students mention on the board and check with the class that they understand the vocabulary.

Exercise 4b

- Write the following on the board:
  We both often have …
  We both had … this morning/yesterday, etc.
  We both like …

- Tell students they will have to tell the class what they have in common. Give them some time to prepare and tell them to use the phrases on the board.

- Adapt this exercise to the size of your class. If you have a large class, put pairs into a group of four or six and tell them to describe what they have in common to the group.

- If you have a small class, you could ask pairs to take turns to report their ideas to the class.

EXTENSION If you ask pairs/groups to tell the class their ideas, make sure everyone can see and hear the speakers. Give the listeners a task, e.g. listen and write the foods that are mentioned, or listen and see if they have the same things in common as the speakers.

Exercise 5

> **Background note:** Camden market is a famous market in London, which started at the beginning of the 20th century as a small food market, but now is very big and consists of lots of smaller markets joined together. They sell clothes, furniture and other things. There are also lots of food stalls with food from different countries. Camden Market is popular with people from London as well as tourists.

- As a lead-in, ask students to name some nationalities whose food is internationally famous and eaten in lots of different countries, e.g. *Italian, American, Chinese, Middle Eastern, Japanese, Greek, Thai, Indian*.

- Put students into groups of three or four.

- Refer them to the photos and ask them to discuss the questions.

- Ask two or three groups to report on what their group said to the class. You could encourage them to use *both* where applicable.

EXTENSION Ask students to list as many foods from those countries as they can. Possible answers:
Italian food: pasta, cheese, pizza, cooked meats, salad, lasagne, olive oil, wine
Chinese food: rice, noodles, beef, pork, fish, prawns and other seafood, vegetables

Exercise 6 9.2 🔘

> **Audio summary:** This recording is of a conversation between two people at Camden market in London.

- As a lead-in, ask students if they have been to a market and what they bought there. Tell them the background about Camden Market. Some students may have been there or know about it.

- Play track 9.2 and ask students to say which stall the speakers went to.

ANSWERS
The Chinese stall in photo 2. They order Kung Pao chicken and a Coke.

AUDIOSCRIPT 9.2
L Wow! Look at all this different food!
C I know. I can't decide what I want.
L Well there's some pizza over there.
C No! We can have pizza any day. Let's try something different.
L OK, what about this place?
C Mmmm … that looks delicious but what is it?
L Excuse me, what is this?
M It's Kung Pao chicken.
C It smells so good! What does it come with?
M It comes with some noodles.
C I don't really like noodles. Is there any bread?
M No, we don't have any bread, sorry. But we have some rice.
C Great. So could I have a small Kung Pao chicken with some rice please?
L And the same for me, but I'd like some noodles, please.
M OK, and would you like any drinks?
L Can I have a bottle of lemonade?
M We don't have any bottles of lemonade, I'm afraid. We have Coke or water.
L OK. Well, just a Coke, please.
C And for me too.

Exercise 7a

- Ask students to read through the sentence beginnings and endings.

- Tell them to complete the matching exercise and then ask them to compare answers with the person sitting next to them.

ANSWERS
1 d 2 a 3 f 4 b 5 c 6 e

Exercise 7b 9.3 🔘

- Play track 9.3 and ask students to check their answers.

AUDIOSCRIPT 9.3
1 It comes with some noodles.
2 Is there any bread?
3 We don't have any bread.
4 We have some rice.
5 Would you like any drinks?
6 We don't have any bottles of lemonade.

Exercise 8

- Refer students to the Grammar focus box and ask them to read the information and complete the exercise.

- To check understanding, elicit an example of *some* and *any* in positives, negatives and questions.

ANSWERS
1 some 2 any 3 some 4 any 5 any 6 some

- Refer students to exercises 2 & 4 in *Grammar reference* on p152. Students can do these for homework.

Exercise 9a

- Ask students to complete the exercise and then to compare their answers with a partner.

1 any **2** some **3** some **4** some **5** a **6** any
7 any **8** some **9** a **10** any **11** any

Exercise 9b 9.4

- Play track 9.4 and ask students to listen and check their answers.

EXTENSION You could ask students to practise the conversation in pairs. For an extra challenge, tell them to change the ingredients each time they practise it. You could also teach students that we often say *toppings* for the ingredients we put on a pizza. They may see this word on a menu.

AUDIOSCRIPT 9.4

A Hello. Can I help you?

B Hi. Yes, please. Do you have any beef?

A Yes, we have some nice steaks here. We also have some small beef cubes.

B OK. Can I have some beef cubes? About a kilo, please. And I'd also like a small steak.

A Just one?

B Yes, just one. Thanks. Also, do you have any yoghurt?

A No, I'm afraid we don't.

B What about rice? Do you have any rice?

A Yes, we have some bags of rice, but we also do rice salad.

B No, I'll just have a bag of rice, please.

A OK. Anything else?

B Yes, do you have any lemons?

A No, we don't sell any fruit or vegetables, I'm afraid.

B OK. That's everything then, thanks.

Pronunciation sentence stress

Exercise 10a 9.5

- Refer students to the sentences and play track 9.5.
- To help raise awareness, you could try reading the sentences to the students putting equal stress on each syllable and then ask them to notice the difference.
- Some students have problems with the consonant sound /ʤ/, which is often said when we say 'Do you'. This exercise helps students recognize the way we blend the words together. Tell students they do not have to produce this sound but should be able to recognize it as *Do you …* when they hear it in questions.

Exercise 10b 9.6

PRONUNCIATION In this exercise, students try to produce /ʤ/. Some students don't have this sound in their own language. If they have problems with it, write the words *July* and *juice* on the board.

Tell students to relax their lips and make them slightly rounded. Tell them to put their tongues on the top of their mouths behind their teeth and to push air out and release their tongues to make the sound. It is a voiced sound.
To help them notice the difference between voiced and voiceless consonants, write *juice* and *choose* on the board.

Tell them to say the words and put their fingers in their ears. Ask them if they can notice a vibration on one of the words. There should be a vibration when they say *juice. Choose* has the voiceless consonant sound /tʃ/.

Drill these words and make sure students can produce /ʤ/. Then show students how we sometimes push *do* and *you* together to make the sounds /ʤə/. The audio recording shows what this sounds like.

- Play track 9.6 and ask students to repeat, focusing on the weak forms.

EXTRA SUPPORT If you think your students will find this difficult, ask them to listen first and mark the words that are stressed.

Exercise 11

- As a lead-in, refer students to the photos on page 87 and ask them to find four differences and make sentences using *some* and *any*, e.g. *On the Italian stall there are some pizzas. On the Chinese stall there aren't any pizzas.*
- Put students into pairs and ask them to decide who is A and who is B. Refer them to the relevant pages. Tell them to read the instructions and look at their photo.
- Demonstrate the activity with a more confident student.
- Tell students to complete the exercise.

There are four differences:
Student A's picture has jam; Student B's picture has honey.
A has two pears; B has three pears.
A has chicken; B has pasta.
A has no drink; B has a bottle of lemonade.

EXTRA ACTIVITY Ask students to role-play *a market stall holder* (= the person who works on a market stall) and a customer. You could ask students to work in pairs and first write a short conversation with a customer asking for food from a specific country. If they are unfamiliar with the food from other countries, they could talk about food from their own country. Students could perform their conversation for another pair or for the class. For an added challenge, ask listeners to guess the nationality of the food.

EXTRA ACTIVITY This activity could be set for homework. You could ask students to choose one country from Unit 8 or this lesson and research a local dish from that country. They could tell a partner about it as a lead-in to the next lesson.

GRAMMAR REFERENCE ANSWERS

Exercise 1
1 any meat **2** a milk **3** olives **4** pasta **5** spoon
6 breads **7** money **8** vegetable **9** oranges
10 apples

Exercise 2
1 some **2** some **3** any **4** any **5** any **6** any **7** a
8 any **9** some **10** a

Exercise 3
1 two; a **2** a; an **3** two **4** Two; a **5** a

Exercise 4
1 some **2** some **3** any **4** some **5** a/some **6** any
7 a **8** some

9.2 In the kitchen

Goals

- Use quantifiers
- Talk about cooking

Lead-in

1 Closed book. Revise countable and uncountable nouns relating to food.

- Write the question starters below on the board:
  Is there any …?
  Are there any …?
  Can I have some …?

- Make sure students understand that *Is there any …?* is followed by uncountable nouns like bread, and *Are there any … ?* is followed by plural countable nouns like apples. *Can I have some … ?* can be followed by either uncountable nouns or plural countable nouns (*bread* or *apples*).

- Ask students to complete the questions with countable and uncountable nouns. You could do this with the whole class or ask students to work in small groups and then share their ideas with the class.

2 Closed book. Discuss how to make some different foods.

- This activity will help you assess how well students can talk about making food. Use the vocabulary that comes up in this lead-in later in the lesson if you can.

- If you can, find photos of these foods and distribute them to the class. If not, write the dishes on the board and check students know what they are. If these are unfamiliar foods, choose other better known foods.
  Omelette   Lasagne   Pizza   Pancakes

- Put students into pairs and ask them to discuss how to make each of the foods. Ask different pairs to explain their ideas to the class. Write useful vocabulary on the board and go over it.

Reading & Grammar   quantifiers

Exercise 1

- Draw students' attention to the questions and give example answers which are true for you.

- Go over expressions to describe frequency, e.g. *once a day/ week/month, sometimes, quite often, all the time, every day.*

- Put students into groups of three or four and ask them to discuss the questions using the adverbs.

- Ask one or two students to report any interesting things they heard.

Exercise 2a

> **Text summary:** A magazine article about how the ability to cook affects our health. Fewer young people know how to cook nowadays and this is affecting their health in a negative way, according to the article.

- Draw students' attention to the title of the article. Check they remember the meaning of *health*. Give an example to show the adjectives, e.g. *Healthy people do lots of sport. Unhealthy people don't do any exercise.* This will help them discuss the questions.

- Put students into pairs and ask them to discuss the questions.

Exercise 2b

- Pre-teach the meaning of *ready-made meals* (= food that is already cooked; you only have to heat it up to eat it), and *takeaway food* (= food you buy from a shop or restaurant that is ready to eat immediately). Don't pre-teach the methods of cooking (*fry, bake, boil*). These are practised later in the lesson. If students ask, say they are methods of cooking and they will learn more later on.

- Tell students to read the article and check if their predictions were correct.

- Ask one or two students to say if they were correct and why or why not.

> **ANSWERS**
> When we cook, we think more carefully about what we are eating and how much we are eating, and we usually eat healthy meals and eat well.

Exercise 3a

- Ask students to read the instructions and the example answer. Tell them to read through the notes and draw their attention to the fact that sometimes they have to include a subject and at other times the subject is already there.

- You may want to give a time limit for reading to encourage them to focus on finding the correct information.

- Students read and complete the notes.

> **ANSWERS**
> Cooking in the past: (1) People spent a long time preparing meals.
> Cooking now: (2) People spend just 27 minutes a day preparing meals.
> When we buy ready-made meals or takeaways we (3) don't really think about what we are eating and (4) we eat more than we need. When we cook, we (5) think more carefully about what we are eating and (6) we usually eat healthy meals and eat well.

Exercise 3b

- Ask students to compare their answers with their partner and then discuss the questions together.

- Check answers with the class.

- Ask a few students to report their partner's opinion.

CRITICAL THINKING Relating information from a text to personal experience in order to give reasons for an opinion is a useful skill. Encourage students to give reasons for their opinion by comparing the information in the text to their own life and context.

Exercise 4

- Ask students to read sentences 1–6 and underline the words which describe quantity (*many, a lot of, much*). Do the first sentence as an example: We have quite *a lot of* health problems today …

- Refer students to the Grammar focus box and ask them to read through the information.

- Students can work alone and complete the rules and the diagram. Ask them to compare answers with a partner.

ANSWERS

1 a lot of 2 many 3 a lot of 4 much 5 a lot of
6 much 7 many

- You could ask students to make sentences using the quantifiers for the ideas they discussed in exercise 3b, e.g. *Not many young people cook in my country.*
- Refer students to *Grammar reference* on p153. There are three more exercises here that students can do for homework.

Exercise 5a

- Refer students to question 2 in exercise 4. Show them how we can answer this using only the quantifiers:
  A *How many young people know how to cook?*
  B *None!/Not many./Some./A lot.*
- Ask students to read the questions and circle the correct quantifier – *much* or *many*. Tell them to look at the nouns and decide if they are countable or not to do this.

ANSWERS

1 much 2 much 3 many 4 much 5 much

- Tell students to circle the answers that are true for them.

Exercise 5b

- Put students into groups of three or four.
- Refer them to the instructions and example. Draw attention to the instruction that they should give more information. You could give your own answer to the first question to give them another example of how to add information, e.g. *A lot! I cook every day for my children.*
- **FEEDBACK FOCUS** Listen for correct use of *much* and *many*. Students often make mistakes when using quantifiers with countable and uncountable nouns.
- Ask one student from each group to explain an interesting thing they heard.
- **EXTENSION** Ask students to make sentences to summarize the habits of their group, e.g. *We don't spend a lot of time in the kitchen. We own some cookbooks but not many.* Students could write their sentences on the board and compare habits with other groups. You could then ask students to vote on the healthiest group.
- **EXTRA ACTIVITY** Ask students to consider how we can create healthier nations through education. Ask them to work in groups (you may want to put them into new groups). Ask them to think of two to four ideas to encourage more young people to start cooking. They could think about education, asking supermarkets to help in some way or getting local markets and other local communities to help.
- Ask students to present their ideas to the class and have a class vote for the best ideas.

Vocabulary & Listening in the kitchen

Exercise 6a 9.7 🎧

- Refer students to the photos and ask them to tell their partner any words they know to describe things in the photos.
- Play track 9.7 and ask students to write the letter of the correct photo next to each person's name.

ANSWERS

Brigit b Laila c Joe a

AUDIOSCRIPT 9.7

B Um ... what do I have in my kitchen? Not much really! I have a kettle because I make a lot of tea. And I have one frying pan and two saucepans. I don't really need anything else. Oh! I forgot the most important thing in my kitchen – the microwave!

L Well, there's nothing special about my kitchen. I have all the usual things. Oh, but I have a beautiful old set of plates and bowls for when people come for dinner. I have a lot of dinner parties!

J I love my kitchen. It's my favourite room in the house! I have a very modern oven and I use it a lot. I have an expensive food-processor, too – I use it to make soup. My flatmates sometimes get angry with me because I spend hours in the kitchen and they can't come in to cook their dinner!

Exercise 6b

- Ask students to compare their answers with a partner before you check with the class.

Exercise 7a

- Ask students to work with a partner to read the vocabulary in the box and try to label the images.

ANSWERS

1 oven 2 food-processor 3 frying pan 4 saucepan
5 microwave 6 kettle 7 fork 8 knife 9 spoon
10 plates 11 bowls

Exercise 7b 9.8 🎧

- Play track 9.8 and ask students to check their answers.
- Go over any unknown vocabulary.
- **PRONUNCIATION** Students sometimes have problems with the *au* spelling and pronounce it /aʊ/ instead of /ɔː/. Check their pronunciation of *saucepan*.

Check the pronunciation of the vowel sounds in other words. You could play track 9.8 again to help students match the spellings with the pronunciation.

In compound nouns we stress the first word. This is true for *food-processor* and *frying pan*. Show students how we stress the first words.

AUDIOSCRIPT 9.8

1 an oven
2 a food-processor
3 a frying pan
4 a saucepan
5 a microwave
6 a kettle
7 a fork
8 a knife
9 a spoon
10 plates
11 bowls

EXTRA ACTIVITY Ask students to make a quick drawing of their kitchen and describe it to their partner. Tell them to use vocabulary from exercise 7a. Listen and write any new vocabulary they use on the board and go over it after they finish speaking.

Exercise 8a

- Depending on your group, you could pre-teach unknown vocabulary or allow students to use their existing knowledge to work out the answers to the exercise. If you think your students won't know any of the terms in the box, teach the meanings. You could use physical gesture and drawings to do this.

150

- Put students into pairs and ask them to complete the exercise.

1 boil 2 fry 3 roast 4 Mix 5 bake 6 chop

Exercise 8b 9.9 🔘

- Play track 9.9 and ask students to listen and check their answers.
- Clarify the difference between *bake* and *roast*, which are both done in the oven. We roast meat but we bake cakes, bread, pasta (lasagne), fish and some other foods.

AUDIOSCRIPT 9.9
1 You boil water in a kettle to make tea.
2 For breakfast I often fry eggs, mushrooms and tomatoes together in a big frying pan.
3 To roast meat, you need a very hot oven.
4 Mix the water and flour together in a bowl with a spoon.
5 Not many people bake their own bread or cakes at home these days.
6 You need to use a sharp knife to chop the onions.

Exercise 9a

- Put students into pairs and ask them to read the instructions and the example.

EXTRA SUPPORT This may be difficult for students if they don't have any experience of cooking or they cook things using other methods. You could do a short matching exercise to help them. You could also teach relevant cooking methods such as steaming and stir-frying.

- Write some foods and dishes on large pieces of paper – see a possible list below. Write the verbs across the top of the board. Ask students to put the foods and dishes under the correct columns. This may help them to think of other similar examples when they work in their pairs.

Possible foods and dishes:
Boil: vegetables, pasta, water
Bake: cake, fish, lasagne and other pasta dishes, puddings, potatoes
Roast: pork, lamb, beef
Fry: eggs, bacon, steak, fish, vegetables in a stir-fry
Chop: vegetables, fruit

- As students write their sentences, correct their errors on the spot so their sentences are accurate for the next exercise.

EXTRA CHALLENGE You could give them a time limit to add an element of competition and energy to the activity.

Exercise 9b

- Group students together so they are working with another pair. Ask them to describe their methods of cooking to the other pair.
- Give them the goal of finding similar examples.
- Ask students to write any interesting or unusual examples on the board.

POSSIBLE ANSWERS
You can boil potatoes in a saucepan, bake or roast them in the oven, or fry them in a frying pan.
You can boil rice in a saucepan, or cook it in a frying pan with meat and vegetables, or cook it in a microwave.

You can roast meat in the oven, fry it in a frying pan, barbecue it on a barbecue, or stew it in a saucepan.
You can boil an egg in a saucepan, fry an egg in a frying pan, cook scrambled eggs in a frying pan or a saucepan or a microwave, or poach eggs in boiling water.
You can boil carrots in a saucepan, steam them in a pan or a microwave, stir fry them in a wok, or roast them in the oven.

Exercise 10a

- As a lead-in, you could find a photo of mushroom soup and ask students to guess what it is and what ingredients it has.
- Ask students to work in pairs and read the instructions and the list of ingredients. Also, refer them to the example conversation.

EXTRA SUPPORT To help students do this exercise, you could go over how we describe quantity for these items, e.g.
Potatoes – number/kilograms
Water, milk – litres/millilitres/pints
Mushrooms – number/grams
Carrots – number/kilograms
Butter – grams

- Ask students to work with their partner and guess the amounts.
- Ask all pairs to say what quantities they guessed and write their ideas on the board. Compare similarities and differences. Tell students they will find out the answers in the next exercise.

Exercise 10b

- Ask students to decide who is Student A and who is B. Ask them to sit in a position so they can't see their partner's book. Tell them to turn to p129 (Student A) and p134 (Student B).
- Ask them to read the instructions and to ask and answer questions to find the missing information about quantities. You could demonstrate this with a student, e.g. *How many potatoes do we need?*
- After students have completed their tables, ask them to say how close their original ideas were to the actual quantities.
- Ask students to read through their instructions for the recipe. Tell them they need to ask their partner to find the missing information in their recipes. Do an example with a student, e.g.
Teacher What do I cut in step one?
Student The potatoes.

EXTENSION For fast finishers or as an extra activity, ask students to think of other soups they like and what ingredients those soups have. They could write a list of ingredients and instructions for other students.

GRAMMAR REFERENCE ANSWERS
Exercise 1
1 many 2 much 3 much 4 a lot of 5 many
6 many 7 much 8 many 9 a lot of 10 many
11 much 12 a lot of

Exercise 2

1 There's no yoghurt.
2 There are no tomatoes.
3 We have no money.
4 There's no living room in my house.
5 There's no water in the bath.

Exercise 3

1 many 2 much 3 much 4 a lot 5 a lot 6 many
7 None 8 many 9 much 10 much 11 no
12 many 13 much 14 many 15 a lot

9.3 Vocabulary and skills development

Goals

• Understand numbers
• Say numbers

Lead-in

1 Closed book. Review vocabulary from the last two lessons.

• Write *eefb* and *kabe* on the board and tell the class to put the letters in the correct order to make two words from lessons 9.1 and 9.2. To help them, tell them the first is a type of meat and the second is a cooking method. (Answers: *beef* and *bake*).

• Put students into pairs and ask them to choose six words from lessons 9.1 and 9.2 to create their own anagrams.

• Tell pairs to swap their anagrams with another pair.

• Ask fast finishers to test each other on more words from these lessons by writing one more anagram each.

2 Open book. Talking about places.

• Refer students to the map and ask them what they know about this area and if they have been there.

• Ask students to discuss if they would like to go to these places and why.

Listening & Speaking understanding numbers

Exercise 1

> **Background note:** The map shows an area of South-East Asia. The items the students have to add to the map are countries, cities and regions. The Philippines is a country made up of more than 7,000 islands. Indonesia is also a country that is made up of thousands of islands. Java and Sumatra are two of the bigger islands. Jakarta is the largest city in Indonesia and the capital. Surabaya is the second biggest city. Singapore is called a city-state and island country. It is internationally recognized as an independent state. Malaysia is a state made up of two regions. One is on the mainland next to Singapore and the other is in the north of the island of Borneo. Papua New Guinea is an island. The whole island is divided into two parts. The west is part of Indonesia and the east is Papua New Guinea. It's famous for having over 700 languages!

• To help students do this activity, bring in photocopied maps of the area or suggest they use their smartphones to find the answers.

• Draw students' attention to the places in the box and ask them to match them to the places on the map.

• Check answers together as a class.

> **ANSWERS**
>
> a Malaysia b Singapore c Jakarta d Java
> e Surabaya f Indonesia g The Philippines
> h Papua New Guinea

Exercise 2a 9.10

> **Audio summary:** Some sentences about Singapore and Papua New Guinea. The speaker talks about different facts about the two places including population, how much food they grow, their location and when they became independent.

• As a lead-in, ask students which country they think has more people living in it – Singapore or Papua New Guinea. You could teach them the phrase *have a high/low population*. Even though this is higher level language it is very relevant to this lesson.

• Tell students they are going to listen to some information about Papua New Guinea and Singapore. Ask them to read the instructions and the numbers. You may need to pre-teach *per cent* (n) (= a number or amount in each hundred), and remind students how we say 1/4, 3/4 (a/one quarter/three quarters) and simple decimals (e.g. *8.4 = eight point four*).

WATCH OUT! In some languages, years are said differently, e.g. in Spanish 1985 is said *one thousand nine hundred and eighty five*. If you don't speak the students' first language, check this so you can identify issues with first-language interference.

PRONUNCIATION Some students have problems with word stress in *per cent*. Use this listening exercise to focus on the correct stress. *Per cent oO*

• Play track 9.10 and ask students to tick the correct numbers. You may need to play the track twice.

> **ANSWERS**
>
> 1 160 2 10% 3 three-quarters 4 1965 5 19.4
> 6 a quarter

Exercise 2b

• Put students into pairs and ask them to compare their answers.

• If students had different answers, explain that it may be because these numbers sound very similar. Tell students they are going to practise noticing the difference in this lesson.

• Tell students you will play the audio again later in the lesson and they can see then if they can understand the figures better. See the extra activity after exercise 3b.

AUDIOSCRIPT 9.10

1 Papua New Guinea is 160 kilometres north of Australia.
2 Singapore grows less than 10% of its food.
3 Papua New Guinea grows about three-quarters of its food.
4 Singapore got independence in 1965.
5 The coldest temperature ever recorded in Singapore was 19.4 degrees Celsius.
6 Less than a quarter of people in Papua New Guinea live in cities.

Exercise 3a 9.11 🔘

- Refer students to the Unlock the code box and ask them to read it.
- Play track 9.11 as they read and ask them to notice the stress patterns.
- Ask these questions to check their understanding:

1 Can we say *five hundreds*? Answer: No, we can't. We don't make *hundred* plural if we have a number in front of it. We can, however, say *hundreds without a number*, e.g. *There were hundreds of people at the football match*.

2 Where is the stress on teen numbers? Answer: On the last syllable, the *teen* part.

3 Where do we say *and* in big numbers? Answer: Before the last whole number, e.g. 3,250 = *three thousand two hundred AND fifty*.

4 What are two ways we can say 2018? Answer: *two thousand and eighteen* or *twenty eighteen*. (From 2000–2009 we can only say *two thousand and ...*, we can't say *twenty eight*. After 2010 we can say *twenty ten* etc.)

Exercise 3b

- Ask students to work in pairs. Tell them to each write five numbers of different sizes.
- Ask students to take turns to read one of their partner's numbers aloud.

EXTENSION If you think students need extra practice, you could write some numbers on the board and ask students to say them.

EXTRA ACTIVITY Write five dates on the board which are important in your life, e.g. *first year at school, first job, year you got married*. Tell students to ask questions to find out what the dates refer to. You can only say *yes* or *no*, so no *Wh*-questions are allowed. You may want to write some sample questions on the board, e.g. *Did you get married in 2007?*

When students guess a date correctly, give more information about the event, and encourage questions to find out more information. When students have guessed all your dates, tell them to do the same in pairs. Listen and correct any errors with dates.

EXTRA ACTIVITY Play track 9.10 from exercise 2 again and ask students if they can understand the numbers better.

Exercise 4a 9.12 🔘

> **Audio summary:** This recording is about Indonesia, a country in South-East Asia. The audio describes some facts about it such as when it became independent, how many people live there, and the main cities and islands in Indonesia.

- Ask students to read through the text and refer to the map to see where Indonesia, Java, Jakarta and Surabaya are before they listen. Ask them to think about what might go in the gaps. It might be a year or a percentage, for example.
- Check the meaning of *independent*. (= in the context of countries this refers to becoming separate and having their own government, not being controlled by another country) and *largest* (= biggest).

- Play track 9.12 and ask students to listen for the numbers and complete the exercise.

ANSWERS

1 1945 2 240 million 3 6,000 4 18,110 5 60%
6 9.6 million 7 2.7 million

Exercise 4b

- Put students into pairs and ask them to compare their answers.

Exercise 4c 9.12 🔘

- Play track 9.12 again and ask students to check their answers. You may need to play the recording twice.
- Check answers with the class.

AUDIOSCRIPT 9.12

The first country we're going to look at today is Indonesia in South-East Asia. It became independent in 1945 and now one of the most important days for the country is Independence Day on 17th August. There are 240 million Indonesians, and they live on 6,000 of its 18,110 islands. Java is only the fourth largest island, but 60% of Indonesians live on it. Two of the main cities are on Java: Jakarta, the capital of Indonesia, with 9.6 million people, and Surabaya, the second largest city, with 2.7 million.

Exercise 5 9.13 🔘

> **Audio summary:** The second part of the lecture gives more facts about Indonesia, including its climate.

- Ask students to read the instructions and the items in the table.
- Check the meaning of *east* and *west* (draw a compass on the board and show that these are directions and points on the compass. Check this by asking students to point to the east and west.) and *imports* (= an import is something that a country buys from another country and brings in to the country. Imports are usually products.).

DICTIONARY SKILLS Ask students to look up the following words and tell you what they mean in their own words: *temperature, minimum, maximum*.

- Ask students what sort of number might go in each part of the table, e.g. size from east to west will be a number of kilometres. Explain the phrase *degrees Celsius* and show students how we write temperatures (e.g. *25°C*).
- Play track 9.13 and ask students to complete the table.
- Ask them to compare answers with a partner.
- Play the track again and ask them to check their answers.

ANSWERS

Size from east to west: 5,120 km (kilometres)
Indonesians working on farms: 40 million (1/6)
Climate – minimum temperature: 25°C
Climate – maximum temperature: 35°C
Rain a year: 3,175 mm (millimetres)
Maximum rain in mountain areas: 6,100 mm (millimetres)
Rice imports: 3 million tonnes

AUDIOSCRIPT 9.13

Now, moving on, the country is 5,120 kilometres from east to west and 1,760 kilometres from north to south. Forty million Indonesians work on farms, which is 1/6th of all Indonesians. The climate is perfect for growing rice because the temperature is usually between 25 and 35 degrees Celsius, and there is 3,175 millimetres of rain a year. In mountain areas this can be 6,100 millimetres. Indonesia is the third largest rice growing country in the world, but it still imports about three million tonnes of rice a year.

EXTENSION Ask students to work in small groups and discuss the information about Indonesia. What surprised them? What did they find most interesting?

CRITICAL THINKING Ask students to discuss population increases in cities. At A2 level they cannot go into complex detail but they could express simple opinions such as: *Lots of people live in cities because they can find jobs there. It's not good for the countryside because lots of young people leave the villages. The cities are very big and there is lots of traffic and pollution.* You could support this with some simple questions for discussion, e.g. *Do more people live in cities or villages? Is this a good thing? Why? Why not?*

Vocabulary Development say numbers

Exercise 6a

- To support this task, you could look up the numbers for these items before class so you can share information with students. You could also allow students to use smartphones if they have them to search for information.
- Put students into pairs. Ask them to read through the table and write numbers and relevant information for each item.

Exercise 6b

- Put pairs together to make groups of four. Ask a pair to come to the front of the class and write their information on the board. Ask other students to say if they wrote anything different and to suggest alternatives. If there is interest and a lot of differences, open this up to a class discussion.
- If you have the correct information tell the students what you found.

EXTENSION The last item is open and could be any important day. You could ask students to say what they think the most important day is and discuss this with their partner or group. They could also discuss important days for other countries they know about.

Exercise 7a 9.14 🔘

- Test before you teach. If you think your students know some of this vocabulary, write some examples on the board and ask students to work in pairs and discuss how you say these items, e.g. 2/3 = *two thirds*.
- Refer students to the Vocabulary focus box.
- Play track 9.14 and ask them to read and listen to the information.
- Check their understanding with these questions:
  1 *What is two thirds of six?* Answer: four.
  2 *How do you write ten point four?* Answer: 10.4. Ask a student to write it on the board.

WATCH OUT! In some languages they write decimals using a comma. Check this with students and explain that in English we write decimals with a point and thousands with commas. Also in some countries they use Fahrenheit to measure temperature. Teach this as an alternative. Lastly, depending on your context, you may want to teach students more measurements such as feet and inches and pounds and ounces.

Exercise 7b

- Ask students to complete the matching activity.
- Put them into pairs and ask them to compare answers.

ANSWERS
1 c 2 d 3 f 4 a 5 b 6 h 7 e 8 g

Exercise 7c 9.15 🔘

- Play track 9.15 and ask students to listen and check their answers.
- Repeat the track and after each item ask students to repeat.

PRONUNCIATION Students need lots of practice with numbers. Pausing in the correct places can help students say large numbers clearly. Write five large numbers on the board and mark where students should pause. You may want to prepare these numbers in advance and consider the best places to pause, e.g. *2,546,059 two million PAUSE five hundred and forty six thousand PAUSE and fifty nine.*

Exercise 8

EXTRA CHALLENGE Ask students to read through the numbers and write them out in full. This is quite challenging but will help clarify how we say numbers.

- Put students into pairs and ask them to take turns saying the numbers to each other. Encourage peer correction.
- Check answers with the class.

WATCH OUT! Question 5 has the number 0.23. Tell students we often say *nought* for the zero in numbers like this: *nought point two three.* Also, remind them we don't usually say *nought point twenty three*; we say the individual numbers after the decimal point.

ANSWERS
1 Seven point four per cent
2 two and two-thirds
3 the twenty-first of July nineteen ninety-two
4 minus eleven point seven degrees Celsius
5 (zero/nought) point two three
6 the twentieth of February twenty fifteen
7 one hundred degrees Celsius
8 one and a quarter

Exercise 9a

- Put students into pairs. Ask them to look at the information and to work together to guess the answers.

Exercise 9b

- Tell students to turn to page 133 in their Coursebooks to check the answers.
- Ask the class if they found anything particularly surprising or interesting.

Exercise 10

- Tell students they are going to find out about two more places on the map – Malaysia and The Philippines. Ask students if they know anything about these places. Refer them back to the map.
- Put students into pairs and ask them to decide who is Student A and who is Student B. Refer them to the relevant pages.
- Ask them to read their information and see what information is missing from their tables and what questions they have to ask.

EXTRA SUPPORT Allow students to write out the questions in full and practise saying their numbers before they start if you think they will find it difficult.

- Demonstrate one or two examples with a more confident student to model the activity.
- Ask students to work in their pairs and complete the exercise.

POSSIBLE ANSWERS

Student A – The Philippines
1 What is the population? *99 million people*
2 What percentage live in the biggest city? *2%*
3 What is the maximum and minimum temperature every year? *The maximum temperature is 28°C. The minimum temperature is 16°C.*
4 When is Independence Day? *On 12th June*

Student B – Malaysia
1 What is the population? *30 million people*
2 What percentage live in the biggest city? *3%*
3 What is the maximum and minimum temperature every year? *The maximum temperature is 38°C. The minimum temperature is 15°C.*
4 When is an important day? *Hari Merdeka, the National Day, is on 31st August.*

EXTRA ACTIVITY Ask students to choose a country they would like to find out about. Refer them to the tables in the last exercise and ask them to do some research after class to find out the information.

In the next lesson, students could read their information to the class. They shouldn't say which country they researched. The other students should try to guess which country they are talking about.

STUDY TIP You could tell students to practise saying numbers out of class. If they see large numbers in their daily lives, they could say them aloud (or quietly rehearse saying them).

9.4 Speaking and writing

Goals

- Ask about and recommend a place to eat
- Order food in a restaurant

Lead-in

1 Closed book. Revision of vocabulary related to food and recipes.

- Ask students to think of something they cooked recently or something they ate. They have to tell their partner at least three steps in how the food is made, e.g. *chop the vegetables, fry the chicken, boil the noodles.*

2 Open book. Describing a photo and guessing the location.

- Refer students to the photo at the bottom of page 92. Don't tell them where it is and ask them not to read the text on the page.
- Put them into pairs and ask them to describe what they can see in the photo and to guess where it is. To review numbers, you could ask them to guess how many people live there.
- Tell students the city in the photo is Edinburgh, and ask them what they know about the city. Below is some information about Edinburgh you can share with them. Population = about 5.2 million. It's the capital city of Scotland. Edinburgh is a very old city and has a castle, a palace and a cathedral. In the photo you can see the castle on top of the hill and some of the old town.

Reading & Writing asking about and recommending a place to eat

Exercise 1

- Put students into pairs and ask them to discuss the questions.
- Ask two or three students to share interesting things they heard from their partner.

EXTRA ACTIVITY Have a class discussion on the best places to eat in their town. You could ask students to recommend places and find out if the other students have eaten in any of the same places. This could end in a class vote on the best place to eat.

Exercise 2a

> **Text summary:** An email from Stefano to a friend. He's asking for advice on a restaurant to go to, to celebrate his friend Molly's 25th birthday.

- Refer students to the email and ask them to read it and find the answer to the question.
- Check the answer together.

ANSWER

Stefano wants Vera to recommend a good but cheap restaurant in Edinburgh with tables to eat outside and a castle view.

Exercise 2b

- Ask students to read through the questions, and go over any unknown vocabulary.
- Tell them to read the text again, and then put them into pairs and ask them to complete the exercise.
- Check answers together.

ANSWERS

1 directions to get there ☐   2 Vera's favourite place ✓
3 the prices ✓   4 nice food ✓   5 opening times ☐
6 possible to sit outside ✓   7 the waiters ☐
8 the view ✓   9 busy or not ✓   10 need to book ✓

EXTENSION Ask students if these are things they consider when looking for a restaurant. Ask students to discuss what they think is important when choosing a restaurant.

Exercise 3

- If necessary, pre-teach *glad* (= happy), *amazing, brilliant* (= very good), *warm* (= quite hot).
- Ask students to read the email.
- Ask them to work in pairs to find the answers to Stefano's questions and underline them.
- Check answers.

ANSWERS

<u>My favourite place is the Castle Terrace</u> because <u>the food is amazing, but it is quite expensive</u>. There's also a place called 'Kayla's Kitchen' with good, cheap food. <u>You can't eat outside</u> there – it's not often very warm in Scotland! But <u>it has wonderful views of the city from the rooftop</u> restaurant. … P.S. <u>You should book a table on the Saturday night</u> because it's very popular.

Vera doesn't tell him to go to her favourite restaurant, but recommends somewhere cheap and popular with good food, good views and friendly waiters.

Exercise 4a

- Do the first sentence on the board as an example.
- Put students into pairs and ask them to complete the rest of the exercise together.

Exercise 4b 9.16

- Play track 9.16 and ask students to listen and check their answers.

ANSWERS/AUDIOSCRIPT 9.16

1 We're looking for a Thai restaurant.
2 You can sit outside on the roof.
3 What's your favourite café for lunch?
4 Do I need to book online?
5 Where's a good place to have some cake?
6 It has a wonderful menu.
7 You don't need to call them and book.
8 Do you know anywhere that has a garden?
9 There's a place called the Riverside with a nice view.
10 My favourite place is Café Blanc because it sells French food.

Exercise 5a

- Tell students they are going to write an email similar to Stefano's. Refer them to the instructions and situations 1–3 and ask them to choose one of the options.
- Refer them to the Language for writing box and read through it with the class.

SMART COMMUNICATION It's important that students learn the conventions for formal and informal writing. The emails on page 92 have examples of how to open and close an email informally.

- Refer students to the emails on page 92. Ask them to underline phrases which open and close the emails. Phrases they should identify:
  How are you?
  Great to hear from you.
  Everything's good with me.
  I'm glad you're well.
  Thanks for your help!
  Have a brilliant time and let me know how your trip goes!

- Ask students to work with a partner and think of other phrases they could use, e.g.
  How are things? What's up? Hope all is well with you. Hope you're well.
  Take care. Speak soon. Bye for now. Look forward to hearing from you.
- Once students have chosen their topic to write about, tell them to work individually and give them further guidelines, e.g. *write sixty to eighty words/two paragraphs.* Give a time limit too, e.g. fifteen minutes.

STUDY TIP Encourage students to review and check their writing for spelling and punctuation. If you know what typical problems your students have with writing, ask them to check their writing for those issues. For example, many students write sentences that are too long and use lots of commas where they should have a full stop and a new sentence. Other students have problems with capital letters. Encourage students to review and correct their written work so it becomes automatic.

Exercise 5b

- If possible, put students into pairs with someone who chose a different situation. Ask them to swap emails. Tell them to read their partner's email and think of how to reply. Remind them to use appropriate phrases to open the email. For example, if the email asks how they are doing, they should give an answer.
- Refer them to the reply on page 92 for help. Again, give a time limit of fifteen minutes or so and ask them to write their replies and check them for spelling and punctuation.

Exercise 5c

- Tell students to give their emails back and read the reply. Ask them to tell their partner if they would like to eat in the recommended restaurant, and why/why not.

EXTRA ACTIVITY Reading an online review. Go to a local restaurant review website and choose three to six restaurant recommendations (depending on the size of your group). Choose and print out positive reviews and different types of restaurants. You may need to adapt the level of English so that your group will be able to understand the main points of the review. Stick the reviews around the room. Ask students to walk around the room, read the reviews and choose the restaurant they would most like to go to. Tell them to sit with a partner and say which restaurant they chose, and why. Ask three or four students to report their partner's choice and reasons to the class. You could vote for the most popular restaurant.

Speaking & Listening in a restaurant

Exercise 6 9.17

- Refer students to the instructions and check they know what they are listening for.
- Play track 9.17 and ask students to write down the food that is ordered and compare their answers with a partner.
- Check answers together.

ANSWERS

Stefano orders grilled chicken with roast potatoes and mixed green vegetables, and Molly orders fish cakes with a tomato, olive and onion salad. They order some sparkling water to drink.

AUDIOSCRIPT 9.17

S Excuse me?

W Hi, would you like to order?

S Yes, please.

W OK. So, would you like a starter?

S No, thanks. Just a main course, please. Could I have the grilled chicken?

W Certainly. And would you like any side dishes with that?

S Um … yes. Can I have some roast potatoes and some mixed green vegetables, please?

W Of course. And for you, madam?

M Could I have some fish cakes, please? This one …

W The fish cakes, OK. And anything else?

M A tomato, olive and onion salad, thanks.

W And would you like something to drink?

M Yes, some sparkling water, please.

S And the same for me. Oh, and another question. Can we pay by credit card?

W Yes, of course. No problem!

S Oh, good. Thank you very much.

Exercise 7a

- Ask students to read through the phrases from the conversation between Molly, Stefano and the waiter.
- Ask them to work in pairs to complete the questions.

EXTRA SUPPORT Remind students that *Can/Could I/we* are always followed by a bare infinitive (an infinitive without *to*) and *Would you like* is followed by a noun or the infinitive with *to*.

- Explain that 'Could I' and 'Can I' are both correct in 2 & 4, but the answers given reflect the wording in the recording.

ANSWERS

1 Would you like   2 Could I   3 Would you like   4 Can I
5 Would you like   6 Can we

Exercise 7b   9.18 💿

- Play track 9.18 and ask students to listen and check their answers.
- Play the track again and ask students to listen and repeat after each question.

PRONUNCIATION Some students tend to make their voices go up at the end of all questions and this can sound quite unnatural. In *wh-* questions, it is more usual to make your voice go down at the end. The voice usually goes up at the end of *Yes/No* questions. Listen to your students and help them if you hear their voices going up in an unnatural way.

AUDIOSCRIPT 9.18

1 Would you like to order?
2 Could I have the grilled chicken, please?
3 Would you like any side dishes with that?
4 Can I have some roast potatoes?
5 Would you like something to drink?
6 Can we pay by credit card?

Exercise 8a

- Put students into pairs and ask them to complete the exercise. You could do the first one or two questions together to help clarify the exercise.
- Check answers.

ANSWERS

1 Could/Can I/we   2 Could/Can I/we have
3 Would you like   4 Could/Can I/we
5 Would you like   6 Would you like

SMART COMMUNICATION Ask students if we use *can* or *could* when making requests. The answer is we can use both but *could* is more polite.

WATCH OUT! Some students get confused with the word stress and spelling in *desert* and *dessert*. Tell them at the end of a meal they have des**sert** oO and camels live in the **des**ert Oo. You could also draw stress bubbles on the board to help them see the difference. Drill the different word stress and point out the difference in spelling.

Exercise 8b

- Ask students to work alone and identify if the questions are asked by the waiter or a customer. Tell them to compare their answers with a partner.
- Check answers together.

ANSWERS

1 Would you like to order? W
2 Could I have the grilled chicken, please? C
3 Would you like any side dishes with that? W
4 Can I have some roast potatoes? C
5 Would you like something to drink? W
6 Can we pay by credit card? C
1 Could/Can I/we see the menu please? C
2 Could/Can I/we have some bread, please? C
3 Would you like another cup of coffee? W
4 Could/Can I/we order, please? C
5 Would you like some dessert? W
6 Would you like a starter? W

EXTENSION Help students to identify that waiter questions are offers and use *Would you like … ?* and customer questions are requests that use *Can* or *Could*. Ask students to work in pairs and think of more possible waiter and customer questions.

Exercise 9

- Refer students to the prompts and the Language for speaking box and demonstrate the conversation with a confident student.

EXTRA SUPPORT Do two or three demonstration conversations so students get a model and are clear on the task.

- Put students into pairs and ask them to take turns role-playing the waiter and customer.
- Ask them to include some of the questions from the Language for speaking box.

EXTRA CHALLENGE Ask students to think of different food items/questions and to improvise and extend the conversation.

Exercise 10

- In this exercise, students should be encouraged to act out the role-play, looking at the menu but without looking at the notes in the lesson if possible.
- Put students into new pairs and tell them to decide who is the waiter and who is the customer. Refer them to p130, and ask them to read the instructions and the menu. Check any unknown vocabulary.

- Demonstrate the role-play with a more confident student. Tell students to work with their partner and act out the conversation. When they have finished, tell them to change roles and repeat the exercise.
- You could ask a confident pair to act out their scene for the class.

EXTRA ACTIVITY This will work well for strong groups and students who like being creative. Ask students to think of problems that happen in restaurants, and write them on the board, e.g. *cold food, get the wrong food, bill is wrong.* Ask students to think of phrases for explaining this, and write these too. Teach students that we usually say *Sorry* or *Excuse me* before we explain a problem, e.g. *Sorry, my food is cold. Excuse me, the bill is wrong.*

Teach phrases for the waiter to respond, e.g. *I'm sorry. I'll get another one for you. Sorry, I'll check it. Sorry, I'll change it.* Ask students to stand up and walk around the room explaining problems and responding as a waiter.

EXTRA ACTIVITY Write an email to say thank you for the recommendation. This will practise relevant language and the past simple. Ask students to remember the emails they wrote to make a recommendation earlier in the lesson. Tell students they have now been for the meals and they want to write an email to say thank you. Remind them of phrases for opening and closing emails, and tell them to say thank you, describe the restaurant (meal, service and place) and close the email.

9.5 Video

Making a pizza

VIDEOSCRIPT

This is *La Cucina*, an authentic Italian restaurant in Oxford, England.

Italian cuisine is popular all over the world, but one dish is especially well-known – pizza. Its simple recipe and basic ingredients mean that many countries now have their own pizza style. American pizza, for example, is very popular - especially Chicago's deep-pan style. But the original pizza comes from Naples, in the Campania region of Italy.

La Cucina's chefs are very serious about pizza and they make each one to a traditional recipe.

To make the dough, they use wheat flour, yeast and water, and season with some salt. They don't use any other ingredients, and they certainly don't use any additives.

When the dough is ready they make the sauce. They chop onion and fry it in olive oil. Then they add good quality Italian tomatoes and some salt.

When the sauce has cooled, they carefully put some on the base. Then they add the mozzarella, a cheese from southern Italy.

Then the pizza is ready to go into the hot pizza oven.

It stays there for about 10 minutes until the base is golden-brown. A few basil leaves on top and there you are – the perfect pizza!

This is the traditional Pizza Margherita – the original pizza – but *La Cucina* sells many different kinds. There's Pizza Romana with olives and artichokes, Pizza al Funghi with mushroom and garlic, and Pizza alle Verdure, with peppers, onions, aubergine and courgette. They even do a 'Your choice'. Customers can choose how many toppings and how much cheese they want.

Finally – when the pizza is finished – they serve it with … nothing. Pizza is so good they always eat it *solo*!

VIDEO ANSWERS

Exercise 1
aubergine ☐ base ✓ basil ✓ cheese ✓
courgette ☐ dough ☐ flour ✓ ingredients ✓
recipe ☐ restaurant ✓ topping ✓ yeast ✓

Exercise 2
Students' own answers

Exercise 3
1 Oxford 2 Naples 3 traditional 4 south
5 golden brown 6 on its own

Exercise 4a
1 yeast, water, salt 2 onions, olive oil 3 tomato
4 chicken 5 mushrooms 6 peppers, onions
7 toppings, cheese

Review

ANSWERS

Exercise 1a
1 There is some rice.
2 There is a bottle of lemonade.
3 There is an apple.
4 There are some pears.
5 There aren't any mushrooms.
6 There isn't any salad.
7 There is some meat.
8 There isn't any jam.

Exercise 2a
1 How many 2 How many 3 How much
4 How much 5 How many

Exercise 2c 9.19 🔊
1 10,000–25,000 different types of tomato
2 17 calories in a lemon 3 12.3 g of sugar
4 891 kg of food 5 14 billion cups of coffee

AUDIOSCRIPT 9.19
P Welcome to the program, Dr Zhang from the National Food and Health Group.
D Thank you.
P So, you're here today to talk about some interesting numbers about food.
D That's right. Firstly, do you know how many different types of tomato there are in the world? Well, some people say 10,000, but other people say there are about 25,000.
P Oh, really?
D Yes. And staying with fruit, when you're watching your calories, try a lemon. There are only 17 calories in a lemon.
P Only 17? And what about milk?
D Well, it's surprising to hear that a cup of 2% fat milk contains 12.3 grams of sugar – that's about 50 calories.
P That's a lot of calories. How much does the average American eat every year?
D The answer to that was 891 kilograms of food in 2011.
P Wow! That's huge. And there's time for just one more fact.

D Well, I think we should finish in Italy – a country of coffee lovers. They drink 14 billion cups every year. That's over 200 cups for every man, woman and child in the country.

P Well, some of those numbers are amazing. Dr Zhang, thank you very much for coming today …

Exercise 3a
1 He's boiling some potatoes.   2 He's making a cake.
3 He's chopping an onion.   4 He's frying some mushrooms.
5 He's roasting a chicken.

Exercises 4a & 4b   9.20
1 twenty-one degrees Celsius
2 two-thirds
3 forty-five point five per cent
4 two million, four hundred and seventy-eight thousand

Exercise 5a
1 Could I have some roast potatoes, please?
2 No, we don't.
3 Would you like a side dish with that?
4 Would you like to order?
5 Do you have any apple juice?
6 Could I have the baked fish, please?
7 OK, just a bottle of water, please.
8 And would you like something to drink?

Exercises 5b & 5c   9.21
4 Would you like to order?
6 Could I have the baked fish, please?
3 Would you like a side dish with that?
1 Could I have some roast potatoes, please?
8 And would you like something to drink?
5 Do you have any apple juice?
2 No, we don't.
7 OK, just a bottle of water, please.

10

The world around us

Unit overview

Language input

Comparatives (CB p97)	• *It's colder and wetter by the sea.*
Superlatives (CB p98)	• *Victoria Falls is the biggest waterfall on the Zambezi River.*
Grammar reference (CB pp154–155)	

Vocabulary development

The weather (CB p96)	• *cloudy, dry, foggy, icy, rain, snow, wet, windy …*
Nature and geography (CB p98)	• *beaches, coast, desert, islands, river …*
Adjective + noun collocations (CB p101)	• *high/low temperatures; strong/light winds*

Skills development

Reading: understanding comparison (CB p100)

Speaking: giving reasons and preferences (CB p102)

Writing: describe a place (CB p103)

Video

Documentary: The Grand Canyon (CB p104)

Vox pops (Coursebook DVD & TG p258)

More materials

Workbook	• Language practice for vocabulary, grammar, pronunciation, speaking and writing • Listening for pleasure • Review: Units 9 & 10
Photocopiable activities	• Grammar: A mystery sentence (TG p207 & TSRD) • Vocabulary: Island tour (TG p224 & TSRD) • Communication: The ultimate adventure kit (TG p242 & TSRD)
Tests	• Unit 10 test (TSRD)
Unit 10 wordlist (TSRD)	

10.1 The weather

Goals
- Describe the weather
- Use comparative adjectives

Lead-in

1 Closed book. Review countries and talk about living in them.
- Ask the class what countries and cities they learnt about in connection with food in Unit 9. Write them on the board.
- Put students into pairs and ask them to discuss what it is like living in these places.
- Listen to their discussions and, if you hear words related to the weather, make a note of them.
- Ask two or three students to report any interesting things they heard to the class.

2 Closed book. Anagram activity on weather vocabulary.
- Write these anagrams on the board and ask students to work in pairs and work out the words. For an extra challenge, don't tell them they are connected to weather. Tell students it's a race. The first pair to finish can write their answers on the board.
  dloc (cold)   tew (wet)   toh (hot)   irna (rain)   nus (sun)
- Write any other weather-related words you heard in the first lead-in on the board and go over the meaning with the class. Encourage peer teaching. Tell the class they will learn to describe the weather in this lesson.

Vocabulary & Listening the weather

Exercise 1
- Put students into pairs and ask them to discuss the questions.
  FEEDBACK FOCUS This exercise is designed to elicit the comparative. Listen and see if any students can already use comparative adjectives. Use this exercise as a diagnostic tool to adapt how you group students and how you teach the grammar later. Keep any sentences you write down to lead into the grammar focus in exercise 8a.
- Ask two or three students to report what their partner said.

Exercise 2 10.1 🔘
- Refer students to the questions. Ask them how they will identify the different speakers. For example, the news report will sound like a TV/radio presenter, the language in the weather forecast will be predicting the weather in the future, someone talking about the weather on a holiday might be using the past simple, and they might talk about what they (i.e. 'we') did.
- Play track 10.1 and ask students to complete the exercise in pairs.

ANSWERS
a Recording 3   b Recording 1   c Recording 2

AUDIOSCRIPT 10.1

1 So, in Lisbon today it's cloudy this morning but dry, and we don't expect any rain. By the afternoon it's going to be warm and sunny, but not really hot, with temperatures of around 20 degrees Celsius.

2 It was great. We loved Malaysia. We went in the wet season, so we had some storms. The first night we arrived, it was really windy and there was a big storm with very loud thunder and lightning. But most of the time during the day it was lovely.

3 N Let's now go to Rupinder in Chicago. Hello, Rupinder. How's the weather there?
R Well Mike, it's freezing here today. There was a lot of snow last night and the roads are very icy. It's cold and foggy now, and there is more snow to come later today.

Exercise 3a
- Go through the meaning of any unknown words in the box.
- Refer students to the three photos with text. Ask them to describe the weather in each photo.
- You could also focus on pronunciation to help students be able to identify the words when they hear them in the listening exercise.
- Ask students to complete the gaps with the words in the box. Tell them to think about the part of speech to help them decide on the correct word, e.g. in number 1 we need an adjective.

Exercise 3b 10.1 🔘
- Play track 10.1 again and ask students to listen and check their answers.

ANSWERS

Lisbon: 1 cloudy 2 dry 3 rain 4 warm 5 sunny
Malaysia: 6 wet 7 storms 8 windy 9 thunder
10 lightning
Chicago: 11 freezing 12 snow 13 icy 14 foggy

Exercise 4a
- Ask students to work with their partners and complete the table with the correct form of the words.

ANSWERS
1 snow 2 rain 3 sunny 4 windy 5 icy 6 freezing
7 foggy

EXTENSION Tell students to work with their partner. To practise using the words in a sentence, ask them to write six sentences about different countries, e.g. *It's sunny in Italy*.

Exercise 4b 10.2 🔘
- Play track 10.2 and ask students to listen and check their answers.

AUDIOSCRIPT 10.2
snow, to snow, snowy
rain, to rain, rainy
sun, to shine, sunny
wind, to blow, windy
ice, to freeze, icy/freezing
fog, foggy

PRONUNCIATION Some students find the difference between spelling and pronunciation difficult in English. You could teach them the phonemic symbol of the different vowel sounds to help them associate spelling with sounds. To help them remember the sounds, show them how we make the sounds with our mouths. Linking the physical movement to the vowel sounds can help aid memory of the sound. You can also ask them to think of words with a similar sound that they already know.

sunny /ˈsʌnɪ/   snowy /ˈsnəʊɪ/   rainy /ˈreɪnɪ/
windy /ˈwɪndɪ/   icy /ˈaɪsɪ/   foggy /ˈfɒgɪ/

Exercise 5

- As a lead-in, ask the class to give you one sentence about weather using a noun, one using a verb and one using an adjective, using the table in exercise 4a. Make sure that they know how to put each form into a sentence, e.g.
  There is a lot of wind. (noun)
  It is snowing. It snows a lot here. (verb)
  It's windy. (adjective)
- Write their examples on the board.

EXTRA SUPPORT Ask students to change the sentences on the board into past simple and present continuous to talk about the past and today. Write the different tenses on the board to support the next exercise.

- Put students into groups of three or four.
- Elicit the names of the four seasons and write them on the board. Ask students to discuss the two sentences in their groups.

EXTRA CHALLENGE Ask students to come and write sentences that they said about the weather today, yesterday and in the different seasons on the board. Correct any errors.

Grammar & Speaking comparatives

Exercise 6

> **Background note:** These photos show men in the desert in Saudi Arabia. The first photo is unusual because the man is dressed for the desert, but there is snow on the ground. Although it is very hot during the day, in some seasons it can get very cold, especially at night, and it can even snow. The second photo shows a man snowboarding on the desert sand.

- Refer students to the photos and ask them to work with a partner and describe what they can see. Tell them to use words from exercise 4a.
- Ask two or three students to give you some sentences about the photos. Ask them what is surprising about the photos. (Answer: the snow in the desert; snowboarding on sand.)

FEEDBACK FOCUS: This is a good opportunity to check the pronunciation and spelling of *desert* again.

- Ask students to discuss which country they think the photos show.

Exercise 7

> **Text summary:** A straightforward descriptive text about the weather in Saudi Arabia. You might find a text like this in a travel guide.

WATCH OUT! Some students may not know where these three countries are. Saudi Arabia is in the Middle East, Austria is in northern Europe, Mali is in western Africa. Students may think the text is about Mali as it has a lot of desert too and is hot. It's not Mali because there's no coast in Mali. You could show the countries on a map if you can access one.

- Put students into pairs and refer them to the text in the country profile. Tell them to read the text and complete the exercise.

- Check answers together.

ANSWERS
a Saudi Arabia. It's hot and it's by the sea.
EXTRA ACTIVITY Extend the discussion on weather and countries and revise large numbers. If your students have smartphones or tablets, put them into small groups and ask them to choose Mali or Austria and do some research on the country to find out information about its weather and other interesting facts, e.g. population, geography, languages, size, what countries it is next to, etc. Re-group students so they are working with someone from another group. Ask them to share and compare what they found out. Ask students to tell the class the most interesting piece of information they heard.

Alternatively, this task could be done individually as homework and students could compare their results in the next lesson.

Exercise 8a

- If you have noted any good examples of comparatives during the lesson so far, use these as an introduction to the grammar focus.
- Refer students to the Grammar focus box and ask them to read the information. They should refer back to the country profile in exercise 7 to help them complete the rules.
- You could complete the rules together as a class or ask students to work in pairs and do the exercise more deductively.
- Check answers.

ANSWERS
1 -er **2** -er **3** -y; -ier **4** more
- Refer students to *Grammar reference* on p154. There are three more exercises here that students can do for homework.

Exercise 8b

- Refer students to the adjectives and ask them to write the comparative forms.
- Put students into pairs and ask them to compare their answers.
- Ask fast finishers to write the answers on the board.
- Go over any errors.

EXTENSION Test students' ability to compare two things. Write different countries on the board – ask students to suggest countries. Write *cold warm sunny rainy* on the board. Tell students they need a piece of paper and have to decide which person is writing. Put students into pairs and give them three minutes to write as many comparative sentences as possible using the countries and weather adjectives, e.g. *Mali is warmer than Austria.*

Then ask students to work in groups of four. Tell each pair to swap their papers with the other pair. Pairs should read the sentences and tick good examples and underline errors. Tell students to take back their papers and make any corrections. Ask students to share interesting sentences they read with the class.

ANSWERS
smaller, bigger, rainier, more dangerous, sunnier, fatter, more boring, cheaper

Pronunciation *than* in comparative sentences

- Draw students' attention to the Pronunciation box. Play track 10.3 and ask them to read and listen.

Exercise 9a 10.4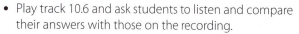

- Tell students to read the two sentences in exercise 9a. Play track 10.4 and ask them to listen to the pronunciation. Repeat the track and ask students to repeat each sentence.

WATCH OUT! As well as reducing the vowel sound in *than*, students need to produce the correct word stress in the adjectives and reduce the weak sound in the *-er*, e.g. **bigg**er.

EXTRA SUPPORT Some students find it hard to produce weak forms. Use back-chaining as a drilling technique to practise this. See Unit 1.3 for instructions on back-chaining.

Exercise 9b

- Draw students' attention to the example conversation and ask them to work with their previous partners and complete the exercise. Encourage them to think of more than one way of answering the questions as in the sample conversation, e.g. *Yes, it's drier. I don't know. I think so.*
- Point out that the recording talks about the size of the population of the cities in question 2.

Exercise 9c 10.5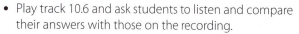

- Play track 10.5 and ask students to listen and compare the answers with their own ideas.

ANSWERS/AUDIOTRACK 10.5

1
A Which city is drier, Dublin or Paris?
B It's close: both cities have a lot of rain, but Dublin's wetter.
2
A Which is bigger, the population of Sydney or Cairo?
B Well, Cairo's population is bigger than Sydney's. Cairo has a population of over nine million, but Sydney's is smaller at just over four and a half million.

Exercise 10a

- Do the first question with the class and then ask students to complete the other questions individually.
- Put students into pairs and ask them to compare their answers.

EXTRA SUPPORT You may want to group faster students with any students who are finding this lesson difficult, to facilitate peer teaching.

- Check answers together.

ANSWERS
1 Are Indian elephants heavier than African elephants?
2 Is Tokyo more expensive than Singapore?
3 Are giraffes faster than humans?
4 Is Canada smaller than the USA?
5 Is the North Pole colder than the South Pole?

Exercise 10b

- Ask students to work in their pairs and take turns to ask and answer the questions.
- Ask students to share any interesting or funny answers they heard.
- Correct any errors you heard.

Exercise 10c 10.6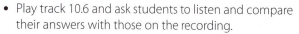

- Play track 10.6 and ask students to listen and compare their answers with those on the recording.
- Students may not have come across the adverb *slightly* before. It's an adverb we use to show a small difference.

EXTRA ACTIVITY Show students *much* and *a bit/slightly* as adverbs to show ways to express a big and a small difference. Write the full sentence which answers question 3 in exercise 10a on the board and ask students if they could or should use *much* or *slightly* in the sentence, e.g. *Giraffes are much/slightly faster than humans.* (Answer: much).

Check that students understand that *much* is a bigger difference than *slightly*.

Ask students to work with their partner and think of two places, two animals and two types of transport. Tell them to write three sentences comparing these things using *much* or *slightly*.

Ask pairs to tell the class their sentences and ask listeners to say if they agree or not and why.

ANSWERS/AUDIOSCRIPT 10.6
1
A Are Indian elephants heavier than African elephants?
B No, they aren't. African elephants are heavier than Indian elephants.
2
A Is Tokyo more expensive than Singapore?
B Yes, it is. Both places are quite expensive, but Tokyo is more expensive than Singapore.
3
A Are giraffes faster than humans?
B Yes, they are. Giraffes can run at 35 miles an hour which is faster than any human being.
4
A Is Canada bigger or smaller than the USA?
B Canada is slightly bigger than the USA.
5
A Is the North Pole colder than the South Pole?
B No, it's warmer. The South Pole is colder than the North Pole.

Exercise 11a

- As a lead-in, you could ask students to say if they live in the city or the countryside. Make sure they remember the meaning of *countryside* (n) (= all the land outside of cities).
- You could also find some photos as a lead-in to create interest and generate ideas.
- Refer students to the table and ask them the question about living in the city or countryside. Encourage students to express some ideas to create interest in the activity – don't worry about correct grammar at this point.
- Put students into pairs and ask them to complete the table with their own ideas. You could give them a time limit of five minutes for this. Tell them to check their comparatives are correct before you go on to the next exercise. Encourage peer correction and monitor to help students correct any errors.

City	Country
more interesting	quieter
noisier	more peaceful
more expensive	cheaper
bigger	safer
busier	more boring
more dangerous	slower

Exercise 11b

- Put pairs together to make groups of four and tell pairs to tell the other pair about their ideas. Encourage discussion and agreement and disagreement by modelling the exercise using your own list to demonstrate.

EXTRA CHALLENGE/EXTRA SUPPORT Write phrases for agreeing and disagreeing on the board, e.g.
I agree.
I suppose so.
I'm sorry, I don't agree.
I'm not sure about that.

Ask fast finishers to write some sentences to summarize their group's ideas, e.g. *We agreed that living in the city is more interesting than living in the countryside.* Ask students to share their ideas with the class after the discussions have finished.

GRAMMAR REFERENCE ANSWERS

Exercise 1
1 icier   2 dirtier   3 worse   4 more dangerous
5 better   6 more friendly   7 foggier   8 easier

Exercise 2
1 The sun is brighter than the moon.
2 Canada is bigger than the UK.
3 Cooking is more difficult than eating.
4 Planes are faster than trains.
5 August is windier than July.
6 Vegetables are healthier than sweets.
7 Your country is more interesting than my country.
8 His clothes are more expensive than her clothes.

Exercise 3
1 more famous   2 warmer   3 drier   4 colder
5 further   6 icier   7 windier   8 longer   9 shorter
10 more beautiful

10.2 Natural wonders

Goals
- Describe nature and geography
- Use superlative adjectives

Lead-in

1 Closed book. Review comparatives. Places to visit.
- Tell students you want to visit somewhere beautiful this weekend. Ask students to suggest places and write them on the board. Put students into pairs and ask them to discuss which places are better to visit in their opinion and why.
- Ask students to tell the class their ideas. Write sentences using comparatives on the board and remind students of the correct forms where necessary.

2 Open book. Discussing photos.
- Refer students to the photos and ask them to work in pairs and discuss which features they can see. Write the names on the board (*mountain, waterfall, lake, river, beach, desert*).
- Tell them to decide which photo(s) they prefer and why.

Vocabulary & Speaking nature and geography

Exercise 1a
- Refer students to the photos and ask them to think about what they show and where they might be. Go over the pronunciation of the places in the box. (You can find the correct pronunciation on track 10.7.) This will help students to complete the activity and help them listen to the audio in exercise 2.
- Put students into pairs and ask them to complete the matching exercise and discuss which countries the natural wonders are in.
- Ask one or two students to share their ideas with the class.

ANSWERS
a Mount Kilimanjaro, in Tanzania
b Victoria Falls, between Zimbabwe and Zambia
c Lake Baikal, in southern Siberia, Russia
d the Amazon (Jungle), Brazil and Ecuador/Peru/Bolivia
e Phuket, in Thailand
f the Gobi Desert, in China and Mongolia

Exercise 1b 10.7 🔘
- Play track 10.7 and ask students to listen and check their answers.

AUDIOSCRIPT 10.7
a Mount Kilimanjaro is in Tanzania in East Africa. Its name means 'mountain of light' and it's a very beautiful place. It's the highest mountain in Africa, but it's not difficult to climb.
b Victoria Falls are beautiful! It's a very big waterfall on the Zambezi River between Zimbabwe and Zambia.
c Lake Baikal is in the south of Siberia in Russia. It's the biggest and deepest lake in the world, but it often freezes in winter because Siberia has a very cold climate.
d The Amazon Jungle is the biggest area of rainforest in the world. It is mostly in Brazil, but some parts of it are in other South American countries such as Ecuador, Peru and Bolivia. About half the world's plants and animals live in rainforests.
e The Andaman Sea has some very beautiful tropical islands, with white sandy beaches, near the west coast of Thailand. The biggest and most famous is Phuket.
f The Gobi Desert is a very large desert in north-west China and Mongolia. It's a cold desert because it's so far north and it sometimes snows there.

WATCH OUT! Punctuation – capitals. Capitals are used differently in different languages. You could show students how names of rivers, mountains, lakes and other natural features are written with capital letters in English when they form part of the name. Encourage students to discuss if this is the same in their first language, to encourage analysis and help them remember differences and similarities between the languages.

Exercise 2a

- Ask students to read through the sentences from the recording and go over any unknown vocabulary with them.

  PRONUNCIATION Some students tend to pronounce the *s* in *island* and put the stress on the wrong syllable in *desert*. They also may have problems with the long /i:/ sound in *beaches*.

- Ask students to work with their partner and complete the exercise.

  ANSWERS

1 mountain 2 waterfall; River 3 lake 4 rainforest
5 islands; beaches; coast 6 desert

Exercise 2b 10.7

- Play track 10.7 again and ask students to check their answers.

  EXTENSION You could ask students to discuss which of the places in the recording they would rather visit. Encourage them to use comparatives so you can further assess their use of this grammar point.

Exercise 3

- Put students into pairs and ask them to discuss the question. Tell them to refer back to the photos in exercise 1a to help them think of features.
- Ask one or two students to share any interesting things they heard with the class.

Exercise 4a

- Put students into pairs and ask them to read the sentences and do the matching exercise.

  ANSWERS

1 b 2 c 3 a

Exercise 4b 10.8

- Play track 10.8 and ask students to listen and check their answers.

AUDIOSCRIPT 10.8

1 Lake Baikal is in the south of Siberia.
2 The Gobi Desert is in north-west China and Mongolia.
3 Phuket island is near the west coast of Thailand.

Exercise 4c

- Refer students to the compass and check they know what it is. Teach them that we call the different directions the *points* of the compass.
- Ask them to complete the points of the compass and compare their answers with the person sitting next to them.

  ANSWERS

1 north 2 east 3 west 4 south

Exercise 4d

- Refer students to page 130 to check their answers.

  PRONUNCIATION If your students have problems producing the /θ/ sound in *north* and *south,* tell them to stick their tongue between their teeth and blow out. Show them how to do this. The /θ/ sound is not voiced. You could show them the difference between the voiced /ð/ and the unvoiced /θ/ by asking them to say the sounds in the words *this* and

south. In *this,* the sound is voiced. If they put their fingers in their ears and say these two words, they should notice a vibration when they say the *th* sound in *this* but not when they say *south*. Ask them to say the sounds /ð/ and /θ/ quickly one after the other to practise.

Exercise 5

- Put students into pairs and ask them to decide who is Student A and who is Student B.
- Refer them to the relevant pages and ask them to read the instructions. Demonstrate the activity by asking a student to come to the board and follow your instructions to draw an island that includes some mountains, a lake, a rainforest and a beach. Don't use the same instructions as the exercise.
- To support this activity, ask students to sit back to back so they are only listening and can't use gestures to aid their instructions.
- When students have finished, tell them to compare their maps and talk about how easy/difficult the exercise was.

  ANSWERS

Student A: river, mountain, lake, waterfall
Student B: island, forest, beach, desert

Grammar & Speaking superlatives

Exercise 6a

EXTRA SUPPORT Ask students to say the numbers in the box. As well as helping with their pronunciation, this will assist them when they listen to the recording to check their answers.

- Pre-teach the meaning of *deep* (draw a swimming pool and label the shallow and deep end), *fresh water* (= water that has no salt in it), *climb* (demonstrate this by miming), *roof* (draw a house and label the roof).
- Ask students to read the information about the three features. You may want to give them a time limit.
- Ask students to work with a partner to read the texts again and insert the numbers they think go in the gaps.

  ANSWERS

Lake Baikal: 1 1600 2 25 3 20
Kilimanjaro: 4 5,895 5 87
Al-Hasa: 6 12 7 3

Exercise 6b 10.9

- Play track 10.9 and ask students to listen and check their answers. You may need to play the track twice.
- Ask students to work with their partner and discuss what they heard. What was most surprising or interesting? Why?

AUDIOSCRIPT 10.9

Lake Baikal in Siberia is the biggest, deepest and oldest lake in the world. It's more than 1,600 metres deep and more than 25 million years old. It has almost 20 per cent of the world's freshwater, and thousands of different kinds of plants and animals live there.
Mount Kilimanjaro, in Tanzania, is one of the largest volcanoes in the world. It's 5,895 metres tall – the highest mountain in Africa. It's sometimes called the 'Roof of Africa'. It's also one of the easiest mountains in the world to climb, even for tourists. The oldest person ever to climb to the top was a French man, Valtee Daniel, who was 87 years old.

An oasis is an area of water in a desert and Al-Hasa is the largest oasis in Saudi Arabia. It covers over 12 km² and gives water to over 3 million trees and a million people, even at the hottest times of the year. Many Saudis believe Al-Hasa is the most beautiful and best area to visit in the country.

Exercise 7a

- Refer students to the Grammar focus box and ask them to read the information.
- Refer students to *Grammar reference* on p155. There are two more exercises here students can do for homework.

Exercise 7b

- Ask students to look at the table and complete the superlative form for each adjective. Do one or two examples together to support students who are finding it difficult. Point out that they can check their answers in the texts in exercise 6a. Tell them to remember the correct spelling.
- Check answers.

ANSWERS

	Adjective	Superlative form
short adjectives	big deep old large hot	biggest deepest oldest largest hottest
adjectives ending in -*y*	easy	easiest
longer adjectives	beautiful	most beautiful
irregular adjectives	good	best

EXTENSION Ask students to come up with two to four more examples for each type of adjective. Tell them to add them to the table. Go over their ideas on the board.

Pronunciation *the ... -est* in sentences

- Ask students to listen to you as you say the superlative adjectives in the table. Ask them to mark the stressed syllables, e.g. the **bigg**est, the **deep**est.
- Ask students to practise saying the adjectives with the correct emphasis.
- Refer students to the information in the Pronunciation box.
- Play track 10.10 and ask them to read and listen.

Exercise 8 10.11 💿

- Refer students to the short conversation and play track 10.11. Ask students to listen the first time you play it and notice the stress.
- Play the track again and ask students to repeat. Pause after each part of the conversation. It may help if you ask them to mark the stress on the longer words: **Am**azon and Missi**ssi**ppi.

PRONUNCIATION When we say a superlative starting with a vowel, e.g. *the easiest, ugliest, oldest*, we say *thee* /ði:/. Point this out to students before the extension activity.

EXTENSION Practise the weak forms in superlative adjectives. Ask students to look at the adjectives in the table in exercise 7b. Ask them to tell you the opposites of these adjectives and write them on the board. Tell students to work in pairs and write the superlative forms. Ask students to practise saying the pairs of adjectives with their partners, e.g.
Student A the oldest
Student B the youngest

Exercise 9a

- Put students into pairs and ask them to read the instructions.
- Demonstrate the conversation with a student.
- Ask students to complete the exercise.

ANSWERS
1 The busiest airport is Beijing, then Dubai, then Los Angeles.
2 The biggest island is Greenland, then Madagascar, then Sumatra.
3 The oldest monument is the Great Pyramid of Giza, then the Parthenon, then the Colosseum.

Exercise 9b 10.12 💿

- Play track 10.12 and ask students to compare their discussions with those in the recording. You could stop the recording after each point and ask students to say if they were correct in their discussions or not.

AUDIOSCRIPT 10.12
1 The busiest airport of the three is Beijing, then Dubai and then Los Angeles.
2 Of these islands, Greenland is the biggest, and Madagascar is bigger than Sumatra.
3 The Great Pyramid of Giza isn't the oldest monument in the world, but it's the oldest in this group. It's older than the Parthenon, and the Parthenon's older than the Colosseum.

Exercise 10a

- Ask students to work with a partner and complete the sentences.
- Check answers together.

ANSWERS
1 **The nearest** bank is …
2 **The cheapest** place to eat is …
3 **The best** place to go shopping is …
4 **The oldest** part of the town is …
5 **The most interesting** art gallery/museum is …
6 **The busiest** street is …

Exercise 10b

- Ask students to work in groups of three and discuss the different items from exercise 10a. Refer them to the sample conversation for extra support.
- Ask two or three students to report their ideas to the class and ask them to discuss different answers.

EXTRA ACTIVITY Role-play a local resident and visitor. Ask students to work in pairs and decide who is the visitor and who is the resident. Model questions the visitor can ask, e.g. *Where's the nearest post office? What's the best place to eat local food?* Ask students to role-play a conversation between the visitor and resident discussing things about the city/town.

You could ask students to write an email recommending places, in order to review informal email writing from Unit 9. Remind them of the emails between Stefano and his friend.

GRAMMAR REFERENCE ANSWERS

Exercise 1

1 This watch is the most expensive thing in the shop.
2 Mount Everest is the highest mountain in the world.
3 My notebook is the neatest notebook in the class.
4 The High Street is the busiest place in my city.
5 The beaches on the north coast are the most beautiful beaches in my country.
6 My frying pan is the most useful thing in the kitchen.
7 My house is the smallest house in my street.
8 Ling-Fan is the tallest student in my class.

Exercise 2

1 the best   2 in   3 the tallest   4 in   5 the largest
6 in   7 more interesting   8 than   9 older   10 than
11 more beautiful   12 than   13 the most beautiful
14 the most expensive   15 hotter   16 than   17 more comfortable   18 than   19 worse   20 than

10.3 Vocabulary and skills development

Goals

• Understand comparison
• Use adjective + noun collocations

Lead-in

1 Open book. Review points of the compass, and nature and geography.

• Ask a volunteer to draw a compass on the board. Ask the class to complete the points of the compass together.
• Practise the pronunciation.
• Ask students some questions about the town or city you are in, e.g. *What's in the south of this city?*
• Tell students you are going to test their memory of the last lesson.
• Ask students to work in pairs. Tell one of them to open their books at Unit 10.2 and ask their partner questions about the geography they learnt, e.g. *What lake is in the south of Siberia?*
• Ask students how much their partner could remember.

2 Open book. Use a photo to elicit and review vocabulary.

• Refer students to the photo of the polar bear. Ask them the questions below and try to review weather vocabulary from lesson 10.1.
What animal is this?
Where does this animal live?
What's the weather like there?
• Write relevant vocabulary on the board and check meaning and pronunciation.

Reading & Speaking understanding comparison

Exercise 1

• Ask students to read through the question and the categories. Elicit an example for each category and write it on the board.
• Put students into pairs and ask them to complete the task. Alternatively you could do this as a whole class activity and write vocabulary on the board. Go over any new vocabulary and encourage peer teaching where possible.

POSSIBLE ANSWERS

1 very cold places: the North Pole, the South Pole, the Arctic, the Antarctic, Siberia, Russia
2 very hot and dry places: The Sahara Desert, the Gobi Desert, places in Africa
3 places with dangerous animals: the ocean near Australia has sharks, some places in Africa have lions, India has tigers, jungles like the Amazon have lots of dangerous snakes and poisonous animals
4 very wet places: tropical areas like the Amazon, Hong Kong and places with a rainy season or monsoon season

EXTENSION Review comparatives and superlatives. Tell students they are going to show the class what they know about natural places and animals. Put them into groups of three or four so they can share what they know. Tell them to write three to five sentences about natural places and animals, similar to the sentences in exercise 2b.

They could pass their sentences to another group who could underline the adjectives and things being compared. They could also discuss if they knew this information already. They could choose the most interesting fact they read about.

Exercise 2a

• Refer the students to the Unlock the code box and ask them to read the information.
• As a lead-in to the next exercise, ask the following questions:
1 What things are being compared in each sentence?
(Answers: the Arctic and Antarctic, lions and cheetahs, north Africa and central Africa, adults and students)
2 What comparative form is given? (Answer: colder)
3 What superlative form is given? (the fastest)
4 What two other words are used to compare? (different, less)

Exercise 2b

• Refer students to the instructions and do the first question with the class to check they are clear about the exercise.
• Put students into pairs and ask them to complete the exercise.
• Check answers together.

ANSWERS

1 The Burj Khalifa in Dubai is one of the tallest buildings in the world, but Everest is much taller.
2 We went on a tour of a mountain and a lake. They were both beautiful, but I enjoyed the lake more.
3 We don't really have winter. The weather in July is hot and February is similar.
4 The south of the island was wet but the north was wetter.
5 We get a lot of wind in the summer, and the autumn is the same.

EXTRA CHALLENGE Adverbs and comparatives review. Draw students' attention to the first sentence in exercise 2b and ask them what *much* is used for in the sentence. (Answer: it's giving information about the size of the comparison. It means a big difference.) Write *way, much, slightly, a little* on the board and ask students to identify the extent of the difference. *Way* and *much* indicate a big difference and *slightly* and *a little* a small difference. Ask students to write a sentence for each adverb, e.g. *Angela is way taller than Bex.* Check answers and explain that *way* is very informal.

Exercise 3

- Ask students to read the information in all five sentences and go over any unknown vocabulary with them.
- Draw students' attention to the example answer. Put them into pairs and ask them to complete the other four questions.
- Check answers together.

ANSWERS
1 (surviving) with no water   2 group (of runners)
3 when he started (walking), when he was 28   4 food (on the journey)   5 before the swim

- Ask extra questions to check comprehension:
1 How long do you think you can survive without food? (Gandhi survived without food for 21 days apparently. So, we can go for about 3 weeks.)
2 How many runners were in the second group? (The same, 50.)
3 How old was Masahito when he finished? (He was 32 and a half.)
4 (no question)
5 How many kilos do you think Strel was when he finished? (He was about 96 kilos according to various websites about him.)

Exercise 4

> **Text summary/Background note:** An article based on a real event, the Marathon des Sables. It's the same as six regular marathons and is called an ultramarathon. Mauro Prosperi is a police officer and pentathlete who became famous for getting lost in the Sahara Desert during this race.

- Draw students' attention to the photo of the runners and ask them to guess where the photo was taken and what the men are doing.
- Ask students to read the headline and check they understand that *v* means *versus* (= against). Ask them what they think the headline means.
- Pre-teach *equipment* (= things you need to do an activity), *to not be finished with something* (v) (= you really want to continue with something, e.g. when you are angry with someone you say *I am not finished with you! I will talk to you later!* To further clarify meaning, contrast this with *I finished talking to him*, meaning the conversation has stopped.)
- Ask students to read the text quickly and see if their ideas were correct.
- Put students into pairs. Tell them to read the true/false statements 1–6 and then to read the article again to

complete the exercise. Remind them to correct the sentences that are false.
- Check answers together.

ANSWERS
1 T
2 F – It is the second largest desert.
3 F – It is sometimes hotter than 50°C.
4 F – Mauro was one of the fastest runners.
5 T
6 F – He returned a few years later and finished the race.

Exercise 5

- Tell students to work with the same partner. Ask them to read and discuss the questions.

CRITICAL THINKING These questions ask students to give their opinions about the text. Encourage them to give reasons and explanations for their opinions. You may want to discuss the first question as a class to show them how to extend the discussion and give an explanation, e.g.
Teacher   I think Mauro was a bit crazy to run in this race. He nearly died. What do you think?
Student   I'm not sure. I don't think he was crazy. Maybe he is very brave.

EXTRA SUPPORT/EXTRA CHALLENGE Teach extra adjectives to describe Mauro's actions: *brave, mad, strong,* etc. Students can use these in their discussions.

- Ask two or three students to share any interesting things they discussed with the class.

EXTRA ACTIVITY Ask students to research other races like this for homework (two are mentioned in the article). They could present their information in the next class and you could compare the races they researched.

Vocabulary & Speaking   adjective + noun collocations

Exercise 6a

- Ask students to look back at the article and to find the highlighted words.
- Put students into pairs and ask them to discuss the questions.

DICTIONARY SKILLS Ask students to look up *high* and look at the information provided. Ask them where they can see the part of speech. (Answer: it comes after the phonemic transcription in many dictionaries and in others may be in the margin.) In some dictionaries the comparative and superlative forms are provided too. Some dictionaries may also include whether the adjective is gradable or not. A gradable adjective is one we can make stronger or weaker with comparatives or adverbs of degree, e.g. *It's cold, colder, quite cold.* Non-gradable adjectives cannot be made stronger or weaker, e.g. *It's freezing today. He's alive.*

- Write these words from the text on the board and ask students to find the part of speech in a dictionary.
later (adverb)
crazy (adjective)
danger (noun)
dangerous (adjective)

ANSWERS
1 adjectives   2 nouns

Exercise 6b

• Refer students to the Vocabulary focus box and ask them to read the information and check their answers.

• Go through the answers together.

Exercise 7a

• Ask students to work in the same pairs and complete the exercise.

• Check answers together.

ANSWERS

1 c   2 d   3 b   4 a

Exercise 7b

• Ask students to complete the gaps with the correct adjective and noun collocation.

WATCH OUT! Remind students to write the correct form of the noun according to whether the answer is plural or singular.

• Tell students to compare their answers with the person sitting next to them.

ANSWERS

1 close friends   2 hard workers   3 strong accent
4 mild weather

EXTENSION To develop vocabulary, ask students to work in pairs and look at the nouns in exercise 7a. Tell them to think of other possible adjectives. Ask them to share their adjectives with the class and write good examples on the board, e.g. *Weather: bad, good, nice, hot, cold; Friend: good, best, old; Worker: good, fast, slow, great; Accent: French etc., good, strange, lovely*.

STUDY TIP Ask students to write these collocations in their notebooks and make sentences that will help them remember the words. Encourage them to personalize this exercise to aid memory.

Exercise 8a

• Refer students to the example. Put them into pairs and ask them to read through the sentences and identify the adjective and noun collocations, and then match the opposite adjectives.

WATCH OUT! The adjective in question 4 is a superlative. Tell students to write the opposite in the same form.

Exercise 8b   10.13

• Play track 10.13 and ask students to listen and check their answers.

ANSWERS/AUDIOSCRIPT 10.13

1 Is there usually ~~light~~ heavy traffic on your way to this class?
2 Did you have a ~~low~~ high score in your last test?
3 Do you like ~~weak~~ strong coffee?
4 Which jobs usually have the highest ~~lowest~~ salaries?
5 Are you a ~~light~~ deep sleeper?

Exercise 9

• Put students into groups of three or four.

• Refer them to the sample conversation and model this with a confident student.

• Ask students to discuss the questions.

FEEDBACK FOCUS As students speak, write examples of good grammar (comparative and superlatives) and errors on the board. Go over this after they have finished speaking or use the examples for revision at the start of the next lesson.

EXTRA ACTIVITY Discuss crazy things. In 'Man v Desert' students read about a man doing a crazy thing. Ask students if they have done a crazy thing or if they know someone who has. Give them an example, telling a story from your own life or about someone you know, if you can. Give students one minute to think about their own example.

Put students into small groups of three or four and ask them to tell each other their stories. Don't focus too much on grammar here. Focus on fluency in this activity. Afterwards you could put students into new groups and ask them to tell their group about crazy stories from their previous group discussions.

10.4 Speaking and writing

Goals

• Give preferences and reasons
• Write a description of a place

Lead-in

1 Closed book. Review superlatives and create interest in the lesson.

• Put students into pairs and ask them to discuss these questions.
1 Where is the best place to go in your town if there is bad weather? Why?
2 Where is the best place to go in your town if there is good weather?

• Ask one student from each group to share their ideas with the class and decide on the best places as a group.

2 Closed book. Brainstorm indoor and outdoor activities to lead in to exercise 1.

• Draw two columns on the board and write *indoor* and *outdoor* at the top of the columns.

• Check the meaning of these terms with the group and ask for one example of an activity you can do in each space. Write the examples on the board.

• Put students into groups of three and give them three or four minutes to come up with as many indoor and outdoor activities as they can.

• Write their ideas on the board and go over any new vocabulary.

STUDY TIP Draw attention to any useful collocations and ask students to write down the collocations. You could focus on verb and noun collocations, e.g. *go camping/to the cinema/ for dinner*.

Speaking & Listening reasons and preferences

Exercise 1

• Ask students what an outdoor person is and check they understand the term. (Answer: someone who prefers doing things outside and likes being outdoors.)

- Put students into pairs and ask them to discuss the question. Refer them to the list of indoor and outdoor activities on the board to help them think of examples.
- Ask two or three students to tell the class about their partners.

Exercise 2

This exercise reviews vocabulary from previous lessons such as *compass*, *equipment* and *plates*, *bowls*, etc. If students are not clear on the meaning of these words, go over them with the class.

- As a lead-in, ask students to think of a definition for something in the class, e.g. *board pen/chalk: You use it for writing on a board* or *It's for writing on a board*.
- Tell students they are going to teach each other some new words using definitions. Refer students to the illustration in the exercise and ask how many items there are. (Answer: ten)
- Tell them they will find the definitions for five items each. Put students into pairs and tell them to decide who is Student A and who is Student B. Refer them to the relevant pages and ask them to complete the exercise and write the correct words next to each item.
- Check answers.

ANSWERS
1 a map   2 a first-aid kit   3 a tent   4 a torch   5 a GPS
6 a stove   7 a sleeping bag   8 a compass   9 a lighter
10 pots and pans

PRONUNCIATION This is a good opportunity to practise saying the letters of the alphabet. Remind students to use the correct wording when asking their partner to spell out these words. *How do you spell … ?* Listen to their pronunciation while they are spelling aloud and correct any errors on the spot.

EXTENSION To help students remember the vocabulary, tell them to take turns testing each other. One person closes their book and the other tests them on vocabulary, e.g.
Student A   What do we use to help us see in the dark?
Student B   A torch.

Exercise 3

Background note: This information is about a survival weekend. This is a trip where people do difficult activities, like long walks and camping in places far from a city.

- Refer students to the instructions and ask them what people do on a survival weekend and why people go on them.
- Ask students to read the information about the weekend and find out what people need to do to pass the course.
- Check answers together.

ANSWERS
To pass the course, Ted, Alex and Zoe need to survive for three days and two nights, and find their way back to the main camp.

Exercise 4   10.14 🔘

- As a lead-in ask students what they think Ted, Alex and Zoe will take with them.

- Refer them to the illustration again and play track 10.14. Tell students to tick the items they take.

ANSWERS
a stove   a lighter   cooking equipment   a GPS   a first-aid kit

AUDIOSCRIPT 10.14
A   OK, so we can take a tent and sleeping bag each and we need to decide on the five most important things to take as well.
T   Well, we need cooking equipment – we have to eat – but I think we should take one stove instead of three because we don't need one each.
A   I think a lighter is more important than a stove because we can make a fire for cooking with wood from the forest.
Z   I'm sorry, but I don't agree. Taking a stove is a better idea than making a fire because what happens if it rains? If we have the lighter and the stove – then we can cook inside the tent.
A   OK, so a stove, lighter and cooking equipment makes three things. We can have two more.
Z   Well, we need to find our way to the camp. I think a map and compass are the most useful things for this because a GPS could break or run out of battery.
A   But that's two more things and we can't have any more than that. What happens if we need the first-aid kit? I'd prefer to take the GPS instead of the map and compass because then we can have the first-aid kit.
T   But what about the torch? I don't like the forest at night time!
A   It gets dark quite late, and we should to go bed early after a long day walking in the forest, so I don't think we need the torch.
Z   OK, let's take the GPS and the first-aid kit.
T   OK.
A   Good idea.

Exercise 5a

- Pre-teach *instead of* (= to indicate a preference, e.g. *I want to go on survival course A instead of survival course B because it is easier and more interesting*).
- Put students into pairs and ask them to complete the sentences.

ANSWERS
1 most important   2 we should; because
3 a better idea   4 I'd prefer; because

Exercise 5b   10.14 🔘

- Play track 10.14 again and ask students to listen and check their answers.

Exercise 6a

- Do the first question together with the class.
- Put students into pairs and ask them to complete the exercise. Tell them to write sentences in their notebooks as they will need to refer to them in exercise 6c.

Exercise 6b   10.15 🔘

- Play track 10.15 and ask students to listen and check their answers.
- Play the track again and ask students to repeat each sentence.

1 I think a compass is better than a GPS.
2 I'd prefer to stay in a hotel.
3 The most important thing to take is food.
4 I think we should only take one torch.
5 Taking a first-aid kit is more important than taking a knife.
6 I'd prefer to have my own tent.

Exercise 6c

- Refer students to the example. Ask them to suggest other reasons why a compass is better than a GPS.
- Ask students to work in pairs and say the other sentences, adding extra information.
- Ask two or three students to explain their ideas to the class.

EXTENSION Ask students to work with a different partner and think of four more items they could use on a survival weekend. These could be used in the next exercise.

Exercise 7a

EXTENSION To give this exercise more context, ask students to think of rules for their own survival weekend. You could do this as a class or put students into pairs and ask them to think of:
Where it is
How long
What people have to do
What they can take

- Refer students to the Language for speaking box. Model the exercise with a student, e.g.
Teacher What do you think we should take, Sara?
Sara I think we should take a compass because it's important and it's small and easy to carry.
Teacher OK, but I'd prefer a GPS.
Sara I'm not sure. It's bigger and more difficult to carry.
Teacher OK, perhaps a compass is a better idea.

EXTRA SUPPORT Giving individual thinking time before a speaking activity can help students produce more language. Ask students to think alone for one minute or so about what they will say.

- Tell students to work in their pairs and discuss the exercise. You could give them a time limit to agree on the order.

Exercise 7b

SMART COMMUNICATION Students may disagree on the items they want to take, but remind them of the importance of politeness in this type of situation. The expressions in the Language for speaking box will help them.

- Put the pairs of students into groups of four and ask them to explain their ideas to the new pair.
- Tell students they have to decide on a final list of five items.

EXTRA ACTIVITY Ask students to write an information text for people coming on their survival course, telling them what to bring. Tell students to refer to the text on page 102. They should have the same headings and include their lists in the equipment section.

EXTRA ACTIVITY If you did the extra exercise above, either stick the texts on the walls around the room and ask students to walk around and read them, or ask students to pass their texts to others to read. Ask students to discuss who wrote about the most interesting/most difficult/easiest/funniest survival weekend. Put students into groups and ask them to choose one weekend for each adjective.

Writing & Reading   describe places

Exercise 8a

Background note: This website review gives information about what to do and see in Zambia. Zambia is a country in southern Africa, with a tropical climate. It does not have any coastline. Many people live in cities but people also live as farmers in the countryside. It's famous for the Victoria Falls on the Zambezi River.

- As a lead-in, ask students to read the title of the review and look at the photos. Ask them what they know about Zambia. Tell them to work with a partner and discuss the question.
- Go over ideas with the class.

Exercise 8b

- Ask students to read the text and see if their ideas were correct.

ANSWERS
You can see at least seventeen amazing waterfalls (including Victoria Falls), five big lakes, a lot of rivers, elephants, lions and many other animals and birds. You can fish, go swimming, and canoe.

Exercise 9a

- Refer students to the questions about paragraph number and content. Ask them to read the review again and answer the questions. You could ask them to underline the most important information in each paragraph.
- Go over the answers together.

ANSWERS
The review has three paragraphs. Paragraph 1 describes the waterfalls, lakes and rivers in the country, and some of the activities you can do on them. Paragraph 2 is about the National Parks and some of the animals to be seen in them. Paragraph 3 is about the climate, weather and the three seasons in Zambia.

Exercise 9b

- Refer students to the diagram and ask them to work in pairs to complete it.
- Check answers together.

WATCH OUT! Question 4 requires them to identify an adjective which comes after the noun in the text. Tell them to read the whole sentence about temperatures.

ANSWERS
1 rivers   2 canoe   3 animals   4 comfortable
5 seasons

Exercise 10a

- Ask students to read the text again and complete the exercise in pairs.
- Go over answers on the board, writing examples under each category (adjectives, comparatives, superlatives).

ANSWERS

Come to Zambia

We have over seventeen <u>amazing</u> waterfalls (including Victoria Falls, the world's <u>largest</u> waterfall), five <u>big</u> lakes and a lot of rivers. Lake Tanganyika is the second <u>deepest natural</u> lake in the world. You can fish, go swimming, or even canoe on it.

Zambia also has some of the <u>best national</u> parks in the world – you can see elephants and lions as well as many other animals and birds.

Temperatures in Zambia are <u>more comfortable</u> than <u>many tropical</u> areas because of the height of the country. There are three seasons, <u>cool</u> and <u>dry</u> from May to August, <u>hot</u> and <u>dry</u> from September to November, and <u>warm</u> and <u>wet</u> from December to April.

Exercise 10b

- Refer students to the Language for writing box and ask them to read it and discuss the question in pairs.

ANSWER

We use adjectives to make the writing more interesting.

Exercise 11a

CRITICAL THINKING Ask students how using diagrams like the one in exercise 9b can help plan a piece of writing. (Answer: it helps you plan a number of paragraphs and think of examples to add to each paragraph. This makes your writing clear and easier to read.) Explain that some students find diagrams useful, but others prefer to write headings. Ask students what they prefer.

- Ask students what they know about Australia. Write relevant information on the board and go over any new vocabulary that comes up.
- Put students into pairs. Refer them to p131 and tell them to draw a diagram similar to the one in exercise 9a. They can add more information if they want.
- Put pairs into groups of four and ask them to compare what they have written with the other pair. They can add information that they don't have to their diagram.

Exercise 11b

- Explain that students are going to use the information in their diagrams to write a review for a tourism website. Refer students to the text in exercise 8 for support. Give them a word limit of forty to fifty words.
- Write *Australia has a barrier reef* on the board and ask students to add an adjective to make the sentence more interesting. Remind them that adjectives go before the noun.
- Tell students to write their reviews individually. They shouldn't compare work with a partner now as they will do this in exercise 12. You could monitor and point out any errors and good language as you read their work.

Exercise 12

- Put students into new pairs and ask them to swap reviews with each other. Tell them they are going to read each other's reviews to make sure they included all the necessary information.
- Encourage them to identify errors with adjectives and word order if you think the class will respond well to peer correction.

EXTRA ACTIVITY Ask students to work with their partners and compare Australia and Zambia. Ask them to make notes of similarities and differences. Tell them to work with another pair and compare their ideas.

Ask them to stay in their groups of four and discuss the similarities and differences between Australia or Zambia and their own country.

10.5 Video

The Grand Canyon

VIDEOSCRIPT

This is the Grand Canyon, one of the world's natural wonders.

The Grand Canyon is in Arizona in the south-west of the United States.

It's one of the most popular tourist attractions in the world and each year over four million visitors come here. They usually drive to the Canyon's Southern Rim and enjoy the famous views from Lipan Point.

They take photographs of the Palisades, the south-eastern wall of the canyon, and look out at the Echo and Vermilion Cliffs.

Tourists also visit the historic buildings along the South Rim, such as the Desert View Watchtower and Lookout Studio. Some even take the Grand Canyon railway, which stops in Grand Canyon village.

Afterwards they go to the Grand Canyon Visitor Centre. Here they can learn all about the canyon's history, geography and wildlife. There are maps, interactive displays and games for children.

People like looking at the canyon, but very few visitors travel *into* the canyon. There is so much more to see inside.

The bottom of the canyon is much warmer than the top. At the top there are cool fir forests. But as you go further, it becomes hotter and drier, and it looks like nowhere else in the world.

The Colorado River runs through the canyon. It is 300 feet wide and 100 feet deep. Over millions of years it cut through the rock and created the canyon. In fact, the river is still changing the inside of the canyon today.

The canyon is beautiful. There are incredible views here and because there isn't any pollution, it has some of the cleanest air in the country. It's an amazing place and everybody should come at least once in their lifetime.

It's great fun too, and there are lots of activities for any age. Visitors can go rafting down the river or go on a helicopter ride over the canyon's amazing landscape.

The Grand Canyon isn't the longest canyon in the world. There are others that are wider and deeper, too. But there are very few places that are so spectacular.

Exercise 1
building ☐ canyon ✓ cliff ✓ forest ☐
helicopter ☐ landscape ✓ map ☐ rafting ✓
river ✓ rock ✓ tourists ✓ wildlife ✓

Exercise 2
Students' own answers

Exercise 3
1 south-west
2 four
3 drive
4 views
5 wildlife
6 A lot of
7 warmer
8 still changing the canyon today
9 cleanest
10 most spectacular

Review

Exercise 1a
1 Cairo is hotter than Bangkok.
2 Canberra is foggier than London.
3 The pollution in New Delhi is worse than in Beijing.
4 Rome is older than Damascus.
5 Ottawa is snowier than Moscow.
6 Mexico City has a bigger population than Tokyo.

Exercises 1b & 1c 10.16 🔊
1 F 2 T 3 T 4 F 5 T 6 F

AUDIOSCRIPT 10.16
1 Bangkok is hotter than Cairo.
2 Canberra is foggier than London.
3 The pollution is worse in New Delhi than in Beijing.
4 Damascus is older than Rome.
5 Ottawa is snowier than Moscow.
6 Tokyo has a bigger population than Mexico City.

Exercise 2a
1 The **biggest** city is …
2 The **oldest** university is in …
3 The **longest** river is the …
4 The **hottest** time of year …
5 The **best** place to live is …
6 One of the **most beautiful** areas is …
Students' own answers

Exercise 3a
1 cloudy 2 foggy 3 freezing 4 icy 5 lightning
6 snow 7 sunny 8 windy 9 rain

Exercise 4a
1 c 2 a 3 e 4 d 5 b

Exercise 5a

	coffee	price	salary	accent	temperature	traffic
heavy	✗	✗	✗	✓	✗	✗
high	✗	✓	✓	✗	✓	✗
light	✗	✗	✗	✓	✗	✓
low	✗	✓	✓	✗	✓	✗
strong	✓	✗	✗	✓	✗	✗

Exercise 6a
1 idea 2 more 3 most 4 should 5 prefer

11

Working together

Unit overview

Language input

going to (CB p107)	• *What are you going to do? We're going to sell tickets.*
Infinitive of purpose (CB p109)	• *I go to the gym to keep fit.*
Grammar reference (CB pp156–157)	

Vocabulary development

Verb + noun phrases (1) (CB p106)	• *plant a tree; give money to charity; organize a sports event …*
Technology (CB p108)	• *app, smartphone, tablet, GPS, website …*
Making adjectives stronger (CB p111)	• *Brazil is a really huge country.* • *She's very good at tennis.*

Skills development

Reading: unknown words (CB p110)	
Writing: a notice (CB p112)	
Speaking: offering to do something (CB p113)	

Video

Documentary: Silicon Fen (CB p114)	
Vox pops (Coursebook DVD & TG p258)	

More materials

Workbook	• Language practice for vocabulary, grammar, pronunciation, speaking and writing
Photocopiable activities	• Grammar: What are you going to do? (TG p208 & TSRD) • Vocabulary: Can you recommend? (TG p225 & TSRD) • Communication: Division of labour (TG p242 & TSRD)
Tests	• Unit 11 test (TSRD)
Unit 11 wordlist (TSRD)	

11.1 Community spirit

Goals

- Use verb + noun phrases (1)
- Use *going to* for plans and intentions

Lead-in

1 Closed book. Review comparatives and superlatives.

- Ask students to work with a partner and discuss these questions.
  What's the friendliest area of your town/city to live in? Why?
  What's the noisiest area to live in? Why?
  What's the prettiest area to live in? Why?
- Tell students to write one sentence to answer each question using comparatives or superlatives.
- Go over ideas with the class and correct any errors with comparatives and superlatives.

2 Open book. Predict what the lesson is about.

- Tell students to read the title of the unit and the lesson. Make sure they understand what *community spirit* is. (= A positive feeling of helping each other and friendship between people who live in the same community, usually between neighbours.)
- Put students into pairs or small groups. Tell them to talk to their group and discuss what people can do to show community spirit.

Reading & Vocabulary   verb + noun phrases (1)

Exercise 1

- Ask students to work in groups of three and read the questions. Ask one student the questions to model the conversation. Encourage students to give examples in their answers by asking questions such as:
  When was the last time you helped someone?
  Can you give me an example?
  Who did you help/speak to? What about?
- Tell the group to discuss the questions together and remind them to give examples.
- Ask two or three students to explain their group's answers to the class. Decide as a class how helpful they are and how often they speak to their neighbours.

Exercise 2a

> **Background note:** A text about Mandela Day. This day was created to recognize Nelson Mandela's birthday, and started on the 18th of July 2009. It was inspired by something Mandela said in 2008 – he asked the next generation to be leaders in changing things, to make things better and more equal for everyone. On this day people around the world do different things to try and make the world a better place. Some organize food parcels, some do activities related to education and others build homes and communities. You can find out more information on the Mandela Day website.

- Refer students to the text title and the photo of Nelson Mandela.

- Ask them to work with a partner and discuss the two questions.
- Go over ideas with the class.

Exercise 2b

- Pre-teach *improve* (v.) (= to make something better), *repair* (v.) (= to fix something that is broken), *elderly* (adj./n.) (= a polite way of saying an old person), *homeless* (adj./n.) (= to describe a person without a home).
- Explain that the text is an advertisement to try and get people interested in Mandela Day. Ask students to read the text and discuss with their partner if their ideas were correct.
- Ask the class how close their ideas were to the article.

  ANSWERS
  1 Nelson Mandela worked to change and improve South Africa.
  2 People celebrate Mandela's life by doing things to help their local area.

Exercise 2c

- Tell students to work with their partners and discuss the questions.

  CRITICAL THINKING Encourage students to give their opinions and support these ideas with reasons. You could help this by giving an example, e.g. *I think Mandela Day is a good idea because it helps people to get to know their neighbours.*

- Ask some students to explain what their partner thought.

  EXTENSION Ask students if there are any days in their country dedicated to a famous person and what that person did.

Exercise 3a

- Refer students to the example. Remind them that a collocation is two or more words that often go together. You could explain that learning vocabulary in this way can help them see how to use the language in a context.
- Ask them to read the advert and work with their partners to find more verbs to complete the exercise.
- Check answers with the class.

  ANSWERS
  1 teach   2 plant   3 organize   4 improve   5 help
  6 look after   7 repair   8 visit   9 give   10 make

Exercise 3b

- Tell students they are going to use the same verbs, and match them to new nouns to make more collocations.
- Ask them to work in the same pairs and complete the exercise.

Exercise 3c 11.1 🔘

- Play track 11.1 and ask students to listen and check their answers.
- Play the track again and ask students to repeat.

  ANSWERS
  1 organize   2 give   3 repair   4 visit   5 make   6 help
  7 plant   8 look after   9 teach   10 improve

AUDIOSCRIPT 11.1

1 organize a party
2 give a present to someone
3 repair your friend's bike
4 visit someone in hospital
5 make a cake for a colleague's birthday
6 help a classmate with their homework
7 plant some flowers
8 look after a friend's children for the evening
9 teach someone to drive
10 improve your local area by picking up rubbish

EXTENSION Test vocabulary by asking students to work in pairs. Tell one person in each pair to close their book. Tell their partner to test them on the collocations, e.g. Student A: *organize;* Student B: *A party and a sports event.*

STUDY TIP To help students remember collocations, tell them to make cards. Use small cards and write the verb on one side and nouns that the verb goes with on the other side. Students can test themselves at home by looking at one side and remembering the collocation(s). They can then quickly check if they were correct.

Exercise 4

- Ask a more confident student the two questions to model the exercise. Refer students to the example answers.
- Put students into small groups and ask them to take turns to ask and answer the questions and give reasons where possible.

Grammar & Listening *going to*

Exercise 5a 11.2 🔘

- Ask students to read the activities 1–6 before they listen. Go over any unknown vocabulary.
- Play track 11.2 and ask them to listen and tick the activities the people talk about.
- Check answers together.

ANSWERS
1 walk to work ✓   2 organize a marathon ☐
3 make some cakes ☐   4 repair a bike ☐
5 organize a game of football ✓   6 help a neighbour ✓

AUDIOSCRIPT 11.2

1 We aren't going to use any electricity or use the car tomorrow. I'm going to walk to work and … Arturo? Are you going to cycle to work tomorrow morning? Yes, my husband's going to work by bike.
2 Next Saturday, I'm going to organize a game of football for the kids around here. We're going to sell tickets and give all the money to charity.
3 What am I going to do on Mandela Day? Well, I've got a neighbour and he's unemployed at the moment. I know he's a bit unhappy about it so I'm going to help him find work. We're going to improve his CV and spend the day sending emails to companies.

Exercise 5b

- Put students into pairs and ask them to discuss the question. Encourage them to give reasons for their answers.
- Ask students to share their ideas with the class.

Exercise 6a

- Ask students to read the instructions. Do number 1 with the class. Tell them to try to remember the phrases from the recording to help them complete the exercise.
- Ask them to match the phrases.
- Tell them to compare their answers with a partner.

ANSWERS
1 e   2 a   3 d   4 c   5 f   6 b

Exercise 6b 11.2 🔘

- Play track 11.2 again and ask students to listen and check their answers.

Exercise 6c

- As a lead-in, ask students if the sentences in exercise 6a are referring to the present or the future. (Answer: the future.)
- Refer students to the Grammar focus box.
- Ask them to read the information and complete the gaps, using the sentences in exercise 6a to help them.
- Check answers together.

ANSWERS
1 are   2 am   3 is   4 going to

- Refer students to *Grammar reference* on p156. There are three more exercises here students can do for homework.

Exercise 7a

- Tell students to read the instructions and the interview quickly without completing the gaps. Ask the class what the text is about.
- Put students into pairs and ask them to read the interview again and complete the exercise, filling the gaps with the correct form of *going to* and the verbs in brackets.

WATCH OUT! Remind students to change the auxiliary verb *be* according to the subject of the sentence when using *going to,* e.g. *I'm/I am going to; He's/He is going to; We're/We are going to,* etc.

ANSWERS
1 're going to celebrate   2 is; going to do   3 are going to make   4 isn't going to eat   5 's going to collect   6 're going to post   7 Are; going to have   8 'm not going to have   9 are going to have

Exercise 7b 11.3 🔘

- Play track 11.3 and ask students to listen and check their answers.

FEEDBACK FOCUS Ask the class what answers (if any) they got wrong. Go over any wrong answers and do further clarification of the grammar if necessary.

AUDIOSCRIPT 11.3

I So, how are the plans for this year's Mandela Day?

O Great, thanks! We're getting emails from people all around the world telling us how they're going to celebrate the day.

I That's good to hear. So what is everyone going to do?

O Oh, all sorts of things. A lot of people are going to make soup and sandwiches and give them to homeless people. I had an email from a man yesterday – he isn't going to eat for 24 hours and he's going to collect money for his local hospital. And, of course, we're going to post everything on our website for people to see.

I Are you going to have time to do something yourself?

O No, I'm afraid I'm not going to have much time at all. But we are going to have a big party here at the office and everyone needs to buy a ticket to come. And all the money goes to charity, of course.

Pronunciation *going to*

- Refer students to the Pronunciation box. Play track 11.4 and ask students to read and listen.

Exercise 8 11.5 🔊

- Remind students that we usually stress the verbs and nouns in a sentence, but in this exercise we are focusing on the stressed and unstressed words in *going to/not going to*.

- Play track 11.5 and ask students to read and listen to the three sentences and notice the stress in *going to*.

- Play the track again and ask students to listen and repeat.

PRONUNCIATION /gʌnə/ In spoken English *going to* is often pronounced /gʌnə/. This is also very noticeable in songs and popular music and sometimes it will be written *gonna* in song lyrics. Point out to students that this can be seen as a little inappropriate in some situations and they should use a more standard form.

EXTRA CHALLENGE Ask students to write one positive and one negative sentence about their plans for the next weekend, e.g. *I'm going to visit some friends. I'm not going to do any work.* Tell them to work with a partner and tell each other their sentences by asking: *What are you going to do this weekend?*

EXTRA SUPPORT If you think the students need extra practice with this structure, you could ask them to walk around the class asking different people the question. After this, tell them to sit with a new partner and say what they remember about everyone's plans for the weekend. This will help practise using third person *He/She's going to … .*

Exercise 9a

- Tell students they are going to participate in Mandela Day and do something good for their community. Ask them to think about who needs help in their community.

- Ask students to read the instructions and make sure they are clear that they need to think of three things they are going to do. Refer them to the examples in the advert to help them with ideas.

Exercise 9b

- Put the students into groups of three or four.

- Tell each student to explain what they are going to do.

EXTRA SUPPORT Give students a format for their explanations and discussions, e.g. say what three things you are going to do. Remember to use *going to*. Then, say why you are going to do these things. Explain the result of the actions, e.g. *We are going to teach young people about cooking and eating more healthy food. We think lots of young people eat very bad food and this is bad for their health. We are going to do this so young people stop eating unhealthy food.* After this, listen to other groups and ask a question, e.g. *What are you going to teach them?*

Exercise 9c

- Ask students to decide on the best three ideas from their group and prepare to explain them to the class.

- Ask each group to tell the class their best ideas. Make sure you arrange the class so everyone can see the group speaking. Give the listeners a job, such as listening and asking a question.

- End the lesson by choosing the best three ideas in the class with a vote.

EXTRA ACTIVITY Put students into pairs or small groups and ask them to think of one other famous person who should have a day where everyone does something to celebrate that person. Students should think about why that person was special, and what people should do on that day. Ask them to share their ideas with the class. You could vote on the best idea.

GRAMMAR REFERENCE ANSWERS

Exercise 1
1 Are you going to make
2 My friends are going to help
3 Is he going to plant
4 I'm going to run
5 Are they going to have
6 I'm not going to work
7 We aren't going to play
8 She's not going to learn

Exercise 2
1 'm going to repair
2 's going to start
3 are going to rent
4 are … going to eat
5 is … going to sell
6 Is … going to teach
7 isn't going to come
8 'm not going to have

Exercise 3
1 are we going to do
2 are going to organize
3 am going to buy
4 are going to come
5 are you going to carry
6 is going to lend
7 Are Helena's cousins going to sing
8 aren't
9 are going to play
10 Are you going to help
11 am
12 'm not going to dance
13 Are you going to buy
14 am
15 are we going to make

11.2 Challenges

Goals

- Talk about technology
- Say why you do things
- Use the infinitive of purpose

Lead-in

1 Closed book. Review some useful language.

- Ask students what vocabulary they can remember from lesson 10.4 that might help someone who is on an outdoor adventure, e.g. *tent, sleeping bag, compass, GPS*. Write the words on the board and check understanding.
- Write *GPS* on the board and ask students what the letters stand for. (Answer: Global Positioning System.)
- Ask students to work in groups of four. They have to think of as many uses for GPS as possible. Encourage them to be creative. Possible uses could be using it to find your way around a new city or to find a restaurant near you. Lots of apps use geo-location technology nowadays. You could ask students what they know about this.
- Go over ideas with the class and tell students they are going to read about an interesting use of GPS in this lesson.

2 Closed book. Discuss apps.

- Ask students for some examples of apps (not necessarily ones that use GPS) and write them on the board.
- Ask students to tell each other about their favourite apps.
- Ask students what other types of technology they use, E.g. mobile phones, tablets and computers. Don't teach any vocabulary at this point; just make a note of what students already know.

Vocabulary & Speaking technology

Exercise 1

> **Background note:** Geocaching is a game which is based on the idea of a treasure hunt. It encourages people to go on adventures and then post about them online. People use an app on their smartphone or tablet to guide them to the treasure. The app uses GPS technology.
>
> The treasure is a box with small gifts inside. When you find the box you have to leave something and take something. You then take a photo and send a message to the app saying you have found the treasure. You can post images and stories online to talk about finding the treasure.
>
> The game has more than 6 million members. There are some good videos and lots of information on the geocaching website.

- Put students into groups of three or four and ask them to look at the illustrations and discuss the question.
- Go over some ideas with the class.

Exercise 2a

- Pre-teach *hide* (v.) (= to put something somewhere where you can't see it), *coordinates* (n.) (= the numbers that show location on a map).
- Ask students to complete the matching exercise.
- Check answers together.

1 b 2 e 3 a 4 c 5 d

Exercise 2b

- Make sure all students understand what geocaching is. You could show students the 'What is Geocaching?' video from the geocaching website if you have access to technology in your classroom.
- Put students into groups of three or four and ask them to discuss the questions.
- Ask some students to report back to the class.

CRITICAL THINKING You could ask students to think of two advantages and two disadvantages of geocaching to extend the discussion, e.g. *One disadvantage is that you need a smartphone to play the game. An advantage is that you can practise English when you write online.* They can do this in the same groups. Ask the groups to share their ideas with the class. Go over any new vocabulary that comes up with the class.

Exercise 3a

- Refer students to the highlighted words in the text.
- Ask them to read through sentences 1–5 and find the words for each gap from the geocaching text. Remind them that the nouns may need to be in singular or plural form.

ANSWERS
1 smartphone 2 apps 3 tablet 4 website 5 GPS

Exercise 3b 11.6

- Play track 11.6 and ask students to listen and check their answers.

AUDIOSCRIPT 11.6

1 I have a smartphone, so I can use the internet when I'm out.
2 I often buy apps for my phone.
3 I take my tablet everywhere, so I can work or study when I'm not at home.
4 I check the news every day on my favourite newspaper website.
5 I have GPS on my phone because I drive to lots of different places for work.

Exercise 3c

- Put students into pairs and ask them to read the instructions and the sample conversation. Tell them to discuss the questions with their partners. Remind them to react to what their partner says and ask for more information.
- Ask two or three students to tell the class what they have in common with their partner and what is different. You could ask them to use these phrases:
  We both …
  I … but she/he doesn't …

Exercise 4a 11.7

- Play track 11.7 and ask students to listen as they read, and to complete the matching exercise. You may need to play this a few times.

ANSWERS

1 @ at   2 / forward slash   3 . dot   4 _ underscore
5 – dash

PRONUNCIATION Drill the sounds /æ/, /ʃ/ and /s/ in isolation and then ask students to find them in the words in the box in exercise 4a (at /æt/, slash /slæʃ/, dash /dæʃ/). Ask students to say these words. Listen and praise good pronunciation. Try to use a good student as a model for the rest of the class to follow.

Exercise 4b

• Ask students to check their answers with a partner.

Exercise 4c

EXTRA ACTIVITY Ask students to close their books. Say one of the symbols from exercise 4a and ask the students to draw it. You could ask for a volunteer to come and draw it on the board. Repeat with the other symbols from exercise 4a.

• Put students into pairs, Student A and Student B, and ask them to find their exercises on p131 and p135 and read the instructions.

EXTRA SUPPORT Saying the alphabet can be hard for students. They learn it at beginner level and then sometimes don't practise it again. If you think your students will find this difficult, go over the pronunciation of the alphabet before they start this exercise.

• Tell them to complete the exercise. Listen and go over any errors after they have finished.

ANSWERS
Student A
www dot myspace dot com forward slash zootwoman
Jack underscore memperton 456 at hotmail dot com
www dot chrisbrock dot co dot uk forward slash personal forward slash
star dash student 74 at thetopschool dot org
Student B
s dot Lorenzo dash Jefferson at hgg dot org
www dot theblacksea dot eu
every underscore apple333 at gmail dot com
www dot national theatre dot gnbo dot com dot ng forward slash

Grammar & Speaking infinitive of purpose

Exercise 5a

Audio summary: Four people talk about their reasons for going geocaching.

• Put students into pairs and ask them to discuss the question.
• Ask some students to share their ideas with the class. You could write ideas on the board using infinitives to help students notice the grammar, e.g. *People go geocaching … to speak English, … to meet friends.* Don't explain it at this point. Focus on content.

Exercise 5b 11.8 💿

• Ask students to read the four reasons.
• Play track 11.8 and ask students to complete the matching exercise.
• Check answers together.

ANSWERS
1 b   2 d   3 a   4 c

AUDIOSCRIPT 11.8
1 I go geocaching to keep fit. I choose caches in the countryside and I walk for miles to find them! It's better than going to the gym.
2 I do it to meet new people. I go on to the website and I arrange to meet them in a café in town and then we look for the cache together. I met my best friend geocaching!
3 Well, it's a good way to find some interesting places. Yeah, I go geocaching to see different places.
4 Why do I go geocaching? That's a good question. Um … because I really enjoy it. I love running around looking for presents. It's like being a kid again!

Exercise 5c

• Ask students to discuss the question. You could do this as a pair work exercise or as a class.

Exercise 6a 11.9 💿

• Ask students to read the sentences.
• Play track 11.9 and ask students to listen and complete the gaps.

ANSWERS
1 to keep   2 to meet   3 to see

AUDIOSCRIPT 11.9
1 I go geocaching to keep fit.
2 I do it to meet new people.
3 I go geocaching to see different places.

Exercise 6b 11.9 💿

• Play the track again and ask students to check their answers.
• Ask them what they notice about their answers (they are all to + infinitive).

PRONUNCIATION We stress the verbs and nouns and not the to when we use this grammar. Ask students to underline the verbs and nouns in each sentence, e.g. I go geocaching to visit different places.

• Repeat the recording and ask them to listen and repeat.

Exercise 7

• Refer students to the Grammar focus box and ask them to read the information and complete the gaps, using the sentences from exercise 6a to help them.
• Check answers together.

ANSWERS
1 to   2 To

• Refer students to Grammar reference on p157. There are three more exercises here students can do for homework.

Exercise 8a

Background note: Easter Island is a Polynesian island in the Pacific Ocean. The island is famous for its 887 large statues of human-like heads. Many people visit the island to see these statues.

• Draw students' attention to the photo. Ask them to read the information next to the photo and discuss the question with a partner.

Not many people visit because it is hard to get there. It takes 5.5 hours by plane or 35 days by boat!

Exercise 8b

- Refer students to the instructions and the items in the box. Ask them to read the first sentence, which is done for them. You could do number 2 with the class for extra support.
- Remind students to use *going to* and *to* + infinitive for all their answers.
- Ask students to work alone and complete the exercise.
- Check answers together.

ANSWERS

1 **I'm going to take a torch to** see in the dark.
2 **I'm going to take a pen to** write some postcards to my family and friends.
3 **I'm going to take (some) presents to** leave in the cache for other people.
4 **I'm going to take a camera to** take some pictures of the statues.
5 **I'm going to take some plastic bags to** take my rubbish back to my hotel.
6 **I'm going to take a GPS to** help me find the cache.

EXTENSION Ask students to work in pairs and think of other things they would take. Ask them to write two to four sentences and explain why they are taking those items. Tell them to compare their sentences with another pair.

Exercise 9

As a lead-in, explain that using the infinitive of purpose can help students write more efficient, shorter sentences. Refer them to the example to illustrate how we change *because they want to* into just *to*.

- Ask students to rewrite sentences 2–7 to make them shorter by using the infinitive of purpose.
- Check answers together.

ANSWERS

1 People go to the gym to keep fit.
2 People shop online to find the cheapest price.
3 People take taxis to save time.
4 In the future, more people are going to cycle to work to do more exercise.
5 People grew vegetables at home in the past to feed their families.
6 People are going to learn more foreign languages in the future to help them find a job more easily.
7 In the past, people moved to the city to find a job.

WATCH OUT! In sentences 3 and 6 there is no longer an *s* on the verb as we are using the infinitive now instead of the third person with 'it'. Make sure students understand this.

EXTENSION Ask students to work in small groups and discuss if they agree or not with these sentences. They could also think of alternatives, e.g. *I agree with number 5. I think people buy food to feed their families now*.

Exercise 10a

- Refer students to the verbs in the box and the example. Ask students to read the instructions carefully and think of their own examples. Tell them to write short sentences and point out that they don't need to use infinitives of purpose at this point (that will be covered in 10b).

WATCH OUT! There is a mixture of regular and irregular verbs here. You may need to check the past forms of *bring* and *buy* (*brought* and *bought*).

Exercise 10b

- Ask students to look at the example and think of reasons for their sentences. Give them about two minutes to think about this.

Exercise 10c

- Put students into groups of three or four. Encourage them to work with someone they haven't spoken to so far in the lesson.
- Refer them to the example conversation. To model the exercise, you could ask two confident students to do a couple of examples for the class.

EXTRA SUPPORT Help students by going over the grammar they will need to use in this exercise. Write the questions on the board to remind them to use the correct tenses:
Why did you + verb …?
Why do you + verb?
Why are you going to + verb?

- Ask students to ask and answer questions in their groups. Remind them to start their answers with *to*.

GRAMMAR REFERENCE ANSWERS

Exercise 1
1 to save   2 to book   3 to see   4 to make   5 to invite
6 to tell   7 to buy   8 to improve

Exercise 2
1 to   2 to   3 to   4 because   5 because   6 to
7 because   8 to

Exercise 3
1 We went to Malaysia to go sightseeing.
2 … we sometimes went to the town centre to use the internet café.
3 I went to the café to email my sister …
4 I walked around to look for another café …
5 I went in to ask them if they had internet …
6 … his wife went to the front of the restaurant to close the front door.
7 I took the statues to a shop to sell them.

11.3 Vocabulary and skills development

Goals

- Deal with unknown words
- Make adjectives stronger

Lead-in

1 Closed book. Review infinitives of purpose.

- Write *I learn English to …* on the board and ask students to complete the sentence. (Possible answers are *get a job, go to university*.)
- Remind them that we use *to* + infinitive to give reasons for doing things. Ask students to tell a partner three more things that they do and the reasons for them. They can be daily activities, e.g. *I walk to my English class to get exercise*.
- Listen and write some good examples on the board to help consolidate the grammar.

2 Closed book. Brainstorm collocations of team.

- Write _____ a team, a _____ team, team _____ on the board.
- Put students into pairs or small groups and ask them to think of verbs that can go before a team, adjectives that can go before team and nouns that go after team, e.g. play for a team, a good team and team player. Get one example of each before you ask them to start.
- Ask one person from each team to come and write their ideas on the board.
- Go over unknown vocabulary. Below are some level-appropriate collocations.
  Verbs: be in, support, lead, choose, organize, play for, have
  Adjectives: a good, a strong, a young/old
  Other nouns: team player, member, game, sport, captain, leader

Reading & Speaking unknown words

Exercise 1

- Refer students to the words in the cloud. Ask them to work with a partner and say what languages they think the words are from and how they might be pronounced.
- Get some feedback and ask students to try saying the words.
- Ask students to work with a partner and discuss the questions.
- Go over some ideas with the class.

STUDY TIP You could use this feedback discussion to talk about reading skills and how sometimes it is good not to look up words you don't know, unless the words are important for understanding the text. You could ask students to compare how they read in their first language and how they read different texts in different ways, e.g. we skim magazines and news articles. Suggest that they try to read texts in English out of class in a similar way, to read more fluently.

Exercise 2a

- Refer students to the sentence and the highlighted word.
- Ask students to read the questions and think about possible answers. Ask them to discuss their ideas with a partner.

Exercise 2b

- Ask students to check their answer by turning to p131.
- Ask two or three students to say how they guessed the meaning. Don't explain strategies now; they will look at this in the next exercise.

Exercise 2c

- Draw the students' attention to the Unlock the code box. Ask them to read the information.
- Ask students to explain how they can identify the part of speech. Try to elicit that the position in the sentence shows the part of speech, e.g words after an article are usually nouns; before a noun we can have an adjective. The word formation can also help, e.g. if the word has a suffix such as -er or -ion, this shows it is a noun.

EXTENSION Ask students to look at the example sentence in exercise 2a and identify three nouns, a verb, and an adjective (nouns: rice, breakfast, Japan; verb: have; adjective: common).

Exercise 3a

- Ask students to work with a partner and identify the parts of speech in sentences 1–6.
- Check answers together.

ANSWERS

1 *flissy:* adjective – describes the noun phrase 'part of the city', and comes before the noun
2 *flisser:* noun – 'new' is the adjective describing this person/thing
3 *fliss:* verb – is an action word, an object pronoun follows this verb, and it is used with the auxiliary verb *can*
4 *flissed:* verb – is an action word, follows the subject *We*, and has an -ed regular past simple ending
5 *flissly:* adverb – describes the action 'my brother's driving', and has a typical -ly ending
6 *unflissy:* adjective – describes the noun 'people'

Exercise 3b

- Draw students' attention to the example answer. Do the second question on the board to model the exercise.
- Tell students to work alone to complete the exercise.
- Then ask students to compare their answers with the person sitting next to them.

FEEDBACK FOCUS Monitor the exercise closely and write good, funny or interesting examples on the board. Ask students to identify their examples on the board and ask them to read them and explain them, if relevant.

POSSIBLE ANSWERS

1 noisy/quiet, expensive/poor, old-fashioned/modern
2 caretaker/principal/teacher, lift/security system
3 call/meet/visit/tell/ask
4 washed/repaired/used/crashed
5 well/fast/badly/slowly/carefully
6 unhelpful/untidy/bossy

EXTRA CHALLENGE Ask students to work in pairs and write their own sentences with a nonsense word like *flissy, flissly,* etc. in them. Tell them to swap their sentences with another pair and guess some possible meanings for the words.

Exercise 4a

- Put students into pairs and ask them to read the first sentence. Identify the part of speech and the meaning of *strict* (= not allowing bad behaviour) as an example with the class. Ask suitable questions to guide students, e.g.
  1 How do you know it's an adjective?
  2 Is it a negative or positive adjective? How do you know?
- Ask pairs to complete the rest of the exercise.

Exercise 4b

- Put pairs together to form groups of four.
- Ask them to compare their answers and explain what helped them guess. Do they all agree?

ANSWERS

1 strict: adjective – describes the noun 'teacher'
2 tax: noun – is a thing people pay
3 barks: verb – A dog does this action loudly.
4 scared: adjective – describes the noun 'sister'

5 **constantly**: adverb – tells us how often the phone rings
6 **soil**: noun – is described by the adjective 'good'
7 **annually**: adverb – says how often the visit needs to be done
8 **massive**: adjective – describes the noun 'house'

DICTIONARY SKILLS Some words can be more than one part of speech. Students will need to know which part of speech they are looking up. To help them with this, write these sentences on the board and ask them to say what part of speech the word in bold is (verb, noun, adjective) and what they think it might mean:
He **crossed** *the road.*
She marked the answer with a **cross.**
She was **cross** *with her daughter when she didn't tidy her room.*

Ask them to look up the word and check the meanings. Tell them that identifying the part of speech before they look up a word can help them to find the correct definition in the dictionary.

Exercise 5a

Text summary: A magazine article about the teams that work with successful people. It asks the reader to think about how important the team, rather than just the individual, is.

- Refer students to the photo and the title of the magazine article and ask them to work in pairs and discuss their ideas.
- Get some ideas from the class.

Exercise 5b

- Ask students to read the questions and think what the answers might be.
- Give students a time limit and tell them to read the article.
- Put students into pairs and ask them to discuss the questions.

ANSWERS
1 They think that scientists today work in teams rather than alone, and that the Nobel Prize for Physics' limit of three prize winners excludes other crucial members of the team.
2 Sport is another area where there are teams of people working hard to support individuals and help them succeed.
3 The article thinks we should stop focusing only on the individual's success and reward (more of) the team.

Exercise 6

- Put students into new pairs and ask them to guess the meaning of the words highlighted in yellow. Remind them to refer to the Unlock the code information.
- Ask students to check the answers in a dictionary if they have one. If not, go over the meanings with the class.

ANSWERS
brilliant: *really good* – The adjective describes a scientist famous for excellence.
award: *to give as a prize* – The infinitive verb 'to award' acts on the noun 'the prize' similarly for individuals and teams.
individual: *one person* – The noun refers to 'one person' and compares to 'team' in the same sentence.

maximum: *the most* – The noun suggests an upper limit 'of three'.
crucial: *very important*. – The adjective hints at the (most) important members of the team.
great: *really good* – The adjective suggests 'the very best' tennis players and F1 drivers.
coach: *trainer/person who helps the players with their game.* – support staff who help/teach individuals
dietician: *person who tells players what to eat and drink* – a noun derived from the word 'diet'
focusing: *action of concentrating only on a part* – verb, derived from 'focus', narrowing scope/vision
huge: *very big* – The adjective includes the 'many more people' working.

Exercise 7

CRITICAL THINKING Ask students to think alone about the questions first and consider examples they could use to support their ideas. This will encourage them to reflect on the questions before answering. It also gives them time to think about what they will say. This often produces better conversations.

- Put students into small groups of three or four. Tell them to think about what they are going to say for one minute.
- Ask them to discuss the questions, giving reasons where appropriate.

Vocabulary & Speaking making adjectives stronger

Exercise 8a

- Students may know *really* or *very* already but avoid using them in their spoken English. As a lead-in, you could find out what they know about making adjectives stronger by asking this question:
  How important are the teams behind winners of Formula One?
- Listen to their answers and write any examples of adverbs and adjectives on the board. Use this later in the vocabulary focus to show what students can already do.
- Ask students to work with a partner and complete the exercise.
- Check the answer together.

ANSWER
c huge (adjective): very big

Exercise 8b

- Ask students to complete the exercise and compare answers with a partner.

EXTRA SUPPORT Ask students to match *brilliant, crucial* and *great* with these synonyms to clarify the meaning: *very good* (brilliant, great); *very important* (crucial).

ANSWER
really

Exercise 8c

- Refer students to the Vocabulary focus box and ask them to read the information and check their answers.

WATCH OUT! Remind students they cannot use *very* with stronger adjectives, e.g. you can't say *It was very brilliant.* You have to use *really* with stronger adjectives.

Exercise 9a

- Go over the meaning of the words in the box.
- Put students into pairs. Ask them to complete the exercise, reminding them to read the context to get clues about the meaning of the missing words.

ANSWERS

1 delighted   2 lovely   3 excellent   4 awful   5 tiny

Exercise 9b   11.10 🔘

- Explain that when we use *really* we always stress it. *Really* is used to make an adjective or verb stronger and more emphatic.
- Play track 11.10 and ask students to listen and notice the emphasis on *really*.
- Play the audio again and ask students to listen and check their answers.

AUDIOSCRIPT 11.10

1
A Were you very glad to get the job?
B Of course! I was really delighted!
2
A Was the weather very nice on your holiday?
B Yes, it was really lovely! We were very lucky.
3
A Is she very good at tennis?
B Yes, she's really excellent! She always wins.
4
A What's wrong? You don't look very happy.
B It's really awful! I failed my driving test.
5
A Let's use my car. Your car is too small for five people.
B You're right. My car is really tiny!

PRONUNCIATION   Do some back-chaining to help students produce the stress correctly, e.g.
Teacher: delighted
Students: delighted.
*Teacher: **rea**lly delighted*
*Students: **rea**lly delighted*
*Teacher: I was **rea**lly delighted.*
*Students: I was **rea**lly delighted.*

Exercise 9c

- Ask students to work with a partner and take turns to practise the conversations. They should say each conversation twice, swapping roles, so each person gets to practise saying *really*.

EXTENSION   Ask students who finish quickly to choose some of the conversations and extend them by writing two more lines.

Exercise 10a

- Put students into pairs and ask them to think of three topics that people often talk about, e.g. the weather, sport and hobbies and how they are feeling that day.

EXTRA SUPPORT   If you think students will find this difficult, then give them topics to write about and some ideas of what adjectives they could include, e.g. The weather: *warm, hot, wet, windy*; Sport event: *brilliant, exciting, great*; Hobbies: *excellent, brilliant, awful, interesting*; How you're feeling: *happy, unhappy, tired, great, awful*.

- Refer them to the conversations in exercise 9a and tell them they are going to write similar conversations. Each conversation must have *really* in it.
- Ask them to work with their partner and write the conversations.

EXTRA CHALLENGE   Ask fast finishers to write a short conversation with gaps after *really* for other students to fill in. They can swap their conversations with other fast finishers, or save the activities for later in the lesson or as a revision exercise in a future lesson.

Exercise 10b

- Put students together to work in groups of four and ask the pairs to swap their conversations with the other pair.
- Tell students to practise the other pair's conversations with their partner.
- Check students are clear on the rule: *really* and *very* come before an adjective.
- Ask students to tell the other pair how well they used *really* and *very*.

EXTENSION   Ask students to read out their dialogues to the class. Tell them to focus on the pronunciation of *really*. Encourage them to exaggerate when pronouncing it.

11.4 Speaking and writing

Goals

- Write a formal/informal notice
- Offer to do something

Lead-in

1 Closed book. Review nouns we can use with *organize*.

- Write *organize* on the board. Ask students to think of nouns we can use with it, e.g. *a party, a sports event*. Teach the meaning of *event*.
- Go over any errors with meaning or pronunciation.

2 Closed book. Discussion about local groups and clubs.

- Ask students to think of local groups and clubs that exist, or groups/clubs you might have in your neighbourhood, e.g. study groups, walking groups, discussion groups, community groups, music groups, chess clubs.
- Ask students if they are members of any groups now or if they have been in the past. Put students into pairs and ask them to share experiences.

Reading & Writing   a notice

Exercise 1

- Put students into pairs and ask them to discuss question 1. Ask them to give examples to support their answers, e.g. *I think I'm really organized because I always plan things and I have a very tidy desk.*
- Ask some students to share any interesting things they heard with the class.
- Ask students to discuss question 2. Encourage them to give examples by describing things they have organized in the past.
- Ask some students to share some ideas with the class.

FEEDBACK FOCUS Encourage students to use *really* and other adjectives from lesson 11.3, e.g. *Sandra is really organized. Last week she planned a huge party!* Write good examples on the board to help students remember them.

Exercise 2

- Refer students to the notices. Ask them to read them quickly and say where you might see these advertisements (Answer: on a notice board in a school or library, or in a local newspaper/magazine).

WATCH OUT! Students might get confused by the way *wanted* is used in the title. You could help explain this by referring to the notices in Wild West films: *Wanted! Criminal … Reward $10,000.*

- Ask them to discuss the questions.

ANSWERS

Notice 1
1 A member of the committee wrote it.
2 A member of the local community/a neighbour/a resident may answer it.

Notice 2
1 Someone at a language school or a college wrote it.
2 Someone who wants to learn English/someone who is not English but is living in the UK may answer it.

Exercise 3a

- Ask students to work with the same partner, read the texts again and discuss the questions.
- Check answers and ask for examples to support their ideas.

ANSWERS

1 Notice 2 is more informal. Words have been removed (ellipsis) and it uses exclamation marks.
2 Notice 1 is more formal. The sentences are full: no contractions or use of ellipsis. The expressions are formal in style, e.g. *Would you like …?*

Exercise 3b

- Ask students to read the Language for writing box and check their ideas about the notices.
- *Ellipsis* will be a new word for students at A2. Explain what it is, e.g. *Ellipsis is when we make a sentence shorter by taking out auxiliary verbs (be, do, have) and pronouns.* Explain what auxiliary verbs are to your students. Ellipsis is common in less formal writing in advertisements and newspaper articles, especially headlines.
- Other points should be familiar to students and can be checked in the proceeding exercises.

EXTRA SUPPORT Write some full questions on the board, e.g.
Are you happy in your job?
Do you like television?
Do you want to go on holiday soon?
Do you live in this area?
Ask students to use ellipsis to make them shorter and more informal. You could do this as a whole class activity and ask students to come to the board and write. Or, you could ask them to complete the exercise in pairs and then check answers. (Answers: Happy in your job? Like television? Want to go on holiday soon? Live in this area?)

Exercise 4a

- Explain that sentences 1–8 have been taken from two different notices. Ask students to read the sentences and decide if they are formal or informal. Refer them to the information in the Language for writing box for help. Remind them to look for ellipsis, contractions, full sentences and exclamation marks.
- Check answers together.

ANSWERS

1 I   2 I   3 F   4 F   5 I   6 F   7 F   8 I

Exercise 4b

- Ask students what the notices are about. (One is about a university basketball team and the other is about organizing a youth club in the local community.)
- Ask students to put the sentences in order to make the two notices.
- Check answers together.

POSSIBLE ANSWERS

Notice 1: 8, 5, 2, 1
Notice 2: 3, 6, 7, 4

EXTRA SUPPORT To help reinforce the different grammatical features of the writing, ask students to identify the features for each sentence in exercise 4a.

POSSIBLE ANSWERS:

1 Use of imperative, not a full sentence: ('Come to …' = 'If you are interested, come to …'– the first part is missed out.)
2 Same as number 1, also if it were formal it would probably be a question: Would you like to join the …?
3 It's a full sentence and no contractions are used.
4 As 3.
5 As 2.
6 Full question, no ellipsis.
7 No contractions used, full sentence.
8 As 1.

Exercise 5a

EXTRA ACTIVITY Ask students to think about notices they have seen or things they might see notices for. Give some examples: job adverts, lost/found things, things for sale. Ask the class to give more examples and write them on the board.

- As a lead-in, ask students what the two notices from exercise 2 have in common. (Answer: they both include questions to the reader, they include details of how to get involved, they explain what the notice is for. They get the reader's attention with the questions and headings.)
- Ask students to work in pairs. Explain they are going to plan a notice using some of the features in the Language for writing box.
- Go through the ideas in the box and ask students to choose one of them, or their own idea, to write a notice for.
- Refer students to the checklist sentences 1–4. Ask pairs to discuss these questions and make notes as they go.

Exercise 5b

- Tell students to work in their pairs and write their notices. You could give them a word limit and encourage them to add some design features to get the reader's attention.

- When they have finished writing, ask them to check the features using the Language for writing box.

Exercise 6

- Put students into groups of four or six and ask them to read each other's notices.
- Ask them to discuss which notices are the most interesting.
- Ask one person from each group to say which advert they found most interesting and why.

EXTRA CHALLENGE Post the notices around the room and ask students to walk around the class and read all the notices. They have to choose one they would like to respond to. Tell them to sit with a partner and say which notice they would reply to and why.

EXTRA ACTIVITY Write an email. Ask students to read the notices written by their classmates as in the reading gallery idea above or from their group discussions. They must choose one they would like to respond to.

Tell them to write an email saying they are interested and asking any questions they have. They could then give the email to the person who wrote the notice and ask them to write a reply, answering the questions.

Listening & Speaking offering to do something

Exercise 7a

- Refer students to the photos and ask them to work in pairs to match the photos to the notices in exercise 2.
- Check answers together.

ANSWERS
1 b   2 a

Exercise 7b 11.11

- Tell students they are going to hear conversations related to the photos and that the conversations are in order. Ask them to read the statements for each conversation.
- Play track 11.11 and ask students to write T or F next to each statement.

ANSWERS
1 F   2 T   3 F   4 T

AUDIOSCRIPT 11.11

Conversation 1
A So, Ryan and Jan made a list of questions to ask Dr Pedersen.
B Oh, that's great. Can I see it?
A Yeah of course. We've got 5 main questions so far …
B I see, yes, these are really good. I'd like to know about the types of questions in the exam too. Shall I write that down?
A Yes, good idea. And when are we going to ask Dr Pedersen about all this?
C I'm going to have a meeting with him this afternoon. Why don't I give him the list then?
A Yes, that's perfect, Shaz. Then we can talk about it in class tomorrow. Now, the next thing is the homework …

Conversation 2
A So I'll read the list and if anyone would like to do something, please just say. Is that OK?

B I'll take notes so we don't forget.
A Thank you. That's very helpful. OK, first there's the problem with rubbish in the park.
C Oh, shall I do that? I go to the park every day anyway.
A Thank you, Janek.
B Let me help you with that, Janek. It's a big park.
C Thanks.
A Great! What's next? Ah yes, we need someone to paint the walls of the school.
D Oh, my husband and his brother could probably do that. Would you like me to ask them?
A Yes, that would be very helpful, thank you. Now then …

Exercise 7c

- Tell students to compare their answers with their partner.

Exercise 8a

- Ask students to work in pairs to read the sentences and complete the exercise.

ANSWERS
1 Shall   2 Why   3 I'll   4 Let   5 Would

Exercise 8b 11.12

- Play track 11.12 and ask students to check their answers.
- Play the track again, stopping after each sentence so that students can repeat.

AUDIOSCRIPT 11.12
1 Shall I write that down?
2 Why don't I give him the list then?
3 I'll take notes so we don't forget.
4 Let me help you with that.
5 Would you like me to ask them?

Exercise 9a

- Pre-teach *give a lift* (= take someone to a place in your car).
- Ask students to complete the matching exercise on their own.
- Check answers together.
- Ask what the phrases a–e have in common. (Answer: they are offering to do something as a reply to what someone said.)

ANSWERS
1 b   2 c   3 d   4 e   5 a

Exercise 9b

PRONUNCIATION In yes/no questions our voices usually go up at the end of the question. In statements and *wh-* questions our voices usually go down. Some students have problems with falling intonation and tend to go up at the end of sentences and all questions. This can make them sound unsure and can cause confusion as the listener does not know when to respond. If we hear rising intonation it can mean the speaker is going to carry on speaking.

To practise intonation, ask students to listen to you saying the phrases a–e and to notice if your voice goes up or down. Your voice should only go up on b and e as these are yes/no questions. Ask students to repeat the phrases after you and then to practise with a partner.

- Ask students to work in pairs and practise saying the conversations.

Exercise 10a

SMART COMMUNICATION   We have specific phrases in English that we use to offer help or a solution to a problem someone has. Some are more formal than others. In the Language for speaking box the more formal phrases include:
Would you like me to …?
Shall I …?
The other phrases are more direct and less formal.

- Refer students to the Language for speaking box and ask them to read the information. Draw students' attention to the use of the infinitive with and without *to* after different verbs. We only use the infinitive with *to* after *Would you like me …?*

EXTENSION   To practise the different phrases, ask students to write alternative responses to the situations 1–5 in exercise 9a, e.g. *A: It's really hot in here. B: Shall I put the air-conditioning on?*

EXTRA CHALLENGE   Sentence drills. Drill some sentences by saying some problems to your students and asking them to reply using one of the phrases for making offers. To support this, write the phrases for making offers on the board and point to the one you would like students to use.

Exercise 10b

- Put students into new pairs and refer them to the relevant pages.
- Ask them to read the information, choose a situation and prepare to do the exercise.

WATCH OUT!   Students need to explain the problem in their own words, not read out the sentences in the book.

- Demonstrate the first example in the work section to model the exercise. Do this with two or three students so they are clear on what to do.
- Ask students to take turns saying their problems to their partners and giving a response using the phrases for making offers.

EXTRA ACTIVITY   Ask students to invent one or two different problems from the ones in 10b. Ask them to write these down. Then, ask them to speak to different people in the class. Tell them to take turns saying their problems and responding. You could demonstrate this with an amusing problem that you've invented yourself. Make sure students keep their problems quite simple and short. You could encourage them to think of funny problems and less serious problems.

11.5 Video

Silicon Fen

VIDEOSCRIPT

Hi, I'm Alicia. Welcome to the Fens. This area doesn't look very modern but it's one of the biggest technology hubs in the world.
This is Silicon Fen, Europe's silicon valley. There are over 1,500 science and technology companies around here. One of the most famous companies here is the processor design company ARM. The business began in a small office on Cambridge Science Park in 1990.

Today the company's headquarters are still only a short drive from Cambridge, but the building is much bigger and a lot more people work here. ARM also has offices in continental Europe, North America, Asia and the Middle East, and employs more than 3,000 people.
It provides technology to some of the world's most popular electronics companies, including Apple and Samsung. The company's technology is in 95% of smart phones. In fact, around 4.3 billion people use a device with an ARM chip every day. That's 60% of the world's population!
Companies like ARM have made this area of the fens one of the most important innovation centres in the world. But why are there so many technology companies in this remote area?
There are several reasons for this. First of all, it's near London and there are airports to the west, and several major sea ports to the east.
Another reason is that there are excellent local facilities. There are fantastic roads and a great rail system.
But the most important reason is Cambridge University. It is one of the oldest and most successful universities in the world.
Some of the world's most brilliant scientists have worked here, such as Isaac Newton and Stephen Hawking. Over hundreds of years the university has made many exciting scientific discoveries.
All of these businesses are only a few miles from Cambridge and most have a connection with the university.
The university provides talented graduates and new technology, so it's a great place for small businesses to start and big businesses to grow.
Experts call this the Cambridge Phenomenon. The university encourages small businesses to start. These businesses become successful big businesses and more small businesses start around them. All of these companies are connected and they can share information, knowledge and resources.
And this is the real secret to Cambridge's success – businesses work well when they work together. Thanks to this collaboration Silicon Fen is going to grow and develop, making it a better place to do business in the future.

VIDEO ANSWERS

Exercise 1

1 the Fens
2 to connect
3 a processor
4 resources
5 to provide
6 an innovation
7 a device
8 a graduate

Exercise 3

1 Silicon Fen is 'Europe's Silicon Valley' because it has so many (famous) science and technology companies/ it is one of the biggest technology hubs in the world.
2 The company ARM is different now than when it began in 1990 because it is in a big office, more people work there, it has offices around the world.

3 There are many technology companies in the area because it is near London, airports and sea ports; the local facilities are excellent, e.g. road, rail; and it is close to Cambridge Uni.

4 The University helps Cambridge Science Park to develop because it provides talented graduates and new technology, it helps small businesses to start and big ones to grow.

5 Cambridge is successful because the businesses work well together.

Exercise 4
1 F doesn't look
2 F 1500
3 T
4 T
5 F 60%
6 T
7 F

Review

ANSWERS

Exercise 1a 11.13 🔘
Wanda promised herself that she will spend less time at work and more time with her brother. She and Johan won't join a gym but will save money for a trip to Italy.

Exercises 1b & c 11.13 🔘
1 I'm going to spend less time at work.
2 Are you going to spend more time with your family and friends?
3 Is he going to look for a new apartment?
4 We're not going to join a gym.
5 We're going to save some money.

AUDIOSCRIPT 11.13
M Do you have any New Year's Resolutions this year?
W Yeah, I'm going to spend less time at work.
M Really? Are you going to spend more time with your friends and family?
W Yes, I want to spend more time with my brother because he's going to move next year.
M Really? Is he going to look for a new apartment?
W Oh, I didn't tell you. He's going to move to Italy.
M Wow! Great! Are you and Johan going to visit him?
W That's my other resolution. We're not going to join a gym this year because it's too expensive. So we're going to save some money for a trip to Italy instead!

Exercises 2a & b 11.13 🔘
1 to paint   2 to teach   3 to look after   4 to repair
5 to organize   6 to make   7 to visit   8 to plant

AUDIOSCRIPT 11.14
1 He got up early to paint the living room.
2 She's going to move to Greece to teach English.
3 I go to Bob's house every weekend to look after his dog.
4 I went to my parents' house to repair my Mum's car.
5 I'm going to call all our friends to organize a birthday party for my best friend.
6 We're going to buy some eggs and sugar to make a cake.

7 I'm going to take the afternoon off work tomorrow to visit my aunt in hospital.
8 I went to the garden to plant some flowers.

Exercises 3a & b
a 3; I agree. They're very/really tiny.
b 5; Yes, it's very/really brilliant.
c 4; Yes, I did. It's very/really good.
d 1; It's very/really cheap.
e 2; Thanks. I think it's very/really lovely.

Exercise 4a
1 Why don't I make some sandwiches?
2 Would you like me to repair it?
3 Shall I teach you some new words?
4 I'll look after the children.
5 Let me organize the documents for the meeting for you.

Exercise 4b 11.15 🔘
1 What are we going to have for lunch?
    a Why don't I make some sandwiches?
2 I want to go out tonight, but I can't.
    d I'll look after the children.
3 I can't speak much Japanese.
    c Shall I teach you some new words?
4 I'm really busy at the moment.
    e Let me organize the documents for the meeting for you.
5 I broke my washing machine last night.
    b Would you like me to repair it?

AUDIOSCRIPT 11.15
1 What are we going to have for lunch?
2 I want to go out tonight, but I can't.
3 I can't speak much Japanese.
4 I'm really busy at the moment.
5 I broke my washing machine last night.

Culture and the arts

Unit overview

Language input

Present perfect simple (CB p116)	• *He has drawn many fantastic pieces of art.* • *She's danced in more than 75 countries.*
Present perfect and past simple (CB p118)	• *Have you ever been to China? Yes, I went last year.*
Grammar reference (CB pp158–159)	

Vocabulary development

Verb + noun phrases (2) (CB p117)	• *go to art galleries, a music festival, the opera …* • *see a film/a play …*
Films (CB p118)	• *action films, comedies, horror films, musicals …*
Past participles (CB p120)	• *visited, begun, grown, drunk, given, bought …*

Skills development

Listening: past simple and present perfect verb forms (CB p121)

Speaking: on the phone (CB p122)

Writing: a review (CB p123)

Video

Documentary: Park Theatre (CB p124)

Vox pops (Coursebook DVD & TG p258)

More materials

Workbook	• Language practice for grammar, pronunciation, vocabulary, speaking and writing • Reading for pleasure • Review: Units 11 & 12
Photocopiable activities	• Grammar: Honestly! (TG p208 & TSRD) • Vocabulary: Culture club (TG p225 & TSRD) • Communication: On the phone (TG p243 & TSRD)
Tests	• Unit 12 test (TSRD) • Progress test: Units 10–12 • Exit test
Unit 12 wordlist (TSRD)	

12.1 Artistic ability

Goals

- Talk about past experience and events using the present perfect
- Use verb + noun phrases (2)

Lead-in

1 Open book. Review aspects of culture from previous lessons. This exercise will encourage students to look back through their books. This might be a nice lead-in to the final unit and help them see how much they have learnt.

- Ask students for some examples of culture (art, music, theatre, opera, dance).
- Tell them to work in pairs and look back through their books to find as many examples of culture as they can in five minutes. Tell them to mark the pages.
- Ask the class for examples from different pages of the book.

2 Open book. Discussing the title of the lesson.

- Ask students to read the title of the lesson and tell you what they think artistic ability means.
- You could ask them to name as many different people as they can (past, present, from any countries) who became famous for their artistic ability.

Grammar & Reading present perfect simple

Exercise 1

- As a lead-in, ask one or two students the questions.
- Put students into pairs and ask them to discuss the questions.

FEEDBACK FOCUS Some students find it difficult to remember the correct preposition in the phrase *be good at*, e.g. they say *I'm good in drawing* instead of *I'm good at drawing*. Correct any incorrect uses of prepositions when you give feedback on this activity.

Exercise 2a

> **Background note:** Stephen Wiltshire is a famous artist from London who draws and paints city views. He is autistic, and is known for being able to draw detailed illustrations of cities after seeing them for only a brief period of time. He was born in 1974.
>
> Tai Lihua was born in 1976 in Tichang city in China. When she was two she became deaf but she has managed to become a famous dancer. She dances by feeling the vibration of drums and bass sounds.

- Refer students to the photos and ask them to work in the same pairs and discuss the question.

ANSWERS

Stephen Wiltshire draws detailed pictures of cities.
Tai Lihua is a dancer.

Exercise 2b

- Pre-teach *autistic* (= describes someone who finds it hard to communicate and form relationships with others).

WATCH OUT! Teach students the pronunciation *artistic* /ɑːtɪstɪk/ and *autistic* /ɔːtɪstɪk/. They are very similar but have a different vowel sound at the start.

- Tell students to read the articles quickly to get as much information as they can and see if their ideas were correct.
- Ask them to read the questions and then read the articles again to find the answers.

Exercise 2c

- Ask students to compare their answers with their partner.

ANSWERS

1 Stephen couldn't speak until he was five.
  Tai couldn't hear from the age of two after an illness.
2 Stephen draws pictures of cities.
  Tai dances – she is one of the most famous dancers in China.
3 He started drawing pictures of London when he was at school.
  She joined a dance company when she was fifteen.
4 His teachers called him 'the human camera'.
  Her teacher asked the class of deaf children to feel the sound of a drum through their feet.
5 Stephen has his own art gallery in London, wants to open another in New York, and has sold his pictures all over the world.
  Tai has danced in more than seventy-five countries and danced at the Beijing Paralympics.

CRITICAL THINKING Ask students to reflect on how these people became successful. Ask them to work in small groups or pairs and discuss these questions: *What made these people successful? Hard work, their teachers and families or something else?* Go through ideas with the class.

Exercise 3a

- Put students into pairs and ask them to read sentences 1–4. Refer them to the Grammar focus box and ask them to complete the exercise.
- Check answers together.

ANSWERS

1 have 2 has 3 hasn't

- Clarify meaning by asking these questions:
  1 When did people start watching Tai? (Answer: We don't know except it was at some point in the past. It's not the most important information.)
  2 What's the most important information in sentence 1? (Answer: The number of people.)
  3 When did Stephen draw the fantastic art? (Answer: We don't know. It was in the past but when is not important.)
  4 Does Stephen have a gallery in New York? (Answer: No, he hasn't opened one in New York.)
  5 When did Tai dance in these countries? (Answer: We don't know. The number of countries is more important.)
- Refer students to *Grammar reference* on p158. There are four more exercises here that students can do for homework.

Exercise 3b

- Refer students back to the articles and ask them to identify one example of the present perfect. Write it on the board.

- Tell them to find and underline more examples. Tell them to compare their examples with a partner and then ask the class to read out some of the sentences.

POSSIBLE ANSWERS

Stephen: He has drawn; he's sold; he hasn't opened
Tai: this hasn't stopped; she's become; she's danced; people have watched

EXTRA ACTIVITY Ask students to work alone and write two positive and two negative sentences about what they have and haven't done this week. Give some examples of your own, e.g. *I've bought new shoes. I haven't finished my work*. Put students into groups of four and ask them to tell each other the sentences. Ask students to find out if they have done the same things.

Exercise 4a

> **Background note:** Nobuyuki Tsujii is Japanese. He was born in 1988. In addition to being a pianist, he's a composer. Aged 12, he performed his own piece, *Street corner of Vienna*.

- As a lead-in, ask students to look at the photo and read the text quickly to find out what kind of art Nobuyuki does. (Answer: he plays the piano and writes music.) Teach the words *pianist* and *composer*.
- Ask students to read the text again and complete the gaps with the present perfect.

Exercise 4b 12.1 🎵

- Play track 12.1 and ask students to listen and check their answers.

ANSWERS

1 has given **2** has won **3** has written **4** has not/hasn't seen **5** has learnt **6** have said

AUDIOSCRIPT 12.1

Nobuyuki Tsujii was born blind, but he started playing on a toy piano at the age of just two. He began learning the piano two years later, and he gave his first big concert in Tokyo when he was twelve years old. He's in his twenties now, but he has given concerts all over the world, and he has won many prizes and international competitions. He has written music for film and TV, too. He hasn't seen the written music, but he has learnt to play some of the most difficult pieces of music in the world only through sound. His classical music fans have said this is amazing

EXTRA ACTIVITY Ask students to tell you the different types of artist that appear in the lesson: *Artist Dancer Pianist Composer*. Draw their attention to the suffixes we use to describe the profession/job: *-er* and *-ist*. Write these words on the board and ask students to say if we add *-er* or *-ist*: *photograph, design, write, sing*. (Answer: all end in *-er*.) Explain that *-er* is the most common ending for professions, but many professions end in *-or*, e.g. *actor* and *director*.

Pronunciation sentence stress

Exercise 5a 12.2 🎵

- Ask students to read the explanation and the sentences with the stress bubbles on them. You could ask students to work with a partner and to try saying the sentences with the correct stress.

- Play track 12.2 and ask students to read and listen.

Exercise 5b

- Ask students what kinds of words are stressed in exercise 5a, apart from the verbs. The answer is nouns: *concerts, written music*.
- Ask them to read sentences 1–4 and mark the stressed syllables. Ask them to compare with a partner.
- Tell students to practise saying the sentences to each other.

Exercise 5c 12.3 🎵

- Play track 12.3 and ask students to listen and notice the stress. Play the track again and ask students to repeat. Students should compare the recording to the way they were saying the sentences and correct any errors.
- Encourage them to repeat the sentences as many times as they want to try and get it right.

ANSWERS/AUDIOSCRIPT 12.3

1 He's sold them all over the world.

2 He hasn't opened a gallery in New York.

3 This hasn't stopped her dream of dancing.

4 Thousands of people have watched her.

PRONUNCIATION In shadowing, students attempt to repeat what the speaker is saying while they are speaking. It can help students notice the rhythm and stress and produce them more naturally. Encourage students to say the sentences in exercise 5b at the same time as the recording if you want to try this. They need to listen to the recording a number of times to notice the pronunciation and become familiar with the content before they repeat.

Exercise 6

- Ask students to read the instructions. Model the exercise with one student.

EXTRA CHALLENGE Encourage students to show agreement and disagreement when they speak, e.g.
A I think Tai is the most amazing.
B Really? I disagree. I think Stephen is the most amazing. It only takes him 20 minutes to remember the details of a city.

- Put students into small groups and ask them to discuss the question. Encourage them to give reasons for their opinions.
- Ask two or three students to report what their groups said.

Vocabulary & Speaking verb + noun phrases (2)

Exercise 7 12.4 🎵

- Asking students to predict what they will hear can help them listen more effectively. Ask students to read questions 1–5 and think about what people might say about those categories. Ask students to discuss their ideas with a partner, e.g. in number 1 the speaker might talk about a family member who is good at art, or who is an artist.
- Play the recording and ask students to complete the exercise. You may need to play it twice, or three times.
- Check answers together.

1 Jimmy   2 Phil, Albina   3 Phil, Albina   4 Albina
5 Jimmy

AUDIOSCRIPT 12.4

P I've always loved music. I don't play an instrument, but I've always wanted to play in a band. I like pop music, rock and jazz, and since I was a child I've had a big music collection. In my free time I often go to rock concerts and I usually go to two or three music festivals a year. I haven't been to a classical music concert before, but I'm going to my first one next week!

J My parents are artists, so I've had lots of drawing and painting lessons. I enjoy painting a lot and I often do it in my free time. I like going to art galleries, too. I also like writing – I've started writing two or three books, but I haven't finished any of them!

A I had dance lessons at school, but I wasn't very good, so I stopped going. But I've always wanted to dance, so I've started going to salsa classes. I love it! I also enjoy going to the theatre to see plays, and especially to see musicals. I live in a big city, so I've been to see all the big musicals – they're fantastic!

Exercise 8a

- Draw students' attention to the noun phrases in the box and tell them they are going to practise putting verbs and nouns together.
- Put students into pairs and ask them to complete the exercise.

go to: 1 the cinema/theatre   2 a music festival
3 a salsa class   4 art galleries   5 a rock/classical music concert   6 the opera
see: 7 a film/movie   8 a play   9 a musical
play: 10 the guitar   11 in a band
have (… lessons): 12 music   13 painting   14 dance
15 drawing   16 singing

Exercise 8b 12.5

- Play track 12.5 and ask students to listen and check their answers.
- Play the track again and ask students to repeat.

AUDIOSCRIPT 12.5

1 go to the cinema / go to the theatre
2 go to a music festival
3 go to a salsa class
4 go to art galleries
5 go to a rock concert / go to a classical music concert
6 go to the opera
7 see a film / see a movie
8 see a play
9 see a musical
10 play the guitar
11 play in a band
12 have music lessons
13 have painting lessons
14 have dance lessons
15 have drawing lessons
16 have singing lessons

EXTENSION   Ask students to work with their partners and think of other activities that can follow go to/see/play/have.

You could give them a time limit and see who can think of the most examples. Ask the pair with the most examples to write them on the board. Ask other pairs to add any different examples and go over any vocabulary students don't know.

Exercise 9a

- Put students into different pairs.
- Do the exercise with a student to model the conversation for the class. Use the information in boxes 1–3 to ask the student questions e.g. *Have you written something? Have you been to many galleries?* When the student answers your questions, ask for more information.

EXTRA SUPPORT   Write some questions students can ask to get more information on the board, e.g.
When did you start playing the … ?
What do you like about … ?
What's your favourite … ?
Why don't you like … ?

- Ask students to tell each other about their experiences using the information in boxes 1–3.
- Ask some students to report back on what their partner does or has done.

Exercise 9b

- Refer students to the example sentence with *both*. Ask them to find at least three things they have in common.
- Put students into groups of four and ask them to tell the other pair what they have in common with their partner.

EXTENSION   Ask students to repeat exercise 9a with another partner and to find another three things they have in common.

EXTRA ACTIVITY   To further practise using the present perfect in first and third person, ask students to write sentences about themselves or other people they spoke to in exercise 9b, e.g. *I've had some piano lessons, Jules hasn't seen a musical.* Put them into pairs and ask them to compare their sentences.

GRAMMAR REFERENCE ANSWERS

Exercise 1
1 She's become   2 You've drawn   3 He hasn't opened
4 I haven't been   5 We've taken

Exercise 2
(infinitive; past simple; past participle)
1 give; gave; given
2 put; put; put
3 drink; drank; drunk
4 go; went; gone/been
5 grow; grew; grown
6 hear; heard; heard
7 break; broke; broken
8 drive; drove; driven
9 wake; woke; woken
10 win; won; won

Exercise 3
1 's broken   2 haven't seen   3 have been   4 've swum
5 've organized   6 haven't made   7 hasn't bought
8 's repaired

Exercise 4
1 have always loved   2 have had   3 have played
4 have won   5 have written   6 hasn't won   7 has given   8 has earned   9 have gone   10 haven't stopped

12.2 At the movies

Goals

- Talk about films
- Use the present perfect and past simple

Lead-in

1 Closed book. Review present perfect.

- Put students into pairs and ask them to take turns to ask: *What have you done today/this week?*
- Ask students to say what their partner has done, e.g. *Bonson has done his homework and he's been to the beach.*

2 Closed book. Create interest in film and revise grammar.

- Ask the class if they have been to the cinema, watched a DVD or seen a film on television in the last week or month.
- Ask students who say yes to tell the class what they saw and if they liked it or not, and why.

Vocabulary & Speaking films

Exercise 1

> **Background note:** The author, Nicole Yatsonsky, was born in the United States. She writes short stories, novels and screen plays. She loves film and writes for film websites.

CRITICAL THINKING Exercise 1 asks students to reflect on the meaning of the quote and say if they agree with it. To encourage students to reflect in this activity, you could teach them some phrases:
I suppose that's true. I'm not sure that's true. I don't think that's true. That's nonsense/rubbish!

- Put students into pairs and ask them to read the quote. Tell them about the author.
- Ask students to discuss the first question. This requires them to reflect and give their opinion.
- Ask some students to share their opinions with the class or report what their partner thought.
- Ask students to discuss questions 2 and 3. These are more practical questions. Ask one or two students to share any interesting things they heard with the class.

Exercise 2a 12.6 ⊙

- Refer students to the types of films in the box and go over any unknown vocabulary.
- Play track 12.6 and ask students to number the types of films. Ask students to compare their answers with a partner.

AUDIOSCRIPT 12.6

1 Sometimes you don't want to look because they are scary, e.g. *The Blair Witch Project, Dracula* films.
2 They tell a love story, e.g. *Titanic, Gone with the Wind*.
3 You laugh at them because they are funny, e.g. *Mr Bean, The Mask*.
4 They tell a story about something that happens in people's lives and sometimes they are very sad, e.g. *The Help, Forrest Gump*.
5 People fight and drive fast cars, e.g. *Speed*, James Bond films.

6 They have spaceships and are set on other planets or they're about the future, e.g. *Avatar, Star Wars* films.
7 They don't have real people and nowadays they're usually made with computers, e.g. *Shrek, Finding Nemo*.
8 People sing and dance, e.g. *Mamma Mia, Grease*.

Exercise 2b 12.7 ⊙

- Play track 12.7 and check answers after each description.
- Play the track again. Stop it after each phrase or sentence and ask students to repeat.

ANSWERS/AUDIOSCRIPT 12.7
1 horror films   2 romantic films   3 comedies
4 dramas   5 action films   6 science fiction films
7 animations   8 musicals

Exercise 2c

- Ask students to work in small groups and think of more films for each type.

EXTENSION You could follow up this activity with a whole class discussion on who has see each film and which are the most popular. Write the films on the board. Check pronunciation and understanding.

Exercise 3a

PRONUNCIATION Refer students to the example sentences and ask them where the stress is in each sentence.
*I **don't** like **ac**tion **films** .... I pre**fer com**edies.*
Remind them that the stress goes on the auxiliary verb when the sentence is negative.

- Put students into small groups of three or four.
- Refer students to the types of films in exercise 2a. Ask them to discuss what types of films they like and don't like. Encourage them to give reasons.

Exercise 3b

- Ask students to read the list of phrases. Check understanding of *everybody* and *nobody*. Ask students to make similar sentences for their groups.

WATCH OUT! Point out that *nobody* is followed by a positive verb and *everybody* is followed by a third person singular verb, e.g. *Nobody likes chocolate* NOT ~~Nobody doesn't like chocolate~~ and *Everybody likes chocolate* NOT ~~Everybody like chocolate~~. In some languages these rules are different.

- Ask each group to read their sentences to the class.
- Finish the exercise by writing sentences on the board that are true for the whole class using the phrases in the list.

Exercise 4 12.8 ⊙

- Ask students to read the instructions.
- Play track 12.8 and ask students to write down the type of film for each speaker.
- Ask them to compare answers with a partner.

ANSWERS
1 dramas/romantic films
2 science fiction films

AUDIOSCRIPT 12.8

1 My favourite film is *Titanic*. It's a drama, but also a love story, and it stars Kate Winslet and Leonardo DiCaprio. It's about a huge ship and all the people on it.

2 The film that's made more money than any other in the world is *Avatar*. It's a science fiction film and it's set in the future.

Exercise 5a

- Ask students to read sentences 1–5 and complete the exercise with their partner.
- Tell students that *set in* describes the time and the place where the story happens.

ANSWERS

1 favourite **2** stars **3** about **4** It's **5** set

Exercise 5b 12.8 ⊚

- Play track 12.8 again and ask students to check their answers.

Exercise 5c

- Write the title of a famous film on the board. Ask students to change the information in the sentences to describe that film, e.g. *Star Wars*:
  My favourite film is Star Wars. It's a science fiction film. It's set in space in the future. It stars Harrison Ford. It's about an adventure in space. There are good people and they fight the bad people.
- Ask students to work alone and complete the exercise about their own favourite film.
- Put students into pairs and ask them to tell each other their sentences and discuss their favourite film.

Grammar & Listening present perfect and past simple

Exercise 6a

Text summary: A web film review about *The Artist,* a French romantic comedy. It was released in 2012. It was unusual because it was silent. It won an Oscar for best film.

- As a lead-in, ask students to look at the photo from a film. Ask them if they think it is an old or a recent film.
- Ask them to read the text quickly to find out if the film is old or recent. (It looks old but is from *The Artist,* which is a recent film.)
- Ask students to read the questions and then read the text again to find the answers.

ANSWERS

1 *The Artist* is a silent black and white film.
2 They walked out because they didn't know the film was silent when they bought the tickets.

Exercise 6b

- Ask students to read the information from the website.
- Draw their attention to *ever* and explain that we use this when we are referring to someone's past, or all their life, e.g. *Have you ever been to Paris? = In all your life, have you been there?*
- Pre-teach *annoy* (= make you feel a little angry).

WATCH OUT! *-ed/ing* adjectives: *annoyed/annoying*. Tell students that we can use the verb *annoy* to make the adjectives *annoyed* and *annoying*. We use *-ed* endings when we are describing how someone feels. We use *-ing* endings when we are describing the thing that makes the person

feel like that, e.g. *I was annoyed. The film was annoying*. Point out other common examples, e.g. *interested/ing, bored/ing* and *tired/ing*.

- Put students into pairs and ask them to discuss the questions.
- Ask two or three students to report what their partner said to the class.

FEEDBACK FOCUS Check the pronunciation of *annoyed* /əˈnɔɪd/, and that students are using *annoyed/annoying* and any other *-ed/-ing* adjectives correctly.

EXTRA ACTIVITY Ask students to work with a partner and discuss any other behaviour that annoys them at the cinema, e.g. people opening sweet packets, people talking, people using their mobile phones.

Exercise 7

- Refer students to the questions in the second part of the web page and ask them to read the Grammar focus box and complete the gaps.

ANSWERS

1 Have **2** Has

- Refer students to exercise 1 in *Grammar reference* on p159. Students can do this for homework.

Exercise 8a 12.9 ⊚

Audio summary: Four speakers responding to the web page. They talk about experiences of leaving the cinema early.

- Ask students to read the instructions.
- Play track 12.9 and ask students to write ticks or crosses in the first column.

Exercise 8b 12.9 ⊚

STUDY TIP Help students to take notes while they listen by telling them to focus on the most important words . As an example write *He thinks it's rude to walk out of a film* on the board. Ask students to identify the key words: *thinks/rude/ walk out*. Tell them to write only the key words when they are taking notes while listening, not whole sentences.

- Play track 12.9 again and ask students to fill in the second column with notes. You may have to repeat the recording. Ask students to compare answers with a partner.
- Check answers together.

ANSWERS

	Have they ever left the cinema early?	Why/Why not?
Speaker 1	✓	The film was really bad – life's too short.
Speaker 2	✗	You have to watch the whole film or you don't know if it's good or bad.
Speaker 3	✓	The film was really boring, and it was a beautiful day.
Speaker 4	✗	It's OK to fall asleep, but it's rude to other people to walk out.

AUDIOSCRIPT 12.9

I Have you ever left the cinema early?

S1 Oh yes! I've left in the middle of a lot of films. I don't want to sit in a cinema watching something really bad – life's too short!

S2 I've never left the cinema early, but I've often wanted to. A few months ago, I went to see a terrible film. Someone walked out every five minutes. At the end of the film, I was the only person left! But I think you have to watch the whole film or you don't know if it's good or bad!

S3 Yes, I have. I walked out once – it was last summer and it was a beautiful day. The film was really boring, so I just decided to leave.

S4 No, I haven't, but I've fallen asleep in a lot of cinemas! When the lights go out, and the seats are comfortable, and the film is slow, then I just can't stay awake! I've never walked out of a film, though. I think it's rude to other people who are watching.

Exercise 9a 12.10

- Ask students to read the sentences and think about what might go in each gap.
- Play track 12.10 and ask students to listen and complete the gaps.
- Ask them to compare their answers with a partner.
- Check answers together.

ANSWERS
1 I've; left
2 went
3 A Have; left
   B have; walked

AUDIOSCRIPT 12.10

1 I've never left the cinema early, but I've often wanted to.
2 A few months ago, I went to see a terrible film.
3
A Have you ever left the cinema early?
B Yes, I have. I walked out once – it was last summer and it was a beautiful day.

Exercise 9b

- Ask students to read the information in the Grammar focus box. Tell them to use the sentences in exercise 9a to find the answers.
- Check answers together.

ANSWERS
1 present perfect   2 past simple   3 present perfect
4 past simple

- Refer students to exercises 2 and 3 in *Grammar reference* on p159. Students can do these for homework.

Exercise 10a

> **Text summary:** A transcript of an interview done at the Rio de Janeiro film festival. An actor and a director are asked about a film they have made which is showing at the festival.

- Ask students to read the interview quickly. Give a time limit of one minute. Ask students to tell you quickly what the conversation is about by answering these questions:

Where are they? At a film festival in Rio de Janeiro.
Do people like Pavel's film? Yes, they do.

- Ask students to work with a partner and complete the conversation by choosing the correct tenses.

ANSWERS
1 Have you visited   2 I have   3 I came   4 was
5 Have you ever been   6 've never been   7 saw
8 thought   9 enjoyed   10 finished   11 stood
12 clapped   13 have said   14 told

Exercise 10b 12.11

- Play track 12.11 and ask students to listen and check their answers.

EXTRA SUPPORT/EXTRA CHALLENGE Remind students of the rule about present perfect and past simple: If we know/say when something happened in the past, we use past simple. If we don't know/say when it happened, we use present perfect. Ask students to go through each answer in exercise 10a and decide if there is a known time or not. Check answers with the class.

AUDIOSCRIPT 12.11

I So Pavel, you're here for the Rio de Janeiro film festival. Have you visited Brazil before?

P Yes, I have – twice. Actually, I came here when I was a child and I was here three years ago for work, too.

I Interesting. And what about you, Wanda? Have you ever been to Rio before?

W No, I've never been here before, but it's a beautiful city.

I I'm very pleased to hear that! So, I saw your latest film *Inbox Me* last night and I thought it was really wonderful.

P Well, thank you very much!

I And everyone else in the cinema enjoyed it, too. When it finished, people stood up and clapped - I couldn't believe it!

P Really? I'm delighted to hear that. A lot of people have said some lovely things about it.

W Last week someone told me it was their favourite film of the year!

I Great! So, tell me …

Exercise 11a

- Draw students' attention to the example conversation and the ideas in the box. Demonstrate the conversation with a student, using one of the ideas in the box, to model the task.
- Put students into small groups and ask them to discuss their experiences.

FEEDBACK FOCUS A sandwich correction slot is when we stop a speaking activity, correct any errors we have heard and then tell students to carry on with the speaking activity, trying not to make the same errors. You could try this during exercise 11a.

Exercise 11b

- Ask students from each group to tell the class some interesting things they heard in their group. Remind them to use *has* for the third person singular.

EXTENSION Choose eight to ten past participles (*played, eaten*, etc.) and write them on the board. Drill: *Have you ever + past participle + object you choose*, e.g. *Have you ever played football?* Students repeat chorally and individually.

Put students into pairs and ask them to take turns asking the questions, using one of the participles on the board, and answering with a short answer, e.g. *A Have you ever eaten snails? B No, I haven't.*

Put students into new pairs and ask them to say what their partner has and hasn't done to give further practice of repeating the structure in the third person, e.g. *Mario has eaten snails. He hasn't played tennis.*

GRAMMAR REFERENCE ANSWERS

Exercise 1
1 Have you ever cried during a film?
2 I've never acted in a play.
3 I've stayed up all night with friends many times.
4 She's watched the same film eight times.
5 Has he ever been to a big concert?
6 I've never wanted to see a horror film.
7 They've never been to the opera.
8 You've met a lot of famous people.

Exercise 2
1 Have you ever been   2 went   3 Did you enjoy
4 did you go   5 've been   6 've never been
7 've watched   8 Have you ever been   9 I haven't
10 have

Exercise 3
1 've been   2 saw   3 walked   4 took   5 swam
6 have done   7 ever eaten   8 drank   9 lost
10 bought   11 broke

12.3 Vocabulary and skills development

Goals
- Form past participles
- Understand past simple and present perfect verb forms

Lead-in
1 Closed book. Review and practise present perfect and past simple.
- Prepare sentences with present perfect and past simple before the lesson. Some sentences should be correct and others should have errors. Write them on pieces of paper.
- Put students into pairs and give them three to six sentences (a mixture of correct and incorrect sentences).
- Ask them to identify correct and incorrect sentences, and to correct the sentences with errors.
2 Open book. Describe photos.
- Ask students to look at the three photos and discuss these questions with a partner.
  1 Where are the people?
  2 What are they doing?

Speaking & Vocabulary past participles

Exercise 1
WATCH OUT! Students can get confused about *have been* and *have gone*. Tell students we only use the past participle of *go* when the person is still in the place, e.g.
She's gone to Hong Kong. This means she is still there and has not returned yet.
She's been to Hong Kong. This means that she has been there and come back.

- Ask students to read the sentences and decide which are true for them. Ask them to look at the second sentence in each example and to think about the last time this happened.
- Ask them to change the sentences where they can to make them true. Do an example on the board, e.g.
I went to a fantastic musical last year.
I went to a fantastic music concert last year.
- Put students into pairs and ask them to compare their sentences and try to find what they have in common.
- Ask students to tell the class what they have in common with their partner.

FEEDBACK FOCUS Encourage students to use *We both* and *We have both* to recycle this language from previous lessons.

PRONUNCIATION Show students how to use stress to show contrast in short answers by writing these sentences on the board:
I've **nev**er **written** a **poem**.
I have. I wrote one **last year**.
I **wrote** a **lot** of **emails** yesterday.
Oh, **I** didn't. I **wrote two** or **three**.

Mark the stress. Explain that in longer phrases we don't usually stress the pronoun – we stress the main verb. In short answers which disagree with the main sentence we stress the pronoun, and we use a full vowel in the auxiliary verb, i.e. *have* /hæv/, *has* /hæs/, *do* /duː/, *am* /æm/ and *are* /ɑː/, not a schwa.

Ask students to practise using stress to show contrast. Ask them to work with their partner and practise giving short answers about their sentences from exercise 1.

EXTRA CHALLENGE Practise turning statements into questions. Do an example on the board. Take a sentence from exercise 1 and make it a question using:
Have you ever …?
When was the last time you …?
Did you … yesterday/last week, etc.?

Ask students to choose three more sentences from exercise 1 and change the statement into a question using one of the forms above.

Put students into small groups of three or four or ask them to walk around the class taking turns to ask and answer their questions.

Exercise 2a
- Refer students to the Vocabulary focus box.
- Ask students to read the information about regular and irregular verbs.

Exercise 2b
- Ask students to work in pairs.

- Check students understand the information in the Vocabulary focus box. Refer them to the table and ask them what they need to look for to complete the exercise. (Answer: they need to look for examples for each rule.) Do one or two examples with the class to clarify the exercise. Tell students to work with their partner and complete the table.
- Check answers together.

Rule	Past simple	Past participle
1 no change	heard won bought met	heard won bought met
2 vowel change	began drank ran	begun drunk run
3 add -n	broke woke spoke	broken woken spoken
4 vowel change + -n	grew gave drove	grown given driven
5 different word	ate went saw did	eaten gone seen done

PRONUNCIATION Write these vowel sounds on the board:
/æ/ /ʌ/ /ɔ:/ /ɜ:/ /əʊ/ /ɪ/ /e/ /i:/ /u:/ /eɪ/

Drill the sounds and ask students to repeat chorally and individually. Help students make the sounds by asking them to look at your mouth when you make the sounds. Ask students to match the verbs from exercise 2b to the sounds. Practise saying the words. You could ask students to make sentences with words with the same sound if they find a vowel particularly difficult.
/æ/ *began drank ran*
/ʌ/ *begun drunk won done run*
/ɔ:/ *bought*
/ɒ/ *gone*
/ɜ:/ *heard*
/əʊ/ *woke woken broke broken grown drove spoke spoken*
/ɪ/ *did*
/e/ *met*
/i:/ *eaten seen*
/u:/ *grew*
/eɪ/ *gave ate*

EXTENSION Ask students to think of nouns that go with the verbs. Give them two or three minutes to work alone and think of collocations. Put students into pairs and ask them to compare answers and make a note of collocations in their notebooks. Go over examples on the board and check meaning and pronunciation.

EXTRA ACTIVITY You could also think of nouns that collocate with these verbs and write them on the board in the wrong order. Ask students to match them to the correct verbs.

DICTIONARY SKILLS Ask students to use a dictionary to look up other collocations. Tell them to look up the infinitive of the verbs, not the past simple form, e.g. *see a film, hear a noise*. Explain that many dictionaries will list the verb in its infinitive form, not in past forms.

STUDY TIP Putting new vocabulary into the context of sentences helps students remember language. This is even more effective if the sentences are meaningful and personal to the students. Ask students to choose six verb–noun collocations and write a sentence for each. Tell them to write something that is true for them, or memorable.

Listening & Speaking past simple and present perfect verb forms

Exercise 3a 12.12 🔘
- Play track 12.12 and ask students to listen and write the verb phrases to complete the sentences. You may need to play the recording twice.

1 opened 2 've opened 3 's run 4 ran 5 've met
6 met 7 've watched 8 watched

AUDIOSCRIPT 12.12
1 I opened the door.
2 I've opened the door.
3 She's run a marathon.
4 She ran a marathon.
5 We've met him.
6 We met him.
7 I've watched Star Wars twice this month.
8 I watched Star Wars twice last month.

Exercise 3b
- Ask students to check their answers with a partner.
- Go through the answers together.

Exercise 4 12.13 🔘
- Refer students to the Unlock the code box.
- Play track 12.13 and ask students to read and listen to the information.
- Ask students if they were able to hear the differences and which was hardest to catch as they listened.

Exercise 5a

> **Background note:** Bollywood refers to the Hindi-language Indian film industry. It's based in Mumbai (this used to be called Bombay). It takes its name from Hollywood in California mixed with Bombay. It is one of the largest film industries in the world, and can make many hundreds of films a year. The films usually involve singing and dancing.

- Ask students to work in pairs and tell each other what they know about Bollywood. After they have spoken, tell them the background information given above about Bollywood.

Exercise 5b

> **Audio summary:** An interview between a presenter and an actor. They talk about how popular Bollywood is. The interview is in two parts. Students will hear the first part in exercise 5c and the second part in exercise 6.

- Ask students to read the text and complete the gaps with the correct tenses.
- Ask students to compare their answers with a partner.

Exercise 5c   12.14 ◉

- Play track 12.14 and ask students to listen and check their answers.

ANSWERS

1 have heard   2 has made   3 's/has sold   4 produced
5 made   6 have become   7 've/have made

AUDIOSCRIPT 12.14

P Good evening. Our guest tonight is Mark Russell, who is going to talk about the Indian film industry, Bollywood, and one of its biggest stars. Mark, welcome.
M Thanks, Steffi.
P Tell us a little bit about Bollywood. Many of us have heard of it, but perhaps we don't all know much about it. Is it bigger than Hollywood these days?
M Yes, it is. In the last ten years, Bollywood has made more films and it's sold more tickets, too. For example in 2009, Bollywood produced over 1,200 films and Hollywood made only about 500. Also, Bollywood films have become popular all over the world and they've made them in lots of countries.

Exercise 6   12.15 ◉

> **Background note:** Hema Sardesai is a playback singer. Playback singers record songs and then actors lip-sync (mime, or pretend to sing) the songs in the films. The singers do not appear on screen.

- Refer students to the photo.
- Ask them to read the verb phrases before they listen, and think about how the phrases are pronounced differently. Encourage students to say the sentences quietly to themselves.
- Play track 12.15 and ask students to identify the correct phrases.

EXTRA SUPPORT   You may need to pause the recording immediately after the point where the phrases below are said.

- Ask students to compare answers with a partner.
- Check answers together.

ANSWERS

1 I've never heard   2 She's recorded   3 she's also had
4 she's been   5 she's visited   6 India celebrated
7 she sang   8 people watched

AUDIOSCRIPT 12.15

M One of the biggest names in Bollywood is Hema Sardesai.
P I've never heard of her. Is there a reason for that?
M Well, she's a playback singer. This means that she records the songs that other actors use in their films.

The actors move their mouths, but they are not singing. The voice is really the voice of a playback singer like Hema.
P So we never see her.
M Not exactly. She's recorded playback songs for over sixty Bollywood films, but she's also had a few successful albums. Also, she's been in shows all over India, and she's visited a lot of different countries.
P So, she's quite famous in India outside Bollywood.
M Oh yes. When India celebrated fifty years of independence she sang her own song and three million people watched her live.

Exercise 7   12.15 ◉

- Ask students to read the questions before they listen.

WATCH OUT!   Question 3 is not answered on the recording. Students have to reflect on this question and give their opinion based on what they heard. Questions 1 and 2 are answered.

- Play track 12.15 again and ask students to write the answers as they listen.
- Ask them to work with a partner and discuss the answers to the questions.
- Go over the answers with the class.

ANSWERS

1 Hema is a playback singer. She records the songs that other actors use in their films. The actors mime the songs, but you hear Hema's voice not theirs.
2 Hema has recorded songs for over sixty Bollywood films and she's had a few successful albums. She's been in shows all over India, visited lots of different countries and sang to an audience of three million people when India celebrated its independence.
3 Students' own answers

Exercise 8a

- Model this exercise by reading aloud five sentences of your own: three true, two false, e.g.
  I went to Australia last year/I learnt to ride a horse last month/I've been to France five times/I haven't seen an opera/I ran a race last summer.
- Ask students to say if they heard past simple or present perfect.
- Read out the sentences again. Tell students to guess the sentences that are false, and to ask questions to find out which sentences are true and which are false, e.g. *Where did you go in Australia? What did you see?*
- Tell students to write their own sentences. Monitor and check that their grammar is correct. Encourage them to write some positive and some negative sentences.

Exercise 8b

- Put students into pairs and ask them to take turns reading their sentences. Tell them to identify if the sentences are in the past simple or present perfect.
- Tell students to ask questions to help them guess which sentences are false.

EXTENSION   Put students into new pairs and tell them to explain what they heard about their partner. Ask them to repeat the exercise if you think they need extra practice with this grammar.

Ask students to think of a famous person they are interested in and know something about. If some students find this hard, group them separately from the others. Ask the students who do know something about a famous person to prepare some information about that person to tell the class. Give them five minutes to prepare the information. Ask the rest of the class to think of some questions to ask. To give extra support, write some general questions they could ask on the board, e.g.

How did you learn about the person?

Where was the person born?

What has the person done?

Ask the question group to then interview the others about the person they chose. This could be done in pairs or as a whole class milling activity (this is when the whole class stands up and walks around speaking to different people in the class) depending on numbers. If only one or two students have prepared information about a person, ask them to tell the whole class their information and tell the class to ask questions to find out more information. Encourage students to use the past simple and present perfect where possible.

EXTRA ACTIVITY If students are interested in Bollywood, you could ask them to find out more about it at home by searching online in English. Ask them to write three facts about Bollywood for homework, and in the next class put students into groups and ask them to compare their facts.

12.4 Speaking and writing

Goals

- Speak on the phone
- Write a review

Lead-in

1 Closed book. Practise the past simple and present perfect in the context of phone calls.

- Ask students to think about a formal and an informal phone call they made recently in their own language. Ask them to tell their partner who they spoke to and what they spoke about. You could give your own examples to lead in to this exercise.

- Ask the class if they have ever done any of these things over the phone: bought something, made a complaint, booked a restaurant, had an argument, arranged a date, applied for a job, told a telephone company about a problem, etc. Ask them which calls were more formal. Encourage students to tell the class any interesting stories about the phone calls and to share similar experiences.

- You could extend this by asking if they make calls to automated response lines where they have to press numbers to choose different options. Encourage them to give their opinions on this type of service.

2 Closed book. Discuss making phone calls in English.

- Put students into pairs.

- Ask them to discuss these questions with a partner:
  1 *Do you ever have to speak in English on the phone?*
  2 *How do you feel about speaking on the phone in English?*
  3 *Why is it difficult?*

- Ask students to share their ideas with the class. Tell the class you are going to practise making phone calls today to make them feel more confident.

Listening & Speaking on the phone

Exercise 1

- Put students into pairs and ask them to discuss the questions.

SMART COMMUNICATION In English we introduce ourselves in an indirect way: *It's Nicola. Nicola here. Nicola speaking.* This may be strange for some students, who might be more used to saying *I'm Nicola.* We are also quite formal on the phone. In some languages you can be quite direct when you answer the phone, but in English we tend to be quite polite even in more informal situations. For example, when we answer the phone at home we would ask *Who's speaking/calling?* not *Who is this?* If we are at work we will start with the name of the company and we might give our own name too, e.g. *Original solutions (company name). Mark speaking. Can I help you?*

- Open this up to a class discussion to compare first language habits and habits in English.

Exercise 2 12.16

- Ask students to read the questions.

- Play track 12.16 and ask students to write the answers. You may need to play the track two or three times.

- Tell students to compare their answers with a partner, and then check answers together.

ANSWERS

1 Marcus wants to know if Caitlin has booked the tickets for the Comedy Club that night.
2 Caitlin is going to call the club to ask about returned tickets.
3 Could I speak to the ticket office manager, please?/Your website says it's sold out, but has anyone returned any tickets?
4 The ticket office manager is not available.

AUDIOSCRIPT 12.16

F Hello?

M Hi Francis, it's Marcus. Is Caitlin there?

F She's not here at the moment.

M OK, well can you tell her to call me back, please?

F Yes, sure. Oh wait, she's just come back. Hang on a minute. I'll just get her.

C Hi, Marcus.

M Hi, Caitlin. Have you booked tickets for the comedy club tonight?

C No, I haven't. Their website said they're sold out tonight.

M Oh no. Well why don't you call them and ask about returned tickets? Sometimes people return tickets because they can't go.

C Oh yes, I didn't think of that. Good idea! I'll call them now and I'll call you back in a minute.

M Thanks, Caitlin. Speak soon.

C OK. Bye.

R Good afternoon. Phoenix Comedy Club. How can I help you?

C Hello. Could I speak to the ticket office manager, please?

R I'm afraid he's not available at the moment. Can I help?

C Maybe. I'm calling about the show tonight. Your website says it's sold out, but has anyone returned any tickets?

R Oh, I'm not sure. You'll need to speak to the ticket office manager about that.

C Right, well could you ask him to call me back, please?

R Yes, of course. Could I have your number, please?

C Yes, it's 0 … 7 … 5 …

Exercise 3a

- Ask students to read the sentences and work with a partner to complete the gaps.

ANSWERS

1 it's **2** speak **3** here **4** afraid **5** Can; back
6 Could; back **7** have **8** Hang

Exercise 3b 12.17 🔘

- Play track 12.17 and ask students to listen and check their answers. Play the track again and ask students to repeat.

- Point out that both 'can' and 'could' are correct in 5 & 6, but note that they will hear 'can' in 5 and 'could' in 6.

AUDIOSCRIPT 12.17

1 Hi Francis, it's Marcus. Is Caitlin there?

2 Hello. Could I speak to the ticket office manager, please?

3 She's not here at the moment.

4 I'm afraid he's not available at the moment.

5 Can you tell her to call me back, please?

6 Could you ask him to call me back, please?

7 Could I have your number, please?

8 Hang on a minute. I'll just get her.

PRONUNCIATION Raise awareness of polite intonation by reading the sentences to the students in a very flat voice. Ask them to compare this with the recording. Elicit the idea that using a flat voice can make the speaker sound bored and uninterested and even rude. Play the track again and ask students to listen to where the voice goes up and down. Ask them to take turns reading the sentences with polite intonation.

Exercise 3c

- Ask students to work with a partner and discuss the question. You could tell them to write I or F next to each sentence.

- Draw students' attention to the Language for speaking box. Ask them to check their answers using the information in it.

- Check answers together.

ANSWERS

Formal: 2, 4, 6, 7
Informal: 1, 3, 5, 8

Exercise 4

- Refer students to the information and diagram. Make sure they are clear on how to develop the conversation using the phrases from the Language for speaking box.

- Model the conversations with two different students to demonstrate the exercise – first model the informal conversation with one student and then the more formal conversation with another student.

- Put students into pairs and ask them to take turns having the two conversations.

EXTRA CHALLENGE If students have smartphones, ask them to record themselves having the conversations. Ask them to listen to the recording with their partner and think about how they could improve their pronunciation. Ask them to re-record the conversations and see if they can improve them.

EXTRA ACTIVITY Disappearing dialogue. Write a short dialogue of a phone conversation (six lines is enough) on the board, using the phrases from the Language for speaking box. Put students into new pairs and ask them to practise the dialogue, taking turns to be the caller. Explain that you are going to test their memory so they have to keep practising as long as they can.

After a few minutes, start to erase parts of the dialogue (a few words at a time, not too much). Tell students to keep practising and trying to remember the words you erase. Keep erasing the dialogue until there is nothing left. Ask students if they were able to carry on doing the dialogue.

Exercise 5

- You could put students into new pairs at this point to give them practice at working with different people.

- Refer them to the relevant pages and ask them to decide who is Student A and who is Student B.

> **Background note:** In one of the conversations, students have to talk about sharing a flat and speak about their flatmate. It is common to live with friends and share a flat in the UK and some other countries. This is popular in cities where young people cannot afford to live alone.

- Pre-teach *flatmate* (n.) (= someone you live with in a flat – not your partner. They are often a friend.) and *to share a flat* (v.) (= to live in the same house with someone who is not your family).

- Ask students to read their information and think about what they will say for each conversation. Ask them to identify which conversations are formal and which are informal before they start, so they know which phrases to use.

EXTRA SUPPORT If you think your students will find it difficult to do this exercise, tell them to write down some phrases they will use for each conversation.

- Tell them to take turns having the conversations.

Reading & Writing **a review**

Exercise 6

- Put students into pairs and ask them to look at the photos. Tell them to discuss which type of entertainment they would prefer to go to and why.

CRITICAL THINKING In exercise 6, students need to decide on their preferences and then explain these choices to their groups. You could demonstrate the exercise by explaining your preferred order to the class, giving reasons for your decisions.

- Put students into small groups of three or four and ask them to read the different types of entertainment. Tell them to work alone at first and order them 1 to 8.

- Tell students to explain their order to their group, giving reasons.

- Ask some students to explain the order that someone else in their group chose.

EXTENSION Talk about things you have in common. Ask students to find any top or bottom choices they have in common with other people in their group or in the whole class (via a whole class milling activity – see an explanation of this in lesson 12.3 after exercise 8b). When they find someone with the same top or bottom choice, ask them to discuss their reasons and see if they are similar. To round off the exercise, ask two or three students to report who they have something in common with, e.g. *Eliza and I both like …*

Exercise 7

> **Text summary:** These short texts are website reviews of events. They are not written by official critics but by people who went to the event. They could be found in blogs or a 'what's on' guide website. The first reviewer enjoyed the circus but the second reviewer didn't enjoy the concert.

- Ask students to read the instruction and compare answers with a partner.

ANSWERS
Photo 1 – Review 2   Photo 2 – Review 1

Exercise 8

- Ask students to work with their partners to read the reviews and discuss the questions.
- Ask them to give reasons for their answers.

ANSWERS
Review 1: positive – the article is positive, and it recommends the circus
Review 2: negative – the review is negative, and it does recommend the concert.

Exercise 9

- Draw the students' attention to the answers in the first example. Ask students to find phrases 1 and 5 in the reviews. Tell students both these phrases show what the writer thought before going to the show – they felt negative in the first and positive in the second.
- Ask them to complete the other three categories.
- Check answers together.

ANSWERS
a 1, 5   b 3, 8   c 2, 6   d 4, 7

Exercise 10a

- As a lead-in to this exercise, ask students to think back to exercise 6 and remember their ideas. Tell them to choose one event to write notes about.
- Ask students to work alone and write notes for points 1–4.

Exercise 10b

- Put students into pairs.

WATCH OUT! There are some more difficult verb patterns in the phrases in the Language for writing box. Draw students' attention to the patterns with *recommend*. *Recommend* can be followed by the *-ing* form of the verb OR by a noun, e.g.
I recommend seeing that concert.
I recommend that concert.
Expect is followed by *to* + infinitive. Sometimes we put a noun before the infinitive, e.g.
I didn't expect to see a famous actress.
I expect the concert to be good.

- Refer students to the Language for writing box and tell them to read the information and think about how they could use the phrases. Ask them to explain their ideas about their event to each other, using the phrases.

EXTRA SUPPORT Model the exercise by giving your own example to the class using the phrases. You could also ask students to write out the sentences before they speak. Encourage them to ask questions to get extra information and details.

Exercise 11a

- Ask students to write their reviews of the event they chose. They can refer to the example reviews from exercise 7. Tell them to write between eighty and one hundred words and include all the information in their notes from exercise 10a.

STUDY TIP Encourage students to get into the habit of checking their writing for spelling and punctuation errors when they have finished. If necessary, go over typical mistakes your students make in both areas.

Exercise 11b

- Put students into pairs and ask them to swap reviews.
- Ask them to read their partner's review and discuss the questions.

EXTENSION Ask students to use the review they read and write a response to give an opposite description. So, if the review was negative, they write a positive review saying why they disagree with their partner's review and what was good/bad about the event.
Tell them to use the phrases from the Language for writing box. When they have finished, tell them to give the review to their partner to read.

EXTRA ACTIVITY Only do this if you feel your group are comfortable with correcting their peers' writing. Tell them to read the reviews and underline good examples of language and errors that they see. Ask them not to correct the errors. Tell students to give back the texts and ask them to notice the examples of good language and to try and correct the errors. Tell students to check their corrections with their partner. Go over any problems with the class.

EXTRA ACTIVITY Find some reviews (in your students' first language) of events from a local magazine or website. Bring them to class. Put students into pairs and give each pair a review. Ask them to translate it, not word for word but in a summary. Put students into larger groups of four or six. Tell them to describe their event and summarize the review. Listeners should say if they would go to the event or not and why/why not.

12.5 Video

Park Theatre

VIDEOSCRIPT

People have enjoyed the theatre for thousands of years. From Ancient Greece to Shakespeare's London, people have always watched plays.
But some things have changed. In Shakespeare's time most people could afford the theatre.

The rich sat in the balconies and the poor sat on the floor – but they all watched the same play.

Today many theatres are very expensive. Ticket prices have increased a lot over the last few years. In London's West End, for example, the average ticket price is 81 pounds sterling and on Broadway it's just under 100 US dollars.

Many of us can't afford these prices.

So there are lots of people, especially young people, who have never been to the theatre.

But some theatres are changing this. Park Theatre is in Finsbury Park in north London.

It's a very modern theatre in an old office block.

It has several different spaces, including Park 200, a large theatre with 200 seats, Park 90, a smaller theatre with 90 seats, and The Morris Space, an area for rehearsals, workshops and classes.

The organizers of the project, Jez and Melli Bond, started Park Theatre to help more people see good plays.

They encourage everyone – theatre fans and first timers – to come and enjoy the theatre. They do this in different ways.

First, they keep prices low. Every ticket costs less than twenty pounds so it's affordable.

They also make sure there's lots of variety. They stage all kinds of plays, from old classics to modern musicals, so it's got something for everyone.

At the moment, for example, they are showing Crystal Springs. This is a modern play about teenagers, parents and social media.

They are also preparing for the children's pantomime Jack and the Beanstalk.

In its short history Park Theatre has been very successful. It has attracted large audiences from all kinds of backgrounds. So just like in Shakespeare's time, everyone can enjoy the theatre.

VIDEO ANSWERS

Exercise 2
Ancient Greece ✓   audience ✓   balcony ✓   floor ✓
pantomime ☐   seats ✓   Shakespearean theatre ✓
theatre ✓   ticket ☐   stage ✓

Exercise 3
1 Negative. Only rich can go now. In Shakespeare's day rich and poor watched the same play. Nowadays, many young people have never been to theatre.
2 Positive. Park Theatre has different bigger and smaller spaces for plays. Keeps prices low. More variety of plays for different kinds of people.

Exercise 4
1 could
2 at the same time as
3 modern, an old
4 two
5 twenty
6 musicals
7 teenagers
8 very successful

Review

ANSWERS

Exercise 1a
1 go, c   2 play, e   3 have, b   4 see, f   5 go, d
6 see, a

Exercise 2a
1 Hang on a minute.
2 Could I speak to Ms Martinez, please?
3 Can you tell her to call me back, please?
4 I'm afraid she's out of the office at the moment.

Exercise 2b 12.18 ⊙
You heard sentences 2 and 4.

AUDIOSCRIPT 12.18
A Right Insurance. How can I help you?
B Hello. Could I speak to Ms Martinez, please?
A One moment, please. I'm afraid she's out of the office at the moment. Would you like to leave a message?
B No, that's fine. I'll call back later.
A OK, thank you.
B Thanks. Bye.

Exercises 3a & b 12.19 ⊙
1 has been   2 built   3 were   4 were   5 came
6 was   7 didn't use   8 decided   9 have come
10 have performed

AUDIOSCRIPT 12.19
These days, Verona coliseum is famous for its opera festival, but it has been a place to see other types of entertainment over the years. The Romans built the coliseum almost two thousand years ago for sports and games called 'ludi'. The most famous of these games were fights between gladiators. These events were very popular and people came from far away to see them. In 1117, there was a big earthquake in Verona and people didn't use the coliseum for a long time. However, centuries later, the Venetians decided to repair the building and use it for concerts. From that time, hundreds of thousands of people have come to Verona to listen to music and many famous opera singers and ballet dancers have performed there.

Exercise 4a
1 comedies   2 romantic films   3 animations
4 action films   5 musicals   6 horror films
7 science fiction films   8 dramas

Photocopiable worksheets: contents

Grammar

Unit 1 All over the world

Paired activity, correcting information about penfriends by asking and answering questions

Language
Present simple *to be*
Nationalities

Preparation: Make one copy of the worksheet for each pair and cut the sheets in half. You will also need some spare paper for each student.

Non-cut alternative: Make one copy of the worksheet for each pair and fold the sheets in half. Tell students not to look at the other halves.

1 Write the word *penfriend* on the board, and elicit its meaning from the class. Tell them that you have a penfriend called Carla. Write on the board: *Spanish/Italian/German*, and encourage students to identify a question they could ask to find out which of these nationalities Carla is, e.g. *Is she Spanish?* Then write the following on the board: *Her neighbours = Chinese/Japanese/Vietnamese.* Elicit the question they could ask to find out Carla's neighbours' nationality, e.g. *Are they Chinese?*

2 Divide the class into pairs. Allocate each partner a letter (A or B) and give them the relevant half of the worksheet, as well as a piece of spare paper to each student. They should not show these to each other. Tell students that they each have information about their partner's penfriend, but there are mistakes. Students correct these mistakes by asking their partner questions (as demonstrated in stage 1). Their partner should answer positively, *Yes, he/she is.* or *Yes, they are.* or negatively *No, he/she isn't.* or *No, they aren't.* If they answer negatively, they should give the correct answer, e.g. *No, she isn't. She's Chinese.*

3 When they have both corrected the mistakes, students work independently to write a short paragraph on the spare paper about their partner's penfriend, using the information they have in their table. They can then compare their paragraph with their partner's table to check their answers are correct, as well as reading each other's paragraphs.

ANSWERS
Student A
Adrian: (~~Greek~~) Polish, (~~Paris~~) London, (~~Turkish~~) Greek
Student B
Luisa: (~~Los Angeles~~) Mexico City, (~~Nigerian~~) Spanish, (~~English~~) French

EXTRA CHALLENGE   Tell students to imagine they have a penfriend living abroad. Ask them to write a paragraph about that penfriend, similar to the paragraph they wrote in instruction 3 above. Once they have written their descriptions, encourage the rest of the class to take turns asking questions to find out about the penfriends.

Unit 2 My day

Paired activity, completing graphs to illustrate a typical day

Language
Adverbs of frequency: *always, usually, often, sometimes, hardly ever, never*
Daily activities

Preparation: Make one copy of the worksheet for each student.

1 Write three sentences about your daily routine on the board (using adverbs of frequency) – two that are true and one that is false. Students work in pairs to guess which one is false. Take a vote and confirm answers as a class.

2 Give a copy of the worksheet to each student. Students label the scale with the adverbs, using the percentages as a guide. Confirm answers as a class.

ANSWERS
1 usually   2 often   3 sometimes   4 hardly ever
5 never

3 Now encourage students to add their own ideas for daily activities at the end of the graph, e.g. *go out for dinner, go to the gym.* Once they have done this, explain that they should complete the graph to illustrate their typical day by drawing bars to show how often they do things. Explain that they should choose a day in the week rather than the weekend. If necessary, demonstrate how they should draw bars on the graph.

4 Divide the class into pairs. Explain that they should take turns to look at their completed graphs in exercise 2 and tell their partner about their day, without letting each other see their graphs. They should then complete the empty graph for their partner, drawing appropriate bars on the graph.

5 When they have finished, students compare graphs to check they have drawn the information accurately. They can also compare their graphs with other students in the class.

EXTRA SUPPORT   Before moving on to exercise 2, draw your own typical day in graph form on the board as an example to illustrate the activity.

EARLY FINISHERS   Students tell each other what their ideal daily routine would be, e.g. *I never get up early.* They draw new graphs to show their partner's improved routine.

EXTRA CHALLENGE   Ask students to tell the class about their partner's day without looking at their worksheets.

Unit 3 Party talk

Group activity, with students mingling to exchange information about themselves

Language
Wh- questions
Yes/No questions

Preparation: Make one copy of the worksheet for each student.

1 Give a copy of the worksheet to each student. In class or for homework, students match the questions with the answers in exercise 1.

ANSWERS

1 e **2** d **3** b **4** c **5** f **6** a **7** h **8** g

2 Ask students to look at exercise 2. Tell them they are going to a party and should imagine they are somebody else. Ask them to complete the sentences with a new name and information about themselves based on the questions in exercise 1.

3 Divide the class into groups (maximum of six students per group) and explain that they are going to a party. Explain that they need to complete the table with information about the other people at the party by asking and answering questions. They should answer any questions using the identity they created for themselves in exercise 2. Ask them to look at the prompts in the table in exercise 3 and think of the questions they will need to ask. They should use their own ideas to think of a question at the bottom of the table, e.g. *Where do you work?*

4 In their groups, ask them to stand up and talk to the other people, asking and answering questions and completing their tables with as many people's information as possible. If possible, put on some background music to create a party atmosphere.

5 After a short while, stop the activity and put students into pairs within their groups. Ask them to compare their answers.

6 Finish with whole-class feedback. Encourage students to talk about who they met at the party and what information they found out. Who has an interesting job? Who has something in common with them?

EXTRA SUPPORT Students can complete exercise 1 in pairs. Additionally, to prepare for exercise 3, model asking and answering questions at a party.

EXTRA CHALLENGE Cut or fold the worksheet so students are unable to see the questions in exercise 1 when they perform exercise 3.

Unit 4 World cities

Paired activity, with students describing famous cities for their partners to guess

Language
There is/are …, There isn't/aren't …, Is/Are there …?

Preparation: Make one copy of the worksheet for each pair and cut the sheets in half.

Non-cut alternative: Make one copy of the worksheet for each pair and fold the sheets in half. Tell students not to look at the other halves.

1 As a class, brainstorm famous cities around the world and what they are famous for. Discuss their ideas.

2 Divide the class into pairs. Allocate each partner a letter (A or B) and give them the relevant half of the worksheet. They should not show these to each other. Focus students on exercise 1 and ask them to choose the correct verb form, *is/are/isn't/aren't* for each sentence/city, referring to the illustrations and word prompts. Check answers as a class, but be careful not to reveal what the cities are at this stage.

ANSWERS

Student A: isn't, are   **Student B:** aren't, is

3 Before moving on to exercises 2 and 3, revise the question form with the class, if necessary: *Is/Are there …?* and the use of *a/an* and *any*. Student A then describes their cities to student B, using the completed sentences in exercise 1, and making more sentences using *There is/are* or *There isn't/aren't* and the word prompts. They can also use their own ideas, if they wish. Student B tries to guess which city it is, and they can also ask questions, e.g. *Are there a lot of parks?* Student A confirms student B's correct guesses or gives the answer after four wrong guesses. Students then swap roles, with student B describing their two cities for student A.

4 After all students have correctly identified the four cities, elicit feedback from a few pairs. Which cities were easy/difficult to guess? What did they learn that they didn't know before?

EXTRA SUPPORT Ask student As to work in pairs with other student As, and the same for student Bs. In their pairs, they complete exercise 1 together.

EARLY FINISHERS Students discuss which cities they want to go to and why.

EXTRA CHALLENGE Pairs write a description of another famous city, e.g. Paris. Encourage pairs to read their descriptions to the class for them to guess the city.

Unit 5 Find someone who can …

Whole-class activity, with students mingling to practise affirmative, negative and question forms of *can* and *could*

Language
can/can't/could/couldn't

Preparation: Make one copy of the worksheet for each student.

1 Give a copy of the worksheet to each student. Students independently complete conversations 1–4 in exercise 1.

2 Check the answers as a whole class.

ANSWERS

a Can b can c Could d couldn't e Can f can't
g Can h can i Could j couldn't k could

3 Focus students on the table in exercise 3. Encourage them to write their own phrases for 8–10. Provide support by eliciting a few ideas, if necessary. Encourage students to use three different forms of *can/can't/could/couldn't*, where possible.

4 Focus students on statements 1–4 and show how they link to conversations 1–4 in exercise 1. Encourage students to identify what you would write in the *Name* and *Extra information* columns for these conversations. For example, for statement 1, they would write *Tim* in the *Name* column and *Likes making chocolate cake* in the *Extra information* column. Check that students understand why Yuki doesn't ask for extra information, i.e. because Ali's answer doesn't match the *Find someone who …* statement.

5 Now explain that students are going to mingle as a whole class and ask and answer questions in order to fill in the table. You may want to outline the following rules before you start the activity:

- If the person's answer does not match the *Find someone who …* statement, students shouldn't write their name in the table.
- We don't usually use the negative form for questions.
- Students should answer a question with a short answer, not just *yes* or *no*.
- After writing someone's name, students should try to obtain extra information by asking another question. Give students fifteen or twenty minutes to mingle. Monitor and check that students are following the procedure correctly.

6 As a whole class, ask for feedback about what students have learnt about their classmates, including the extra information.

EXTRA SUPPORT Exercise 1 can be done in pairs.

EARLY FINISHERS Divide the class into pairs and give each pair a category of people: *children, teenagers, old people, students, teachers, parents*. In their pairs, ask them to brainstorm what these people usually *can* and *can't* do.

EXTRA CHALLENGE Encourage students to fold the top section of their worksheet so they can't see the conversations in exercise 1 while performing the mingling activity. Monitor as they ask and answer questions.

Unit 6 Three in a row

Paired activity, using regular past simple verbs in a noughts and crosses-style game

Language
Past simple regular verbs
was/were

Preparation: Make one copy of the worksheet for each pair. You will also need some spare paper for each student.

1 Divide the class into pairs. Give a copy of the worksheet to each pair, as well as a piece of spare paper to each student. Give students five minutes to complete exercise 1. Review answers as a class and quickly recap pronunciation of *-ed* endings.

ANSWERS

1 1 We add *-ed*.
  2 We add the letter *-d*.
  3 We add *-ed*. We change the *y* to *i*.
  4 *be*. It is not a regular past simple verb – it changes to *was* or *were*.

2 Copy the grid from exercise 2 on to the board and ask two students to play a quick game of noughts and crosses with each other. They tell you where they want to place their nought or their cross using the grid references, e.g. *A2, C3*. They should try to get three noughts or crosses in a row, horizontally, vertically or diagonally.

3 Pairs should now look at the *How to play* instructions in exercise 2. Student A chooses one of the verbs from the box in exercise 1, question 4. Student B formulates a past tense sentence with the verb and a time phrase, such as *last night*, using the spare paper to write down the sentence, if necessary. They read the past simple sentence to student A and tell them where to write it in the grid (by saying a coordinate). Student A writes the sentence in the grid if it is correct, you may need to act as a referee in some cases. Students then switch roles. They can use each verb once only – except for the verb *be*, which they can use as often as they like. Pairs continue the game until one of them has three sentences in a row, or when it is no longer possible to do so. Ask students to play the game another two times by copying the grid on to spare paper.

4 After fifteen minutes, ask them to stop. The winner is the partner with the most rows of three.

EXTRA SUPPORT At the end of the previous lesson, students can take the worksheets home with them to check the meanings of the verbs.

EARLY FINISHERS In their pairs, students give each other the beginning of a sentence, e.g. *Yesterday, I received a …* Their partner should think of as many ways of completing this sentence as possible, e.g. *… phone call from an old friend./… an email from my brother.*

EXTRA CHALLENGE In their pairs, students give their partner three of the verbs from the box in exercise 1, question 4. Their partner then has two minutes to try to formulate one sentence that uses all three verbs in their past simple form. For each verb they are able to use, they award themselves one point. They can repeat this as many times as they like.

Unit 7 What's the question?

Paired activity, playing a question-and-answer game to practise irregular past simple verbs

Language
Past simple irregular verbs

Preparation: Make one copy of the worksheet for each pair and cut the sheets in half.

Non-cut alternative: Make one copy of the worksheet for each pair and fold the sheets in half. Tell students not to look at the other halves.

1 Write the following verbs on the board: *finish, open, start, do, leave, make*. Ask students what the difference is between the first three verbs and the last three verbs when forming the past simple – the first three are regular; the last three are irregular. Ask students what the past simple forms of *do, leave* and *make* are *did, left* and *made*, and then ask them to brainstorm other irregular verbs and their past simple forms.

2 Divide the class into pairs. Allocate each partner a letter (A or B) and give them the relevant half of the worksheet. They should not show these to each other. Give students ten minutes to independently write the answers to the questions in exercise 1 without using the words in bold. The first answer has been done as an example.

3 In their pairs, give students fifteen minutes to take turns to read their answers from exercise 1 to each other. Their partner should decide what the question was in each case, completing the questions on their own section of the worksheet using the correct form of the verb in box 1 and the other words in box 2.

4 Once students A and B have both written the questions, they should check answers by reading them to their partner, who tells them if they are right or wrong. They award themselves one point for each correct question. The winning pair is the pair with the most points between them.

EXTRA CHALLENGE In their pairs, students write a short story or sequence of events. They should use the irregular verbs from the worksheet, but they also alternate between regular and irregular verbs, e.g. *I visited my friend last night. We had a great evening. We watched a film on TV and afterwards we ate a wonderful meal that we prepared together …*

Unit 8 Rules and advice

Paired/Group activity, discussing rules and advice for people visiting a country for the first time

Language
should/shouldn't, have to/don't have to

Preparation: Make one copy of the worksheet for each student.

1 Give a copy of the worksheet to each student. Encourage them to explain what the words/phrases *should/shouldn't* and *have to/don't have to* in exercise 1 mean. Then ask them to complete one of the sets of rules/advice for them, as appropriate. After a few minutes, ask for whole-class feedback.

2 Divide the class into pairs. Give students ten minutes to think about the country where they are learning English, and complete each section of the table with three pieces of rules/advice for people visiting the country for the first time.

3 Ask pairs to then work with another pair, and take turns to tell each other about the rules/advice they wrote in exercise 2. Explain that pairs should award themselves one point for each rule or piece of advice that only they thought of. The winning pair is the students in the group with the most points.

EARLY FINISHERS Students think of other categories and brainstorm more rules/advice that would be important/useful for visitors to the country they wrote about it in exercise 2.

EXTRA CHALLENGE Students imagine they are the founders of a 'perfect' society. In groups, they should write rules/advice for their new society. The rules/advice should be as realistic or attainable as possible, e.g. *People don't have to pay for medical and dental treatment.* would be realistic but *People don't have to pay for anything in the shops.* wouldn't be. They can then write a *People's charter*, which they describe to the rest of the class. Students vote on which society they would most like to live in.

Unit 9 Perfect pairs

Group activity, matching and completing sentences, and making mini-conversations

Language
Countable and uncountable nouns: *olives, beef, pasta,* etc.
Quantifiers: *a, an, some, any*
Food words

Preparation: Make one copy of the worksheet for each pair and fold the sheets into three sections.

1 On the board, write the words: *a, an, some* and *any*. Ask students when we use these words: *a* and *an* with countable singular nouns; *some* with countable and uncountable plural nouns in positive statements, etc. If necessary, they can refer back to Unit 9.1 in their Coursebooks.

2 Divide the class into groups (four students per group) and sub-divide each group into pairs. Allocate each pair a letter A or B and give them the relevant section of the worksheet. They should not show these to the other pair. In their pairs, students decide which word, *a, an, some, any* or –, can be used to complete each sentence.

3 Once they have completed their sentences, pair A reads out their completed sentences one by one. Pair B then looks for a suitable response to each sentence and reads it out. Go through the example with the class. Together as a group, they decide if it is the correct response; there is only one appropriate response per sentence. If they both agree, they match the sentences and responses by writing the appropriate letter/number in the boxes.

4 Review answers as a class.

ANSWERS

Pair A: **1** (an) e   **2** (some) f   **3** (a) j   **4** (any) d
5 (any) a   **6** (an) b   **7** (some) l   **8** (an) k   **9** (a) i
10 (any) g   **11** (some) h   **12** (some) c
Pair B: **a** (any) 5   **b** (–) 6   **c** (–) 12   **d** (some) 4
e (some) 1   **f** (some) 2   **g** (a) 10   **h** (any) 11
i (some) 9   **j** (any) 3   **k** (any) 8   **l** (–) 7

5 Now tell students to unfold their worksheets and look at the *All students* section. Working individually at first, they should decide what they would like for dinner tonight and complete the menu. They should then work in their groups again to try to choose a menu that they would all be happy with.

EXTRA SUPPORT If students make mistakes during stage 1, point this out to them. Focus their attention on whether the object is countable or uncountable, singular or plural, and whether the sentence is a question, a positive statement or a negative statement.

EXTRA CHALLENGE Write on the board: *picnic hamper*, and elicit from students what this is. Tell students to imagine that they are going on a picnic. They should independently make a list of ten to fifteen food items to put in their picnic hamper. Then divide the class into pairs and encourage students to play a guessing game. They should take turns asking questions to try and find out what they each have in their hamper, e.g. *Have you got any meat?* Their partner should answer using full sentences, e.g. *Yes, I've got some meat.*

Unit 10 A mystery sentence

Group activity, completing sentences, then playing a game to practise comparative adjectives

Language
Comparative adjectives: *drier, worse, more dangerous,* etc.

Preparation: Make one copy of the worksheet for each student.

1 Divide the class into groups (maximum of four students per group) and give a copy of the worksheet to each student. Students work in groups to complete sentences 1–13 with the comparative forms of the adjectives in the box. Remind them that, in some cases, they will need to add *more* before the adjective to make it comparative.

2 Once they have done this, students find the mystery phrase in sentences 1–13 by using the letters from the shaded spaces to complete sentence 14.

ANSWERS

1a **1** more famous   **2** worse   **3** drier   **4** cheaper
  5 better   **6** more expensive   **7** heavier
  8 sunnier   **9** wetter   **10** more interesting
  11 more comfortable   **12** more dangerous
  13 cooler
  b **14** more beautiful

3 Give students five minutes to independently complete the table in exercise 2, writing an example for each category.

4 Back in their original groups, students then take turns to ask one another questions to try to find out what they had chosen in exercise 2. They should use *yes/no* questions e.g. *Has it got four legs? Does it live in this country?* and comparative adjectives, e.g. *Is your animal bigger than a cat? Is it more dangerous than a tiger?* Give the groups a maximum of ninety seconds to identify each item, and twenty minutes in total to do the activity. Students win a point for each item they identify, and the winner is the student in each group with the most points.

EXTRA SUPPORT Students can refer to Unit 10.1 in their Coursebooks for extra help with the target grammar, if necessary, during stage 1.

EXTRA CHALLENGE With multinational classes, students work in pairs and tell each other about different aspects of their country or region, using comparative adjectives, e.g. *My home town is Cannes, which is a very expensive place. The towns and villages nearby are cheaper.* Partners should then tell others in the class about their country from memory.

Unit 11 What are you going to do?

Whole-class activity, predicting what other students are going to do in certain situations

Language
Future with *going to*
Verb and noun collocations: *plant flowers, look after a pet*, etc.

Preparation: Make one copy of the worksheet and cut it into twelve cards.

1 Tell students that your friend is going for an important job interview next week, and that you are going to help and support him. You are going to practise the interview with him, you are going to drive him to the interview, and you are going to take him out for lunch afterwards, but do not tell students this yet. Students should ask what you are going to do by asking questions with *going to*, e.g. *Are you going to practise the interview with him? Are you going to lend him a tie?* You should answer with full sentences, stressing *am* or *not*, e.g. *Yes, I'm going to practise the interview with him./No, I'm not going to lend him a tie.* Let students ask about ten questions or until they have found out what you are going to do.

2 Give each student a card, if you have more than twelve students, some will have to share a card. Explain that each of their cards shows a different situation, and two things that they are going to do. They should choose and write an appropriate third thing that they are going to do, completing their card.

3 Students or pairs/groups then take turns to read out their situations. The other students/pairs/groups take turns to ask questions to find out what they are going to do. Each student/pair/group is allowed one question only. For each positive answer they receive when they ask a question, e.g. *Are you going to cook some food? Yes, I am.*, they win one point. The winning team is the one with the most points once everyone has had a turn at reading their situations to the class.

EXTRA SUPPORT Students can refer to Unit 11.1 in their Coursebook for useful verb and noun collocations to use while making guesses, if necessary.

EXTRA CHALLENGE Play a memory game as a class. One student begins by saying what another team is going to do, e.g. *Sofie and Tomas are going to make some food for their class party.* The next student repeats the sentence and adds a sentence about what another team is going to do, e.g. *Sofie and Tomas are going to make some food for their class party. Esra and Alvaro are going to buy some new furniture for their home.* The game continues with each subsequent student adding a sentence to the list. How much can they remember?

Unit 12 Honestly!

Paired/Group activity, with students playing a guessing game to discover what experiences they have each had

Language
Present perfect simple and past simple for past events: *I've met Steven Spielberg. I met him last summer.*, etc.

Preparation: Make one copy of the worksheet for each pair. You will also need some spare paper for each student.

1 Divide the class into pairs. Give a copy of the worksheet to each pair, as well as some spare paper to each student. Give students five minutes to complete the conversation with the correct form of the verbs from the box. Review answers as a class. Ask students why the first sentence uses the present perfect simple, and the rest of the conversation uses the past simple. Because the first sentence is about an event in the past where the speaker is interested in what happened more than when it happened. The rest of the conversation gives the details.

ANSWERS
1 met 2 did, meet 3 were 4 was 5 were 6 was
7 did, meet 8 went 9 was 10 was 11 wanted
12 Did, say 13 was 14 came 15 said 16 did, say
17 said 18 happened

2 Tell students to now work independently. They write three true experiences they have had on their pieces of spare paper. Encourage them to think of funny, interesting or unusual experiences as well as usual ones.

3 They should then work with their partner again. They read each other's sentences and copy out all six on a separate sheet of paper, mixing up the order.

4 Ask pairs to join with another pair to form small groups. Explain that they are going to play a guessing game. The first pair says one of their six sentences, together, at the same time, e.g. *I've been to Australia.* Students in the other pair ask them questions, e.g. *Gregor, where did you go in Australia? Carola, what did you do in Australia?* to establish which student is telling the truth. Once they have come to a conclusion, they complete the first two columns in the table by writing the student's name, together with the relevant sentence about them.

5 Pairs then switch roles, with the other pair reading one of their sentences for students to guess which experiences they really had. Pairs continue in this way, taking turns to read their sentences until all the sentences have been read.

6 After both pairs have completed their tables, students check answers by revealing who was telling the truth and ticking or crossing (and correcting) their entries in the table for each sentence. Pairs award themselves a point each time they correctly identified who was telling the truth. The winning pair is the one with the most points.

EXTRA CHALLENGE Working independently, students write a paragraph about a life experience that may or may not be true. They then read this to the rest of the class, who should decide by asking questions whether it is true.

1 Grammar All over the world

Student A

1   Ask student B questions about their penfriend Adrian. Find and correct the mistakes.

Examples: *Is Adrian Greek? Is his home in Paris?*

Adrian	
Nationality	Greek
Home	Paris
Job	Doctor
Married/Single	Married
Nationality of husband/wife	Turkish
Neighbour(s)	Mr and Mrs Ahmed
Nationality of neighbour(s)	Pakistani

2   Answer student B's questions about your penfriend Luisa.

Luisa	
Nationality	Mexican
Home	Mexico City
Job	Student
Married/Single	Married
Nationality of husband/wife	Spanish
Neighbour(s)	Ms Dubois
Nationality of neighbour(s)	French

Student B

1   Answer student A's questions about your penfriend Adrian.

Adrian	
Nationality	Polish
Home	London
Job	Doctor
Married/Single	Married
Nationality of husband/wife	Greek
Neighbour(s)	Mr and Mrs Ahmed
Nationality of neighbour(s)	Pakistani

2   Ask student A questions about their penfriend Luisa. Find and correct the mistakes.

Examples: *Is Luisa Mexican? Is her home in Los Angeles?*

Luisa	
Nationality	Mexican
Home	Los Angeles
Job	Student
Married/Single	Married
Nationality of husband/wife	Nigerian
Neighbour(s)	Ms Dubois
Nationality of neighbour(s)	English

2 Grammar My day

1   Fill in gaps 1–5 on the graph with the words from the box.

> ~~always~~   hardly ever   never   often   sometimes   usually

2   Draw bars on the graph to show a typical day for you.

My day

1 ___always___   100%
                 90%
2 _____   80%
                 70%
3 _____   60%
4 _____   50%
                 40%
                 30%
                 20%
5 _____   10%
6 _____   0%

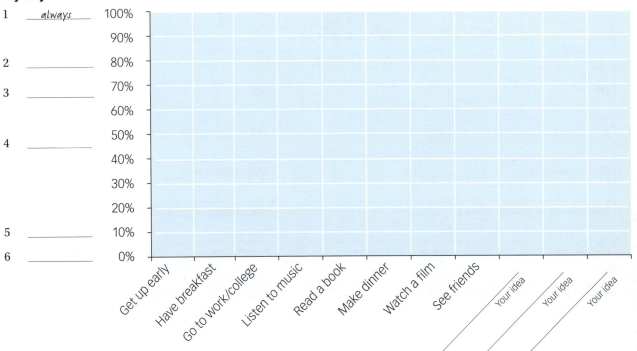

Get up early · Have breakfast · Go to work/college · Listen to music · Read a book · Make dinner · Watch a film · See friends · Your idea · Your idea · Your idea

3   Work with a partner. Describe your day using your graph in exercise **2**.

4   Complete the graph for your partner.

My partner's day

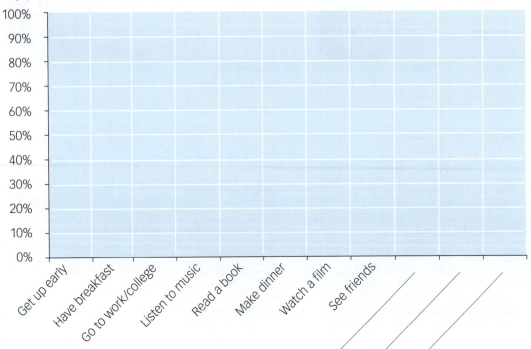

100% · 90% · 80% · 70% · 60% · 50% · 40% · 30% · 20% · 10% · 0%

Get up early · Have breakfast · Go to work/college · Listen to music · Read a book · Make dinner · Watch a film · See friends

3 Grammar Party talk

1 Match the questions 1–8 to the answers a–h.

1 What's your name?

2 Where do you live?

3 What do you do?

4 Do you like your job? Why/Why not?

5 When do you relax?

6 What do you do in your free time?

7 How often do you go to parties?

8 Are you married?

a I watch films.

b I'm a musician.

c Yes, I do. I meet a lot of interesting people.

d I live in London.

e My name's Shasi.

f At the weekend.

g Yes, I am.

h About twice a month.

2 Imagine you are somebody else. Complete the information using the questions in exercise **1**.

1 My name's _____ .

2 I live in _____ .

3 I'm a _____ .

4 I *like/don't like* my job because _____
_____ .

5 I relax _____ .

6 In my free time I _____ .

7 I go to parties _____ .

8 I'm *married/single*.

3 Work in small groups. Ask and answer questions to complete the table.
Answer using your information from exercise **2**.

Name?				
Live?				
Job?				
Like job?				
Relax?				
Free time?				
Parties?				
Married?				

4 Grammar World cities

Student A

1 Look and choose the correct word in the sentences.

There *is / are / isn't / aren't*
a beach in this city.

There *is / are / isn't / aren't*
13 million people in this city.

2 Describe your two cities to student B using *There is/are* or *There isn't/aren't*. Answer student B's questions.

3 Listen to student B describe two cities. Ask questions and guess the cities.

Student B

1 Look and choose the correct word in the sentences.

There *is / are / isn't / aren't* many
tall buildings in this city.

There *is / are / isn't / aren't*
a famous park in this city.

2 Listen to student A describe two cities. Ask questions and guess the cities.

3 Describe your two cities to student A using *There is/are* or *There isn't/aren't*. Answer student A's questions.

5 Grammar Find someone who can …

1 Complete the conversations with *can, can't, could* or *couldn't*.

Conversation 1
Ana ᵃ_____ you make a cake?
Tim Yes, I ᵇ_____ .
Ana What kind of cake do you like making?
Tim Chocolate cake.

Conversation 3
Yuki ᵍ_____ you swim?
Ali Yes, I ʰ_____ .

Conversation 2
Ella ᶜ_____ you dance well when you were younger?
Max No, I ᵈ_____ .
Ella ᵉ_____ you dance well now?
Max No, I ᶠ_____ .

Conversation 4
Ali ⁱ_____ you drive when you were sixteen?
Tim No, I ʲ_____ . How about you?
Ali Yes, I ᵏ_____ .
Tim Is that normal in your country?
Ali Yes, it is.

2 Complete the table below with your own ideas (8–10).

3 Work as a class. Ask and answer questions to complete the table.

	Find someone who …	Name	Extra information
1	can make a cake		
2	couldn't dance very well when they were younger		
3	can't swim		
4	could drive when they were sixteen		
5	can speak three languages		
6	can't see without glasses		
7	could run very fast when they were a child		
8			
9			
10			

6 Grammar Three in a row

1   Work with a partner. Read and answer questions 1–4.

     1   What do we add to these verbs to make them past simple?
        call   collect   finish

     2   What do we add to these verbs to make them past simple?
        believe   close   love

     3   What do we add to these verbs to make them past simple? What do we change?
        carry   copy   try

     4   Which verb from the box is the odd one out? Why?

> be   believe   call   carry   close   collect   copy
> enter   finish   like   look   love   move   notice
> open   post   prepare   receive   return   shout
> start   thank   use   visit   wait   walk   want   work

2   Play the game.

> **How to play**
> 1   Student A: choose one of the verbs from the box in question 4.
> 2   Student B: use the word in a past simple sentence.
>   Say the sentence to student A and tell him/her where to write it in the grid.
> 3   Student A: write student B's sentence in the grid if it is correct.
> 4   Switch roles. Try to get three sentences in a row.

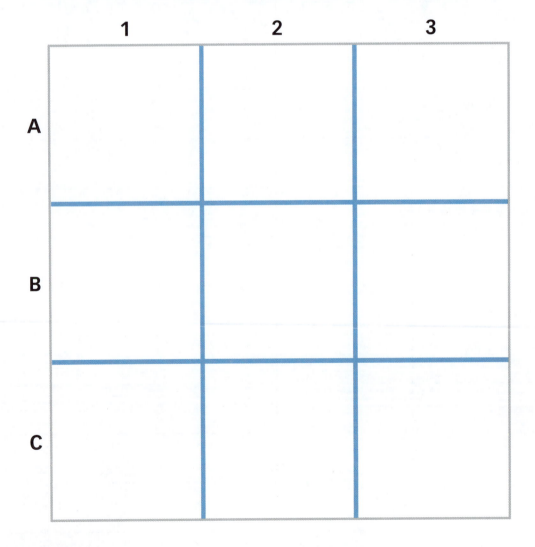

7 Grammar What's the question?

Student A

1 Read and answer the questions. Do not use the words in **bold**.

1 When was the last time you **gave** someone a **present**?

Last week. It was my mum's birthday and I bought her a scarf.

2 When was the last time you **rode** a **bicycle**?

_____

_____

3 When was the last time you **did** some **exercise**?

_____

_____

4 When was the last time you **had** a **holiday**?

_____

_____

5 When was the last time you **ate** a **healthy meal**?

_____

_____

2 Say your answers from exercise **1** to student B.

3a Listen to student B's answers. What were the questions? Complete the questions with the correct form of the verbs from box 1 and the words from box 2.

1

> buy   drink   fly   go   sleep

2

> coffee   for eight hours   on a plane
> something expensive   to the cinema

1 When was the last time you _____

_____ ?

2 When was the last time you _____

_____ ?

3 When was the last time you _____

_____ ?

4 When was the last time you _____

_____ ?

5 When was the last time you _____

_____ ?

b Check your answers with student B.

- -

Student B

1 Read and answer the questions. Do not use the words in **bold**.

1 When was the last time you **slept** for **eight hours**?

At the weekend. I was really tired.

2 When was the last time you **went** to the **cinema**?

_____

_____

3 When was the last time you **bought** something **expensive**?

_____

_____

4 When was the last time you **flew** on a **plane**?

_____

_____

5 When was the last time you **drank coffee**?

_____

_____

2 Listen to student A's answers. What were the questions? Complete the questions with the correct form of the verbs from box 1 and the words from box 2.

1

> do   eat   give   have   ride

2

> a bicycle   a healthy meal
> a holiday   a present   some exercise

1 When was the last time you _____

_____ ?

2 When was the last time you _____

_____ ?

3 When was the last time you _____

_____ ?

4 When was the last time you _____

_____ ?

5 When was the last time you _____

_____ ?

3 Say your answers from exercise **1** to student A.

4 Check your answers in exercise **2** with student A.

8 Grammar Rules and advice

1 Complete one set of rules/advice.

In the school/college/university where I am learning English:

- Students should _____ .
- Students shouldn't _____ .
- Students have to _____ .
- Students don't have to _____ .

In the company where I work:

- Workers should _____ .
- Workers shouldn't _____ .
- Workers have to _____ .
- Workers don't have to _____ .

2 Work with a partner. Think of the country where you are learning English.
Complete the table with rules/advice for people visiting the country for the first time.

Visiting famous sites (e.g. museums, galleries)	1
	2
	3
Eating out	1
	2
	3
Getting around (e.g. buses, trains)	1
	2
	3
Visiting someone's home (e.g. for dinner)	1
	2
	3

3 Work with another pair. Tell each other about your rules/advice in exercise 2.

9 Grammar Perfect pairs

Pair A

1 Complete the sentences with *a, an, some, any* or –.

   1 [e] Would you like _____*an*_____ apple for dessert?
   2 [ ] I've made you _____ toast.
   3 [ ] Could I have _____ glass of lemonade, please?
   4 [ ] Have we got _____ food in the fridge?
   5 [ ] Did you buy _____ honey when you went shopping?
   6 [ ] I usually just have _____ orange for breakfast.
   7 [ ] I bought _____ lovely beef at the market yesterday.
   8 [ ] There's _____ olive on my pizza. I hate olives!
   9 [ ] That's _____ nice-looking sandwich. What's in it?
   10 [ ] Have we got _____ bread in the cupboard?
   11 [ ] Can I have _____ bread with my soup?
   12 [ ] I had _____ really nice noodles for dinner last night.

2 Say your sentences and listen to pair B. Match their responses a–l to your sentences 1–12.

Pair B

1 Complete the sentences with *a, an, some, any* or –.

   a [ ] No, the supermarket didn't have _____ left.
   b [ ] Me, too. I love _____ fruit!
   c [ ] So did I. I prefer them to _____ rice.
   d [ ] Well, there's _____ cheese, milk and orange juice, but that's all.
   e [1] No, thanks. I'd rather have _____*some*_____ yoghurt, if we have any.
   f [ ] Thank you. Could I have _____ jam on it?
   g [ ] Yes. Would you like _____ sandwich?
   h [ ] Of course you can, but I'm afraid we haven't got _____ butter to put on it.
   i [ ] There's _____ chicken and sweetcorn, but it isn't very tasty.
   j [ ] I'm sorry, but we haven't got _____ left. Amy drank it all.
   k [ ] There aren't _____ on mine, and I love them.
   l [ ] I never eat _____ red meat – I think it's horrible.

2 Listen to pair A and match their sentences 1–12 to your responses a–l.

All students

1 Choose what you would like for dinner tonight. Complete the menu.

   Starter: _____
   Main course: _____
   Vegetables: _____
   Dessert: _____
   To drink: _____

2 Work in small groups. Discuss the dinners you chose in exercise **1**. Agree on a menu.

10 Grammar A mystery sentence

1a Work in small groups. Complete the sentences 1–13 with the comparative form of the adjectives from the box.

> bad   cheap   comfortable   cool   dangerous   dry   expensive
> famous   good   heavy   interesting   sunny   wet

1 Who's _ _ _ _ _ _ ▣ _ _ _ in your country, David Beckham or Usain Bolt?

2 The film I saw on Saturday was bad, but the one I saw last night was _ ▣ _ _ _ .

3 It rains a lot in the hills in my country, but it's _ ▣ _ _ _ on the coast.

4 £600 is a lot to pay for a new computer. Have you got anything _ _ ▣ _ _ _ _ ?

5 The weather today has been terrible. I hope it will be ▣ _ _ _ _ _ _ tomorrow.

6 My friend's phone cost a lot of money, but mine was _ _ _ _ _ _ _ ▣ _ _ _ _ _ .

7 My luggage weighed 22 kilos, but my friend's was _ _ ▣ _ _ _ _ .

8 With more than 4,000 hours of sunshine a year, Arizona is _ ▣ _ _ _ _ _ than anywhere else in the world.

9 I tried to dry my washing in the garden, but it rained and now it's even _ _ ▣ _ _ _ !

10 Because there is so much to see and do, I think my town is _ _ _ _ _ ▣ _ _ _ _ _ _ _ _ _ _ _ than others in the area.

11 I love my new sofa. It's much _ _ _ _ _ _ _ ▣ _ _ _ _ _ _ _ than my old one.

12 Swimming in the sea near my town isn't safe, but it can be even _ _ _ _ _ _ _ _ _ _ _ _ ▣ _ when the weather is bad.

13 It's too hot to go outside today, so I'll stay in until it gets _ _ _ ▣ _ _ later on.

b Use the shaded letters to complete sentence 14.

14 The woods are lovely in the spring, but they're _ _ _ _ _ _ _ _ _ _ _ _ _ _ in the autumn when the leaves change colour.

2 Complete the table with your own examples. Do not show the other students in your group.

An animal	
A vehicle	
A country	
An electrical item	
A household item (non-electrical)	
A plant	
A famous building	

3 Work with your group. Guess their examples in exercise **2**. Ask questions with comparative adjectives and *Yes/No* questions.

Examples:

Is your animal bigger than a cat?

Does it live in this country?

11 Grammar What are you going to do?

It's your English-class party this Friday.

1 You're going to make some food.
2 You're going to choose some music.
3 _____

Some new people moved into the house next door to yours yesterday.

1 You're going to take them a cake.
2 You're going to invite them for coffee.
3 _____

You want to make your garden nicer.

1 You're going to plant some flowers.
2 You're going to cut the grass.
3 _____

Your neighbour is going on holiday next week.

1 You're going to take him/her to the airport.
2 You're going to look after his/her pet dog.
3 _____

You're going to improve some rooms in your home.

1 You're going to paint the rooms.
2 You're going to buy some new furniture.
3 _____

Your neighbour is ill in bed.

1 You're going to make him/her some food.
2 You're going to collect his/her children from school.
3 _____

You don't have much money at the moment.

1 You're going to ask your boss for more money.
2 You're going to stay at home in the evenings.
3 _____

It's your friend's birthday tomorrow.

1 You're going to buy him/her a present.
2 You're going to take him/her out for dinner.
3 _____

You're going on holiday on Wednesday.

1 You're going to get some foreign money.
2 You're going to look for your passport.
3 _____

You won a lot of money in a competition last week.

1 You're going to buy a new car.
2 You're going to give some money to charity.
3 _____

The weather forecast says it's going to be warm and sunny this weekend.

1 You're going to go to the beach.
2 You're going to have a barbecue.
3 _____

Your college plans to make some money for a local charity.

1 You're going to organize a fashion show.
2 You're going to sell some cakes.
3 _____

---

12 Grammar Honestly!

1   Work with a partner. Complete the conversation with the correct form of the verbs from the box.

> be (x7)   come   go   happen   meet (x3)   say (x4)   want

Dani   I've [1] _____ the director Steven Spielberg.

Max   Really? When [2] _____ you _____ him?

Dani   Two years ago.

Max   Where [3] _____ you?

Dani   I [4] _____ in London.

Max   Why [5] _____ you there?

Dani   I [6] _____ there for a job interview.

Max   How [7] _____ you _____ him?

Dani   I [8] _____ to a café for a coffee and he [9] _____ there, too.

Max   Why [10] _____ he there?

Dani   For the same reason as me, I suppose. He [11] _____ a coffee as well.

Max   [12] _____ he _____ anything to you?

Dani   Yes. The café [13] _____ very busy and he [14] _____ up to my table and [15] _____ , 'Is this seat free?'

Max   OK, and what [16] _____ you _____ to him?

Dani   In a loud voice I [17] _____ , 'Go away, Steve. Stop following me around.'

Max   I don't believe you!

Dani   Honestly, it really [18] _____ , I promise you!

2   Write three true sentences about experiences you have had. Example: *I've been to Australia.*

3   Work with your partner. Write your six sentences from exercise **2**. Mix up the sentences.

4a   Work in small groups. In your pairs, say your sentences to the other students. Ask and answer questions about the sentences. Guess who is telling the truth and complete 'Name' and 'Sentence' in the table.

  b   Check your answers with the other students. Tick (✔) or cross (✗) the boxes in the table.

Name	Sentence	Correct?
Gregor	... has been to Australia.	✓
Carola	... has met Mo Farah.	✗ (Gregor has met Mo Farah.)
		☐
		☐
		☐
		☐
		☐
		☐

Vocabulary

Unit 1 Who's Marcos?

Paired/Group activity, understanding family vocabulary to complete a family tree

Language
Family: *aunt, brother, son-in-law*, etc.

Preparation: Make one copy of the worksheet for each pair and cut the sheets in half.

Non-cut alternative: Make one copy of the worksheet for each pair and fold the sheets in half. Tell students not to look at the other halves.

1 Ask a selection of students to come to the front of the class and write their name, plus the names of one or two of their family members, on the board, e.g. *Petra + Karel and Sabrina*. Each student should explain to the class how each person is related to them, e.g. *Karel and Sabrina are my cousins.*

2 When the students at the front of the class have done this, see how much the class can remember. Ask students in turn to say how the people named on the board are related to the students, e.g. *Akiko, who are Karel and Sabrina*. Students should answer with complete sentences, e.g. *Karel and Sabrina are Petra's cousins.* Students can correct their classmates if they make a mistake.

3 Divide the class into groups, four students per group and sub-divide each group into pairs. Allocate each pair a letter A or B and give them the relevant section of the worksheet. They should not show these to the other pair. Give pair A ten minutes to complete as much of the family tree as possible by asking pair B about the people on their list, e.g. *Who's Alicia?* Pair B answers pair A's questions by reading the relevant information. Pair A writes the names in the relevant spaces on the tree. Pair A can also ask *Yes/No* questions to confirm their answers, e.g. *Is Alicia Antonio's mother?*, with pair B answering *Yes, she is.* or *No, she isn't.*

4 Once the ten minutes have passed, ask pairs to exchange their worksheet sections, giving pair B a chance to ask the questions.

5 Pairs A and B then work together to identify where Marcos is on the family tree on pair A's section of the worksheet, using the process of elimination. Once pairs have identified this, they should complete the sentence together. The first group to correctly complete the sentence is the winner. Check answers together as a class.

ANSWERS

1 **a** Alicia **b** Maria **c** Antonio **d** Clara **e** Marcos **f** Ana **g** Andrea **h** Yolanda **i** Ricardo **j** Lucia **k** Silvia **l** Fernando

2 Marcos is Clara's husband, Ricardo's father, Edmundo's uncle, Fernando's grandfather and Alberto's son-in-law.

Unit 2 Telling the time

Paired activity, with students exchanging information about what time they do daily activities to find similarities

Language
Telling the time: *half past, o'clock, quarter past/to, twenty minutes past*, etc.
Daily activities

Preparation: Make one copy of the worksheet for each pair and cut the sheets in half. You will also need some spare paper for each pair.

Non-cut alternative: Make one copy of the worksheet for each pair and fold the sheets in half. Tell students not to look at the other halves.

1 Review telling the time by drawing a clock face on the board. Draw the hands of the clock in different positions, asking students to call out the correct times.

2 Divide the class into pairs and give them a piece of spare paper. In their pairs, ask students to write three things they think you do every day, and at what time they think you do them. Ask pairs to read their sentences aloud to the class, and confirm if they are correct.

3 Allocate each partner a letter (A or B) and give them the relevant half of the worksheet. They should not show these to each other. Tell students they are the person on the worksheet and ask them to look at the information. Students take turns to ask and answer questions about what time they do the activities, e.g. *What time do you get up?* They should answer their partner's questions by referring to the clock faces on their section of the worksheet. If they do an activity at the same time, they should tick that activity; if they do it at a different time, they should cross the activity. The first pair to find the three activities done at the same time is the winner.

ANSWER

Activities done at the same time: have lunch (half past one), watch TV (nine o'clock), go to bed (eleven o'clock)

EXTRA SUPPORT Ask student As to work in pairs with other student As and the same for student Bs. In their pairs, they identify the different times for the activities on their section of the worksheet, and prepare questions and answers before the activity begins.

EARLY FINISHERS In their pairs, students compare their own daily routines and times with those on the worksheet. Encourage them to identify any similarities and differences.

EXTRA CHALLENGE In their pairs, encourage students to design an improved daily routine for each other or for you.

Unit 3 Guess the job

Paired activity, completing a puzzle and then asking and answering questions to guess jobs

Language

Jobs: *businessman/businesswoman, cleaner, dentist,* etc.
Conditions: *badly paid, well paid, work inside,* etc.

Preparation: Make one copy of the worksheet for each student.

1 Divide the class into pairs and give each student a copy of the worksheet. Give pairs five minutes to work together and complete the puzzle using the photo clues. Once the puzzle is complete, the first pair to find the mystery job using the letters from the outlined squares is the winner. Check answers as a class.

ANSWERS

1 1 businesswoman   2 musician   3 cleaner   4 chef
  5 student   6 photographer   7 hairdresser   8 pilot
  9 nurse   10 journalist   11 mechanic
2 dentist

2 Explain they are now going to play a guessing game in their pairs. First model exercise 3 by telling the class you are thinking of a job from exercise 1. Encourage the class to ask you *yes/no* questions to guess which job it is. If necessary, brainstorm the type of questions they can ask, e.g. *Does this person work outside?* Students try to guess the job within two minutes.

3 In their pairs, give students fifteen minutes to take turns choosing a job for their partners to guess. Students win a point for each job guessed within the time limit. Students lose a point for any incorrect guesses (thereby encouraging them to ask as many questions as they can first).

EARLY FINISHERS   Students play hangman using the jobs from exercise 1 or their own ideas. The game can be made more challenging if unusual or bizarre jobs are chosen.

EXTRA CHALLENGE   Students talk about the positive and negative aspects of each job in exercise 1, deciding which job(s) have the most positive points.

Unit 4 Design dictation

Paired activity, describing and drawing rooms and furniture in a flat based on floorplans

Language

Furniture: *armchair, bed, chair,* etc.
Rooms: *bathroom, bedroom, kitchen, living room*
Prepositions of place

Preparation: Make one copy of the worksheet for each pair and cut the sheets in half.

Non-cut alternative: Make one copy of the worksheet for each pair and fold the sheets in half. Tell students not to look at the other halves.

1 Ask students to tell you what they have in their bedroom or living room at home. Write their answers on the board and leave the words/phrases on the board for support during the activity.

2 Divide the class into pairs. Allocate each partner a letter (A or B) and give them the relevant half of the worksheet. They should not show these to each other. Elicit a few sentences to describe what is in the floorplans, e.g. *There's a washing machine in the kitchen.* Write some of these sentences on the board.

3 Student A describes their flat for student B. Student B then draws and labels the furniture in the blank floorplan (they can just draw a square and write a label for each item). Encourage students to use prepositions of place to describe where the furniture is, but they don't have to be completely accurate. Students then swap roles, with student B describing their flat for student A to draw.

4 Once pairs have finished, they can check answers by comparing their drawings to their partner's illustrations.

EXTRA SUPPORT   Ask student As to work in pairs with other student As and the same for student Bs. In their pairs, they write five sentences describing their floorplan together before the activity begins. Elicit two or three sentences for each floorplan and proceed with the activity.

EARLY FINISHERS   Students discuss which flat they prefer and why.

EXTRA CHALLENGE   Elicit other furniture vocabulary not covered in this lesson, and ask students to add them to their drawings, e.g. *lamp, desk, bookcase, basin, wardrobe, sofa.*

Unit 5 Who is it?

Group activity, playing a describing/guessing game about what people are wearing

Language

Clothes and accessories: *dress, glasses, gloves,* etc.

Preparation: Make one copy of the worksheet for each student. You will also need a large number of counters (or coins) to use as markers. Alternatively, students can cross out the illustrations in pencil and then rub out the pencil marks before the next round.

1 Describe a number of students in the class in terms of what they are wearing, e.g. *This person is wearing a black hoodie and a yellow T-shirt.* Ask students to guess who you are describing.

2 Students then do the same in pairs: one student describes another student in the room and their partner guesses who it is. Elicit a few sentences from the class and write them on the board, providing any necessary corrections.

3 Divide the class into groups (minimum of three students per group) and give each student a copy of the worksheet. Explain that students take turns to secretly choose a person on the worksheet. The other students in the group take turns to ask *yes/no* questions, e.g. *Is this person a man? Is he wearing a hat?* The student who has chosen the person replies with short answers, e.g. *Yes, he is.* As students ask questions, they can eliminate certain people, either by placing a counter/coin on the people or crossing them out with a pencil.

4 After eliminating people, students can make a guess. They score one point for each correct guess and lose a point for each incorrect guess. Once the person has been correctly identified, the game is repeated. Allow fifteen minutes for the game. The student with the highest score wins.

words (i.e. words from the target language that they can write at the bottom of their worksheet before the game begins). Monitor the game, instructing students to cover up their cheat words as they gain confidence and fluency.

Ask students to imagine more details about the people in the illustrations. Ask questions, e.g. *What is their job? What is their daily routine?* to recycle vocabulary from previous units.

Unit 6 Memories

Whole-class memory game, with students trying to remember where their classmates were at different times

> **Language**
> Time phrases: *at six o'clock, last week, two days ago,* etc.
> *was/were*

Preparation: Make one copy of the worksheet and cut it into sixteen cards.

1 Write the following on the board: *Where were you* _____ *8 p.m.* _____ *Saturday?* Encourage students to identify the missing words, *at, last/on.* Briefly ask some students this question, eliciting complete sentences, e.g. *I was at the cinema at 8 p.m. last Saturday.* Extend to include other questions and time phrases, e.g. *Where were you two hours* _____*? Where were you* _____ *2008?*

2 Give each student one of the cards or students can work in pairs/groups if you have more than sixteen students in the class. First ask them to complete the sentence by circling the correct option for them/their group *I was/ We were* and *my/our* and writing a time phrase. They can combine time phrases, if they like, to give a more specific time, e.g. *at half past two last Saturday.* Explain to students that their sentences do not have to be true for them.

3 The first student reads out their completed sentence to the rest of the class. The second student then repeats where the first student was and when, and then reads out their own sentence, e.g. *Miguel was at a nightclub last Saturday. I was at the theatre two weeks ago.* Each subsequent student repeats where the previous students were and when, before saying their own sentence. If they make a mistake about a previous student, the relevant student should correct them, e.g. *I wasn't at a nightclub last Sunday. I was at a nightclub last Saturday.*

4 The last few students to speak will have quite a challenge, as they will have to remember the most. So when the activity is finished, you could repeat it in reverse, i.e. with the last student to speak being the first student to speak in the new round.

Students imagine that they really were in the situation on their card. In pairs, they ask each other questions about where they were, e.g. *Who were you with? What was it like at the nightclub?* They then write a few sentences on a piece of spare paper about their partner's situation, using *was* and *were*, e.g. *Teresa was at a nightclub last Saturday at ten o'clock. She was with some of her friends. The music was really good, but there weren't many people there.*

Unit 7 A sporting chance

Paired activity, with students telling the class about a sport they do, and guessing which sports other students do

> **Language**
> Sports and fitness: *do yoga, play football, swim,* etc.

Preparation: Make one copy of the worksheet for each pair.

1 Divide the class into pairs and give each pair a copy of the worksheet. Ask them to look at the illustrations in exercise 1 and tell each other the names of the sports/ activities. Review answers as a class.

ANSWERS

1 swim 2 play basketball 3 cycle 4 play tennis
5 do yoga 6 jog/run 7 ski 8 do judo 9 do athletics
10 go fishing 11 play football 12 go to the gym

2 Tell pairs to imagine that they do one of the sports/ activities in the illustrations. They should tick the reasons why they do it in exercise 2a, and write sentences about the sport/activity in exercise 2b.

3 Focus students on exercise 3 and explain that they are now going to read their sentences from both exercise 2a and b to the rest of the class. The other students are going to guess what the sport/activity is. The first pair begins by reading their sentences to the class. As soon as a pair thinks they know what the sport/activity is, they raise their hands. The speaking pair should stop speaking at this point.

4 All pairs in the class should then make a guess, completing the first sentence in exercise 3 by writing down the names of the speaking students and the sport/ activity they think they do. The speaking students should also complete their sentence.

5 The process is repeated for the other pairs, with the rest of the class completing sentences 2–12. Students should continue their answers on the back of their sheet if there are more than twelve pairs in the class.

6 When all pairs have spoken, check answers as a class. Pairs should award themselves one point for each sport/activity they correctly identified. The winning pair is the students with the most points.

Unit 8 Parakeet Island

Paired/Group activity, choosing different things to do on a weekend away

> **Language**
> Holidays: *apartment, beach, swimming,* etc.

Preparation: Make one copy of the worksheet for each student and fold the sheets in half.

1 Divide the class into pairs and give each student a copy of the folded worksheet. Tell them not to look at the folded-over section yet. Give students five to ten minutes to read the advertisement in exercise 1 and rearrange the letters in bold to make words/phrases. Review answers as a class.

ANSWERS

1 hotels 2 apartments 3 guest houses 4 beaches
5 swimming 6 local people 7 museums 8 galleries
9 sightseeing 10 towns 11 tour 12 Trek

2 Ask students to turn over their worksheets and work individually to complete exercise 2. Explain that they are going to visit Parakeet Island this weekend and are going to choose what they want to do. Students read the sentences and tick one option for sentences 1–6.

3 Now divide the class into groups (between four and six students per group). Explain that they are going to Parakeet Island together this weekend and should work out an itinerary. Give students fifteen minutes to tell one another what they want to do and explain why they want to do this, e.g. *On Saturday morning, I want to lie on the beach and go swimming in the sea because I need to relax.* They should try to persuade the others in their group to do the same and agree on what they are going to do together.

4 After fifteen minutes, tell students to imagine that they have returned from their holiday on Parakeet Island. The groups should take turns to tell the others in the class what they did, either by nominating one student in the group to speak, or by taking turns.

EXTRA CHALLENGE Students work in pairs, imagining they are chatting on a social networking site. One student imagines they went to Parakeet Island while the other student stayed at home. The student who stayed at home writes questions, e.g. *Where did you stay? What did you eat?*, and the student who went writes appropriate answers. Give pairs ten minutes to write as many questions and answers as possible.

Unit 9 Let's cook

Paired activity, completing a recipe, then trying to remember it by ordering the kitchen items used in the recipe

Language
Cooking verbs: *boil, chop, fry*, etc.
Kitchen items and utensils: *bowl, saucepan, spoon*, etc.

Preparation: Make one copy of the worksheet for each pair and fold the sheets in half.

1 Ask the class to think of a well-known (but simple) dish. Ask students what the ingredients are, how you would prepare them, and the kitchen items you might need. Then ask students if they can think of other words for preparing food and the kitchen items needed for that type of preparation.

2 Divide the class into pairs and give each pair a copy of the folded worksheet. Tell them not to look at the folded-over section yet. Give students five minutes to complete the recipe by choosing the correct words. Review answers as a class.

ANSWERS

1 a roast b bake c fry d boil e chop f mix

3 Ask pairs to turn over their worksheets and look at exercise 2. They should first label the kitchen items.

4 In exercise 3, working from memory, pairs discuss in which order they would use these items to make the recipe in exercise 1, recycling the cooking verbs, e.g. *We need to fry the tomatoes and the onions so we need a frying pan.* Give students ten minutes to number the items in the correct order. The first pair to finish is the winner.

ANSWERS

2 a bowl b oven c fork d frying pan e kettle
f knife g microwave (oven) h food-processor
i plate j saucepan k (wooden) spoon

3 **Suggested order: a** 7/6 **b** 1 **c** 11 **d** 2 **e** 3 **f** 5
g 9 **h** 4 **i** 10 **j** 8 **k** 6/7

EXTRA SUPPORT Pairs can unfold their worksheet and refer to the recipe in exercise 1 while completing exercise 3.

EXTRA CHALLENGE In their original pairs, students make a list of ten ingredients. They then exchange lists with another pair, and try to think of a dish they could prepare with some or all of the ingredients they can add other ingredients if they like, but they must try to use as many of the ingredients as they were given. Encourage students to write the recipe, using the recipe in exercise 1 as a model.

Unit 10 Island tour

Paired activity, identifying islands that will be visited on a tour

Language
Nature and geography: *beach, coast, mountain*, etc.

Preparation: Make one copy of the worksheet for each pair and cut the sheets in half.

Non-cut alternative: Make one copy of the worksheet for each pair and fold the sheets in half. Tell students not to look at the other halves.

1 Write the following places on the board and ask students which words can precede or follow each one: *Copacabana _____ ; the Kalahari _____ ; _____ Geneva; the Andaman _____ ; Niagara _____ ; the Yellow _____ ; _____ Olympus; the Ivory _____ (Beach, Desert, Lake, Islands, Falls, River, Mount, Coast).* Ask them what *Mount* and *Falls* are short forms of *mountain* and *waterfalls*.

2 Briefly review *north, south, east* and *west* with the class, ask students where places are in the country where they are studying.

3 Divide the class into pairs. Allocate each partner a letter (A or B) and give them the relevant half of the worksheet. They should not show these to each other. Explain that they are going on a tour of an island group called the *Chilli Islands*. On their sections of the worksheet, they both have maps of the five islands they will visit. Student A has the names of the islands and the order in which they will visit them. Student B has the maps, but in a different order and with no names and numbers.

4 Student A begins by describing the islands in order and their features, e.g. *There are two lakes on Naga. They are in the west. There is a mountain in the middle of the island.* Student B asks questions to help them identify the islands and the order of the tour, e.g. *Are there any beaches on Naga? Where are they?*, labelling and numbering the islands in order.

5 When student B thinks they have matched the islands and numbers, they should compare their sections of the worksheet to check answers. The first pair to correctly name and number the islands is the winner.

EXTRA SUPPORT Ensure the student A section of the worksheet is allocated to less-able students, as their task is less complicated.

EARLY FINISHERS In their pairs, ask students to choose one of the islands and write a brief description for a travel brochure or website.

EXTRA CHALLENGE In their pairs, students write a travel blog describing their tour of the Chilli Islands and what they did while they were there, e.g. *On our first day, we visited Naga. In the morning, we walked through the rainforest in the east of the island, and then went to a beautiful beach on the west coast where we had lunch and swam in the sea …*

Unit 11 Can you recommend …?
Paired activity, with students finding out useful information about each other's towns

Language
Saying websites and email address
Technology

Preparation: Make one copy of the worksheet for each pair and cut the sheets in half.

Non-cut alternative: Make one copy of the worksheet for each pair and fold the sheets in half. Tell students not to look at the other halves.

1 Write the following information on the board:
   www.pizza-place/london.com
   info@pizza_place.com
   07628 866012
   Ask the class how we say the website, the email address and the phone number. It may also be helpful to review the following technology words before the activity begins: *GPS, website, smartphone, tablet, app*. Write the words on the board, jumbling the letters. Ask students to rearrange them to make the words.

2 Divide the class into pairs. Allocate each partner a letter (A or B) and give them the relevant half of the worksheet. They should not show these to each other. Explain that student A is going to visit student B's town, and student B is organizing a conference in student A's town. They are going to ask and answer questions about each other's towns in order to complete the tables on their sections of the worksheet.

3 Student A begins by asking student B to recommend somewhere to eat and an interesting place to visit in Westbridge. They will also need to ask for information about these places, e.g. *Where is it? What's the website? What's the email address?* Student B will answer student A's questions using the information on their section of the worksheet. Student B then asks student A to recommend somewhere to stay and a good taxi service in Eastport, finding out the information needed to complete their table.

4 After twenty minutes, stop the activity and check answers as a class. Try checking answers as choral drills, so that students can hear/practise the stress and intonation.

EXTRA SUPPORT Monitor students while they do the activity, and point out any mistakes they make, but do not correct them; instead, ask them questions, e.g. *Are you sure there should be a dash there?*

EXTRA CHALLENGE If students have smartphones (or if you have access to the internet), tell students to find websites for a hotel, a restaurant, a place to visit and a taxi company in the town/city where they are studying. In their pairs, they

then dictate these website addresses to a partner. Their partner checks they have recorded the addresses correctly by checking them online.

Unit 12 Culture club
Paired/Whole-class activity, guessing which activities other students did by matching conversations to photos

Language
Culture and the arts (verb and noun phrases): *go to a concert, see a film,* etc.

Preparation: Make one copy of the worksheet for each pair and fold the sheets in half. You will also need some spare paper for each pair.

1 Write the following on the board:
   _____ the guitar / in a band
   _____ an opera / a play / a film / a musical
   _____ to a rock concert / to a classical musical concert / to an art gallery / to a salsa class
   _____ painting / singing lessons
   Encourage students to identify the missing words (*play, see, go, have*). Leave the phrases on the board.

2 Divide the class into pairs and give each pair a copy of the worksheet and a piece of spare paper. Tell them not to look at the folded-over section on their worksheets yet. Ask them to read the conversation in exercise 1 and try to guess what activity Lottie and Nadine did.

ANSWER
Lottie and Nadine saw an opera.

3 Next, ask students to turn their worksheets over and look at exercise 2. Invite each pair to the front of the class and allocate each pair one of the activities you wrote on the board in stage 1 in secret. Whisper an activity to them or write it down for them, e.g. *You saw a film.*

4 Students imagine that they have just done this activity. In their pairs, they should write a brief conversation (similar to the one in exercise 1 on their worksheet) on a sheet of spare paper. The only rule is that they can't mention the activity in their conversation.

5 Pairs then take turns to read and act out their conversations to the class. The other pairs guess what activity they did and complete the sentences in exercise 2 next to the relevant illustration, using the activities from the board. If you don't have enough students in your class to allocate all the activities, explain that they won't need to complete all the sentences.

6 When all pairs have acted out their conversations, students check their answers by mingling as a whole class and asking each other questions, e.g. *Peter and Samira, did you see a film?* They award themselves a point for each correct answer. The winning pair is the students with the most points.

EXTRA CHALLENGE In their pairs, students imagine that the town or city where they are studying is going to host a cultural festival. They should choose and write about two or three cultural events that they think would appeal to visitors, e.g. a music concert. They should try and include as much detail as possible about the event. Each pair then has a few minutes to tell the others in the class about which events they chose. The class can then vote for four or five of the events to include in the festival.

1 Vocabulary Who's Marcos?

Pair A

1 Ask pair B about the people from the box. Complete the family tree.

Example: Who's Alicia?

Alicia Ana Andrea Antonio Clara Fernando Lucia Maria Ricardo Silvia Yolanda

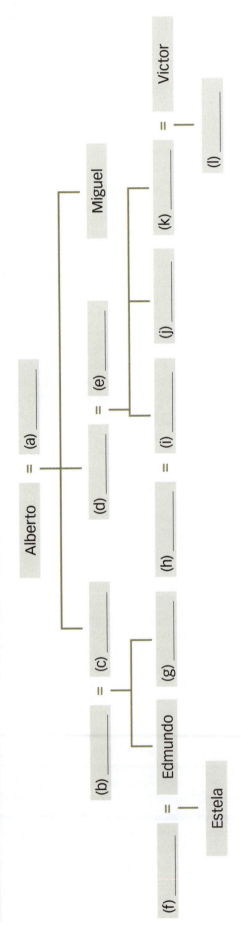

2 Work with pair B. Where is Marcos in the family tree? Complete the sentence.

Marcos is Clara's _____ , Ricardo's _____ , Edmundo's _____ , Fernando's _____ and Alberto's _____ .

- -

Pair B

1 Answer pair A's questions using the information.

Alicia is Alberto's wife and Edmundo's grandmother.

Ana is Edmundo's wife and Estela's mother.

Andrea is Edmundo's sister and Maria's daughter.

Antonio is Alberto's son and Andrea's father.

Clara is Miguel's sister and Andrea's aunt.

Fernando is Lucia's nephew and Silvia's son.

Lucia is Antonio's niece and Silvia's sister.

Maria is Antonio's wife and Edmundo's mother.

Ricardo is Clara's son and Yolanda's husband.

Silvia is Victor's wife and Clara's daughter.

Yolanda is Ricardo's wife and Fernando's aunt.

2 Work with pair A. Where is Marcos in the family tree?

2 Vocabulary Telling the time

Student A

1a You are Maria/Mario. You are a doctor. Here is some information about your day.

Work with student B. Ask and answer questions about your days. Tick (✔) the activities you do at the same time.
Cross (✘) the activities you do at different times.

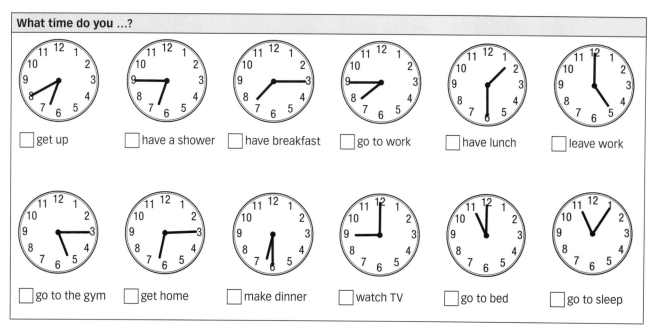

What time do you ...?

☐ get up   ☐ have a shower   ☐ have breakfast   ☐ go to work   ☐ have lunch   ☐ leave work

☐ go to the gym   ☐ get home   ☐ make dinner   ☐ watch TV   ☐ go to bed   ☐ go to sleep

b Which three things do you do at the same time?

Student B

1a You are Chris/Christine. You are a teacher. Here is some information about your day.

Work with student A. Ask and answer questions about your days. Tick (✔) the activities you do at the same time.
Cross (✘) the activities you do at different times.

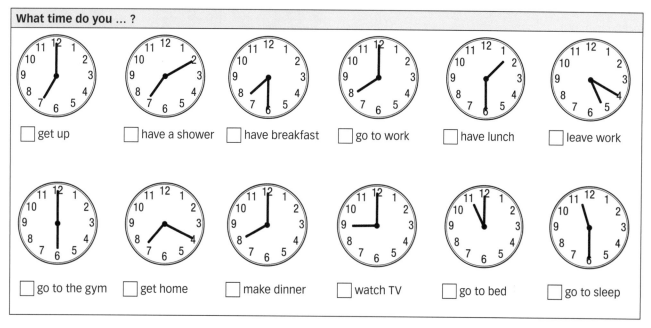

What time do you ... ?

☐ get up   ☐ have a shower   ☐ have breakfast   ☐ go to work   ☐ have lunch   ☐ leave work

☐ go to the gym   ☐ get home   ☐ make dinner   ☐ watch TV   ☐ go to bed   ☐ go to sleep

b Which three things do you do at the same time?

1   Work with a partner. Complete the puzzle with the words 1–11.

2   Find the mystery job in the puzzle.

3   Take turns to choose a job from the puzzle. Ask and answer questions. Can you guess the job in two minutes?

4 Vocabulary Design dictation

Student A

1 Describe your flat and furniture to student B.

2 Listen to student B describe their flat. Draw and label the furniture.

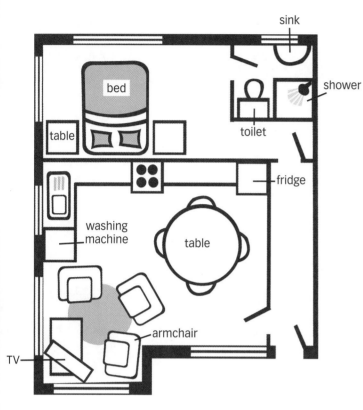

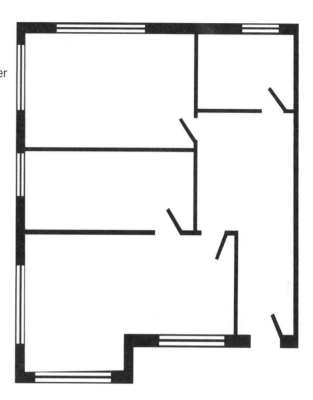

Student B

1 Listen to student A describe their flat. Draw and label the furniture.

2 Describe your flat and furniture to student A.

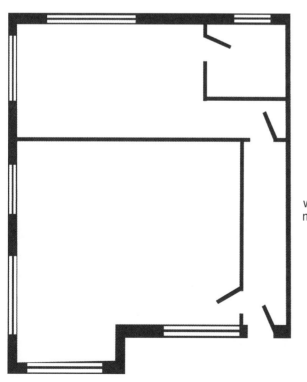

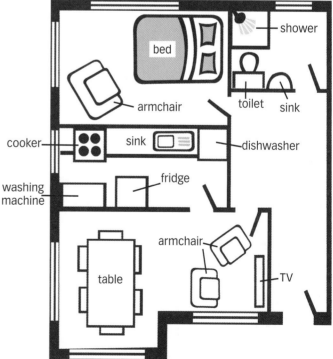

5 Vocabulary Who is it?

Tara	Abdullah	Jun Ho	Valentina
Max	Hong-li	Tatiana	Gizem
Pedro	Takahiro	Sarah	Mei

6 Vocabulary Memories

I was / We were at a nightclub _____ _____ .	*I was / We were* at the theatre _____ _____ .	*I was / We were* on holiday _____ _____ .	*I was / We were* at the swimming pool _____ .

I was / We were in a restaurant _____ _____ .	*I was / We were* at home _____ _____ .	*I was / We were* at a party _____ _____ .	*I was / We were* on *my / our* computer _____ .

I was / We were in the park _____ _____ .	*I was / We were* at a football match _____ .	*I was / We were* at the shops _____ _____ .	*I was / We were* in the car _____ _____ .

I was / We were at work _____ _____ .	*I was / We were* in the garden _____ _____ .	*I was / We were* at the cinema _____ _____ .	*I was / We were* in Australia _____ _____ .

COMING SOON

7 Vocabulary A sporting chance

1   Work with a partner. Look at the illustrations. What are the sports/activities?

1

2

3

4

5

6

7

8

9

10

11

12

2a   Imagine that you and your partner do one of the sports/activities. Tick (✔) the reasons why you do it.

☐ We do it to keep fit.   ☐ We do it to meet friends.   ☐ We do it to have fun.
☐ We do it to win.   ☐ We do it to lose weight.   ☐ We do it to learn something new.

b   Write three sentences about the sport/activity with your own ideas.

We do it outside.

We wear special clothes.

1 _____

2 _____

3 _____

3   Say your sentences from exercise **2** to the class. Do not say the sport/activity.
Listen to the other pairs. Guess the sport. Complete the sentences.

1 We think that _____ and _____ _____ .

2 We think that _____ and _____ _____ .

3 We think that _____ and _____ _____ .

4 We think that _____ and _____ _____ .

5 We think that _____ and _____ _____ .

6 We think that _____ and _____ _____ .

7 We think that _____ and _____ _____ .

8 We think that _____ and _____ _____ .

9 We think that _____ and _____ _____ .

10 We think that _____ and _____ _____ .

11 We think that _____ and _____ _____ .

12 We think that _____ and _____ _____ .

8 Vocabulary Parakeet Island

1 Work with a partner. Rearrange the letters in **bold** to complete the advertisement.

Visit Parakeet Island this summer
The island that has everything you need for a wonderful holiday!

Stay in comfortable [1] **olsthe** _____ ,
[2] **nametrtspa** _____ and [3] **segut oesuhs** _____ .

Lie on beautiful [4] **acbhees** _____ .

Go [5] **mngsmiwi** _____ in the clear, blue sea.

Meet friendly [6] **olcla leeopp** _____ .

Visit interesting [7] **esumsmu** _____ and art [8] **rilgaesle** _____ .

Go [9] **htsigeinseg** _____ in the [10] **wsnto** _____ and villages.

Go on a [11] **orut** _____ of the island.

[12] **kert** _____ in the hills and countryside.

---

2 You are going to Parakeet Island this weekend. What do you want to do?
Choose and tick (✔) one option each from 1–6.

1 You want to stay in:
  ☐ an apartment by the beach.
  ☐ a cheap hotel or guest house in the town.
2 You want to eat and drink in:
  ☐ family restaurants in the town (these are quite cheap, but the food is very good).
  ☐ cafés by or on the beach (these are quite expensive, but the food is very good).
3 On Saturday morning, you want to:
  ☐ lie on the beach and go swimming in the sea.
  ☐ go sightseeing in the towns.
4 On Saturday afternoon, you want to:
  ☐ trek in the countryside.
  ☐ visit a ruined temple in the mountain.
5 On Sunday morning, you want to:
  ☐ visit a museum of local culture.
  ☐ go on a tour of the island with a guide.
6 On Sunday afternoon, you want to:
  ☐ meet local people and learn about the local culture.
  ☐ visit a famous art gallery.

3 Work in small groups. Discuss the things your group chose in exercise **2**. Agree on a plan for the weekend.

4 You have just come back from Parakeet Island. Tell the class about your weekend.

9 Vocabulary Let's cook

1 Work with a partner. Choose the correct word to complete the recipe.

Pasta in a tomato sauce with chicken

1 First of all, you need to ᵃ *bake / roast* a chicken (at the same time, you could also ᵇ *bake / roast* some bread to go with your meal).

2 While the chicken is cooking, you should ᶜ *chop / fry* some tomatoes and onions in a little oil until they are soft.

3 When the tomatoes and onions are soft, ᵈ *boil / fry* about 200 ml of water.

4 Add the water to the tomatoes and onions, and make it into a sauce.

5 When the chicken is cooked, ᵉ *chop / mix* it into small pieces.

6 Then ᶠ *chop / mix* the chicken together with the sauce.

7 Now cook some pasta.

8 When the pasta is ready, warm up the chicken and sauce.

9 Finally, serve the pasta with the sauce and eat it.

----

2 Label the illustrations.

a

b 1

_____ *oven*

c

d

e

f

g

h

i

j

k

3 Remember the recipe in exercise **1**. Put the kitchen items in the order they are used in the recipe.

Student A

1 Tell student B about the islands you will visit on the tour.
They are in the correct order. Answer student B's questions.

The Chilli Islands

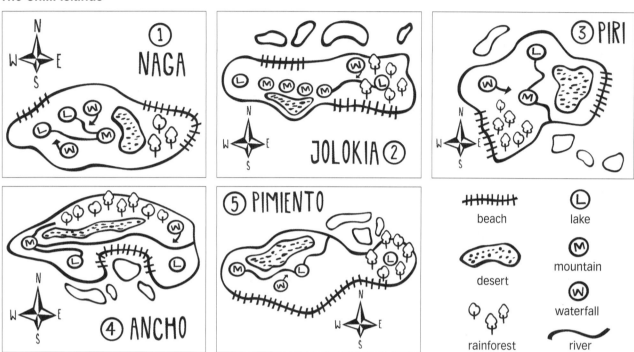

Student B

1 Ask student A questions about the islands you will visit on the tour. Put the
islands in the order you will visit them. Label the islands with names from the box.

Ancho   Jolokia   Naga   Pimiento   Piri

The Chilli Islands

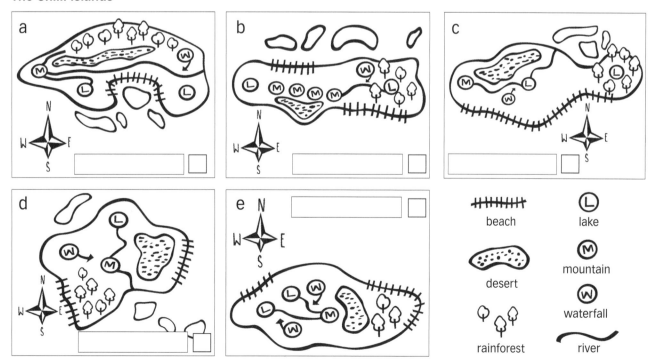

11 Vocabulary Can you recommend ...?

Student A

1 You are going to visit Westbridge. Ask student B questions to complete the table.

Westbridge				
Somewhere to eat			**An interesting place to visit**	
Name of restaurant			Name of attraction	
Where is it?			Where is it?	
Website			Website	
Email			Email	
More useful information				

2 Answer student B's questions using the information about Eastport:

- You think that the Sea View Hotel is very comfortable. It is on High Street. Its website is www.sea-view-hotel/Eastport.com. You can email them at contactus@sea_view_hotel.com.
- The best taxi service in your town is called A to B Taxis. It is on Station Road. Its website is www.a-to-b-taxis.co.uk. You can email them at information@a_to_b_taxis.co.uk.
- Student B can text or call you if they need help. Your mobile number is 0878 621349.

Student B

1 Answer student A's questions using the information about Westbridge:

- You think that the best place to eat in town is a restaurant called The Angry Pepper. It is on Old Street. Its website is www.the-angry-pepper.com. You can email them at theangrypepper/bookings@mymail.com.
- Westbridge Castle is a very interesting place to visit. It is on Castle Hill. Its website is www.westbridgecastle.com. You can email them at visit_westbridge_castle@mailworld.com.
- Your town has a GPS app that you can download to a tablet or smartphone from the website www.westbridge/gps.com.

2 You are going to visit Eastport. Ask student A questions to complete the table.

Eastport				
Somewhere to stay			**A good taxi service**	
Name of hotel			Name of company	
Where is it?			Where is it?	
Website			Website	
Email			Email	
More useful information				

12 Vocabulary Culture club

1   Work with a partner. Read the conversation. What activity did Lottie and Nadine do?

Lottie	What did you think?
Nadine	Well, I don't like that sort of music, but I enjoyed it.
Lottie	Me, too. The musicians were good, and some of the singers were excellent.
Nadine	Did you understand what they were singing about?
Lottie	No. I don't speak Italian!

---

2   Your teacher will tell you and your partner an activity. Write a short conversation
about the activity you did. Do not write the name of the activity.

3a Take turns to act out your conversation to the class. Guess what activities
the other students did. Complete the sentences.

Lottie and
Nadine saw an opera .

1

_____ and
_____
_____ .

2

_____ and
_____
_____ .

3

_____ and
_____
_____ .

4

_____ and
_____
_____ .

5

_____ and
_____
_____ .

6

_____ and
_____
_____ .

7

_____ and
_____
_____ .

8

_____ and
_____
_____ .

9

_____ and
_____
_____ .

10

_____ and
_____
_____ .

11

_____ and
_____
_____ .

b   Check your answers with the other students. Ask and answer questions.

Communication

Unit 1 Something in common

Whole-class activity, with students mingling to obtain personal information about one another, then identifying things they have in common

Language
Asking for personal information: *What's your name/ nationality/job?*, etc.
Asking for clarification: *Can you repeat …? How do you spell …?*, etc.

Preparation: Make one copy of the worksheet for each student.

1 Tell students to imagine they are joining an English language club in their home city. The club needs some personal information about them. Elicit the questions needed to fill in the information on the worksheet, e.g. *What's your name? What's your nationality?* Write students' suggestions on the board, correcting any mistakes.

2 Ask two or three students the questions on the board. Ask for further clarification, if appropriate, e.g. *Could you repeat that, please?* When you have finished, erase the questions from the board.

3 Give a copy of the worksheet to each student. Give students fifteen minutes to walk around the classroom and ask as many students as possible (up to a maximum of ten) questions in order to complete the forms. They should ask one another for clarification if something is unclear.

4 When their time is up, students return to their places. They independently answer questions 1–4 in exercise 2, referring to their completed forms in exercise 1. If necessary, clarify these questions with the class first. Students should add up the numbers they wrote after each question and convert these into points. The student with the most points is the 'winner'.

Unit 2 What's on?

Paired activity, making suggestions and deciding how to spend a weekend away using a *What's on* guide

Language
Making suggestions and arrangements: *Do you want to …?/Would you like to …? Let's …, What time do you want to …? Where shall we …?*, etc.
Accepting: *Yes, I'd love to. Yes, that sounds nice.*, etc.
Refusing: *I'm sorry, but …, Thanks, but I'm afraid I …*, etc.

Preparation: Make one copy of the worksheet for each pair.

1 Write the following three headings on the board: *Making suggestions and arrangements*, *Accepting* and *Refusing*. Ask students for phrases to write under each heading. If necessary, give examples, ensuring all the phrases from the *Language for speaking* box on page 22 of the Coursebook are covered. Drill the phrases, focusing on intonation.

2 Divide the class into pairs, giving each pair a copy of the worksheet. Tell pairs that they are going to spend the weekend in Singapore together. They need to plan how to spend their time. Ask them to read the *What's on* guide and think about what they would like to do.

3 Pairs then take turns to make suggestions and accept or refuse their partner's suggestions, e.g. *Would you like to go to the jazz club on Saturday evening? Yes, I'd love to./ Thanks, but I'm afraid I don't like jazz.* They must agree on six activities to do together and what day and time to do them, making notes on the back of the worksheet.

4 Pairs should join up with another pair and compare their itineraries.

EXTRA SUPPORT Draw a table on the board with three column headings as follows: *Saturday morning*, *Saturday afternoon* and *Saturday evening*. Draw another table and repeat for *Sunday morning*, etc. Encourage students to use the tables to help prompt them while making notes on their itinerary.

EXTRA CHALLENGE Students design their own *What's on* guide for their local area or a city of their choice, which can then be displayed around the classroom.

Unit 3 Ask me something!

Group activity, playing a board game to practise making, accepting and refusing requests

Language
Making requests: *Can/Could I … (, please)? Can/Could you … (, please)?*, etc.
Accepting: *Sure. Yes, of course/that's fine*, etc.
Refusing: *I'm afraid not. No, I'm sorry, but …*, etc.

Preparation: Make one copy of the worksheet for each group (maximum of four students per group). You will also need a counter for each student and a dice for each group.

1 Make requests to students in the class, e.g. *Could you open the window? Can you lend me a pen?* Ask for more examples of requests around the classroom, and ways to accept or refuse them. Write these phrases on the board for extra support during the activity, if necessary.

2 Divide the class into groups, giving them a copy of the worksheet, the dice and counters. Ask students to place their counters on START. Explain that students take turns to roll the dice.

3 Demonstrate the game by rolling the dice and moving a counter along the board. If you land on a square with a verb or an illustration, make a request to the student on your left, using that verb or illustration as a prompt. The student to your left rolls the dice to decide how to answer: for scores of 1, 3 or 5, the student on your left politely refuses your request and gives a reason; for scores of 2, 4 or 6, the student accepts the request. If your request is refused, don't move your counter and explain that it is the next player's turn to roll the dice; if your request is accepted, move your counter one space. It is then the

next player's turn. Also explain that if a player lands on *Ask your teacher*, they should think of a typical classroom request to ask you, e.g. *Could you help me with this exercise, please?* There is no need to roll the dice to decide how to answer in these instances. You can decide whether to give a positive or negative response.

4 Groups play the game until the first player finishes.

EXTRA SUPPORT Write the verbs from the board game on the board before play starts. Students practise making requests with these verbs before playing the game. Also encourage students to identify the requests in the illustration prompts on the board game.

EARLY FINISHERS Encourage students to select a verb from the board game. How many different requests can they think of using just that one verb?

EXTRA CHALLENGE The board game can be played in pairs rather than in groups.

Unit 4 Which hotel?

Group activity, giving directions to different hotels, and deciding which hotel to stay in

> **Language**
>
> Giving directions: *go straight on, it's on the left/right/ corner/at the end of the road, it's opposite the museum/ park/train station, take the first/second left/right, turn left/ right*, etc.

Preparation: Make one copy of the worksheet for each group (maximum of four students per group), cutting the sheet into the four cards.

Non-cut alternative: Make one copy of the worksheet for each student and fold the sheets so that only one card is showing. Tell students not to look at the other cards.

1 Elicit from the class directions from your classroom or school to a nearby location, e.g. *a park*. Write this language on the board. Ensure the key phrases from the *Language for speaking* box on page 43 of the Coursebook are covered, ask for directions to more than one place, if necessary.

2 Divide the class into groups. Allocate each student in the group a letter (A, B, C or D) and give them the relevant section of the worksheet. Explain to the class that each student in the group has a different hotel marked on their map. In their groups, students take turns to give directions to their hotel, starting from the train station. The other students in the group follow the directions and mark the new hotel on their map.

3 Once all students have given directions to their hotels, students check answers by showing each other their maps. If anyone has a hotel in the wrong place, the directions can be repeated and the group can all help correct the problem.

4 Finally, encourage students to imagine they are going on holiday together, and discuss which hotel they would most like to stay at, based on what is near each hotel and what they all like doing on holiday. Encourage students to consider all the options and try to persuade each other that their choice is best until they reach an agreement.

5 As a whole class, discuss which hotel is the most popular and why.

EXTRA SUPPORT Ensure the student A section of the worksheet is allocated to less-able students, as the directions to Hotel A are less complicated.

EARLY FINISHERS Students take turns to give directions to the other places on the map, starting from the train station each time.

EXTRA CHALLENGE Students write directions from their home to a place they like to visit, e.g. *a café*.

Unit 5 High-street shopping

Group activity, playing a board game to practise asking for things in a shop

> **Language**
>
> Language for shopping: *Can I help you? Can I pay by card? Do you sell …? How much is …? Yes, of course./No, I'm afraid we only take cash.*, etc.

Preparation: Make one copy of the worksheet for each group (maximum of four students per group). You will also need a counter for each student and a dice for each group.

1 Write the following shops on the board and ask students which ones they go to most often: *baker's, book shop, butcher's, clothes shop, newsagent's, shoe shop, supermarket.* They should work as a class to order the shops by how often they are visited on average by the whole class.

2 Divide the class into groups, giving them a copy of the worksheet, the dice and counters. Ask two students to place their counters on *The Real Deal Supermarket*, and the other two students to place their counters on *Flowerdales Supermarket*. Explain that students take turns to roll the dice. The aim of the game is to collect all the items on their shopping list (point to the table on the worksheet).

3 Demonstrate the game by rolling the dice and moving a counter along the board (the squares on the high street). At each square on the street, there are one or two adjacent shops that a player can choose to visit to try and buy the items on their shopping list. (They can't enter more than one shop on each turn.)

4 To buy something in the shop, the student talks to the player on their left, who acts as the shop assistant. Before starting the conversation, the shop assistant rolls the dice to determine the outcome of the conversation (referring to the *Shop assistants* prompts on the worksheet). If there are no problems, the student can buy the item and tick it off their shopping list. If the shop doesn't have the item, it is too expensive or the shop takes cash only, the student can't buy that item, and play moves to the next player. If necessary, roll the dice a couple of times with a confident student and model typical conversations between the shopper and the shop assistant, e.g. *Hello. Can I help you? Do you sell cookbooks? Yes, we do. Here you are. How much is this one? It's £5.00. Can I pay by card? No, I'm afraid we only take cash.*

5 When they get to the end of the high street, the supermarkets count as a square, and they then move back along the street in the other direction. If a student lands exactly on one of the supermarkets, they can buy one item only without needing to have a conversation with a shop assistant – they can simply choose one item from their shopping list and tick it.

6 The game continues in this way, with students moving up and back down the high street trying to buy the items on their shopping list. The winner is the first student to successfully buy everything on the list. Monitor students while playing the game to ensure they are carrying out a full conversation and using the phrases from Unit 5.4 of the Coursebook.

Unit 6 The right response

Paired/Group activity, practising showing interest as a listener, and making appropriate responses

Language
Showing interest as a listener: *Really? That's great! That's terrible!*, etc.

Preparation: Make one copy of the worksheet for each pair and fold the sheets in half. You will also need some spare paper for each pair.

1 Divide the class into pairs and give each pair a copy of the worksheet as well as a piece of spare paper. Ask them to focus on the conversations in exercise 1. Give students five minutes to complete the responses with a word from the box. Review answers as a class. Ask them to identify which phrases are used to respond to bad news, which are used to show interest and which are used to respond to good news. Drill the phrases with your class, paying particular attention to the stress and intonation.

ANSWERS
1 no   2 awful/terrible 3 nightmare   4 terrible/awful
5 Really   6 you   7 interesting   8 great/brilliant
9 brilliant/great

2 Tell students to unfold their worksheets and look at exercise 2. In their pairs, give students fifteen minutes to complete the table by writing nine mini-conversations. They should begin by filling in the responses (speaker B) using the phrases in exercise 1, but in a different order. They should then write sentences (speaker A) that would elicit this response from speaker B.

3 Once their tables are complete, ask each pair to join with another pair. Pairs take turns to read out their speaker A sentences. The other pair writes down an appropriate speaker B response on the spare sheet of paper. The first pair then reads out their sentence again, and the other pair says their response. The first pair should tell them if they are right or wrong, but remind students that phrases like *That's great!* and *That's brilliant!* have a similar meaning, so either answer would be correct.

4 The winning pair is the students in each group who gave the most correct responses.

EXTRA CHALLENGE In their groups of four, students should tell one another about something that really happened to them. This could be a sentence or a short story. As a group, they choose one student's story and tell it to the rest of the class. After listening and responding appropriately, as in the main activity, the class should guess which student in the group it really happened to.

Unit 7 What do you think?

Group activity, talking about ways of improving an international college

Language
Agreeing and disagreeing: *You're right. Yes, but …*, etc.
Asking for and giving opinions: *What do you think (of …)? I think …*, etc.

Preparation: Make one copy of the worksheet for each group (maximum of three students per group), cutting the sheets into the three sections.

Non-cut alternative: Make one copy of the worksheet for each student and fold the sheets so that only one section is showing. Tell students not to look at the other sections.

1 Tell the class that you think students learn more when they enjoy their studies. Ask them what they think about this, and review phrases for agreeing/disagreeing and asking for/giving opinions from the *Language for speaking* box on page 72 of the Coursebook.

2 Divide the class into groups. Allocate each student in the group a letter (A, B or C) and give them the relevant section of the worksheet. Tell students to imagine that they are either studying or working at a college called Hampton International College, and that the people who run the college are going to make it a better place for its students. The illustrations on their sections of the worksheet show some of the suggestions that are being considered.

3 Students independently choose one of the four suggestions on their section of the worksheet that they think will make the college a better place. Then give students ten minutes to take turns to tell the other students in their group about all the illustrations on their section of the worksheet, i.e. all the suggestions for improving the college, then explain which one they chose and why, e.g. *I chose a cinema. I think this is a good suggestion because students can watch films in English.*

4 Now give the groups ten minutes to choose just one suggestion from the three proposals they have independently chosen. They will do this by asking for/giving opinions and agreeing/disagreeing, as necessary, e.g. *I don't know about that. For me a minibus is really useful. Students can go to museums and different places.*

5 After ten minutes, ask each group which one suggestion they chose, and write these on the board.

6 Extend this to a whole-class activity, if possible, by telling students that of the suggestions you wrote on the board, they can only choose one proposal. What one suggestion can they all agree on (if any) that will make the college a better place for the students?

EARLY FINISHERS Groups think of some proposals other than those shown in the illustrations that could make the college a better place.

Unit 8 South Port to North End

Paired activity, asking for and giving information at a train station

Language
Asking for information: *How much does a ticket cost? When is the next train to …? When would you like to come back …? Which platform does it leave from? Would you like a single or return?*, etc.

Preparation: Make one copy of the worksheet for each pair and cut the sheets in half.

Non-cut alternative: Make one copy of the worksheet for each pair and fold the sheets in half. Tell students not to look at the other halves.

1 Tell students to imagine they are in a ticket office of a large railway station in London and want to catch a train. What language might they need to book a ticket? Write their suggestions on the board, correcting any mistakes. Erase these from the board before moving on to the next stage.

2 Divide the class into pairs. Allocate each partner a letter (A or B) and give them the relevant half of the worksheet. They should not show these to each other. Ask students A and B to read their sections of the worksheet. Summarize that student A needs to make a train journey with their young nephew, and is going to book some tickets. Student B works at the station ticket office and is going to help them do this. Point out that it is currently 7.15 a.m., as this will affect the first part of their exchange. Also point out that student A has a budget of £60.

3 Student A begins by explaining to student B where they want to go, when they need to be there and who they are travelling with. They should use the prompts in the table on their section of the worksheet to ask questions, e.g. *When is the next train to North End? What platform does it leave from? How much is an adult return? How much is a child single?* Student B tells them their options, using the information on their section of the worksheet, and gives other information that student A asks for or which may be useful or important (platform numbers, ticket prices, etc.). Give student A ten minutes to fill in their table with the relevant information.

4 Once the ten minutes have passed, ask students to exchange their worksheet sections, giving student B a chance to ask for information.

5 When students have completed their tables, they should check their answers with you. Point out any mistakes they have made, but do not correct them. The activity continues until the first pair has all the correct answers.

ANSWERS

Next train to North End leaves at	7.35 a.m.
Train arrives in North End at	9.25 a.m.
Train leaves from platform number	7
Train from North End leaves at	6.10 p.m.
Train arrives in South Port at	7.45 p.m.
Train leaves from platform number	2
Ticket price	Adult return: £40 Child single: £15 Class: second
Total cost of tickets	£55

EXTRA SUPPORT Ensure the student B section of the worksheet is allocated to less-able students, as this person has a slightly easier task.

EXTRA CHALLENGE Ask students to write *True/False* statements about the journey. They take turns to read these to the class for them to identify as true or false, e.g. *The next train leaves at 7.35 a.m. (True) An adult second-class return costs £55. (False)* Students could also think of other questions they might ask when booking a journey by train, bus, plane, etc., e.g. *Can I buy food on the train? Do I need to change anywhere?*

Unit 9 Ten conversations

Paired activity, acting out different situations in a restaurant

Language
Ordering food in a restaurant: *Would you like a starter/ some dessert/more drinks? Can/Could I/we see the menu/ order?*, etc.

Preparation: Make one copy of the worksheet for each pair and cut the sheets in half.

Non-cut alternative: Make one copy of the worksheet for each pair and fold the sheets in half. Tell students not to look at the other halves.

1 Tell students to imagine they are in a restaurant in an English-speaking country. Go through the different stages of the meal with the class, from the customer entering the restaurant to asking for the bill at the end. Elicit the phrases from the *Language for speaking* box on page 93 of the Coursebook and write these on the board. Erase these from the board before moving on to the next stage.

2 Divide the class into pairs. Allocate each partner a role (customer or waiter) and give them the relevant half of the worksheet. They should not show these to each other. Explain that they are in a restaurant, and they are going to have ten short conversations together. Demonstrate how the activity works by modelling the example conversation with you as the customer and a student as the waiter. Read out the first question in bold: *Can I sit outside?* The student then chooses the appropriate response in bold in the Waiter table: *I'm sorry, but there are no free tables outside at the moment.* You then ask the question in bold from the Customer table: *Never mind. Can I sit by the window instead?* The student ends the conversation using their other bold sentence from the Waiter table: *Of course. I think there's a free table.* Point out that each conversation has four parts to it.

3 Give pairs fifteen minutes to act out as many conversations as possible, using the other questions and responses. Once they have used a question/response, they should cross it out.

4 Review answers by choosing pairs to act out their conversations.

ANSWERS

Customer

1 Can I sit outside?
   I'm sorry, but there are no free tables outside at the moment.
   Never mind. Can I sit by the window instead?
   Of course. I think there's a free table.

2 Could I see the menu?
Certainly. Here you are. And as well as the dishes on the menu, there are also some on the board.
Where's the board?
It's on the wall by the door.

3 Can I order now?
Certainly. What would you like?
I'd like the steak, please.
Would you like any chips with that?

4 Could I have some more bread, please?
Of course. I'll bring some over. Would you like some butter, too?
Yes, please. And can I have a glass of water, too?
Yes, would you like some ice in that?

5 Excuse me, could I pay now?
Of course. I'll get your bill.
Can I pay by credit card?
I'm sorry, but the machine is broken and we can only take cash at the moment.

Waiter

1 Would you like to order now?
I'm not quite ready. Could you give me another minute?
Yes. Just call me when you're ready.
I will, thanks.

2 Would you like a starter?
Yes, please. What's the soup of the day?
It's tomato and red pepper.
That sounds nice. I'll have that, please.

3 Would you like any side dishes with that?
Yes, please. Could I have a green salad with it?
Would you like anything on the salad?
A little olive oil and lemon juice would be nice, thanks.

4 Would you like something to drink?
Yes, could I have some apple juice, please?
I'm afraid we don't have any. Would you like orange instead?
Yes, that would be fine. With lots of ice, please.

5 Would you like some dessert?
No, thank you. I couldn't eat another thing.
How about a coffee?
No, thanks. I don't want to be awake half the night.

5 Finally, ask pairs to have their own conversations using the opening sentences on their sections of the worksheet. This time, the customers and waiters should switch roles.

EXTRA CHALLENGE Students act out a customer/waiter situation in which the customer is very awkward or demanding.

Unit 10 The ultimate adventure kit

Paired/Group activity, choosing items for a kit for outdoor adventure activities

Language
Giving preferences: *The most important/best/most useful thing is …, I'd prefer to … because …, X is a better way than Y because …*

Preparation: Make one copy of the worksheet for each pair.

1 Ask students if they have ever been on an outdoor activity holiday, e.g. camping, trekking. What items did they take with them? Write a few of their suggestions on the board.

2 Divide the class into pairs. Ask students to imagine they are going to spend a week walking in the hills. They can take just one of the items on the board. What would they take? Let them discuss this in their pairs for a few minutes, ensuring they use the language for giving preferences and reasons from the *Language for speaking* box on page 102 of the Coursebook. Then ask them for feedback. What did they choose and why? Why did they choose one thing over another?

3 Give each pair a copy of the worksheet. Explain that they and their partner run a company that sells equipment for people who enjoy adventure activities. They have decided to sell an ultimate outdoor adventure kit of twelve items. In their pairs, give them fifteen minutes to choose eight items from the illustrations on their sheet. They should also choose four more items of their own choice (i.e. items not shown on the worksheet). Working together, and using language of preference, they make their choices and write these at the bottom of the worksheet.

4 Once they have done this, ask students to join with another pair to form small groups. They compare their twelve items. Give the groups ten minutes to prepare a new list of twelve items, writing the list on the back of one of their worksheets, selecting the best items from their two lists. This will involve pairs persuading each other of the benefits of their preferred items, and why these might be better or more useful than others.

5 The groups then tell the rest of the class about their kit. The class votes for which kit is the best, with the winning group being the one with the most votes.

EARLY FINISHERS In their original pairs, students choose and put on the desk a selection of everyday items they have with them, e.g. in their bag. They should think of a reason why they might find these useful on an outdoor adventure holiday and tell their partner, e.g. *I could use my car keys to get stones out of my shoes.*

EXTRA CHALLENGE In their original groups, students design and write a magazine or website advertisement for the kit they finally decided on in exercise 3. Alternatively, they could present their kit as an advertisement to the rest of the class.

Unit 11 Division of labour

Group activity, arranging a weekend conference and dividing tasks

Language
Making offers: *Shall I (do) …? Why don't I (do) …? Would you like me to (do) …?*, etc.

Preparation: Make one copy of the worksheet for each student.

1 Tell the class that you have got a problem, or that you need some help, e.g. *I'm really hungry. I've got a headache. This shopping is really heavy. I need to go to the airport tomorrow. I'm going to move house at the weekend.* Briefly review the phrases for making offers, e.g. *Shall I …? Why don't I …?* and invite students to offer help. You should respond to their offers with typical responses, e.g. *Thank you. That would be great.* Also write these responses on the board, if necessary.

2 Divide the class into groups (maximum of four students per group), giving each student a copy of the worksheet. Ask each group to nominate a leader.

3 Tell students to imagine that they all work for the same company, and that they are organizing a weekend conference. Some important visitors from another country will be coming to the event. The worksheet lists the different jobs they have to do during the event, and roughly how long each job will take. There are just over 35 hours of jobs in total. The aim of the activity is to divide the jobs equally (or as equally as possible) among students in the group. As a guide, explain and write on the board, if necessary that each student should aim to do eighteen to twenty hours of work each (if there are three in each group), or fifteen to eighteen hours (if there are four in each group). They should also share some of the jobs, such as the meetings and the party on Sunday.

4 The group leader should list the jobs on the sheet, and the members of the group should each offer to do the different jobs. They should also try to allocate jobs sensibly (e.g. the student who has dinner with the visitors on Friday night will also probably take them back to the hotel afterwards). They should complete the table by writing their names next to each job. The first group to complete their table is the winner.

EARLY FINISHERS Students independently think of some other problems or situations in which they might need help (as in stage 1). Then, in their groups, they say what their problem/situation is, and the other students in their group offer to help.

EXTRA CHALLENGE In their groups, students think of another situation where there are a lot of things to do and where sharing the work would be desirable (e.g. a party). Working together, they should all offer to do different jobs before and during the event.

Unit 12 On the phone
Paired activity, acting out phone calls

> **Language**
>
> On the telephone: *Can you tell her to call me back, please? Hang on a minute. I'll just get her. Could I speak to the manager, please? I'm afraid he's not available at the moment.*, etc.

Preparation: Make one copy of the worksheet for each pair and cut the sheets in half. You will also need some spare paper for each student.

Non-cut alternative: Make one copy of the worksheet for each pair and fold the sheets in half. Tell students not to look at the other halves.

1 Elicit from the class useful phrases for when making phone calls, e.g. to say who is calling, to ask to speak to people, to ask people to call you back. Write the phrases on the board, dividing them into formal and informal, as in the *Language for speaking* box on page 122 of the Coursebook. Erase these from the board before starting the activity.

2 Divide the class into pairs. Allocate each partner a letter (A or B) and give them the relevant half of the worksheet, as well as a piece of spare paper. They should not show

their sections of the worksheet to each other. Explain that they are going to call each other on the phone, using the information on their sections as prompts. In each call that they start, they have a specific objective (in bold in their prompts) which involves leaving a message for someone who is not there and making sure the person on the other end of the line takes down the message correctly. Explain to students that calls 1 and 2 are informal, but calls 3 and 4 are more formal, so remind them to be careful with their choice of language during those calls.

3 Students take turns to make their calls and try to obtain their objectives. Encourage students to write any messages on their spare sheets of paper. Each time a student successfully achieves an objective in bold, they tick the box by their prompt to indicate it is complete.

4 The first pair in the class to complete their calls and tick all of their boxes is the winner.

EXTRA SUPPORT Rather than erasing everything from the board, leave the phrases on the board in stage 1, for support during the activity.

EXTRA CHALLENGE In their pairs, students imagine and write prompts for other phone calls where a caller needs something or wants someone to do something. The person who answers the phone can agree/refuse, or can say that the person their partner wants to speak to is not there and take a message. Students swap their prompts with other pairs to act out.

1 Communication Something in common

1   Ask and answer questions to complete the personal information.

Name: _____	Name: _____
Nationality: _____	Nationality: _____
Job: _____	Job: _____
Email address: _____	Email address: _____

Name: _____	Name: _____
Nationality: _____	Nationality: _____
Job: _____	Job: _____
Email address: _____	Email address: _____

Name: _____	Name: _____
Nationality: _____	Nationality: _____
Job: _____	Job: _____
Email address: _____	Email address: _____

Name: _____	Name: _____
Nationality: _____	Nationality: _____
Job: _____	Job: _____
Email address: _____	Email address: _____

Name: _____	Name: _____
Nationality: _____	Nationality: _____
Job: _____	Job: _____
Email address: _____	Email address: _____

2   How many students did you find ...

1   whose first name begins with the same letter as your first name?
Example: *Alberto / Anna*

2   whose last name begins with the same letter as your last name?
Example: *Schneider / Sanchez*

3   who have the same nationality as you? _____

4   who use the same email provider as you? _____

2 Communication What's on?

1 Work with a partner. Read the *What's on* guide.

2 Plan your weekend in Singapore. Take turns to make suggestions and accept/refuse your partner's suggestions. Arrange six activities.

What's on Singapore

TRIP TO SENTOSA ISLAND

SEE PINK DOLPHINS, SEALS AND MORE!

OPEN: 9 A.M.–4 P.M. DAILY

TICKETS: $11 PER PERSON
$5 FOR CHILDREN

Book online at www.sentosaisland.com

International restaurant

All you can eat lunch!
Try food from all around the world!

12 p.m.–2 p.m.

Singapore Art Museum

Open: 10 a.m.–7 p.m. daily

ONLY $10

Sushi For You

Japanese restaurant

12 p.m.–2 a.m.

Live music at the Jazz Club

Come and hear some great live jazz!

Open: 9 p.m.–9 a.m.

CLUB LATINO

Live Latin music until 2.30 a.m.

Latin nights

Free Salsa classes 7–8 p.m.

Drinks half price before 8 p.m.

Singapore Zoo

See monkeys, penguins, beautiful birds.

Say 'hello' to our new baby giraffe!

Tickets: adults $28
children $18

Singapore city tour

Saturday: 11 a.m., 1 p.m. and 3 p.m.
Sunday: 1 p.m. and 3 p.m.

3 Communication Ask me something!

29 **Pay**	28 **Help**	27	26 **Sit**	25 **Go forward one space**	24	23 **Go back two spaces**	22 **Use**	21 **Ask your teacher**

30								20 **Open**

31 **Park**					17 **Lend**	18 **Go forward four spaces**	19

32 **Call**	2	3 **Go back two spaces**	4 **Use**	16			

33 **Bring**	1 **Leave**	5	15 **Tell**	14 **Call**	13 **Bring**

FINISH	**START**	6 **Go forward one space**	12 **Go back three spaces**

7	8 **Open**	9 **Help**	10 **Park**	11 **Pay**

How to play

1 Roll the dice and move your counter.

2 Make a request to the player on your left.

3 The player on your left throws the dice.

   For a score of 1, 3 or 5: refuse the request and give a reason. (Don't move your counter.)

   For a score of 2, 4, or 6: accept the request. (Move your counter one space.)

4 The first player to finish is the winner.

4 Communication Which hotel?

Student A

1 Give directions from the train station to Plaza Hotel.

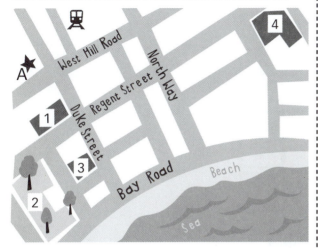

Key

🚉 Train station
A ★ Plaza Hotel
1 Science and Technology Museum
2 Victoria Park
3 Museum of Modern Art
4 Stonelanes Shopping Centre

2 Listen to students B, C and D give directions.
Draw the hotels on your map.

Student B

1 Give directions from the train station to King's Hotel.

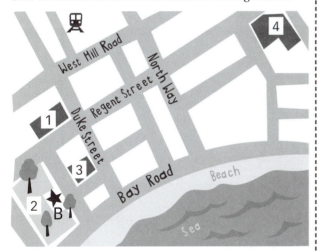

Key

🚉 Train station
B ★ King's Hotel
1 Science and Technology Museum
2 Victoria Park
3 Museum of Modern Art
4 Stonelanes Shopping Centre

2 Listen to students A, C and D give directions.
Draw the hotels on your map.

Student C

1 Give directions from the train station to Blue Sky Hotel.

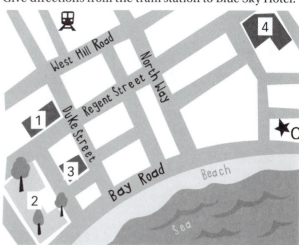

Key

🚉 Train station
C ★ Blue Sky Hotel
1 Science and Technology Museum
2 Victoria Park
3 Museum of Modern Art
4 Stonelanes Shopping Centre

2 Listen to students A, B and D give directions.
Draw the hotels on your map.

Student D

1 Give directions from the train station to City Hotel.

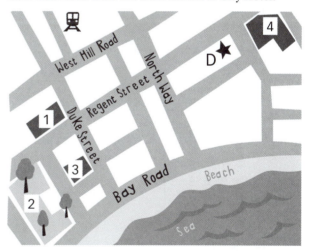

Key

🚉 Train station
D ★ City Hotel
1 Science and Technology Museum
2 Victoria Park
3 Museum of Modern Art
4 Stonelanes Shopping Centre

2 Listen to students A, B and C give directions.
Draw the hotels on your map.

How to play

1 Place your counter in one of the supermarkets.
2 Roll the dice and move your counter.
3 Go into a shop next to your counter. Try to buy something on your shopping list. You can't buy things that are too expensive and you can only pay by card.
4 Supermarkets: if you land on a supermarket, you can buy one thing on your shopping list. You don't need to talk to a shop assistant.

Shop assistants

⚃ You don't have it.	⚁ No problems.
⚄ No problems.	⚅ You only take cash.
⚂ It's very expensive (say a price).	⚅ No problems.

Shopping list	Player 1	Player 2	Player 3	Player 4
A cake				
A cookbook				
A newspaper				
Some trainers				
A jacket				

6 Communication The right response

1 Work with a partner. Complete the conversations with words from the box.
More than one answer may be possible.

> awful brilliant great interesting nightmare no really terrible you

1 **Sofia** My horrible boss moved into the house opposite mine last week.
  Rita Oh _____ !

2 **Lisa** I cooked a meal for my friends last night, and then they were all ill.
  Marcel That's _____ !

3 **Michele** I missed the last train on Saturday night and had to walk home.
  Klaus What a _____ !

4 **Lucas** I failed all of my exams last summer.
  Tosh That's _____ !

5 **Luigi** I'm going to New York on business next month.
  Justine _____ ?

6 **Zoe** It was so hot last night that I couldn't sleep.
  Renata Poor _____ !

7 **Nadine** Tom asked Eva to the cinema at the weekend.
  Nina That's _____ !

8 **Jessica** Yesterday, my boss agreed to give me more money.
  Kim That's _____ !

9 **Carlo** My neighbour works in a garage, and he repaired my car for free.
  Tan That's _____ !

---

2 Complete the table with mini-conversations. First write the responses for speaker B using phrases from exercise **1**.
Then write sentences for speaker A using your own ideas.

1	Speaker A	4	Speaker A	7	Speaker A
	Speaker B		Speaker B		Speaker B
2	Speaker A	5	Speaker A	8	Speaker A
	Speaker B		Speaker B		Speaker B
3	Speaker A	6	Speaker A	9	Speaker A
	Speaker B		Speaker B		Speaker B

3 Work in small groups. Take turns to read out the speaker A sentences. Guess the speaker B responses.

7 Communication What do you think?

Student A

1   Look at the illustrations. Choose one suggestion you think will make Hampton International College a better place.

A swimming pool	Free bicycles for students to use	A garden where students can relax	A cinema

2   Tell students B and C about the illustrations, what you chose and why.

3   In your group, discuss the suggestions you all chose. Choose one thing.

Student B

1   Look at the illustrations. Choose one suggestion you think will make Hampton International College a better place.

A language centre where students can practise English	A gym	A quiet room where students can relax	A free tablet computer for every student

2   Tell students A and C about the illustrations, what you chose and why.

3   In your group, discuss the suggestions you all chose. Choose one thing.

Student C

1   Look at the illustrations. Choose one suggestion you think will make Hampton International College a better place.

A café selling healthy food and drinks	A minibus	An indoor sports room	A tennis court

2   Tell students A and B about the illustrations, what you chose and why.

3   In your group, discuss the suggestions you all chose. Choose one thing.

8 Communication South Port to North End

Student A

1 Read the information. Book train tickets with student B. Complete the table.
- You and your 10-year-old nephew are at South Port station. It is 7.15 a.m.
- You both need to be in North End by 9.30 a.m.
- Your nephew is not coming back to South Port (he is staying with family).
- You need to be back in South Port by 8 p.m.
- You have £60 for both tickets.

Next train to North End leaves at	
Train arrives in North End at	
Train leaves from platform number	
Train from North End leaves at	
Train arrives in South Port at	
Train leaves from platform number	
Ticket price	Adult return: Child single: Class:
Total cost of tickets	

Student B

1 Help student A book train tickets. Use the information.
- The time is 7.15 a.m.

Timetables

South Port → North End	
Depart	Arrive
6.55 a.m.	8.45 a.m.
7.35 a.m.	9.25 a.m.
8.35 a.m.	10.25 a.m.
10 a.m.	11.50 a.m.
11 a.m.	12.50 p.m.
All trains depart from platform 7	

North End → South Port	
Depart	Arrive
4.50 p.m.	6.40 p.m.
5.30 p.m.	7.20 p.m.
6.10 p.m.	7.45 p.m.
7.30 p.m.	9.45 p.m.
8.30 p.m.	10 p.m.
All trains depart from platform 2	

Ticket prices

First class	Second class
Adult single: £35	Adult single: £25
Adult return: £55	Adult return: £40
Child single: £25	Child single: £15
Child return: £45	Child return: £25

9 Communication Ten conversations

Customer

1 Have ten conversations with the waiter. Use opening questions 1–5 and make suitable responses.

1 **Can I sit outside?**
2 Could I see the menu?
3 Can I order now?
4 Could I have some more bread, please?
5 Excuse me, could I pay now?

Responses		
Yes, please. What's the soup of the day?	I'm not quite ready. Could you give me another minute?	**Never mind. Can I sit by the window instead?**
Can I pay by credit card?	Where's the board?	Yes, could I have some apple juice, please?
I'd like the steak, please.	Yes, that would be fine. With lots of ice, please.	I will, thanks.
That sounds nice. I'll have that, please.	Yes, please. And can I have a glass of water, too?	No, thank you. I couldn't eat another thing.
Yes, please. Could I have a green salad with it?	No, thanks. I don't want to be awake half the night.	A little olive oil and lemon juice would be nice, thanks.

- -

Waiter

1 Have ten conversations with the customer. Use opening questions 1–5 and make suitable responses.

1 Would you like to order now?
2 Would you like a starter?
3 Would you like any side dishes with that?
4 Would you like something to drink?
5 Would you like some dessert?

Responses		
Of course. I'll get your bill.	Would you like any chips with that?	It's on the wall by the door.
Of course. I'll bring some over. Would you like some butter, too?	**I'm sorry, but there are no free tables outside at the moment.**	How about a coffee?
Yes. Just call me when you're ready.	Certainly. What would you like?	Certainly. Here you are. And as well as the dishes on the menu, there are also some on the board.
Of course. I think there's a free table.	Would you like anything on the salad?	It's tomato and red pepper.
I'm sorry, but the machine is broken and we can only take cash at the moment.	I'm afraid we don't have any. Would you like orange instead?	Yes, would you like some ice in that?

10 Communication The ultimate adventure kit

1   Work with a partner. Look and choose eight items for an outdoor adventure kit. Write the items below 1–8.

2   Choose four more items of your own. Write the items below 9–12.

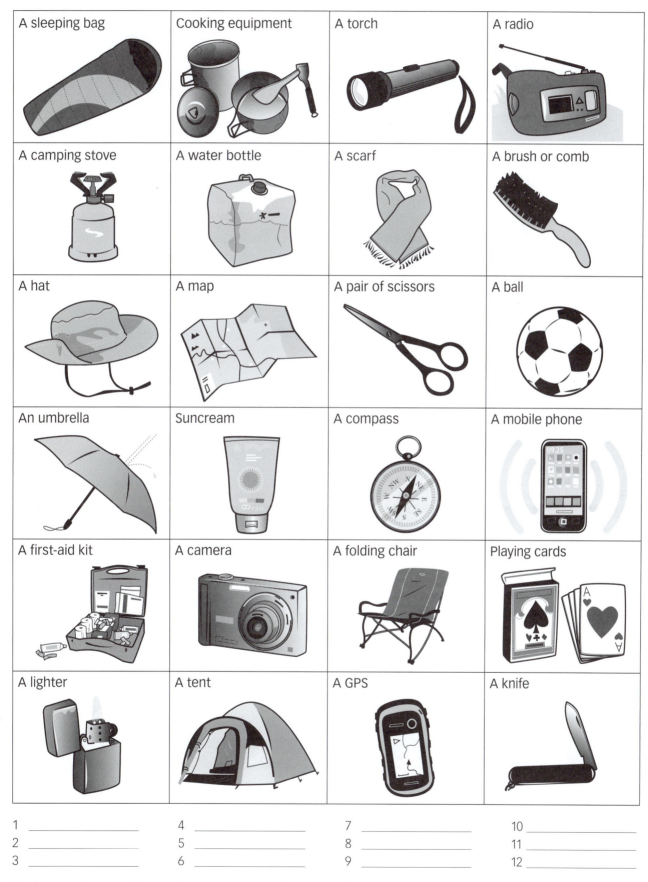

A sleeping bag	Cooking equipment	A torch	A radio
A camping stove	A water bottle	A scarf	A brush or comb
A hat	A map	A pair of scissors	A ball
An umbrella	Suncream	A compass	A mobile phone
A first-aid kit	A camera	A folding chair	Playing cards
A lighter	A tent	A GPS	A knife

1 _____   4 _____   7 _____   10 _____
2 _____   5 _____   8 _____   11 _____
3 _____   6 _____   9 _____   12 _____

3   Work in small groups. Discuss the items you chose for your outdoor adventure kits. Choose twelve items.

1   Work in small groups. Take turns to make offers. Complete the tables.

Friday

Job	Time	Name(s)
Meet the visitors at the airport in the morning and take them to the hotel.	2 hours	
Take the visitors for lunch at a local restaurant.	2 hours	
Take the visitors on a guided tour of the town in the afternoon.	3 hours	
Go to dinner with the visitors.	2 hours	
Take the visitors back to the hotel.	30 minutes	

Saturday

Job	Time	Name(s)
Meet the visitors for breakfast at the hotel in the morning and take them to the office.	1 hour	
Meeting 1: talk about the new products.	3 hours	
Eat lunch with the visitors at the office.	1 hour	
Meeting 2: talk about the company problems.	3 hours	
Go to dinner with the visitors.	2 hours	
Take the visitors to an evening show.	3 hours	
Take the visitors back to the hotel.	30 minutes	

Sunday

Job	Time	Name(s)
Meet the visitors for breakfast at the hotel in the morning and take them to the office.	1 hour	
Meeting 3: talk about the company's future.	3 hours	
Take the visitors on a trip along the river (lunch included).	3 hours	
Evening party.	3 hours	
Take the visitors back to the hotel.	30 minutes	

Monday

Job	Time	Name(s)
Meet the visitors for breakfast at the hotel in the morning.	1 hour	
Go to the airport with the visitors and say goodbye.	1 hour	

12 Communication On the phone

Student A

1 Act out the phone calls and tick (✔).

<table>
<tr><td>

1

- Call your friend Thomas.
- You want to meet him at half past six tomorrow evening.
- If Thomas is not there, leave a message: you want Thomas to call you back, but he hasn't got your number (your number is 0875 237 4456).
- ☐ **Ask student B to read back the message to you and check the information is correct.**

</td><td>

3

- Call your boss Mrs Jenkins.
- You are going to be late for a meeting.
- If Mrs Jenkins is not there, leave a message: you are going to be an hour late. Explain why.
- ☐ **Ask student B to read back the message to you and check the information is correct.**

</td></tr>
<tr><td>

2

- Student B calls and asks to speak to Mariko, who shares a house with you.
- Tell student B that Mariko is not there.
- Offer to take a message.
- Listen and write student B's message on a piece of paper.

</td><td>

4

- Student B calls the college where you work and asks to speak to Mr Watson, an English teacher.
- Tell student B that Mr Watson is in class at the moment.
- Offer to take a message.
- Listen and write student B's message on a piece of paper.

</td></tr>
</table>

Student B

1 Act out the phone calls and tick (✔).

<table>
<tr><td>

1

- Student A calls and asks to speak to Thomas, who shares a flat with you.
- Tell student A that Thomas is not there.
- Offer to take a message.
- Listen and write student A's message on a piece of paper.

</td><td>

3

- Student A calls the office where you work and asks to speak to Mrs Jenkins, your boss.
- Tell student A that Mrs Jenkins is in a meeting at the moment.
- Offer to take a message.
- Listen and write student A's message on a piece of paper.

</td></tr>
<tr><td>

2

- Call your friend Mariko.
- You want to ask her to come to your new house for dinner on Thursday.
- If Mariko is not there, leave a message: you want Mariko to call you back, but she hasn't got your number (your number is 0287 143 8851).
- ☐ **Ask student A to read back the message to you and check the information is correct.**

</td><td>

4

- Call your English teacher Mr Watson.
- You can't come to his class.
- If he's not there, leave a message: explain that you can't come to his class this afternoon because you have to go to the dentist's.
- ☐ **Ask student A to read back the message to you and check the information is correct.**

</td></tr>
</table>

Vox pops

Aim: Each of these video worksheets aims to provide students with extra listening and speaking practice on topics connected to the corresponding unit in the Coursebook.

Preparation: Make one copy of the worksheet for each student and cut or fold in half as shown.

Unit 1 Family

1 Give a copy of the worksheet to each student. Students work independently to complete the answers for their own family. Put students in pairs and ask students to compare their families. Conduct class feedback.

2 Ask students to read through section 1 in exercise 2. Elicit that Amsterdam and Leiden are cities in the Netherlands. Play the video and allow time for students to discuss their answers. Next ask students to read section 2. Can they answer any questions from memory? Play the video again. Check answers.

ANSWERS

1 1 Amsterdam 2 18 3 53 4 brothers 5 Griffin
2 1 T 2 F/South London 3 T 4 F/mid-30s
  5 F/elder brother is called Graham

3 Pair students with a different partner to the one they had for exercise 1. Ask students to read the questions and encourage them to share opinions and give reasons for their answers. Elicit ideas and share feedback in open class.

Unit 2 My day

1 Give a copy of the worksheet to each student and ask them to look at exercise 1. Students work independently or in pairs to match the verbs in the box with the phrases. Do the first one together. Elicit that *cook* and *have* are both possible. Check answers with the whole class. (See answers below in step 2.)

2 Ask students to read through section 1 in exercise 2. Play the video and allow time for students to discuss their answers with a partner. Check answers and then ask students to read section 2. Play the video again and pause if necessary to allow for writing time, and encourage students to discuss their answers.

ANSWERS

1
1 cook/have breakfast/lunch/dinner
2 get/wake up
3 play computer games
4 check emails
5 start/finish work
6 go jogging/swimming
7 go to school/to work/to bed
8 have a shower/a bath
9 go shopping
10 watch a film/television
2
1 half past eight 2 a coffee/check emails
3 every morning 4 finish work 5 have a shower
6 watch a film/read a book 7 get up/for breakfast

3 Put students in small groups and ask them to discuss the questions in exercise 3. Conduct class feedback and ask general questions, e.g. *Who gets up very early? What time do you have dinner? Who cooks dinner?*

Unit 3 What do you do?

1 Give a copy of the worksheet to each student. Students work in groups and discuss the question together. If necessary, elicit ideas such as *enjoy helping people, enjoy working with people, earn a lot of money*, etc. Share feedback as a whole class.

2 Ask students to read through section 1 in exercise 2, checking the meaning of *researcher* and *charity*. Then play the video, stopping after the first question and allowing time for students to discuss their answers with a partner. Check answers and then ask students to read through section 2. Play the rest of the video and encourage students to discuss their answers. Go through the answers with the class. Play the whole video through again if appropriate.

ANSWERS

1 1 hospital 2 charity 3 music 4 University
  5 teacher
2 1 d 2 a 3 c 4 b

3 Put students in pairs and ask them to read exercise 3. Check they understand that it is a class (or group if you have a large class) survey. First they need to write the direct questions. Do question 1 together and write it on the board: *Do you like your job/studies?* Elicit the second question and ask students to think of the third question together. Encourage the students to move around, asking and answering the questions, and giving reasons for their answers. Conduct class feedback.

Unit 4 Where I live

1 Write *rooms* and *furniture* on the board and elicit a few words for each category. Give a copy of the worksheet to each student and ask them to read exercise 1. Students work in groups or pairs. Conduct class feedback, checking spelling and pronunciation as necessary.

2 Ask students to read through section 1 in exercise 2. Check the meaning of *share a house*. Then play the video, stopping after the second question to allow time for students to discuss their answers with a partner. Check answers and then ask students to read through section 2. Play the rest of the video and encourage students to discuss their answers. Go through the answers with the class. Play the whole video through again if appropriate.

ANSWERS

1 1 (R) 2 (V) 3 (V) and (E) 4 (R) (K)
2 cooker ✓ fridge ✓ sink ✓ freezer ✓ washing machine ✗
  table ✓ sofa ✓ coffee table ✗ chair ✓ shelf ✗ desk ✓
  cupboard ✗ TV ✓ chest of drawers ✓ armchair ✓

3 Put students in pairs and ask them to discuss the questions in exercise 3, encouraging them to give reasons and examples for their answers. Elicit ideas and conduct class feedback.

Unit 5 Shopping

1 Give a copy of the worksheet to each student and ask them to read exercise 1. Check vocabulary such as *groceries* and *jewellery*. Students work in pairs and discuss their answers.

2 Play the video and stop after the speakers have answered the first question: *Do you shop online?* Check the answer to section 1 in exercise 2 in open class. Play the rest of the video and ask students to complete the table in section 2, discussing their answers together. Finally, ask students to read section 3. Can they match any of the answers from memory? Play the video again to check their answers.

ANSWERS

1 Libby
2 Meriam: shoes/dresses (O); jewellery (S)
  Peter: shoes (S); holidays/clothes (O); clothes (both)
  Jack: clothes/groceries (O); lunch (S)
  Omar: clothes (S); trainers (O)
  Libby: clothes (S); books (O)
3 1 b 2 c 3 e 4 a 5 d

3 Put students in pairs to answer the question in exercise 3. Encourage students to share opinions and give reasons for their answers. Conduct class feedback on the discussion.

Unit 6 Don't give up!

1 Give a copy of the worksheet to each student. Students work in pairs and discuss their answers to the questions, using the adjectives to help them. Check the meaning of *entertaining* and *amusing*.

2 Ask students to look at the table in section 1 in exercise 2. Ask them if they have seen any of the films and which words they think could be used to describe the films, e.g. which film could be described as sad but good. Play the video through once and allow time for students to discuss their answers with a partner. Play the video through again if appropriate and go through the answers with the class.

ANSWERS

Meriam	yesterday	The Devil Wears Prada	very funny
Libby	two days ago	The Grand Budapest Hotel	funny and entertaining
Omar	two weeks ago	Transformers	really exciting
Peter	a week ago	The Wolf of Wall Street	very, very entertaining and amusing.
Jack	last weekend	The Lone Soldier	quite sad, a good film.

3 Put students in pairs or small groups and ask them to read the task in exercise 3. Give plenty of time for discussion and encourage students to give reasons for their choices. Each group can present their ideas to another group or to the whole class. The class then chooses the best idea.

Unit 7 Sporting heroes

1 Ask students what you can do to stay fit and healthy, brainstorming ideas on the board. Give a copy of the worksheet to each student. Tell students they are going to watch a video of some people talking about how they keep fit and healthy. Students read exercise 1 and look at the images in pairs to predict what the speakers will say.

2 Ask students to read through exercise 2, checking any vocabulary, e.g. *wherever you can*. Play the first question of the video through once and allow time for students to discuss their answers to section 1 with a partner. Check answers and play the second question of the video. Encourage students to discuss their answers to sections 2 and 3.

ANSWERS

1 1 F 2 T 3 T 4 F 5 F
2 1 b 2 b 3 a 4 b 5 a

3 Regroup students with a different partner from exercise 1. If some of your students are colleagues at the same company or study at the same college, they may wish to work together. Ask students to read the task in exercise 3. Encourage them to share opinions and give reasons for their answers. Each group can present their ideas to another group or to the whole class. Encourage students to ask questions about the plans.

Unit 8 I went to …

1 Give a copy of the worksheet to each student. Ask them to do the task individually, then discuss with a partner. Check they understand the difference between *go out with friends* and *stay with/visit friends*.

2 Ask students to read through section 1 in exercise 2. Play the first two questions of the video and allow time for students to discuss their answers with a partner. Check answers. Play the third question of the video and encourage students to discuss their answers to exercise 2. Play the video through again if appropriate.

ANSWERS

2 1 three weeks ago 2 last summer 3 Greece
  4 Paris 5 Portugal 6 Switzerland
3 go out with friends (Ch)
  go swimming in the sea (R)
  go to restaurants (R)
  go to the beach (R)
  relax by the pool (T)
  stay with/visit friends (Al)
  visit monuments (Ch)
  walk around a town (Ar)

3 Put students in pairs and ask them to discuss the questions in exercise 3. Share feedback in open class.

Unit 9 In the kitchen

1 Give a copy of the worksheet to each student. Go through the task with them. Encourage them by asking questions such as *What is at the back of your fridge? At the top? Is there any fruit? Sauces? What do you keep in the door?* Then, divide the class into pairs and ask them to compare their lists. Does anyone have anything unusual in their fridge? What do they always have in their fridge?

2 Ask students to read through the questions in exercise 2. Play the video and ask students to do section 1. Check answers. Play the video again and ask students to answer section 2 with a partner, giving reasons. Elicit any interesting points of comparison as a whole class.

ANSWERS
1 1 half an hour 2 very little 3 salads/orange juice
  4 vegetables/yoghurt 5 not much 6 usually
  7 milk/cheese

3 Students work in pairs or small groups and discuss the questions in exercise 3. Conduct class feedback.

Unit 10 Natural wonders

1 Give a copy of the worksheet to each student. Ask students to read the interview questions in exercise 2. Students work in pairs or in groups and share ideas. Do feedback in whole class.

2 Play the first question of the video and allow time for students to discuss their answers to section 1 with a partner. Check answers and then ask students to read through section 2. Play the second question of the video and encourage students to compare their answers with a partner. Play the video again if appropriate and go through the answers with the class.

ANSWERS
1 1 d 2 c 3 b 4 e 5 a
2 1 winter/hot 2 spring 3 summertime/nice
  4 summer/shining 5 summertime/weather

3 Divide the class into small groups of three or four. Ask students to read through the task in exercise 3. Each student presents their ideas to the rest of the group. Encourage the other students to actively listen by getting them to ask questions about each place.

Unit 11.1 Community spirit

1 Give a copy of the worksheet to each student. Tell students they are going to watch a video of some people talking about how they help their community. Students work in pairs or in small groups and discuss the interview questions in exercise 2. Check they understand they need to read both interview questions and to discuss the list of activities. Check any vocabulary, e.g. *marathon, raise money, fun run, homeless, volunteer*. Share ideas as whole class.

2 Ask students to read through section 1 in exercise 2 and explain to them that there are four extra sentences in the list. Play the video and allow time for students to compare their answers with a partner. Check answers and then ask students to look at section 2. Can they match any of the speakers to the activities from memory? Play the video

through again and encourage students to compare their answers.

ANSWERS
1 ✗ 2 ✓/Vicky 3 ✓/Charlotte 4 ✗ 5 ✓/Ken
6 ✗ 7 ✓/Ciorstaidh 8 ✗ 9 ✓/Alastair 10 ✓/Alastair

3 Put students in new pairs or small groups and ask them to read the questions in exercise 3. Encourage them to share opinions and give reasons for their answers. Elicit ideas and conduct class feedback.

Unit 11.2 Challenges

1 Give a copy of the worksheet to each student. Students work in pairs and do the first activity together. You may wish to demonstrate this by choosing a student and writing on the board three things you think they use every day/occasionally.

2 Ask students to look at the table and explain the task. Play the whole video and allow time for students to compare their answers with a partner. Check answers and then ask students to look at section 2. Can they remember what the speakers said? Play the video again and encourage students to discuss their answers.

ANSWERS
Vicky: computer (E)/at work; smartphone (E)
Charlotte: phone (E); tablet (E)/watch favourite programmes; TV (O)
Ken: computer (E)/send emails; GPS (O)
Ciorstaidh: smartphone (E)/keep in contact with friends; tablet/laptop (O)/do research
Alastair: laptop (E)/for work/writing; record player (O)/play music

3 Pair students with a different partner to the one they had in exercise 1. Ask students to read the questions in exercise 3 and encourage them to share opinions and give reasons for their answers. Elicit ideas and conduct class feedback.

1 Video Family

Vox pops

1 How many people are there in your family? Write the number next to each family member, e.g. if you have two sisters, write *2* next to *sister*. Then compare with your partner. Are your families similar or different?

aunt	brother	cousin	daughter
nephew	niece	sister	son	uncle

Meriam

Omar

Izzy

Richard

2 Watch the video. Do sections 1 and 2.
Can you tell me about your family?
1 Circle the correct option.
  1 Meriam's sister lives in *Amsterdam / Leiden*.
  2 Omar's sister is *18 / 20* years old.
  3 Libby's brother is *52 / 53* years old.
  4 Izzy has four *sisters / brothers*.
  5 Richard's nephew is called *Graham / Griffin*.
2 Decide if the sentences are true (T) or false (F).
  1 Meriam's sister is 20 years old.   T F
  2 Omar's sister lives in North London.   T F
  3 Libby's daughter is called Stella.   T F
  4 Izzy's brothers are all in their mid-40s.   T F
  5 Richard's younger brother is called Graham.   T F

3 Interview a partner. Use the questions below or think of your own questions.
  1 Is it good or bad to be in a big family? Why/Why not?
  2 What about a small family? Why/Why not?
  3 Which would you prefer? Why/Why not?
    a lots of brothers and sisters
    b no brothers or sisters

2 Video My day

Vox pops

Isaure

John

Sarah

Stephanie

Brook

1 Write the correct verb(s) next to each phrase.

check	cook	finish	get	go (x3)
have (x2)	play	start	wake	watch

1 _____ / _____ breakfast/lunch/dinner
2 _____ / _____ up
3 _____ computer games
4 _____ emails
5 _____ / _____ work
6 _____ jogging/swimming
7 _____ to school/to work/to bed
8 _____ a shower/a bath
9 _____ shopping
10 _____ a film/television

2 Watch the video. Do sections 1 and 2.
What is a typical day for you?
1 Tick (✓) the activities in exercise **1** that the speakers talk about. Use up to three words in each gap.
2 Complete the sentences.
  1 **Isaure** I have my breakfast and go to school, which starts at _____.
  2 **John** I always start the day with a _____ at my desk, and then check _____.
  3 **Sarah** I go jogging _____.
  4 **Sarah** I _____ at about five o'clock.
  5 **Stephanie** I normally get up at 7.30, then I _____.
  6 **Stephanie** In the evening I usually _____ or _____.
  7 **Brook** I _____ at 7 a.m. and usually have eggs _____.

3 Work with a partner. Discuss the questions.
  • Who in the videos are you most similar to? Why?
  • Choose five activities from exercise 1. What time of day do you usually do them?

3 Video What do you do?

Vox pops

 Vicky  Ken  Ciorstaidh  Rosie  Elaine

1 Work with a partner. Discuss the jobs in the box. What do you think the people who do these jobs enjoy about them?

> businessman/woman   lawyer
> musician   nurse   photographer

2 Watch the video. Do sections 1 and 2.

Where do you work or study?

1 Complete the sentences with the words in the box.

> charity   hospital   music   teacher   university

1 **Vicky**   I work in a _____ as a researcher.
2 **Ken**   I work for a _____ . I'm not studying at the moment.
3 **Ciorstaidh** I study _____ in Manchester.
4 **Rosie**   I study at the _____ of Nottingham and I study music.
5 **Elaine**   I work as a _____ in Leicester.

Do you like your job? What job would you like to have?

2 Match speakers 1–4 to their answers a–d.

1 Vicky   a I enjoy working with the children.
2 Elaine   b ... I want to be a lawyer ...
3 Ciorstaidh   c I'd like to be a professional musician.
4 Rosie   d I love my job.

3 Mini class survey. Find out how many people in your class/group:

• like their job/studies. Why/Why not?
• would like to do their job for the rest of their life. Why/Why not?
• would like to do a different job in the future. What job? Why?

Who gave the most interesting answer? Why/Why not?

- -

4 Video Where I live

Vox pops

1 Work with a partner. Look at the furniture and items in section 2 in exercise **2**. Which rooms in a house can you find them in? Can you think of two more items for each room?

2 Watch the video. Do sections 1 and 2.

Do you live in a house or a flat?
Which is your favourite room?

1 Write the first letter of the correct person's name next to each question: Vicky (V), Ken (K), Ciorstaidh (C), Rosie (R) and Elaine (E).

1 Who shares a house? ____
2 Who lives in a flat? ____
3 Whose favourite room is the kitchen? ____ and ____
4 Who likes to watch TV in their favourite room? ____
5 Who says their favourite room is comfortable? ____

Can you describe your favourite room?

2 Look at the items below and tick (✓) the ones the speakers talk about.

cooker	☐	chair	☐
fridge	☐	shelf	☐
sink	☐	desk	☐
freezer	☐	cupboard	☐
washing machine	☐	TV	☐
table	☐	chest of drawers	☐
sofa	☐	armchair	☐
coffee table	☐		

3 Work with a partner. Discuss the questions.

• Would you change anything (furniture, rooms, garden, etc.) about the place you live in? Why/Why not? What?
• Describe your ideal house or flat.

Do you and your partner have similar or different ideas?

 Vicky  Ken  Ciorstaidh  Rosie  Elaine

5 Video Shopping

Vox pops

1 Look at the items below. Which do you buy online? Which do you buy in a shop? Compare your answers with your partner.

> books clothes films flowers groceries holidays
> jewellery lunch music shoes/trainers

2 Watch the video. Do sections 1, 2 and 3.

Do you shop online?

1 Who doesn't shop online very often? _____

What do you like to buy online?

What do you like to buy in shops?

2 Where do the speakers buy the items below? Do they buy the items online (O) or in shops (S)? One speaker buys clothes both online and in shops. Who is it?

	Meriam	Peter	Jack	Omar	Libby
shoes					
dresses					
holidays					
clothes					
groceries					
books					
trainers					
jewellery					
lunch					

3 Match speakers a–e to answers 1–5.

a	Meriam	1	buys clothes online because of convenience.
b	Jack	2	buys trainers online because of exclusive styles.
c	Libby	3	buys books online because they're easier to find.
d	Peter	4	buys jewellery in shops because you can see how it looks.
e	Omar	5	buys shoes in shops because you can try them on for fit.

3 Which of the speakers are you most similar to? Why/Why not? Discuss with a partner.

Meriam

Peter

Omar

---

6 Video Don't give up!

Vox pops

1 Describe the last film you saw. Use the words in the box to help you. Compare your answers with your partner.

> amusing boring entertaining exciting
> frightening funny sad

Libby

Jack

2 Watch the video. Do section 1.

When was the last time you watched a film?

What was it?

Did you enjoy it?

1 Match the speakers with their answers.

	When?	What?	Enjoy?
Meriam	a week ago	*The Lone Soldier*	funny and entertaining
Libby	last weekend	*The Wolf of Wall Street*	very funny
Omar	two days ago	*Transformers*	quite sad; a good film
Peter	yesterday	*The Devil Wears Prada*	very, very entertaining and amusing
Jack	two weeks ago	*The Grand Budapest Hotel*	really exciting

3 Work with a partner or small group. Plan an English-language film night for your language class. Decide what film you will watch and how you will organize the evening. Then share your ideas with another group/the rest of the class. Choose the best idea.

7 Video Sporting heroes

Vox pops

1 Work with a partner. What answers can you give to these questions?

- How do you keep fit?
- What should you do to stay healthy?

2 Watch the video. Do sections 1, 2 and 3.

How do you keep fit?

1 Decide if the sentences are true (T) or false (F).

1 Tony plays football twice a week.	T	F
2 Charlotte does exercise classes in the evenings.	T	F
3 Alastair cycles to work every day.	T	F
4 Rosie likes to swim and to dance.	T	F
5 Alan walks to work and eats healthily.	T	F

 Tony  Charlotte  Alastair

 Rosie  Alan

What should you do to stay healthy?

2 Choose the correct answer.

1 Tony thinks you should eat …
  a less vegetables.
  b fresh vegetables.

2 Charlotte thinks people should …
  a do exercise every day.
  b do exercise a few times a week.

3 Alastair thinks people should …
  a walk wherever you can.
  b go to the gym.

4 Rosie thinks people should …
  a walk to the shops.
  b go to the gym.

5 Alan thinks people should …
  a not eat too much fat.
  b not eat any fat.

3 How many of your ideas from exercise **1** do the speakers talk about?

3 Work with a new partner and do the task.

Your workplace/college wants employees/students to be healthier. Think of three ideas that could help people to be healthy at work or college, e.g. *walk or ride a bike to work/college*. Share your ideas and design a leaflet or email message.

---

8 Video I went to …

Vox pops

 Tony  Charlotte  Alastair  Rosie  Alan

1 Look at the activities in section 2 in exercise **2**. Do you like doing these things on holiday? Why/Why not? What other things do you like doing? Compare your ideas with a partner.

2 Watch the video. Do sections 1 and 2.

When did you last have a holiday?
Where did you go?

1 Circle the correct answers.

1 Charlotte went on holiday *three months ago / three weeks ago / two weeks ago*.

2 Rosie went on holiday *last summer / two months ago / last month*.

3 Tony went to *Spain / Greece / Egypt*.

4 Charlotte visited *Paris / Dubai / Geneva*.

5 Alastair went to *Germany / Portugal / Mexico*.

6 Alan went to *the USA / Thailand / Switzerland*.

What did you do?

2 Write the name of the correct speaker next to each of the activities: Tony (T), Charlotte (Ch), Alastair (Ar), Rosie (R) and Alan (An).

1 go out with friends   _____
2 go swimming in the sea   _____
3 go to restaurants   _____
4 go to the beach   _____
5 relax by the pool   _____
6 stay with/visit friends   _____
7 visit monuments   _____
8 walk around a town   _____

3 Work with a partner. Look at the places in section 1 in exercise **2**. Which places would you like to visit? Why/Why not? Did you go to any of these places on your last holiday? Did you like it? Why/Why not?

9 Video In the kitchen

Vox pops

1   Imagine you are at home standing in front of your open fridge. Now write a list of everything that is in your fridge. Compare with a partner.

2   Watch the video. Do sections 1 and 2.

How much time do you spend in your kitchen?
What's usually in your fridge?

1   Complete the sentences. Use the words in each gap.

   1   Martin spends about _____ a day in the kitchen.
   2   Richard spends _____ time in his kitchen.
   3   Evelyn has dairy, _____ and _____ in her fridge.
   4   Martin has chicken, fish, a lot of _____ , milk and _____ .
   5   Izzy says there's _____ in her fridge.
   6   Richard _____ just has prawns in his refrigerator.
   7   Paul says there is _____ , orange juice and _____ in his fridge.

2   Watch the video again. Compare your answers in exercise 1 with the speakers'. Who are you most similar to? Why?

3   Work with a partner or in small groups. Discuss the questions.

   When did you last cook a meal? Who for? What's your favourite meal to cook? Why/Why not? What ingredients does it need? How do you make it?

10 Video Natural wonders

Vox pops

1   Answer these questions. Talk to your partner/group and share your ideas.

   • What is the most beautiful part of your country?
   • When is the best time to visit?

2   Watch the video. Do sections 1 and 2.

What's the most beautiful part of your country?

1   Match speakers 1–5 to places a–e.

   1   Evelyn   a   The Lake District, UK
   2   Martin   b   Yorkshire, England
   3   Izzy   c   North Devon, UK
   4   Richard   d   Florida, USA
   5   Paul   e   Costa Brava, Spain

When's the best time to visit?

2   Complete the sentences.

   The best time to visit ...

   1   Florida is in the _____ because it's less humid and less _____ .
   2   North Devon is in the _____ so you can surf.
   3   Yorkshire is in the _____ when the weather is _____ .
   4   the Costa Brava is in the _____ because the sun is always _____ . But the winter is also _____ and peaceful.
   5   the Lake District is the _____ for the _____ .

3   Work in small groups. Some English-speaking friends of yours would like to visit the place you talked about in exercise 1. Make some notes about the best time to visit, how to get there, where to stay, what to do, local food, etc. Share them with your group.

11.1 Video Community spirit

Vox pops

1 Work in pairs/small groups and discuss the interview questions in exercise **2**. Look at the activities in the list. Have you ever done any of them? When? Who for?

2 Watch the video. Do the sections 1 and 2.

Have you ever done something to help your community?
What did you do?

1 Tick (✓) the sentences you hear. There are four extra sentences.

  1 I ran a marathon to raise money for charity.
  2 I have given money to charity.
  3 I did a fun run with my family.
  4 I always give my old clothes and shoes to charity shops.
  5 I helped manage money for a charity.
  6 I helped homeless people find somewhere to sleep.
  7 I served soup and pudding to help raise money.
  8 I played in a charity table tennis match.
  9 I volunteered for a church.
 10 I helped prepare food for poor people.

2 Write each speaker's name next to the activities in exercise **1**: Vicky (V), Charlotte (Ch), Ken (K), Ciorstaidh (C) and Alastair (A).

3 Work with a partner or in small groups. Discuss the questions.

- What are the common ways of helping the community in your local area/ country?
- Do you know anyone who works/ volunteers for a charity? What do they do?
- Are there any problems in your community that you think a charity could help solve? What? How?

11.2 Video Challenges

Vox pops

1 Write down three items of technology that you think your partner uses every day and three items that you think they only use occasionally. Talk with your partner and compare your answers.

2 Watch the video. Do sections 1 and 2.

Do you use technology a lot in your life?
What do you use every day and what for?
What do you use occasionally?

1 Write (E) in the table if the speaker uses the technology every day, and (O) if the speaker uses it occasionally.

2 Watch again and make notes in the table on what the speakers use the technology for, e.g. for work, do research, etc.

3 Work with a partner or in small groups. Discuss the questions.

- Which speaker are you most similar to?
- Which technologies in exercise **2** do you think will still exist in ten years' time?

Vicky	computer *E*	MP3 player	tablet	smartphone
Charlotte	GPS	phone	TV	tablet
Ken	phone	computer	GPS	TV
Ciorstaidh	smartphone	TV	laptop	tablet
Alastair	laptop	MP3 player	record player	phone